6⁵⁰

3-25-64   (63-14450)

# PRAIRIE REBEL

# PRAIRIE REBEL

*The Public Life of William Lemke*

*by*

EDWARD C. BLACKORBY

UNIVERSITY OF NEBRASKA PRESS · LINCOLN

1963

Publishers on the Plains

UNP

MANUFACTURED IN THE UNITED STATES OF AMERICA

To Jewel and Chuck

# Acknowledgments

In making acknowledgments I am conscious of obligations incurred over a period of years during which a first version of this study was a doctoral dissertation and an earlier project concerning the Nonpartisan League was a masters thesis. I owe a special debt of gratitude to Louis G. Geiger, whose assistance and suggestions have given me the inspiration to undertake and the guidance to complete this biography. The assistance given by William Koenker, Eric Selke, Elwyn B. Robinson, and Mr. and Mrs. Glenn Matott was so time-consuming that I remember it most appreciatively and their interest provided encouragement when it was needed. Robert B. Wilkins, Felix A. Vondracek, Peter A. Munch, Robert Campbell, Ross Talbott, Henry Tomasek, J. L. Sayre, M. Beatrice Johnstone, Lloyd Stone, William W. Phillips and many others provided thoughtful advice and direction or assisted in locating materials during various periods when I was engaged in research or writing. Jon R. Ashton and his staff of the University of North Dakota library, Matilda Stoxen and Mrs. Eve Wienbergen of the Dickinson State Teachers College library, Margaret Rose with the assistance of Mrs. B. D. Wetmore of the North Dakota State Historical Society library, Mrs. Hazel Webster Byrnes of the State Library Commission, Gertrude Voldal of the Dickinson City Library, Albert G. Anderson of the Masonic Library at Fargo, Roy P. Johnson of Fargo, T. Buford Rowland of the Legislative Section of the National Archives, and the staff members of the Agricultural Section of the National Archives, of the Library of Congress, the University of Minnesota library, of the libraries of the State Historical Societies of Minnesota and Wisconsin, and of the library of Wisconsin State College at Eau Claire were most cooperative and their suggestions led to material I otherwise would not have been able to use. Herman Kahn of the

Franklin Delano Roosevelt library at Hyde Park replied fully to my requests. I am indebted to the family of Gutzon Borglum for permission to see his papers in the Library of Congress. George Dynes and Glenn Brudvig courteously checked some citations.

The interviews and correspondence with such public figures as Gerald P. Nye and such leaders of the Nonpartisan League as A. C. Townley are obviously of such invaluable assistance that I do not need to acknowledge these to indicate their helpfulness. They and many others are listed in the bibliography. The citations referring to them, however, represent only a token portion of their actual contribution to my understanding of William Lemke and the history of the Nonpartisan League, and I wish to express my sincerest appreciation for the assistance all of them have given. Some, such as O. B. Burtness, I interviewed many times. His willingness to give of his time on these many occasions was characteristic of all whom I interviewed, without a single exception.

There are others whose names were not centers of political controversy over such an extended period of time such as Ole Gunvaldsen, Fred McLean, and John Nystul and still others such as Russell Reid, Kathrine B. Tiffany, Charles Liessman, W. O. Skeels, Earl Duell, and E. E. Kennedy who were situated so as to have an intimate understanding of some phase of Lemke's career. These and others of this group were equally generous of their time, and their understanding of Representative Lemke and the period in which he lived contributed immeasurably to mine. Because they lived where it was convenient for me to interview them and because of their close association with and their understanding of Mr. Lemke, Mr. and Mrs. Herbert Swett were of special assistance, and I remember most appreciatively their cooperation in numerous interviews. There are many other North Dakota political figures whom I have known but whom I have not formally interviewed and acquaintances, associates, and colleagues who have contributed significantly. I am deeply conscious of my obligations to them.

The decision to preserve the William Lemke Papers by Mrs. William Lemke and her family and to permit me to use them on an unrestricted basis both before and after they were placed in the Orin G. Libby Historical Manuscripts Collection at the University of North Dakota Chester Fritz Library was most generous. The opportunity this decision provided does not always occur, and I wish to acknowledge it as basic to the writing of this biography. The interviews with Mrs.

Lemke, with her sons, William, Jr., and Robert, and with other relatives of William Lemke provided me with understanding and with guidance to sources of material which otherwise I would have overlooked.

My father, C. E. Blackorby, shared his intimate understanding of the pioneer circumstances surrounding William Lemke's boyhood, providing a vivid description and an understanding I could not have gained as well in some other manner, and I am deeply indebted to him for this and for many insights into the political and economic history of North Dakota. An uncle, C. C. Converse, was a member of the North Dakota Legislative Assembly in the 1915 session that rejected the terminal elevator proposal and served as State Tax Commissioner during the gubernatorial terms of R. A. Nestos, experiences which enabled him to assist me which he did most generously.

The advice, assistance, and encouragement given me by my wife has enabled me to bring this to completion, and my son has assisted with some of the research work. I am indebted to them more than I can ever repay.

# CONTENTS

# CHAPTER I

# Prairie Heritage

In the years just prior to 1917, William Lemke emerged as one of the leaders of the farmer rebellion known as the Nonpartisan League. Subsequently identifying himself with more extensive political movements based on agrarian discontent, he displayed an understanding of the grievances of debt-ridden spring wheat farmers and, to a lesser degree, those of all debtor classes throughout the nation. He was one of the authors of A. C. Townley's Nonpartisan League legislative program, and in 1920 he was a successful candidate for Attorney General of North Dakota. Recalled from office in 1921, it was not until 1932 that he again won an election, this time to the United States House of Representatives. In the late 1920's he drafted a program of bankruptcy and monetary legislation designed to assist debtor farmers. With these measures as a platform he was elected to Congress on the Republican ticket in 1932, but he found President Franklin D. Roosevelt, whom he had supported, opposed to his proposal for farm mortgage refinancing.

Embittered by the President's attitude, he made the political error of accepting the 1936 Presidential candidacy offered him by splinter groups. His campaign met little public response, and he was not an important factor in the election. His influence diminished by his unsuccessful candidacy, he remained—with the exception of one term—a member of the House of Representatives until his death in 1950. During these years he continued his support of farm legislation, at the same time supporting the isolationist movement and North Dakota public works and conservation programs.

Severe financial reverses in the years between 1910 and 1914 had compelled Lemke to abandon a business career based on land speculation, and it was during this time that he chanced upon, or chose, the role of agrarian radical. Once this role became his career, he proved to be a natural leader of a farm-protest movement. His

1

parents had been among the first settlers in a frontier area. The
Lemke children had vivid memories of empty country where land
was free; it was natural for William Lemke to accept the idyllic
concept of a virtuous yeomanry, an interpretation so typical as to be
referred to as the "agrarian myth." Lemke accepted as its corollary
the "agrarian demonology" which attributed farm problems to conspiracies originating among Wall Street or London bankers.[1] His own
investments in land and the problems of his relatives who were
farmers gave him a continuing interest in the difficulties experienced
by debtor farmers.

In 1881, when the Lemke family came to Dakota, the northern
half of the territory was sparsely settled—a fringe of homesteaders
along the Red River Valley; a few towns along the Northern Pacific
railroad, which ran from Fargo to Beach. The St. Paul and Pacific,
now known as the Great Northern, had just entered the territory at
Grand Forks. These were the avenues of immigration and commerce
for immigrants from Minnesota, Wisconsin, Iowa, and states farther
East. Mingled with them were those direct from Scandinavia, Germany,
other European areas, and Canada. Many who were originally from
Europe had lived in other states, sometimes for a generation, before
turning to the chief remaining areas where the Homestead, Tree
Claim, and Pre-emption laws held forth a possibility of proprietorship
without a lifetime of debt. In 1870 the population of the area that
now comprises North Dakota consisted of scattered hunters and
trappers. By 1880 the Twelfth Census showed a population of 34,896,
which increased to 152,199 in 1885 and 182,719 in 1890. The increase
in the amount of land filed on was phenomenal. About two million
acres were assigned to settlers by the land offices in 1880; in 1884
title to over eleven million acres was transferred by the government.[2]
In a few years the area was transformed from an empty land peopled
by buffalo hunters, trappers, and Indians to a territory looking toward
statehood.

The rapidity of settlement, however, created its own difficulties. The
opportunity was great for those who came with cash reserves or who,
through thrift and careful use of the labor resources of a large family,
accumulated cash. For them the hardships they were enduring,
though intense enough to create lifelong memories and attitudes,
could be relatively transitory. Within the period of a few years the
sons and daughters of the most successful settlers could experience
both the bitterest struggles of lonely pioneering and the luxury of

frame houses and college educations. But then there were those who were just successful enough to stay and the many who, not quite that successful, turned eastward again. The homesteads of these latter families were often acquired by more fortunate individuals through evasions of the commutation feature of the Homestead Act. The settler who had accumulated cash would, in return for a quitclaim deed, lend the discouraged homesteader enough money to pay the costs of commutation and the expenses of returning East. The settler who was leaving would first take title to his quarter section and then depart. The creditor would then file the quitclaim deed at the county courthouse and take possession of the land. Whether it was by a truly selective process or by the chance hand of fortune, the established families and community leaders of North Dakota for a generation to come were being chosen.

The frontier fostered the conviction that only an economic system out of harmony with the "natural order" would prevent every man from being successful, and economic conditions that stood in the way of the new settlers were resented by them. Capital was short and brought a premium. High interest rates were prevalent. There were no amortization plans, and renewal was uncertain. Many farmers lost their property after having paid the principal on their debts in the form of discounts, fees, and high interest rates, and the title of banker was often a symbol of oppression. Fluctuation of the supply of credit, sensitive to financial changes in the East, contributed to the suspicion that there was a Wall Street conspiracy afoot.[3] The credit agencies, the railroads, and the corporations which marketed the farmers' crops were often regarded as the demons interfering with the natural economic order, thus bringing hardship, failure, and bankruptcy.

North Dakota became a state in 1889. One movement of protest, The Farmers Alliance, had become strong during the last years of the territorial period. Practically every farmer in the county in which the Lemkes had settled belonged to the Alliance. A political group known as the Independents resulted from it, which in 1892 was successful in electing a governor and other state officials for one term.[4] William Lemke thus had an early opportunity to hear Populist viewpoints, an experience that was to be repeated during the free silver campaign of 1896.

The settlers were conscious of their dependence on Eastern capital and foreign markets, but Europe's political problems seemed to them to be remote indeed from the Dakota frontier. Even the recent immigration groups who retained traditions and memories from the lands of their origin felt that they had made a sharp break with the past that would never be bridged. At first the Indians were the threat to security that disturbed the homesteaders; but following the death of Sitting Bull, the defeat of the Sioux at Wounded Knee in 1890 firmly established the reservation system. Distance was credited with providing security that was actually due to the world situation. There was "the feeling of deep peace . . . the effort to forget Old World problems and the craving for isolation."[5] The environment provided an ideal medium for the growth of the attitudes that would later support isolationism.

It was here that William Lemke matured. He had been born at Albany, in Stearns County, Minnesota, on August 13, 1878. In early 1881 his parents, Frederick and Julia Lemke, moved to Grand Forks in what was then Dakota Territory, where they purchased and for a time operated the Goldberg Hotel. Grand Forks was a gateway city, an Ellis Island for the new territory, and most of the hotel guests were homesteaders on their way to where the land lay open. It was only a year later that the Lemkes sold their hotel and joined in the land rush. Frederick Lemke used his rights under the Pre-emption Act to acquire a quarter section of land near Crystal, a town in southwestern Pembina County. A year later, in the spring of 1883, the Lemkes moved again, the father driving one ox-drawn covered wagon and the mother another. They followed during part of their journey a newly built railroad that led from Grand Forks into Devils Lake, where they stayed long enough to see the first train arrive before turning their wagons northward toward the Big Coulee country in the newly constituted Towner County.[6]

The Lemkes, though of German origin, were not recent immigrants. Frederick Lemke had come from Stettin, Germany, in 1851 with his parents. He had been born at Ottendorf, Prussia, in 1843. After leaving Germany, the Lemkes made their first home in Wisconsin, later moving to Minnesota, where they lived on a farm near Farmington before moving to the Albany area. Julia Lemke was born in 1852 at Jefferson, Wisconsin, the oldest daughter of Anthony and Theresa Klier. Her father, who was originally from Bavaria, had lived in the United States since before the Mexican War and was a veteran of that conflict. Despite the fact that she was born in the United States, her speech, customs, and ideas bore a much closer resemblance to those of the old country than did those of her Prussian-born husband.

Her insistence on living in the original claim house, built in 1883, until her death in 1933 revealed her desire to stay with the old and familiar. Standing nearby was a more substantial home built and occupied by some of her children; her residence in the old home was by choice and not from necessity.[7]

The Lemkes had lived under even more primitive conditions upon their first arrival in 1883. The first task had been to get the crop planted. During the spring and summer of 1883, the family lived in a tent. In the late summer and fall they built the frame building which was to be the only home the family knew until after the father's death in 1901. The house, which was to hold a total of twelve people, was two stories high with one room on each floor.[8] A ladder made of bars nailed between the studdings was the only way to get to the second floor. Fuel was a problem on the treeless prairie, for the banks of the Big Coulee on which they had settled were not wooded. For the long cold season that lay ahead, the necessary food and other supplies had to be obtained before winter began. There was no "neighboring" this first of those years of struggle and lonesomeness which were to be such a vivid memory to William Lemke, then five years of age.

There were nine members of the family in 1883. Three more children, Caroline, Charles and Lillian, were born to the Lemkes after that time. Caroline, at first named Dakota, was the first white child born in Towner County. Charles died of croup at the age of four years; the other nine children grew to maturity. The family's religious background was divided between the German Lutheran and Roman Catholic communions. The parents had compromised by rearing the boys according to their father's Lutheranism and the girls in the faith of their mother.* Despite the religious difference, family training was strict. Children in the Lemke home were to be seen and not heard. Neighbors testified that they were shy and fled to the loft at the approach of strangers, and they would usually remain there until the guests had gone.[9] Their shyness was not surprising, for there were few neighbors, and trips to the town of Cando were rare.

* Years later, in a letter to Lemke pleading with him to affiliate with the Roman Catholic Church, Bishop Vincent Wehrle related that during early prairie missions he had urged Julia Lemke to alter the arrangement by which the boys were being raised as Protestants, but that she had told him that it was a situation which could not be changed without disturbing family harmony (Bishop Vincent Wehrle to William Lemke, July 14, 1938, Lemke Papers).

There was no neighborhood church, and education was in a one-room school which was attended by three families, the Lemkes and the children of the brothers Dave and James McCanna.

The fact that the Lemke family had arrived so early in Towner County had enabled them to select good land. It was rich, level prairie not too dissimiliar from the Red River Valley land near Grand Forks and Crystal. The Lemkes knew some very hard years. Drought caused crop failures in both 1889 and 1890, and they were in difficult circumstances at that time. The father farmed extensively. The land was free of stone and easy to cultivate. Instead of plowing, he "stubbled in" much of his crop. It was risky farming, but a good year would bring big returns. One of the most successful crop seasons the Towner County area experienced was in 1891. The farmers who had managed to stay out of debt were from that time on in better cash position not only to weather the depression years which ensued but also to profit from the misfortunes of others. Many of those who needed to use the returns from the 1891 crop to retire previous obligations did not have the necessary reserves to carry them through the hard years of 1892 and 1893. This was the time of opportunity for William Lemke's father. It was not long before the senior Lemke had accumulated a total of 2700 acres.

By 1896 Frederick Lemke was considered a wealthy man. He was a vigorous man who left a definite imprint on the lives of William and his other sons. He had enlisted in the Civil War in 1861, when he was eighteen years of age, and had served with "Company E, Third Wisconsin Cavalry."* He was proud of having been under the command of Franz Sigel at the time Missouri was saved by turning back the threat to St. Louis. When in Congress, William Lemke recalled that his father distrusted the British because he believed they had prolonged the war by helping the South with the intention of joining France in a subsequent partition of the United States.[10]

By 1900, the year before he died, Frederick Lemke had become a sufficiently prominent public figure to be elected to the lower house of the state Legislative Assembly from the district that included the counties of Rolette and Towner. His legislative career, though cut short by death, was long enough to merit an editorial in the *Bismarck Tribune* denouncing the Lemke bill, a proposal which would have transferred the state capital from Bismarck to the eastern part of the

---

* Company E, Third Wisconsin Cavalry was organized in 1861 by Colonel Barston at Janesville, Wisconsin. (Interview with Mrs. William Lemke, June 3, 1951).

state. He also supported legislation regulating interest rates and defining usury—the type of legislation for which his son was in decades to come, the nation's most determined advocate.[11] It was apparent that Frederick Lemke's Republicanism did not include allegiance to Alexander McKenzie and Judson LaMoure, who were reputed to be the political bosses of the state.

In the fall of 1901 he attended a land sale at the county courthouse with the intention of purchasing a section of state land. The bidding was brisk, as three other people wanted to buy the same land. Shortly after losing the first quarter section to be auctioned, he suffered what was diagnosed as a stroke of apoplexy and died a few minutes after he was carried from the auction room. It was the commonly held conviction of the community, shared by many members of his family, that the shock of losing the land to others had been a contributory cause to his death.* His widow received nine hundred acres of land and each of the surviving children, two hundred.[12] Ben, the oldest brother, took over the farming operations and eventually purchased much of the land from the others.

Schooling for the Lemke children was delayed and existed for the boys only in the weeks or months when there was no farm work to do. An accidental injury which destroyed the sight of one eye was an additional handicap for William, who finished the eighth grade in 1895. Seven of the fourteen children who were in school that year were Lemkes, and the others were from the two McCanna families. Ben, the oldest Lemke, was twenty-one years of age; William was sixteen; and Henry and Fred were fifteen and thirteen, respectively. Isabella was older than William; Julia and Caroline were younger. Ida was no longer in school, and Lillian was too young to attend. The Lemke family had not settled in a community of German origin, and the children, who were accustomed to speaking German at home, were compelled to use English when with other children. The teacher of the school in that year wrote:

Living conditions at home were such that there wasn't much room for them to study at night—so they each—four boys dug . . . a den in the banks of the Big Coulee—and lived in the dugouts so they could study at night. Jim McCanna Jr. was usually boss of the school. He started that on me,

---

* The three who were bidding against him were Albert Gibbens, William Noyes, and George Clerk. Gibbens obtained one-half section and Noyes and Clerk each obtained one of the other quarter-sections of the section of state land that Lemke had wished to purchase. (C. E. Blackorby to author, October 4, 1955).

and it didn't work—when the Lemke boys saw that they were going to have an equal chance . . . they seemingly woke up—got interested in the work—and seemed to really enjoy school—Bill perhaps more than the others—at any rate, I never saw anyone, that was so hungry for knowledge and could assimilate it more and faster than Bill could and did.[13]

In 1895 William transferred to Cando High School, a two-teacher institution, but one with a curriculum which included instruction in debating. His father was willing to spend money for education; when tax money was not available, he had on one occasion paid the teacher himself to secure additional weeks of instruction for his family.[14] He was equally generous in providing a college education for those of his family who desired it.

Three of the Lemke children took advantage of the opportunity for a college education. Isabella enrolled at the University of North Dakota in 1896, William in 1898, and Henry in 1899. The university was actually a small liberal arts college compelled by the poor preparation of its students to give much of its training on the secondary level. The physical facilities were limited, consisting of two classroom buildings and two dormitories.[15] However, the monopoly the college had on student time helped to overcome the handicaps of poorly prepared students, inadequate facilities, and meager salaries. In only a decade or two the leaders of the state were drawn to a surprising extent from among the alumni.

Literary societies which competed with one another in debates were a central feature of campus life. The competition was keen. Lemke "was one of the original members of the ADT Literary Society and he took his work in that very seriously too. He not only worked on his own numbers . . . but he was also a good helper for others, and especially so when they were working on inter-society debates." Although "he was not eloquent . . . fluent, nor . . . a ready speaker" there were compensating qualities, for "he was not the type to enter an oratorical contest; but he was a good debater; he spared no pains to prepare himself, working on both sides of the question in getting the material and then good, very good, in organizing it and trying to think beforehand what his opponents might or might not do and what might affect the judges."[16]

He played football with great enthusiasm. It was an amateur game with a faculty member or an older student doing the coaching. The schedules were arranged on short notice with an informality and a casualness foreign to the sport today. Student interest was spontaneous, and competition was unspoiled by sports writers, commentators, or alumni recruiters. There was nothing lukewarm about Lemke's interest: "He played football to *win;* it was not play to him, but very serious business. He gave every ounce of strength he had, and it was effective."[17] About five feet eight inches tall and weighing only 149 pounds, he was not fast enough for the backfield, so he played in the line. He became known for his grit and his unwillingness to admit pain or injury, becoming an extremely effective player and eventually serving as captain. Many of his teammates, such as W. L. Nuessle, O. B. Burtness, and Lynn J. Frazier, were later to hold positions of leadership in the state. A close friendship with Frazier developed, and the two became roommates. It was a life-long association that resulted in Lemke's backing of Frazier for governor and later for United States senator, and their names were to be linked together in agrarian debtor legislation which they introduced and passed in the national Congress.

One of Lemke's enthusiasms was to result in the introduction of fraternity life to the campus. With a handful of others, he led in the organization of the Varsity Bachelor Club, which took its name from a pledge made by its members to forego marriage. Its executive officer was known as Grand Bachelor, an office Lemke held while on the campus and until 1922. He was the pivotal leader of the club and led in the plans for building a fraternity house. It was his organization and promotion work that led to the adoption of a financing scheme whereby premiums on endowment policies taken out on the lives of prominent public figures would be paid by fees charged to the students who lived in the new home. The club was to be the beneficiary of the policies and it could also borrow funds, using the policies as security. It was Lemke also who had university alumni introduce a bill in the state Legislative Assembly permitting the erection of the present fraternity house on the university campus.[18] The house was built in 1909 in a style and in such proportions that it remains an imposing structure on the campus today—a reminder of the energies of William Lemke.

As was to be true in later life, Lemke had not thought in small terms, and he soon found that he had overreached the financial resources of the club members. To complete the financing of the house, he issued invitations to successful alumni, offering them the opportunity to become members of the Varsity Bachelor Club, with the privilege of initiation and all the privileges of membership when they returned to the campus to visit. That prestige and status had come to be associated with membership was confirmed when a surprising number of these men accepted and paid the fees. In December of 1909, nearly seven and one-half years after he had graduated, Lemke finally had the house completed and ready for occupancy.[19]

Lemke's aggressiveness was also displayed at the university in less constructive ways. At times the student-faculty relationship was closer than desired by the students. Careful supervision, rigid rules, and strict standards of conduct were imposed and enforced. Students well into their twenties expressed irritation at faculty restrictions and felt hostility toward particular faculty members who enforced the rules. Vilhjalmur Stefansson, later a famous Arctic explorer and author, undiscouraged by expulsion, went on to win national and international distinction; decades later he received apologies in the form of an honorary degree. Lemke was never so unorthodox as to merit this severe a disciplinary action, though both Frazier and he lost the privilege of living in the college dormitory.[20] They neither drank nor smoked and thus avoided the type of difficulty that brought more serious results to others.

Lemke was considered an able student, but he did not rank at the top of his class. Chemistry was the only science course he took. In addition to his law courses, he earned credits in Spanish, French, German, philosophy, history, government, public finance, sociology, and English. For some reason his part in student escapades did not lessen the esteem in which he was held by President Webster Merrifield and most of the members of the faculty. Professor Samuel Peterson was certain of the impression Lemke would make as a student at Georgetown University, where he enrolled after completing his studies at the university. M. A. Brannon likewise urged him to go East for further study, and the influence of Merrifield and Peterson may have caused Lemke to select Yale University when he decided to transfer from Georgetown.[21]

In any event the interest of faculty members in Lemke was a continuing one. Many of them later showed their confidence in him by investing in enterprises he had organized. A few years after he graduated, when President Merrifield wanted an alumnus of the university on the Board of Regents, it was to Lemke that he wrote, with copies of his letter to Lemke going to other prominent alumni. In every way it is clear that by the time of graduation Lemke was a quite different person from the not very prepossessing nineteen-year-old country boy whom Dean Joseph Kennedy had enrolled in the fall of 1898.

Lemke's natural vigor of expression was to characterize his later life as well as his student life. Although his reading and training gave him the eloquence and forensic ability that would later enable him to address select audiences such as the United States Supreme Court in restrained and dignified language, the forceful and earthy vernacular with which oxen had been compelled to gee and haw was always at his command. The language of the threshing crews was his so naturally that one hearing him use it might conclude that he knew no other. When occasion demanded, he could be an orator; yet he could also quickly change pace and become an effective stump speaker.

Other forerunners of the coming years appeared. The Lemke family fortune had come from purchasing cheap land, and during his college years Lemke had been bantered about an ambition to invest in Latin America. One of the student publications had referred to him as "King William. . . . He has not given up, but has simply postponed, his plan of going to South America and forming one grand empire out of the republics there." In his own letters he himself referred to this definite ambition. Professor Andrew Bruce of the Law School observed that Lemke's interest in Latin America had been aroused by reading *Soldiers of Fortune* and *Captain Macklin,* books by Richard Harding Davis.[22] Whatever their origin, there is something of Walker filibustering and Austin land promotion in the ideas Lemke expressed while still in college.*

From the very beginning of his legal practice, Lemke held the opinions of a progressive liberal in the La Follette tradition; he was a devotee of the Wisconsin ideas of primary election and popular government. How much his prairie Farmers' Alliance, Populist heritage and how much his instruction from university professors such as Samuel Peterson inclined him in this direction is difficult to ascertain. Peterson later wrote a book, *Democracy and Government,* revealing his idealistic sense of mission and his understanding of political philosophy as well as of the mechanics of government.[23] Lemke's instruction in government was neither mechanical nor mediocre.

Indicative of the influence of its university upon the state of North Dakota is the number of alumni who participated either in the progressive movement in the years before 1916 or in the Nonpartisan

---

* Use of the commutation provision of the Homestead law had enabled Lemke to obtain land near Bisbee.

League. Noteworthy, besides Lemke, were Lynn J. Frazier, William Langer,\* and J. M. Anderson. Even those whose reputations did not come from the Nonpartisan League, such as O. B. Burtness, W. L. Nuessle, Gudmundur Grimson, and R. A. Nestos, were in pre-League days, members of the Progressive faction of the Republican party;† they never affiliated themselves with the stand-pat group which supported and succeeded the Alexander McKenzie machine. Paul Griffith wrote Lemke in later years of the days when they lay on the campus lawn dreaming of the time when they could reform the state government. During Lemke's college years the McKenzie-LaMoure machine was alleged by opponents to be in complete control of the state, and it was not until the first year in which Lemke served as a practicing attorney that the machine suffered a crippling reverse.[24] McKenzie's opposition in the state was led by the editor of the *Grand Forks Herald,* George B. Winship, an advocate of progressive reforms such as primary elections and the short ballot. Winship was politically influential in the Grand Forks area; students at the university were exposed to his influence both directly by means of his paper and indirectly by means of their instructors. Part of the liberal tendency in North Dakota politics attributed to the university may have been the result of Winship's crusading journalism.

While at the university, Lemke participated in military drill with zest and enthusiasm. During his first ten years as an attorney, he wrote to both Presidents Taft and Wilson offering to organize regiments in the Rough Rider tradition for service in Mexico, citing his military training at the university as his qualification for command.

Lemke's student life did not include very much purely social activity.

---

\* William Langer, of Cass County, came from a background remarkably similar to Lemke's. Langer too was of German stock, descended from a family that had known both frontier struggles and later prosperity. Equally brilliant and ambitious, he too had sufficient resources and encouragement to go East to college after leaving the university. Langer was a La Follette Progressive with views on both domestic and international affairs almost identical to those of Lemke. Despite the Roman Catholicism in their religious backgrounds, both men later married Protestants and raised their children in the Protestant tradition. The two were on friendly terms while attending the university, although Langer, being one class behind Lemke and eight years younger, did not challenge Lemke's seniority or leadership at that time. It was not until later that their careers would make them rivals.

† Prior to attending the university, Frazier and Nestos had attended the Mayville Normal School, as had Usher L. Burdick, who, when denied admission to the University of North Dakota, attended the University of Minnesota.

There are numerous letters to and from girls who were fellow students —letters which bespeak genuine liking and respect—but nothing more serious. He was not communicative in the ordinary table chitchat, but he was always courteous and he came alive when more serious subjects, such as politics and world affairs, were introduced.[25] A lover of flowers and poetry, Lemke had to be known to have his gentler qualities appreciated. His stern appearance was accentuated by a strong jaw and rough facial skin. Had his eye been uninjured and had he himself been less serious in mien and manner, he might have found feminine interest more difficult to resist at this time.

Friendships among the students at the University of North Dakota were close. These were the ties which later made it possible for Lemke to promote his investments and to obtain the employment with the Equity Co-operative Exchange that was his steppingstone to leadership in the Nonpartisan League. The alumni were a statewide club of which Lemke was a leading member, one to whom the others turned for leadership not only in the affairs of the Varsity Bachelor Club but in other university legislative and alumni activities.

In the fall of his senior year, Lemke and his brother Henry were called home by the death of their father. In the fall of 1903, after four years of liberal arts and one year of law training at the university, Lemke entered Georgetown University in Washington, D.C. Attachment to his mother's religion or deference to the wishes of his sister Isabella may have dictated his choice of college. Whatever the reason, he was to stay there only a year before transferring to Yale University. At Georgetown, he ranked thirty-fifth in a class of seventy-six students;[26] while there he worked for a time in the office of Senator William B. Allison of Iowa.

Regarding his year of study at Yale Lemke mentioned more often than any other in his correspondence the lectures in constitutional law given by Simeon O. Baldwin, even though this was one of the courses in which his grade score was lowest. His rank in class is not available, but his average grade was several points below that earned at Georgetown. A recommendation written in later years by Dean Henry Wade Rogers of the Law School, in whose classes he had earned very creditable marks, indicated that Lemke had made a good impression as a student. William Howard Taft, then Secretary of War, addressed the 1905 graduating class, and Lemke later recalled having been introduced to him at that time. Living at a boarding house, he did not enter into social life and formed few friendships, although one, with the son of Senator José Castellot of Mexico City, was very significant as Castellot interested Lemke in Mexican land and successfully encouraged him to form Mexican land colonization companies.[27]

After graduating from Yale in 1905 and while looking for an opening to practice law, Lemke temporarily took care of the practice of C. C. Converse, a Cando attorney.[28] When J. E. Robinson, a Fargo attorney, invited him to join his firm, Lemke accepted. Thus he began a career that was to be trying, challenging, hectic, and often disappointing.

Lemke returned to his own state, a young man who had gone abroad and made good, with enhanced reputation among his former teachers and classmates. North Dakota already had attorneys who were graduates of Eastern universities as well as many citizens of erudition, but they had arrived in the state so equipped. Lemke was among the first from North Dakota and from its university to return from the East as a graduate of a famous university law school. He was twenty-eight years of age, ambitious for political recognition as well as for professional and financial success. The Varsity Bachelor Club, the partnership with Robinson, and his Mexican land companies were the three respective vehicles through which he expected to achieve these three objectives.

Lemke hoped that the Varsity Bachelor Club and the other "University boys" could influence the actions of national senators and representatives, the governor, and other elected officials. The political division within the dominant Republican party was between the Progressives and the Stalwarts. Repeated defeats in Republican conventions caused the former to desert the party in the 1906 general election to effect the election of the Democrat John Burke—a defection they repeated in 1908 and again in 1910. Because he feared that return of the governorship to the conservatives would mean abandonment of the Robert La Follette reform program, Lemke supported Burke.[29] The Progressives, however, had also been successful in electing some Republicans to the national House of Representatives. In 1900 Thomas Marshall, who was later considered a Progressive, was elected. In 1904 Asle J. Gronna joined Marshall as one of the state's two representatives.* When the census of 1910 resulted in a third congressional district for North Dakota, Patrick D. Norton, another Progressive, won the post. But the senators, chosen by the state legislature, tended to remain conservative. In 1898, Martin N. Johnson, a representative with Progressive leanings, was defeated by a Stalwart candidate, Porter J. McCumber, although Henry Clay Hansborough, the other senator,

---

* Later, as senator, Gronna was to become one of La Follette's closest associates.

later displayed some sympathy for the Progressives and was disowned by McKenzie and subsequently defeated.*

The role Lemke played in this political situation was in large part determined by his location in Fargo and by the presence of his new law partner, J. E. Robinson. Fargo, the largest city, stood at the gateway of the state. It was the natural center for any statewide organization such as the new agrarian movement then developing. A patriarch with flowing beard and a dignified and pompous manner, Robinson was as ready to preach of the evils of the day as were the Biblical prophets whom he in some respects resembled. He was positive, dynamic, eccentric, and in general a "character." Coming in 1882 from Maryland to Fargo to practice law, he had been identified with the famous divorce-mill era when Fargo was something of a Reno. After his 1916 election to the North Dakota Supreme Court, he discussed the cases before the court in signed newspaper articles. His letters to friends were distinctive. It was not unusual for him to use two or three words, or at best a phrase, to do the work of a sentence; and often there were only six or seven lines to a page written in a large bold hand.[30] If Lemke had searched for a partner who would do less to neutralize his own eccentricities, he could not have been more successful.

Robinson could tolerate the idiosyncracies of others in turn for having his own gruff ones accepted, and he shared both the office work and the pleading with Lemke. Although politically ambitious, he achieved a position on the state Supreme Court only after several election defeats. His greatest enthusiasm was for judicial simplicity, for cutting directly through the law's delays and circumlocutions to give what seemed to him to be the just decision. Instead of the customary involved opinion, Robinson's rulings would be given tersely and to the point in informal English; but what brevity he gained was lost by his comments on extraneous subjects. In his crusading enthusiasm, he published a small monthly magazine entitled *The Common Good,* containing articles of his own and of others, the subscription price of which was one dollar a year. Lemke became co-publisher and editor. The magazine savored of the reform spirit then current and carried on its masthead the motto, "The good of the whole community can be promoted only by advancing the good of each individual composing it. What must we do to be saved?" Underneath the motto the names of

* Johnson was victorious over Hansborough and Marshall in 1908 but died in 1909. Burke's Democratic appointee was displaced by the election of Gronna in 1910.

the magazine's publishers appeared in bold print: "Published by Robinson and Lemke." Articles concerned topics including corruption within the legal profession, low interest rates of government-owned New Zealand banks, election law reforms such as the initiative, and public ownership of utilities and marketing facilities.[31] The general atmosphere of public-spiritedness and moral indignation may well have furthered Lemke's inclination toward the Progressive movement. However, Robinson and Lemke were not revolutionaries. Their motivation was not so much a dislike of capitalism as a desire to have the rules changed to benefit aspirants like themselves. They understood the conflict of interest between rentiers and entrepreneurs, and they realized that the game was being played to benefit the rentiers rather than the entrepreneurs, among whom they classed themselves.

Lemke's legal, business and political activities, however, did not interfere with a newly awakened romantic interest. In 1908 the firm of Robinson and Lemke employed Miss Isabelle McIntyre* as a stenographer; Lemke lodged in the hotel-rooming house owned by Miss McIntyre's mother. Others of the Varsity Bachelor Club had broken their fraternal vows, and it was soon to be Lemke's turn. Miss McIntyre discovered that Lemke was not as stern and unbending as he appeared; he delighted in helping her with the flower garden and yard work on her mother's property. Their engagement was announced and the marriage set for April 16, 1910, in the Protestant Episcopal Gethsemane Cathedral. A trip to look after Lemke's Mexican properties was to be their honeymoon.[32]

This land had been purchased from Senator José Castellot, whose son Lemke had known at Yale, and M. B. Katze. A vast tract on the west coast of Mexico in the state of Sinaloa, it had all the advantages of North Dakota's Red River Valley plus a warm, moderate climate, and Lemke quickly perceived that it could be versatile in production and extremely fruitful. His own experience had taught him that land obtained for almost nothing needed only railways and people to increase in value. This Mexican land could be purchased for a few cents an acre, and the Southern Pacific Railway was being built toward it. Lemke reasoned that Americans, their own frontier gone, would follow the railroad down the west coast of Mexico just as they were then settling in Alberta in Canada.[33]

Once his enthusiasm was aroused, he brushed all doubts aside. Soon he would move there himself. There would be an American area with

* Originally Isabelle McGilvray. McIntyre was adopted as her name upon her mother's second marriage.

American schools. Not tens of thousands but hundreds of thousands of Americans would migrate to Sinaloa. He would be happy to spend his life there, away from the cold climate and the political injustices imposed upon North Dakota and the United States by conservative reactionaries. He organized the Black Earth Finance Company in 1906 and with Castellot's and Katze's assistance he organized tours to Mexico for North Dakotan investors. When in Mexico, these investors were introduced to President Porfirio Díaz and to the governors of many of the states. They were treated with royal courtesy by Díaz, and eventually a total of $400,000 was invested to purchase 550,000 acres. The first 80,000 acres of rich agricultural land was carried on the company's books as worth $20.00 an acre. The rest of the acreage was timber and grazing land located in the territory of Tepic, later to become the state of Nayarit, and was given a value of $1.25 an acre on the books of the Land Finance Company, organized by Lemke and incorporated in 1907, replacing the Black Earth Finance Company.[34]

Lemke and his Mexican colleagues had made the tours so successful that a land boom developed. Robinson had supported Lemke's enterprises by investing in them from the start. Lynn J. Frazier, among others, was willing to go deeply into debt in order to do the same. Other investors were past or current members of the faculty of the University of North Dakota and business or professional men from Lemke's home town of Cando and from the nearest larger town of Devils Lake, in addition to many of the families who farmed in the Big Coulee area of Towner and Ramsey counties, as well as many of Lemke's former fellow students and their relatives and friends. Noteworthy among these latter was William Langer, who invested his own money and persuaded many of his Casselton relatives to invest also.[35]

Because many of those investing also took part in North Dakota politics, the tours had to be arranged in the interims between elections. "I fully appreciate conditions covering election, and all other matters mentioned in your letter, and upon bringing your party down in November, we will arrange for them to meet President Díaz, and the leading members of the cabinet, having them meet the different Governors in case you visit different States on your trip to the Republic, and everything will be done by us to make their stay pleasant and agreeable," Katze wrote about the 1908 tour. In 1909 Lemke took another group, and the additional $40,000 necessary to complete the second purchase was raised. *The Common Good* was now used for promotion of the enterprise.[36] By 1909 Lemke had utilized all of his own funds and all he had been able to raise through the sale of stock.

Lemke had sensed no hint of political instability in the Mexican government. Porfirio Díaz was eighty years of age and had exercised dictatorial powers in Mexico almost continuously since 1878; in 1908 he could not be expected to rule much longer. Under Díaz large land grants had been obtained by his favorites, the inhabitants expelled, and the lands closed, "awaiting the coming of some Yankee prospector in search of vast tracts . . . to be used . . . in bamboozling his countrymen through the organization of . . . agricultural companies." Occasionally the Yankee prospector was himself deceived. Lemke staked his entire fortune and continued to use his own money to protect his investors until his death in 1950.[37]

In 1909, after the investments had been made, Lemke was disturbed by a magazine article entitled "Barbarous Mexico." He protested vigorously, asking for space in which to answer the article, which he alleged was "so full of untruths and half truths. . . . It certainly is to be regretted that you should lend your columns to slander and malign the world's greatest ruler, Porfirio Diaz, the President of Mexico. . . . The slums there are no worse than you find in Chicago and other cities." Statements such as this are difficult to reconcile with the high value placed on Lemke's sagacity by his many friends and by some of his opponents. Readiness to exaggerate and to conceal conditions which, if revealed, would interfere with his interests both marred and limited his career. Unsubstantiated charges, innuendo, and a tendency to invective characterized his political offensive and were not always forgotten. The admiration of his friends stemmed from other qualities. Another inaccurate statement was his description of Mexican travel conditions. To reassure Frank Langer, the father of William Langer, whom the adverse publicity had disturbed, Lemke wrote: "Mrs. Langer will find it as safe and comfortable to travel in Mexico as she does in the states."[38]

His honeymoon trip to Mexico in 1910 refuted his own statement regarding the safety of Mexican travel. His desire to see the wilder portions of the property his company had purchased took him and his bride to areas which lacked the comforts he had described to Langer. Mrs. Lemke later recalled traveling "over a road built by Cortez. . . . When we went over those big rocks we would bounce to the top of the coach and come down with a thud. It was really torture. . . . At night one driver ran beside the mules carrying a lighted pine torch . . . so we would not go over the precipice." They had gone as far as possible by train, but after that they had to utilize almost every means of transportation. "The R.R. was completed as far as the Santiago river. . . . From there . . . we traveled to Tepic by mule . . . . We stayed nights at native shacks and ate their food. . . . I was so tired I was hardly conscious. . . . All I was able to do was hang on to that animal."[39]

As bad as the first trip was, it did not rival Mrs. Lemke's second one, in which the Lemke party became involved in guerrilla warfare that resulted from the overthrow of Díaz and the accession of Madero. The latter was unable to restrain the Indians under Zapata, who moved northward taking land, driving foreigners out, and leaving chaos and often death in their path. Mrs. Lemke recalled: "The next time I went to Mexico with Bill was in Jan., 1911. Quite a number went that time. They were colonists and bought land with the intention of making their homes there. . . . The revolution broke out. . . . The S.P.R.R. gave us two box cars to live in. . . . This was an anxious time. . . . One night there was a battle between the rebels and Federal troops. . . . Bullets hit the house and trees. . . . Rebel soldiers rode to the Ranch House." When they inquired on which side the Americans were, William Langer, who was with the party, answered: " 'Viva William Howard Taft.' That amused them and they went away. . . . The rebels took most of our cattle and horses."[40]

It was on this trip that the rupture between Langer and Lemke took place. Langer was discouraged about the corporation in which he and his family had invested $50,000. He wanted the party to leave; Lemke thought it wisest to stay. Langer subsequently demanded and received approximately $500, all the cash Lemke had available, and left on foot. It was impossible to communicate with the United States to obtain funds, and this, together with the danger of traveling with women and children, compelled the Lemke party to remain another two months, their situation made the more perilous by their lack of funds. Langer started walking and eventually was picked up by two men in an open car. They were all arrested by the Federals and the two men were shot.[41] Langer was able to escape, but the relations between Langer and Lemke were never again the same as before. Each thought the other had been unreasonable and unfair, and the hostility between them, although concealed at times, was to affect the political careers of both.

Americans who had investments in Mexico confidently assumed

that another *caudillo* would arise and that their own country would support him on a *de facto* basis. Accordingly, when Madero failed to maintain order, they were delighted at his overthrow by Huerta, who promised to follow policies similar to those of Díaz. They knew that the American ambassador, Henry Lane Wilson, favored such a policy and that he had recommended that the Huerta government be recognized and supported.[42] For Lemke recognition was vital. His entire enterprise was menaced unless stability was restored soon; the two years since the outbreak of the revolution had nearly ruined him financially. Just when it seemed that all would be well, the murder of Madero caused the Taft administration to withhold recognition, leaving the problem for Woodrow Wilson. The latter's adoption of a *de jure* policy refusing to recognize any regime not chosen by constitutional means was the final blow to Lemke's Mexican dream.

Many liberals in the United States recognized that Wilson was acting from idealistic motives, even though fumblingly so, in an effort to bring true democracy and traditional American political principles of government to Mexico. It was Lemke and not Wilson who was out of character. Up to 1913 American investors in Mexico had recognized the source of Mexican anarchy to be in Mexico, but after that date they felt that just as the Mexicans were about to restore stability, President Wilson interfered and encouraged other generals and bandits to revolt against Huerta.

Lemke's attitude was one of unbelief. Why a President "should virtually form an alliance with murder, rape, and robbery in the name of Villa" was more than he could understand. "Verily this is the age of the school teacher." It was not long before, in Lemke's vocabulary, Wilson was the "he-schoolmarm," an inhumane man to whom "350 Americans that have been murdered mean nothing." Not recognizing his own motives, Lemke accused Wilson of being influenced by the imperialistic Standard Oil Company. Wilson and Bryan were, in Lemke's words, "cowardly dogs."[43]

His own financial situation was becoming desperate. Every cent he could gather was used in meeting taxes and expenses of the Land Finance Company, for otherwise title to the Mexican property would revert to the Mexican government. He found it necessary to postpone payment of a subscription to the *Literary Digest* and to sign notes for his life insurance premiums. When his own lack of funds made it necessary to levy assessments against the stockholders, Lemke's indignation grew greater. When he was unable to borrow funds, Wilson was the scapegoat to whom Lemke assigned responsibility for this and all of the troubles of the company; "his hands, I believe are bood [*sic*] stained, and I can prove it. By this I mean he assisted the men who murdered and robbed in Mexico in every way possible against the established Huerta government." The only solution, he decided, was election of a Republican President in 1916, for then everything would be as it had been before the Madero revolt of 1910. The United States would never stand for confiscation, he argued, and the only chance of loss lay in failure to pay the assessments to meet taxes and interest charges.[44]

Both Huerta, whom President Wilson was opposing, and Díaz had been generous to the Roman Catholic Church, and Lemke found unexpected allies in members of the Roman Catholic clergy who favored Huerta. Everything depended upon maintaining investor confidence and awakening the voters to the need of defeating Wilson. Gathering material from José Castellot and from Father F. C. Kelly of Chicago, Illinois, and drawing on his own information, Lemke wrote a book entitled *Crimes Against Mexico*, denouncing Wilson for his policies and advocating their reversal. Published in 1915, it contained statements bitterly critical, and when Lemke decided on a lecture tour about the Mexican situation, his speeches were in the same vein. Reviewers commented on the bitterness of the book. "That is all the ignorant pup knows" was Lemke's response to a review of his book in the *Fargo Forum*, and he defended his book at length in the columns of another Fargo paper, *The Searchlight*.[45]

At no time in North Dakota's history has any distant speculative project influenced the political history of the state as much as did the Lemke investment in Mexico. The building of the railroads and the bonanza farms of the Dalrymples and others had a greater impact, but they were close at hand. The Land Finance Company was a distant investment comparable in this respect to the Mississippi and South Sea bubbles. For Lemke it was a fatal error. His lifetime's energies, his own accumulations and inheritance, the reserves and often the credit of his friends were all hazarded on the enterprise, and lost. Lemke, no doubt, had intended to charge the colonists high prices for the land, and had justified it by convincing himself that they would prosper. Nor had it disturbed his social conscience that their prosperity might be partly due to cheap labor and Mexican poverty. But he had not intended that his associates should lose money, and he was distressed to know how much hardship he had caused his friends. That distress warped his political convictions, making an interventionist in one area of one who was an isolationist in all others; a colonial-minded man instead of an anti-imperialist; a supporter of a reactionary dictator by a young politician who in domestic politics posed as a liberal and a champion of the underdog; and a seeker of political favor from conservative President Taft by an arch La Follette progressive. Aside from the rupture with Langer that eventually contributed to a defeat of North Dakota's Nonpartisan League, Lemke's hostility to Wilson spared Republicans future worry about a possible coalition of the North Dakota Nonpartisan League with the Wilson administration. Perhaps the greatest effect on North Dakota that this speculative venture had was the transition of Lemke himself to the role of agrarian radical. Had he and his friends grown rich in the Mexican enterprise, it is difficult to imagine him as North Dakota's political prairie rebel. It was the credit stringency during the years when borrowed funds were needed to prevent failure which first occasioned his bitter references to the money trust and Wall Street financiers.

The book he had written made little impact. His lecture tour was too unsuccessful to continue long. Because Woodrow Wilson was in the White House, Lemke could do nothing to help the Land Finance Company. In the fall of 1915, he made one more trip to Mexico, an unhappy experience. He found disorder and banditry everywhere, and for a time he was in the custody of Obregon. An attack of typhus interrupted his trip, and he ventured no farther than Mexico City. Coming home before he was well, he remained seriously ill during January and February of 1916. He found it difficult to forget the scenes he had witnessed and the tragic lot that had befallen former acquaintances. Moreover, Senator Castellot, now a refugee in the United States, was in difficult economic circumstances and constantly harassed Lemke for funds which Lemke owed and was unable to pay.[46]

Lemke needed a new project, one which ultimately was to be supplied by A. C. Townley and in a form that would have the additional appeal to Lemke of threatening to terminate Woodrow Wilson's political career. An additional grievance against Wilson resulted from the form memo with which Lemke's offer to organize a Rough Rider–type regiment for Mexican service had been rejected.[47] This casual response to a labored personal letter, several pages long, seemed to Lemke a personal affront. He was prepared for any opportunity to help defeat the Democratic administration.

In contrast to the disappointment and disaster created by his Mexican venture, Lemke's life had a brighter side. His marriage had ended the personal loneliness and isolation that had been his. On March 7, 1912, a son was born. He was named William after his father, and Lemke's pride and pleasure in the new arrival is apparent in his correspondence.* Lemke liked poetry and would read it by the hour. He belonged to the Eugene Field Society. Sentimentally romantic by nature and easily entertained by well-turned phrases and pithy sayings, he was an especial devotee of anything written or compiled by Elbert Hubbard, purchasing nearly everything Hubbard published. He enjoyed Mark Twain and often referred to *The Mysterious Stranger,* one of Twain's less known works. He now had a yard and garden of his own and could enjoy his hobby, the growing of flowers. He was still active among the university group and was responsible for the fact that Victor Wardrope, one of his closest friends, was on the Board of Regents. The relationship between the Merrifields and the Lemkes was unusually cordial, and it was Lemke who was toastmaster at the 1912 alumni reunion. These reunions were annual affairs, and his trips to the Varsity Bachelor Club home on the campus were frequent.[48]

Although he was of a divided religious background, his personal habits, except in his use of profanity, conformed with those that would be approved by the standards of those faiths which are very strict. However, he was not a regular church attendant and did not worry about the problems associated with religion. To those who inquired as to his personal beliefs, he simply said that he did not know but thought man was placed here for a purpose and that he preferred to leave speculation and debate to others. Born of Lutheran and Roman Catholic parents, married in an Episcopal ceremony, and now adjusting himself to the Christian Science faith that Mrs. Lemke had embraced, Lemke himself had developed a patient kind of deism, one that did not prevent him from using the symbols of other people's faiths to appeal to their emotions, yet one which made it impossible for him to feel dogmatic certainty. He was not a scorner and seemed

---

* Two more children were born to the Lemkes. The second oldest, Robert McIntyre, was born on February 21, 1916; their daughter, Mary Eleanor, on June 18, 1920.

to understand the need of others for a certainty that he neither needed nor felt.* Yet Lemke's family and philosophy could not keep him from being a bitter man. He had always displayed great intensity in anything in which he was engaged; and he could not understand the part his own poor judgment had played in his financial reverses. He had need of an outlet for his indignation and a very definite need for employment.

The Society of Equity had been founded in North Dakota in 1907 with John M. Anderson as its first secretary. When the Equity Cooperative Exchange was organized in 1911 to enter the grain commission business in the terminal market, Anderson became its first president. Through Anderson, an old Varsity Bachelor Club friend, Lemke had been in contact with Equity from its beginning and he had attempted to use Equity to elect Thomas Marshall and to defeat Porter J. McCumber for United States senator in 1910. Anderson had used all of his influence as an Equity officer to arouse interest in Lemke's Land Finance Company.[49]

In view of their close relationship, it is hard to imagine Anderson employing any other attorney than Lemke for Equity's legal work in North Dakota. This professional association brought with it introductions to a great many rising young politicians from outside of North Dakota's borders as well as from within. The friendship with Anderson later cooled and the men ceased to be close friends in 1916, but Lemke's associates in Equity included George Lofthus, the Equity orator and organizer, who in turn introduced Lemke to the issues of the agrarian movement. Other men in Equity legal work included Minnesota liberals who had been elected to Congress, such as James

---

* This is the substance of her memory of Lemke's comments of Mrs. Herbert Swett during an interview on September 10, 1956. A devout Lutheran and an admirer of Lemke's political career, she had asked Lemke about his philosophy.

The author is indebted to both Mr. and Mrs. Herbert Swett for many insights into Lemke's character. They were faithful political followers of Lemke and transported him from one speaking engagement to another during many of his campaigns. Swett was leader of the Nonpartisan League faction in the lower house of the North Dakota legislature in 1923, working closely with Lemke. Through the years that followed he was always identified with the Lemke faction of the League. In 1936 he followed Lemke into the Union party and was in charge of getting Union party electors on the ballot in the mountain and Pacific coast states during that campaign. Later in the year he managed Lemke's congressional campaign in North Dakota. Their long period of association with Lemke and the fact that they were both able, astute observers of what was happening have made them particularly helpful to the author.

Manahan and Charles A. Lindbergh, father of the famous aviator. Other Minnesotans whom he came to know well were Benjamin Drake, Spurgeon O'Dell, and Frederick A. Pike. Their liberal and radical friends throughout the nation further widened Lemke's circle of acquaintances.

One of the most influential forces within this agrarian movement was the Agricultural College at Fargo. Horace E. Stockbridge, its first president, had recruited instructors who were to have a major impact on the state's history. John H. Worst, its third president, had supported these men in the work they did. E. F. Ladd and H. L. Bolley were two of the better known men whom Stockbridge had brought to the state, and Stockbridge had instructed Ladd to make "a thorough and systematic investigation of the composition and physical characteristics of wheat . . . with the hope of establishing a definite and accepted method for the simple and positive determination of the grade in the buying and selling of wheat, the result of which would be the prevention of controversy between buyer and seller, the protection of producer against unscrupulous purchasers and of honest dealers against the unfavorable influence of dishonest buyers."[50] Ladd had very effectively carried out this mandate, and the results of his work were used by Equity leaders in their agitation for marketing reforms. Lemke's work with Equity brought him in much closer touch than ever before with Ladd and with other men at the Agricultural College, and he became interested in the controversies revolving about that institution. Conservative groups in the state were backing Thomas Cooper of the college's extension division in an effort to break the close working relationship of the college with the leaders of the agrarian movement within the state. Ladd had issued many bulletins reporting on his research work, most of which tended to confirm the suspicions of farmers regarding the unfairness of grain grading as then practiced in North Dakota. Conservative business interests were disturbed because of the results of Ladd's work and sought to bring other influences into the college that would either neutralize or terminate it.

But the most important friendship for Lemke at this time was the friendship that developed between him and Fred B. Wood, one of the North Dakota leaders of Equity. It was Wood who gave A. C. Townley the foothold Townley needed to start the Nonpartisan League; and it was Wood who later convinced Townley that Lemke was the legal adviser they needed to complete the triumvirate which controlled the

League.[51] This association with F. B. Wood, a McHenry County member of Equity, was Lemke's entree to Nonpartisan League leadership and state-wide political prominence.

Lemke's battles for Equity were almost a rehearsal for those he later fought for the Nonpartisan League. As his effectiveness in the courtroom became known, many Equity members came to him with their personal legal problems, soon learning that Lemke charged little and often did not collect that. Lemke, either intentionally or through happenstance, began developing the reputation as the legal friend of the farmer—a reputation which was to be a major political asset. There were prominent cases which occasioned newspaper publicity;[52] Anderson employed Lemke to represent him in an action requesting the removal of the head of the Fargo police department. Because this case involved a large convention of farmers, agrarian leaders throughout the state learned of Lemke and became conscious of his legal and forensic ability.

Each year Equity sponsored a Tri-State Grain Growers' Association meeting at Fargo at which farmers from North Dakota, South Dakota, and Minnesota could benefit from the information and the speakers made available by the Agricultural College. On January 23, 1914, the meeting was in full session with a program scheduled to run well into the evening. Conservative business interests recognized that these meetings helped create discontent with both the marketing and credit facilities available to farmers. These businessmen were angered and irritated, and some of them who attended the meetings had heckled the speakers. It seemed to Equity officials that the conservatives were there for no other reason than to create disturbance and trouble. They planned to continue their evening session when members of the Chamber of Commerce, the president of the Civic Auditorium Association, the sheriff, and the city police chief arrived, announcing that another group had made prior arrangements for the use of the hall for that evening, and attempted to take over the platform. A near riot ensued, during which the sheriff was thrown off the platform three times. Anderson quieted the crowd after which the police chief, J. K. Bingham, ordered the meeting to disperse. The farmers left, but they and their leaders focused the resentment they felt on the police chief who had broken up their meeting.[53]

In the ensuing litigation Lemke's talents played a starring role. In the other Equity cases, Lemke had been one of several attorneys. The legal counsel from St. Paul and Minneapolis had been the main attorneys, and his own part had been that of North Dakota consultant.

In this case Lemke was the attorney employed to represent Anderson, who was demanding Bingham's removal as chief of police. Indignation meetings were held where Lemke was the principal speaker. Hearings were held before the City Commission with Lemke presenting the case for Anderson. Only one member favored disciplining Bingham, and it was apparent that the case was accomplishing little besides providing exercise for Lemke's talents. Lofthus recommended that the case be dropped, but Lemke characteristically persisted, next requesting Governor Louis B. Hanna to remove Bingham from office. The governor pleaded a trip to Europe, thus stalling the case until fall, when he finally refused to grant Lemke's request. Meanwhile, newspaper headlines such as "Lemke scores Police Chief" and reported remarks of Bingham that Lemke was a "disgrace to the North Dakota bar" were the best kind of advertising for Lemke in his effort to achieve prominence in the Equity movement. Until this time he had merited few, if any, front page news stories or headlines.[54]

Despite Hanna's failure to act favorably on Lemke's request in the Bingham case, the governor retained Lemke's support in the elections of 1914. Although Lemke continued his disloyalty to the progressive movement by opposing Usher L. Burdick, his opposition to the Progressives in 1914 was not the determining factor it probably had been in 1912, when he had marshaled the forces of the Varsity Bachelor Club in support of Hanna or in 1910 when he left the state during the primary campaign instead of remaining to support the Progressives, Marshall and W. S. Lauder, in their campaigns against McCumber and Hanna. The third party candidacy of J. H. Wishek was responsible for Burdick's defeat, as Lemke and the Varsity Bachelor Club seem to have been for James A. Buchanan's in 1912. Hanna's victories in 1912 and 1914 enabled Arthur C. Townley's Nonpartisan League to take the place of the Progressive faction in North Dakota politics and caused an entirely new political alignment in the state. Lemke's support of Hanna was one of the contradictions in Lemke's record, for he was supporting the man whose conservative views and policies created the farmer rebellion in which Lemke was to be a leading rebel. His obligation to Hanna for assistance with the Varsity Bachelor Club (Phi Delta Theta) home was the explanation for Lemke's action, but it is not an adequate defense of his failure to support the progressive movement in which he believed. Nor does it alter the fact that the primary elections of 1912 and 1914 were two of the most decisive in the history of the state.

World War I had broken out during the late summer and thus

momentarily intensified North Dakota's credit stringency. Two months after the fall election, the legislature met in a session which proved to be one of the most significant in North Dakota's history. Lemke was present for a few days of the session and was there when Lofthus threw down the gauntlet to the legislature and demanded the building of a state-owned terminal elevator, a political issue since Populist days of Lemke's early youth. Lemke wrote: "I did not do anything in Bismarck.... After the reading of the roll call the legislature is not in a mood to do anything more for us than they have to. I believe there is a fair show of getting the Terminal Elevator."[55] Lemke was wrong about the probable action of the legislature on the terminal elevator, but, because the legislature refused to appropriate funds for the proposal, he was able to return to the 1917 legislature as one of the leaders and political bosses of the Nonpartisan League. As an unnoticed spectator, Lemke had no idea that within two years he would be a dominating influence on all three branches of the state government.

A political revolution was impending, preceded, as in the case of all revolutions, by warning symptoms. Lemke had detected some of these symptoms and wrote to a friend: "I am keeping my eye on the western part of this state and feel that conditions will loom up there during 1914."[56] The western part of the state was in the process of replacing cattlemen with homesteaders, whose farms were too small and whose methods of cultivation were not adapted to the low rainfall of the region. It was here that the Socialist party had been having its greatest rural successes. Farmers all over the state were caught in the credit stringency that followed the outbreak of World War I. Lemke was affected by the same business and credit recession, and he was bitter that the future seemed to offer no political alternative to the control he felt that financial interests had on the two major parties. His employment by Equity had revived his memories of the Alliance and Populist movements and of the views his father had supported when in the state legislature. Too, it had trained him in the language and ways of agrarian revolt. The Bingham case had brought him to the attention of discontented farm leaders and had provided him with unprecedented publicity in the daily papers. His efforts to achieve success and prominence through business promotion had met with failure; he was not only ready for a political revolution but qualified by his experience to serve as one of its leaders.

# CHAPTER II

# Inside the NPL

The legislative session of 1915 caused a realignment of political groups in North Dakota. It did this by rejecting a proposed plan for the state to build and operate a terminal elevator. A similar project had been one of the unrealized goals of the agrarian leaders who had captured control of the state government in 1892. The North Dakota Bankers Association had favorably considered it in 1906, and in more recent years the leaders of Equity had endorsed it. The popular vote on the issue on the two occasions when it had been submitted to the public had revealed a considerable unanimity of opinion in favor of the experiment in government ownership. A Board of Grain Commissioners, appointed by a liberal legislature in 1907, had reported favorably to the 1909 legislature, and it was action by the legislature of 1909 that began the legal steps necessary before construction of a terminal elevator system could be begun. An amendment to the state constitution had been necessary before the legislature could authorize the building of an elevator; at that time passage by two successive sessions of the legislature and subsequent ratification by the people were necessary to amend North Dakota's constitution. This had been done twice. The first amendment had authorized the legislature to construct such a terminal in other states and had been ratified in the 1912 election by 73.4 per cent of the total vote cast on the issue; the second amendment had authorized construction of a terminal within the state and had been ratified in November, 1914, by a vote of 73.59 per cent.[1] This last election was just two months before the opening of the 1915 legislative session. The previous legislative session of 1913 had anticipated a favorable vote and had authorized the state Board of Control*

* The official name of the Board of Control was the Board of Control of Charitable and Penal Institutions; the members were R. S. Lewis, chairman, F. O. Brewster, and J. W. Jackson.

to investigate the matter of the location of such elevators and costs of buildings and sites, and to submit plans and specifications of buildings and equipment, machinery and methods and rules of operations of the same to the 1915
Legislative Assembly of this State, it being the duty of the Board of Control
under this act to devise methods of operation and submit plans and specifications covering in detail the establishment of a terminal elevator system in the
states mentioned herein, with recommendations as to the most favorable
location, and estimates of the cost of such system or systems.[2]

The 1913 legislature had levied a tax of one-eighth of a mill on
all property in each of the years 1914, 1915, and 1916 to raise the
necessary funds to begin the operation of a terminal elevator system.
At the time of the election and as late as December, 1914, Equity
leaders had not realized that an adverse report by the Board of Control was causing the Hanna administration to reconsider the wisdom
of proceeding with construction of a terminal elevator system. The
Board of Control had investigated in both Canada and the United
States and reported that the program was so lacking in feasibility that
they had deemed it unnecessary to submit any recommendations as
to location or any plans for proceeding with construction of the elevator facilities.[3]

Had Governor Louis B. Hanna been an advocate of the project,
the Board of Control would probably have gone through the motions
of submitting recommendations on possible locations as well as specifications and estimates regarding actual construction. Even had he had
no influence on the Board of Control, his opinion of its report carried
great weight with many of the legislators whose task it was either
to accept or to disregard this report. It is here that the effects of
Lemke's political defection, and that of the members of the Varsity
Bachelor Club, become apparent. Had they been true to the progressive movement in 1912 or in 1910, a Progressive, more sympathetic to the terminal elevator proposal, might have been governor
at this time.

George Lofthus and the other leaders of the Equity Cooperative
Exchange were determined, experienced agrarian leaders. They had
become convinced that state-owned terminal elevator facilities were
necessary at this time, and they did their best during January, 1915,
to see that all of the work of agrarian leaders over a period of many
years to provide such facilities was not now lost as the result of the
adverse report of the Board of Control.* A convention of the Equity

---

* Fred B. Wood, P. M. Casey, and M. P. Johnson published and signed a full
résumé of the terminal elevator question in the *Cooperators' Herald* of February
12, 1915.

was assembled at Bismarck during the legislative session, and an invitation was extended to the comparatively new North Dakota branch of the Farmers Union to meet with them. The argument of Lofthus and Equity leaders was that the legislature should not surrender its policy-making function to the Board of Control. It was clear to them that Hanna intended to prevent the erection of the terminal elevator.[4]

After the convention adjourned, many of the members stayed in Bismarck. At a meeting of Equity members in downtown Bismarck, Lofthus bitterly attacked many of the legislators, who, he felt, were responsible for doubt as to whether the legislature would authorize construction of the marketing facilities. These attacks by Lofthus were referred to as the roll call. He reserved his most violent criticisms for those who, while pretending support, might actually in the end lend their influence to subterfuges designed to stall further progress toward actual construction. The legislators used Lofthus's tactics to do what they had wanted to do anyway, thus placing the blame for their actions on Lofthus. The daily press went along with them, the implication being that their own anger had given the legislators the courage to ignore pressure politics to which they might otherwise have cravenly submitted. The Hanna administration had defied Equity. All that Lofthus could do now was to carry on a grass-roots campaign to arouse indignation against the offending legislators and to sell stock in Equity marketing enterprises.[5]

Lofthus and the other Equity members left Bismarck with the feeling that they had been treated with thinly veiled contempt. When they were told later that one of the legislators had said that Equity members should "go home and slop the hogs" and leave the making of the laws to those who were elected and qualified to do so, they did not find it difficult to believe. It seemed to them that the progress resulting from decades of agrarian agitation had been lost.

Economic factors at this time made them feel their disappointment even more keenly. This was the winter after World War I had begun and before the inflationary effects brought on by that conflict had overcome the initial deflation. Farm tenancy and indebtedness were increasing.[*] The credit structure was very sensitive to financial tremors at that time; there would be no real attempt to adjust the credit machinery of the country to the needs of farmers until 1916. National

[*] The percentage of the farms operated by tenants increased from 8.5 per cent in 1900 to 25.6 per cent in 1920. The ratio of tenancy to number of farms in 1910 was 14.3 per cent. The reader needs to remember that a credit shortage in the money centers of the nation had the severest effects on rural banks.

banks could not lend on farm mortgages in 1915, and farmers were
dependent on retail store credit, insurance companies, and the Eastern
money that state banks could attract to the state. These three sources
of credit were much less available when the slightest seasonal or other
cyclical change took place in the money markets of the East. Farmers
knew, and their leaders could speak at length, about the disastrous
consequences of a credit system which made credit available when
it was needed least and difficult to obtain when the need was critical.
The economic situation at this time was such as to make farmers
receptive not only to a proposal for a terminal elevator but also to one
for a bank owned by the state which would insure a source of credit
to farmers. Business conditions were not normal and Lemke observed
that nearly eighty people—a large number for such a small city as
Fargo was then—were in his home town bread lines, and that comparatively well-dressed individuals had been seen searching garbage
cans for food.[6] The generally critical credit situation gave many of the
state banks a difficult time.* Credit extended by the retail merchants
was the chief cushion that tided many farm families over until other
sources of credit were again available.

There were some people among those watching Lofthus during the
terminal elevator fight who sensed the situation and who grasped the
possibilities for political action. Arthur C. Townley, a former resident
of Beach who blamed market conditions for the failure of his farming
operations and who had subsequently joined the Socialist party, and
A. E. Bowen had a vision of what might be accomplished. They
created an organization known as the Nonpartisan League and tried
to sell memberships at a moderate price. The first membership they
sold was to Fred B. Wood of Deering. Realizing that he needed an
established citizen in some community and recalling that Wood had
sold enough Socialist memberships at one time to bring in thirty-six
dollars in one payment, Townley selected Wood as the farmer to give
the kind of initial impetus that was needed.† Wood consented to help
sell memberships in the Deering community, and Townley tentatively
arranged to visit the Wood home when he came to that area.[7]

* An officer of a small state bank during this period told the author that his
bank was affected adversely by this crisis, and that this was his first warning of
the serious difficulties that would later affect the banking system of North
Dakota.

† Usually one dollar was collected from each new member as earnest money
of intention to continue paying a similar amount each month. Unless some new

Surprising Wood by coming in late winter rather than after the spring's work was done, Townley found Wood less receptive to the Nonpartisan League proposal than he had been when at the Equity meeting in Bismarck, and Wood refused to accompany Townley until one of the Wood sons went with Townley on a farm-to-farm tour and proved that the memberships would sell. With the senior Wood as a companion, Townley found the sales much easier to make, and they persuaded the first seventy-two farmers on whom they called to join the new organization. This gave Townley a start which aided him in making future sales, and he found he was no longer dependent on the Deering farmer. Because of his increased confidence in the success of the sales campaign, Townley took another organizer, Roy Cooper, with him, and then instructed the organizer to repeat the same sales talk Townley had used. Surprisingly enough, the sales went very well when the new man went out alone. Townley immediately ceased direct selling of memberships and began training organizers. In addition to terminal elevators, flour mills, rural credit banks, hail insurance, and packing and cold storage plants to be provided by the state, Townley had listed reformation of grain grading practices and exemption of farm improvements from taxation as objectives of his new organization. His program was almost an exact restatement of the program for farmers advanced by the North Dakota Socialists, who were following a policy that assumed that every individual except the monopoly capitalist could belong to the Socialist party. It had been on this assumption that Townley's work with the Socialist party had been conducted, and it was from the ranks of that party that Townley recruited many of his organizers.[8]

When League membership appeared destined for a 1915 total of over 25,000, Townley decided that he needed additional assistance. Historians differ as to when and how Lemke was selected. It is difficult to be certain regarding Usher L. Burdick's contention that George Lofthus would have become the man closest to Townley had the Equity leader not become critically ill. Townley, who gave Wood's recommendation as the determining factor in bringing Lemke to his attention, was in later years inclined to minimize the role that Lemke performed within the power structure of the League.[9]

---

member paid more than the usual amount, this meant that Wood had sold thirty-six memberships. Often initial payment was a postdated check, and this made the amount of cash Wood had collected an indication of unusual influence in his home area.

In any event, Lemke was ready for this new opportunity to gain political prestige when it came. While Equity had been very helpful to him during the time when economic disaster had befallen his Mexican enterprise, he had not achieved the place in it that he had hoped would be his.[10] Also, at this time he needed to mollify Langer in order to gain Langer's cooperation in paying taxes and other costs necessary to keep title to the Mexican land, and nothing was better calculated to achieve that objective than an offer to assist Langer in obtaining League endorsement for state attorney general.[*] Too, he hoped to assist his partner in the same way for Robinson's candidacy for the state Supreme Court.[†]

Before he became a permanent salaried employee of the Nonpartisan League, Lemke attempted to salvage the investment in Mexico. The United States had recognized the government of Venustiano Carranza, and Lemke hoped that this might mean a return to stability. He had recently published *Crimes Against Mexico*, and Equity had reimbursed him for his legal services, enabling him to make a trip. It was a most unpleasant experience, for it was at this time that Pancho Villa attempted to embarrass Carranza by attacking Americans. Lemke was fortunate to be in an area where Obregon was in control rather than one in which Villa was carrying on his raids. Despite the Mexican generals and the constant banditry, Lemke eventually arrived in Mexico City. This was the trip during which he became ill with typhus, and he was unable to accomplish anything there or to reach the properties of the Land Finance Company on the west coast of Mexico. He came

[*] Langer asserted that Lemke controlled the League nominations in 1916 and nominated many of those who were mixed up with Lemke in Mexican investments so that Lemke could control them. This leaves little doubt as to whom Langer credits as being responsible for his own nomination. (William Langer, *The Nonpartisan League: Its Birth, Activities, and Leaders* [Mandan, North Dakota: Morton County Farmers Press, 1920], p. 28.

[†] In a letter to J. E. Robinson dated October 6, 1915, Lemke wrote: "I have . . . been doing . . . work for you as a . . . candidate for . . . the Supreme Court. . . . The Farmers movement or the Equity people will be solidly for you. . . . I am satisfied that there is nothing in it for us as far as law is concerned in Fargo" (Lemke Papers). The reference to the Nonpartisan League as "the Farmers movement" is interesting. The reference to their legal practice indicates that their business was not good and that both Lemke and Robinson needed a better method of making a living. Lemke did not abandon a thriving business to devote himself to the League. The League provided him with a welcome alternative to the struggling legal practice in which he was engaged as well as enabled him to assist his partner.

home as soon as he was able to do so and before he had recovered from his illness.

It was when he was back in Fargo in the winter of 1916 and while he was still desperately ill that Townley, Wood, and others came again to see him. Mrs. Lemke recalled that "the nurse and I didn't want these men to bother Bill but he insisted on seeing them." It is probable that it was at this time that Lemke accepted permanent employment with the League on a salaried basis, for, as Mrs. Lemke related: "Before Bill was physically able to he was out making trips regarding the formation of the League."[11]

Conditions had proved favorable both for the initial launching of the League and for its treasury. Not only had the deflation and the credit stringency of the fall and winter of 1914–1915 provided the seedbed of discontent necessary to organize the League, but also the business boom which began in the summer of 1915 combined with the biggest wheat crop the state had produced up to that time to enable the farmers to pay the membership dues they had pledged earlier in the year. During the spring of 1915 Townley had been compelled to accept a substantial portion of membership fees in the form of post-dated checks,* a great portion of which would never have been honored had there been a poor crop and business year.

The next goal for the League was an election victory. A newspaper, *The Nonpartisan Leader,* had been started in the fall of 1915.† During the entire time of organization Townley had been watching for potential candidates and he had set up a procedure for their nomination. Leaguers in each precinct were to hold meetings in February at which delegates were to be chosen to attend legislative district conventions. One delegate was to be chosen from each of the conventions to be held in each of the forty-nine legislative districts. These forty-nine delegates were to be the state nominating convention. After the convention had finished, Townley's plan called for a gigantic mass meeting of Leaguers from all over the state to meet the candidates who had been chosen by the delegates. By this time those whose

---

* PDC became the League code word for these checks. Eventually League leaders found it necessary to have friendly banks handle this paper. Each year large amounts of these checks were accepted. According to Townley failure of Nebraska farmers to make their checks good after the 1920 deflation was one of the most serious blows the national organization of the League suffered.

† One of the most interesting features of the paper was the cartoons of John M. Baer.

interest was in politics were aware that there was a new movement afoot but they were inclined to discount its effectiveness.[12] League leaders themselves, although they knew they had gained a political foothold, were not certain whether their organization would stand the assaults of the established factions at the time of the June primary election. Townley's plan was to run candidates for nomination at that time, and a contingency he feared was that the old voting habits might neutralize the newly found enthusiasm of the farmers for the Nonpartisan League.

The 1916 Presidential primary election was held in March, a few weeks before the League convention and nearly eleven weeks before the primary which was to choose candidates for state office. One feature of the March primary was the choice of national committee-man for each party. In the Republican party this had traditionally caused a contest between the Stalwarts and the Progressives. The Nonpartisan League was as yet not mobilized for political action and would not be until after its convention. If it had been, it might not have endorsed a candidate for national committeeman, for Town-ley had not planned for League involvement in national politics. There was no doubt, though, about his intention to oppose the Pro-gressive and the Stalwart factions in the state primary to be held in June.

Despite League opposition to the two Republican factions, Lemke accepted the nomination for national committeeman from the Progres-sives. His defeat by Gunder Olson, the candidate of the Stalwarts, was an indication in itself that Lemke was not prominent enough in March of 1916 to attract a large number of voters to the League. It was the League which brought Lemke prominence and gave him the forum from which he could win statewide elections. His rise was as rapid as that of the League and a consequence of its activity. In March, 1916, the *Cooperators' Herald* had to explain who the candi-date for national committeeman was, and it described Lemke as being "well known as the Equity attorney and for several years active in Progressive politics." By the fall of the same year Lemke's prominence at the League convention and in other League activities had brought such a change that one man wrote of him: "There is no man in the State who is so well known to the farmers . . . and whose name would have so much influence."[13] Gunder Olson's defeat of Lemke later proved to be a major misfortune for the Nonpartisan League, but at this time League leaders were concerned only with state offices.

Lemke's defeat did not disturb them. Lemke himself was bitter and complained about those who had not supported him.

As the forty-nine delegates gathered for the state endorsing convention of the Nonpartisan League, there was no certainty as to what they would do. The actual process of choosing candidates was unique. Names of all suggested candidates were placed on a blackboard and then discussed at length, one by one. A secret ballot followed with nothing to prevent the delegates from voting as they wished. However, their own political inexperience and the prestige of League headquarters were such that it was unlikely that they would endorse anyone of whom Townley disapproved. But Townley had no specific candidate in mind; he wanted a winning ticket. This uncertainty on Townley's part and the delegates' inexperience made it possible for Lemke to exercise his talent for controlling conventions.*14

The selection of Lynn J. Frazier as candidate for governor ensured Lemke's future in the government which the League was to install in Bismarck. Townley credited Beecher Moore, a League organizer, as responsible for bringing Frazier to the convention's attention. The organizers had been instructed to watch for good candidates as they traveled from county to county, and their reports had led Townley to conclude that John Hagan was the best name. During a casual conversation at League headquarters, Moore spoke up to say he knew of a man who might do. He explained that he had been late getting to the county convention in Pembina County and found that Frazier had the meeting organized and was speaking to the group when he arrived. Lemke was present when Moore was relating this to Townley, and he exclaimed, "I know him; I went to school with him." Townley then asked Lemke for a report on Frazier. The report was good, and Townley instructed Lemke to telephone Frazier to come to Fargo for an interview. Lemke's own statement confirms the common assumption that Frazier was Lemke's candidate. Lemke recalled that Frazier's name occurred to him when Beecher Moore mentioned Pembina County. Asking for the floor, Lemke described the qualifications of the Pembina County farmer so well that the convention

---

* "Bill was a born organizer—not the sort that goes out and speaks to large assemblies or groups of people nor even to single individuals one by one, but rather to confer with a few leaders, to work in top committees" (Kathrine B. Tiffany to author, January 1, 1957). Mrs. Tiffany knew Lemke before he became a skilled speaker, and apparently his skill in influencing group action antedated the development of his forensic abilities.

decided to interview him. Calling Frazier on the pretext that Lemke wanted advice on whether to run for lieutenant governor or not, Lemke persuaded him to come to Fargo. Possibly a day or two intervened before Frazier arrived. The delegates visited with Frazier, and he returned to Hoople not knowing that he was being considered for governor. According to Lemke the convention endorsed Frazier for governor before Frazier knew he was being considered; and Frazier's first knowledge of his endorsement was from reading of it in the paper while on a second trip to Fargo after another call from Lemke.[15] The two accounts agree in assigning Lemke a role in Frazier's nomination but disagree as to that role's importance.

Neil C. Macdonald, who had been one of Lemke's fellow students at the University, was endorsed for superintendent of public instruction. Lemke corresponded with Langer about helping the latter with his candidacy.[16] There seems little question but that Lemke succeeded in having the League endorse his partner, J. E. Robinson, for the state Supreme Court. Other League nominees with whom Lemke had been associated were prominent Equity members P. M. Casey* and M. P. Johnson; Lemke had known Thomas Hall and Carl Kositzky in the Progressive movement. Whether his part was as great at this juncture as the nomination of so many of his friends would suggest is difficult to determine. Townley assigned him a minor role; outsiders assumed it was a major one; and this was the beginning of the reputation which was to give Lemke the nickname of "the political bishop"— the kingmaker—of the Nonpartisan League. His associates of university days and others insisted on believing that he was a major influence inside the Nonpartisan League. Victor Wardrope, a former university student and a fraternity brother of Lemke's who was now a banker in Leeds, wrote:

I was under the impression that Townley, Wood, etc. were running the Non-partisan League. I had heard intimations that you were, at least, one of the powers behind the throne, but I hardly believed it. . . . I have read . . . the story of the Non-partisan League Convention, and I can see the fine Dutch hand of Bill Lempke [sic] written large on every page. Why, you son of a gun, that list of candidates looks like the Muster Roll of your personal friends.[17]

---

* Casey was the only candidate to be run for the Democratic nomination. All other League selections ran for the Republican nomination. Casey's endorsement was to demonstrate the true nonpartisanship of the organization.

One limitation applied to the power of both Townley and Lemke. Townley had set as a basic rule that no officer of the League could become a candidate for state office. This principle became firmly imbedded in the minds of Leaguers, and Lemke had to accept this limiting factor as the price for his position and the influence he had within the League organization. One purpose of the rule had been to answer the argument that Townley himself was seeking public office. At this time there was no effort on the part of either Lemke or Townley to become candidates; their concern was with mobilizing the organization in order to win the Republican nominations by defeating the candidates of the Progressive and Stalwart factions.

Meanwhile the Progressives were planning to head their ticket with Usher L. Burdick, the candidate who had narrowly missed defeating Louis B. Hanna in 1914. Key Progressive leaders, such as O. B. Burtness, felt that the League was playing into Stalwart hands by dividing the liberal vote. Burtness wrote Lemke: "Now, Bill, you know there is not a man anywhere on earth I think more of than Lynn Frazier and whom I would like better to support. This is true of many other of the University boys." Burtness went on to explain that he and the others had promised Burdick their support two years previously, and he suggested a conference of League and Progressive leaders to effect Frazier's withdrawal. "I never thought the day would come when I would have to oppose Lynn Frazier for anything, and it is certainly like going back on my own brother to line up against him," wrote Victor Wardrope. When Lemke explained that Frazier's nomination was the result of the demand of thirty-seven thousand farmers, Wardrope retorted: "Your statement that our old pal is the choice of 37,000 farmers of this State, is equal to the best thing . . . Bill Nye ever wrote. Why bless your innocent heart, Bill, there are not two thousand people in the State who ever heard of Frazier, and when the papers arrived here, announcing his endorsement, all the Nonpartisan League men . . . branded . . . [it] as a base slander by a corrupt press to injure the cause of the down-trodden farmer. . . . To a man they exclaimed 'who in the hell is Frazier?' " The conference was held and consideration was given to having R. A. Nestos withdraw as Progressive candidate for the national Senate to enable Burdick to oppose Porter J. McCumber for that office, but the plan was dropped.[18]

After 1912 George Lofthus of Minnesota had provided the emotional and intellectual leadership in the Equity drive for the terminal elevator.

His death at this time left the leadership to J. M. Anderson, who, though first president of the North Dakota branch, was not an inspiring, dynamic individual, as Lofthus had been. The conservative press, once so opposed to Equity, now found it preferable to the Nonpartisan League. They quoted Anderson, Lemke's fellow officer in the Varsity Bachelor Club and the man responsible for inducting Lemke into the agrarian movement by means of Equity, as being favorable to Burdick and opposed to Frazier. When Anderson failed to deny these reports, Lemke wrote to him, enclosing clippings and asking for a denial. When Lemke countered Anderson's evasive reply by sending a statement he wished Anderson to give the press, Anderson refused and the two were never intimate friends again.[19]

The proposal that Lemke should drop the League candidate for governor in favor of Burdick ignored the fact that Lemke had not supported Burdick in 1914. In any event the League would not have accepted the change easily. Lemke himself found the power that went with his new position gratifying, and this factor alone would have been enough to make him uncompromising. Besides, he was dedicated to the cause he had embraced. He enjoyed the prospect of having helped select a governor taken like a modern Cincinnatus from his plow to come without personal ambition to meet the challenges and responsibilities that the Nonpartisan League was going to urge him to accept. Lemke had confidence that Frazier had sufficient stature. Not forgotten was Frazier's academic record or the fact that but for the death of his older brother, Frazier probably would have succeeded in his plan to become a physician. The two men had complete confidence in one another. Frazier was less dynamic than Lemke; as governor, if it had not been for Lemke spurring him on, he would have been less aggressive. He did not have the ambition to be in the center of things and could have lived happily on his farm for the rest of his life. If there had been a time when such a life would have found Lemke content, it had long since passed. So closely did the two men's outlooks on economic and political philosophies agree that the ideas of one could almost be predicted if those of the other were known. On few things would they ever disagree.* Frazier recognized the superior training, legal

* Only in 1928 was there a sharp divergence. Lemke had perceived earlier than had Frazier that prohibition was not succeeding. Both were ardent "drys" but in the late 1920's Lemke was ready to concede failure. Lemke supported Smith, and Frazier, Hoover. If religious prejudice entered into Frazier's decision, there is no evidence of it; and Lemke refused to believe that it did.

knowledge, and the capacity for sustained intellectual application possessed by Lemke. Knowing that their purposes were the same, their thinking alike, and Lemke's training and capacity for work far superior, and that he was indebted to Lemke for his political career, Frazier sought Lemke's advice and deferred to it. However, Frazier was not incapable of administrative decision or of forming his own opinions. Lemke's influence with Frazier came from the latter's certainty that they were near agreement, from the absolute confidence that their friendship and Lemke's integrity were such that, as governor and later as senator, Frazier could be certain that unfair advantage would never be taken of him. In all their correspondence Lemke was most tactful in avoiding giving offense. For the moment he was satisfied to be behind the scenes helping select the actors and laying out the plot. Soon he was to be talking about making Frazier President of the United States. To anyone who thought that ridiculous, Lemke needed only to point to the feats they had already accomplished.[20]

The League movement was gaining momentum. In the enthusiasm created by its cash resources, it could not prevent the initiating of new enterprises such as the consumers' stores—enterprises which were not original parts of the League program and which Lemke later stated he had strongly opposed. The movement was big, growing rapidly, enthusiastic, and—as Townley later expressed it—"hard to herd." The *Nonpartisan Leader,* the weekly newspaper which had represented the League since the fall of 1915, was soon to be supplemented by the purchase of the *Fargo Courier-News,* a daily. From the beginning the League had recognized the place of the press in molding public opinion against them and had called in top editorial talent such as that of Charles Edward Russell to direct their publications.[21] One of the more important League affiliated enterprises was the Service Bureau, which supplied "boiler plate" and other material to local newspapers.* To provide customers for itself, the Service Bureau helped the farmers either to buy or to organize weekly newspapers. The political campaign of May and June, 1916, antedated some of these developments, but the League was growing very rapidly. Already it was necessary for Lemke to spend part of his time in St. Paul, Minnesota, making plans to establish a large headquarters there.

---

* This organization was originally called Northwest Publisher's Service; near the end of 1918 it was reorganized into the Publisher's National Service Bureau, and both organizations were subsequently referred to as the Service Bureau.

The North Dakota National Guard was called to the Mexican
border, taking their commander, John H. Fraine, who was also the
Stalwart candidate for governor, with them. With only Burdick and
Frazier actively campaigning, the Leaguers thought it best to organize
a Frazier Special Train to carry him over the state, a campaign device
that proved remarkably effective.[22] Frazier's appearance won farmers
and neutralized the charge of opponents that the League was in
control of radicals. Close liaison was established with labor headquarters, for from the beginning the Nonpartisan League had been
sympathetic to labor. Though a farmer organization, it enacted a
program of laws favorable to labor and thus differentiated itself from
the typical agrarian movement. The urban influence of the Socialists
who assisted with the organizing and the liberals imported from
other states by Townley probably account for this. Very early, League
leaders had realized that their chance of building a national party
depended on wooing the labor vote in other states. The breadth of
their approach as compared to that of the typical agrarian movement
makes more plausible the claim that only World War I prevented the
Nonpartisan League from becoming a national party. These experiences had a moderating effect on Lemke's own development. Never
was he at any time opposed to collective bargaining, and he later
criticized the Republican-enacted Taft-Hartley Act as being both
wrong and politically unwise.

As primary election day approached, the opposition was apprehen-
sive yet hopeful that the new movement had been overestimated.
Leaguers themselves were confident yet anxious, a matter of particular concern to them being the weather on election day, for bad
weather meant bad roads and a reduction in the rural vote. The
result was a sweeping victory for Nonpartisan League candidates.
Despite bad weather every candidate they had endorsed, including
P. M. Casey in the Democratic column, had been nominated. The
primary election had a traumatic effect on those accustomed to power.
Temporarily the political situation almost demanded that they support
the Republican nominees, as any other course would make them party
irregulars and would result in conceding the state to Wilson in the
fall election. Lemke's own reputation was enhanced. Comments in
letters to him, such as "How is the Nonpartisan Boss?" "Please accept
my congratulations for the magnificent victory . . . that the League
through your guidance put over;" and "While the successful candidates
are receiving heaps of congratulations, I want to take this opportunity

of extending my felicitations to yourself. The 'Warwick of the West' has nothing on you Bill," were typical ones and indicated the leading role Lemke had played in the victory.[23]

Townley had taken several precautions to convince farmers that the League existed solely for their protection and to refute charges that he was interested in self-aggrandizement. No candidate for national office had been supported; candidates in both parties had been endorsed; no officers of the League had been permitted to run for office; and no effort had been made to capture the party organization machinery.* As the returns came in, a surprising development was the capture of enough precinct committeemen to control the committees of a majority of the counties. Without instruction or planning the farmers had taken care of that matter by themselves.[24]

During the months of the campaign Lemke had not forgotten the Mexican investment or his disapproval of President Wilson. Helpless to do anything about it and fearful that the Republicans would nominate Roosevelt, he had concentrated on the job of nominating the League candidates. The control of the state party machinery opened a new possibility. As state chairman of the Republican party, Lemke could be in a position not only to help the League ticket but also to assist in carrying the state for Hughes, a candidate he could support.

It was an advantage Lemke was quick to grasp. The Nonpartisan League might be nonchalant as to whether Wilson was defeated or not, but there was nothing of indifference in Lemke's attitude.† He had a score to settle, and the opportunity for settling it was at hand. It remained for Lemke only to consolidate the League committee votes and manage to have them cast for himself. As he mobilized the power given him by his Nonpartisan League position to capture the state chairmanship of the Republican party, Lemke could see clearly the chance to defeat Wilson. He believed that a change of President

* Precinct committeemen were elected at the polls at the same time as the primary election. At a time specified by law they later met and chose the county committee from among their number and selected state committeemen. The state committeemen from the various counties then met at a statewide meeting and chose the state chairman of the party. The national committeeman, however, was chosen by election in March.

† A great number of the League leaders and farmer members supported the Democrats and Wilson because they felt that the Republicans and Hughes were too conservative. To prevent a schism within the League, Lemke had to avoid involving the League in the campaign for Hughes.

would mean a foreign policy toward Mexico that would protect his own imperialistic purposes, and he wrote to a friend suggesting that they elect Hughes and move to Mexico.[25]

Surprised by the results of the 1916 primary election, the Republican conservatives fought a rear guard action, attempting to disqualify enough Nonpartisan League committeemen to enable the Stalwarts to control the party machinery. They were able to prevent the state Republican meeting from endorsing the League platform, but they were unable to stop the election of William Lemke as state chairman of the party.[26] Wistfully they could only hope that the choice of Lemke would hold enough League votes in the Republican column to carry the state for Charles Evans Hughes against Woodrow Wilson and for Senator Porter J. McCumber against John Burke, the Democratic candidate. After serving three terms as governor, Burke had accepted appointment from President Wilson as Treasurer of the United States. His long record of public service, the prominent national position he then held, and the fact that Wilson was fairly strong in North Dakota made it seem possible that Burke, North Dakota's leading progressive, might defeat McCumber.

As state chairman, Lemke had only three offices to be concerned about. With the exception of John Steen, who was opposing P. M. Casey, the Democrat whom the League had endorsed for state treasurer, the entire Republican state ticket was safe. The candidates endorsed by the League for superintendent of public instruction and for the state Supreme Court—Neil C. Macdonald and Lemke's law partner J. E. Robinson—were on the no-party ballot.* Although not quite as certain of election as the League-endorsed candidates in the Republican column, these candidates were in a safer position than Steen, McCumber, or Hughes.

The delicate problem resulting from the League's claim that it was neither Republican nor Democrat, but rather an association of farmers who endorsed candidates regardless of party, had to be met. This non-party device, having enabled Townley to avoid the obstacles created by party labels, had contributed greatly to League success in June. Although the state normally cast a much smaller number of Democratic than Republican votes, the nonpartisan concept had enabled farmers who were traditional Democrats to cross over into the Republican column. It was to appease them, and especially those who were very loyal to President Wilson, that Casey had been endorsed by the League for state treasurer. Lemke, as one of the three

---

* Other NPL nominees for the Court were R. H. Grace and L. E. Birdzell.

Cartoonist J. M. Baer, Beach, North Dakota, postmaster discovered by Townley who, after serving one term in Congress, was to become nationally known for his work, here graphically illustrates that the Nonpartisan League platform was designed to support not only the larger Republican party of North Dakota but also the smaller Democratic party.

chief officials of the League and at the same time serving as state chairman of the Republican party, endangered this concept. To avoid defeating Casey and offending Leaguers who were Wilson supporters, it was essential that Lemke's campaign activities as Republican state chairman be dissociated from those of the Nonpartisan League. Despite Lemke's personal antipathy toward Wilson, League activity and advertising had to be neutral.[27]

To Republicans outside of the League this dual role was not only distasteful, it was downright contemptible and dishonest. One of the features of the campaign was the constant effort of Republicans to maneuver Lemke into having League candidates endorse Hughes and McCumber. Their bitterness was understandable. Here were candidates taking the Republican label and demanding the support of conservative Republicans, yet giving nothing in return and often openly admitting that the label meant nothing to them except as a vehicle in which to ride to office.

The attempt to disqualify League committeemen had delayed Lemke's election as state chairman of the Republican party until September 5, a delay he later regarded as a major reason for his failure to carry North Dakota for Hughes. Almost immediately he encountered an obstacle, the refusal of the Republican national committee to release funds to him as North Dakota chairman of the party. Coupled with the delay in choosing him as chairman and the fact that local financial backing was not available, it became impossible for him to open headquarters. With the state candidates safe and amply financed by the League, no funds were coming from within the state. Conservative North Dakota Republicans were the only other possible source of funds within the state, and they were reluctant to give to a party whose chairman was one of the three executive officers of Townley's League. Black stem rust in late July and early August had ruined what had promised to be a repetition of the bumper wheat crop of 1915. If there had been any disposition to give, this crop failure would have made the contributions small. Unfavorably inclined to Lemke in the first place, the Stalwarts, under the impact of the crop failure, were unwilling to contribute anything to the campaign. It is possible also that they were working through Gunder Olson to prevent the National Committee from sending funds to Lemke. In North Dakota, as in so many other states in 1916, the Hughes campaign was impaired by the hostility between conservatives and progressives within the Republican party.

In the latter part of September Lemke went to Republican headquarters in Chicago. When the funds were still not forthcoming, he
threatened to resign.[28] Nothing would have delighted North Dakota
conservatives more than to see Lemke relinquish his hold on the
organization, but it is probable that national headquarters realized
that Lemke's resignation would hurt Hughes badly in both North
Dakota and Minnesota, and they sent funds during the first week in
October in sufficient amount to open party headquarters and to begin
the campaign.

Once headquarters was established and money was available with
which to operate, Lemke devoted himself to the campaign with
characteristic energy. The pressure of time caused by the delay in
opening headquarters and the difficult task of directing two campaigns while appearing to direct only one made the month of October
a frenzied one for him. Party headquarters were set up and close
liaison was maintained with League headquarters. Material and
personnel were used interchangeably. Ostensibly Lemke was running
the Republican headquarters and the League headquarters was an
autonomous unit. Actually Lemke was the policy-maker and the court
of last resort in both. As the campaign progressed, the pressure on
Lemke to use the League influence on behalf of the Republicans
mounted. "Farm vote is for Wilson. Only Frazier and Manahan can
change them,"* wrote one conservative Republican. McCumber
wrote, pleading with Lemke to run Frazier's picture in the advertisements with those of Hughes and McCumber, while others begged
Lemke to sign his personal endorsement to the advertisements, con-
tending that his known leadership in the League would bring League
voters to McCumber and Hughes and that the Democratic state
chairman had signed Democratic campaign material with his name
rather than using the impersonal title of state committee.[29]

Support for McCumber against Burke was another inconsistency.
As a Progressive, Lemke was placed in the anomalous position of supporting McKenzie's senator against the former liberal governor.
Burke's close association with the Wilson administration and his
defense of Wilsonian foreign policy as it related to Mexico and the
German submarine campaign were enough to make the transition to
support of McCumber easy for Lemke. Restraint was not part of

---

* Lynn J. Frazier was the League-endorsed candidate for governor; James
Manahan was one of Lemke's most effective political speakers on behalf of
Hughes and the Republicans.

Lemke's nature. Before the campaign was over, he was making attacks on Burke that implied dishonesty and betrayal of trust while in office.[30]

Lemke did help the Republicans win votes for Hughes among League farmers and German-American groups. He was not as successful in appealing to voters in larger towns. He felt that Wilson talked as a liberal while reorganizing the banking and monetary systems in a manner pleasing to conservatives. Unfortunately, the speeches given by Hughes did not lend themselves to a successful wooing of the liberal vote. When Hughes came to Fargo to speak, League leaders came to hear him; but he spent part of his time discussing the Adamson Act, a subject in which the farmers were not interested and an issue on which the Republicans would almost certainly lose the railroad labor vote in North Dakota. In one other respect Lemke gave strength to the Republican ticket. His known German name and his firm conviction that Wilson's policies would lead to participation in the European war, and that Hughes, once he was elected, would disregard Roosevelt and follow a program of true neutrality, aided in winning the German vote in the state. This vote had been offended by Roosevelt's speeches regarding German violation of Belgian neutrality. The fact that the German counties in the area to which he was able to send a German speaker voted heavily for Hughes was the source of Lemke's conviction that he successfully appealed to the German vote. Lemke knew that Wilson's slogan, "He Kept Us Out of War," was effective in those German communities where no German speakers campaigned, or where Lemke was unable to persuade the local community leaders regarding the fallacy that he felt was contained in Wilson's slogan. Where Lemke was able to reach the community of German origin, the election results indicated that voters were convinced that there was a greater chance of continued peace with Germany under Hughes as President than there would be if Wilson were re-elected. The desire for peace was the overriding consideration in the election.[31]

In the state as a whole the Republicans gained from 26.66 per cent of the vote they had received in 1912 to 46.57 per cent in 1916; in the seven counties with the highest percentage of German-American population, they increased their percentage from 27.3 per cent in 1912 to 61.79 per cent in 1916.* The gain was most striking in McIntosh

* Emmons, Mercer, Morton, McIntosh, Stark, Sheridan, and Logan counties were in the area where Lemke felt that he had been most successful. These

County, where the Republican percentage climbed from 20.97 per cent
in 1912 to 77.36 per cent in 1916. These figures support Lemke's assertion that North Dakota would have voted for Hughes and against
Wilson if the National Committee had supplied more speakers who
could use the German language in their campaign talks. Lemke knew
the ethnic background of the state sufficiently well to understand that

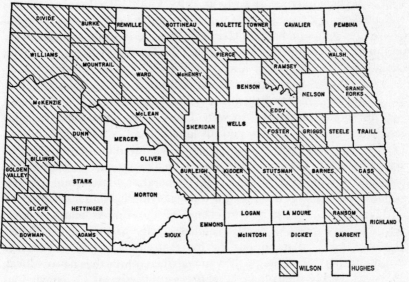

Fig. 1.—Party Votes, General Election, November 7, 1916

there were other counties which, though not nearly as solidly German
in origin as these seven, still had communities which were.

The war issue complicated the campaign picture in North Dakota
in still another manner. With many of its foreign-born inhabitants

counties had populations that were preponderantly German in origin, a large
proportion of whom came from German colonies that had settled in Russia and
that had lived there for several generations before coming to the United States.
These latter were reputed to be more intense in their regard for Germany
than immigrants who came directly from Germany. There were heavy concentrations of such voters in all of these counties, although this was not quite as
true of Morton and Stark, in which the cities of Mandan and Dickinson respectively were located. Both of these towns were railroad and distribution centers.
Their population was more mobile, and the railroad vote probably diminished
the Republican vote in these communities. McIntosh had the greatest concentration of citizens of German origin; the actual figure was 79.2 per cent. Mercer
had 57.3 per cent; Sheridan, 54.1 per cent; and Emmons, 46.5 per cent (Wilkins,
p. 5).

settled in colonies, the state was particularly susceptible to the problems that came with the rising feeling against "hyphenated Americans" during Wilson's exchange of notes with Germany over the submarine sinkings. Although the full fury of the hysteria did not break until after the United States entered World War I, those of German origin who criticized Wilson's policy as pro-British were beginning to have their motives impugned as early as 1916. Until 1915, Lemke's friends had jocularly addressed him as a Dutchman. No offense was intended or taken in such idle banter. Germans, as were most immigrants, were proud of the country of their origin; in Lemke's case, and among other Germans, there was already a decided antipathy toward England. From the very beginning of World War I, Lemke felt that Wilson had acceded to British sea policy in an unneutral manner and that his actions might lead to war. Lemke's correspondence with his family and theirs with him, and his letters to a German officer named Lemke who was interned at Jacksonville, all indicated a decided sympathy with Germany.[32] It was a feeling no more unnatural or unpatriotic than that which a first-generation descendant of any national origin might feel about a war involving his father's homeland.

When Germany became an enemy of the United States, Lemke immediately expressed his unqualified loyalty to the United States. However, as did many others, he found it easier to feel and express loyalty to the United States than to convince others that he was loyal. This was doubly difficult in Lemke's case because of his convictions about the causes of all wars. Lemke believed that all wars were caused by a very few for their own enrichment; he may have been influenced toward this view by passages in Mark Twain's *The Mysterious Stranger*. His conclusion was no different from those of men such as Frazier, Gronna, and La Follette, who were of Canadian, Norwegian, and old American stock respectively. Yet after 1915 the fact that Lemke was of German origin made it more difficult for him than for others to express such views without being accused by some of ethnic bias. Until the United States entered the war in 1917, he had freedom to speak his opinions, but oftentimes they were discounted by those who felt he was governed by sympathies with Germany and not by the other reasons he advanced. His 1916 effort as Republican chairman to appeal to ethnic loyalties in communities of German origin with the argument that the election of Wilson would occasion a greater likelihood of war than would the election of Hughes heightened the suspicions of many.[33]

As he established headquarters, Lemke's first plan was to bring to North Dakota speakers including such prominent people as William E. Borah of Idaho, Albert Beveridge of Indiana, and Theodore Roosevelt. Men such as Senators George Norris of Nebraska, Warren G. Harding of Ohio, Knute Nelson of Minnesota, and Thomas Sterling of South Dakota also were invited and came, as were a number of members of the House of Representatives. Before long, the reports that came in regarding the German vote changed Lemke's plans. Lemke alleged that the Democrats were bringing German speakers into North Dakota. Whatever the *Bismarck Tribune* might say editorially about the issues which were determining votes, its editor was under no illusions privately, and he wrote Lemke: "Some work must be done among the German-Americans. . . . Roosevelt has alienated many." Another letter to Lemke warned that the German vote was going to Burke and Wilson. Indignant because Republican speakers had been too favorable to England, one Republican party worker wrote asking that only "good neutral Americans" instead of "pro-British and anti-German" speakers be sent to his community. Messages such as these made Lemke realize the importance of modifying his original strategy. He ceased trying to bring Theodore Roosevelt to the state and emphasized more frequently the need to appeal to foreign-language groups in their own languages, especially in the case of Germans and Norwegians, giving instructions to the speakers to show Wilson as unneutral in the European wars and urging the speakers to the Norwegians to be more progressive in tone than those to the Germans. To minimize the effect of Theodore Roosevelt's attacks on Germany, Lemke sent out instructions that none of the Roosevelt speech materials be circulated among people of German origin and directed that they be told that "Hughes will be President, not Roosevelt."[34]

Adverse reports continued to arrive. The Republican national headquarters disregarded Lemke's requests for foreign-language speakers. In desperation he decided to find German-speaking orators without waiting for national headquarters to send some. Of the two he was able to obtain, only one proved satisfactory. The other speaker failed to keep his speaking engagements. In Lemke's own estimate, the German-language speaker who stayed for the duration of the campaign, and James Manahan, who was Irish in origin and able to appeal to anti-British feelings, were the most effective in winning votes for Hughes.[35]

A state-wide campaign in the days before radio and television meant speakers in nearly every town in the state. To plan their transportation, schedule their halls, and provide advance publicity became a tremendous managerial task, and, in Lemke's case, there was a very short time in which to do it. The splendid response to Bryan's talks for Wilson was another discouraging piece of news for Lemke. The fact that Lemke was supporting McCumber added strength to rumors among Burke followers of an alliance between McCumber and Townley.[36] There was no logical reason why Townley should make such a bargain. His candidates in the Republican column were certain of election. Lemke's own desire to defeat Wilson governed the position he took, for he would have limited his effectiveness in supporting Hughes if he had deserted McCumber and endorsed Burke.

By the third week in October, the campaign had moved toward its climax, and it was obvious that there was nothing certain about a Hughes victory. Although continuing to talk confidently, Lemke gradually yielded to demands and to his own desire to win. Despite the fact that it was contrary to League policy and against the best interests of the organization which paid him his salary, he took steps which resulted in throwing League support to the candidacy of Hughes. This was contrary to the basic creed of the League as laid down by its founder; the Nonpartisan League's attitude toward national politics was the origin of the name Townley had chosen for it. When campaign anxieties intensified, Lemke bracketed the pictures of Hughes, Frazier, and McCumber in large political advertisements and had his own name printed at the end of them, thus lending the support of the League to Hughes for, to most of the farmers, Lemke was first and foremost an officer of the League and for that reason his name implied League endorsement of Hughes and McCumber.

The June primary which had placed the Republican party in the hands of extremists made the 1916 election one of the more enigmatic in North Dakota's history. Although Republican Governor Hanna issued a statement in behalf of the Republican candidates, there is little evidence in campaign headquarters files of further activities on behalf of Hughes by North Dakota's conservative Republican governor. Another significant feature of the campaign was the inactivity of leading Progressives such as Usher L. Burdick and R. A. Nestos. Former Senator Henry Clay Hansborough, once identified with the McKenzie faction of the Republican party, campaigned for Wilson. William Langer, certain of his own election and perhaps not anxious to increase Lemke's power or to offend either Hughes or Wilson supporters, ceased campaigning or speaking outside of his home county after the middle of October. Constant complaints came from Republicans about the fact that Frazier was not supporting Hughes; none of the League candidates would travel with McCumber. The type of candidate Hughes was and the type of individual Lemke was made the campaign one against Wilson rather than one for Hughes.[37]

As grueling and hectic as the previous four weeks had been for Lemke, the hours of waiting as election returns poured in were even more trying. It was soon apparent that the result would be close, both in the state and in the nation. In a succession of wires from national headquarters, Lemke was cautioned to protect the ballot boxes and to employ inspectors and competent counsel. One wire stated: "Republicans claiming Minnesota and California. Watch your state closely. May determine election." As late as the evening of the day following the election, Lemke was claiming that North Dakota might still vote for Hughes. Returns from the tier of counties along the Canadian border in the western part of the state and other northwestern counties gradually altered the result. By the evening of November 9, Lemke was willing to concede the state to Wilson unless the national outcome depended on North Dakota, in which case he advised asking for a recount. To protect the ballots for such a contingency, he requested $2500 from national headquarters and received it.[38] The vote was close and a shift of less than one-half vote a precinct would have altered the result.

An analysis of the election does not point the way to a single clear-cut theory of why Lemke as state chairman had failed to carry the state for Hughes. All of the counties in the state containing major cities, except Stark, Morton, and Richland, voted for Wilson. McCumber's home was at Wahpeton in Richland County, and Dickinson, the largest city in Stark County, had a heavy foreign-born population as had much of Morton County. This would indicate that Lemke's greatest failure was in the urban, not in the rural areas. Counties with a heavy German-speaking population, such as Emmons, McIntosh, Mercer, Morton, Sheridan, Stark, and Wells, all voted for Hughes, some of them by wide majorities. Lemke himself was quoted as blaming the peace-loving Norwegians but later denied having made the statement. Some, but not all, of the counties along the Canadian border from Towner County westward had substantial Norwegian populations. Traill County in the Red River Valley, the most heavily Norwegian of any county in the state, voted for Hughes by a vote of 1423 to 664, clearly indicating that the Norwegian vote was not the decisive factor. Later Lemke referred to the counties along the Canadian border as those responsible for the failure, implying Canadian or British influence on behalf of England.[39] The inadequacy of this explanation was apparent when it became clear that Pembina and Cavalier counties, two with the heaviest proportion of residents of Canadian origin, voted for Hughes.

Failure of Hughes to win back the Progressives, who had been alienated in 1912, partially explains the Democratic majority in North Dakota.[40] Hughes's failure was most pronounced in the northwestern part of the state, where Burdick's influence would have been decisive had he campaigned among the urban Progressives in the larger towns. Three transcontinental railroads, each with at least four major terminals, and a fourth railroad which crosses one corner of the state and which had one terminal, meant that there was a substantial railroad labor vote in the state. Their defection to the Democrats diminished the total Republican vote.

Burke's candidacy had suffered because of Lemke's participation in the campaign. Lemke had attacked Burke, and the latter had threatened to sue Lemke. Lemke's charge had been that Burke made improper expenditures from state funds which had not been accounted for. Lemke had always supported the former governor in previous campaigns, and Burke had invested and lost money in Lemke's Mexican enterprise.[41] The attacks on Burke seem inexcusable in view of their past relationships and leave Lemke with little to complain about the tactics which were later to be used against him by League opponents. As chairman of the Republican party, Lemke contributed his full share to McCumber's victory over Burke—hardly an accomplishment for a professed Progressive. Lemke could have conducted the campaign with emphasis on support of McCumber; his duties as chairman did not make it necessary for him to attack Burke as he did. Burke's defeat was not without future consequences. Had he been elected, his vote would have been decisive in the organization of the United States Senate in the Sixty-sixth Congress, and Henry Cabot Lodge would not have served as chairman of the Senate Foreign Relations Committee at the time when the Treaty of Versailles was being considered.

Casey's candidacy and the League claim to nonpartisanship both suffered because of Lemke's role as chairman of the Republican party.

The Republican advertisements—over the name of one of the officers of the League—which asked for a straight ticket vote must have influenced many of the *Leader* readers to vote for Steen, who was Casey's opponent for state treasurer.[42] The final tabulations showed the two candidates to be separated by 200 votes, and a shift of half of that number would have resulted in an election tie. This gave League opponents control of one major office and was the last attempt of the League until 1956 to file candidates in the North Dakota Democratic primaries.*

While Lemke may have held rural and German-American votes for Hughes, he probably lost votes elsewhere by his vicious attacks on Wilson. His attacks on the President's record as one of crime and murder were offensive to some. Neither was Lemke a good choice to soothe the ruffled feelings of Progressives. Burdick had not been introduced to Hughes when the latter toured the state. This was in September, before Lemke was in active charge, but Lemke's past record of opposition to Burdick both in 1914 and 1916 meant that Burdick would not feel receptive to overtures from Lemke. Burdick flatly refused to campaign for Hughes, stating that he would leave the task to congressmen who knew more about the issues.[43]

For the moment the defeat of Hughes obscured the great victory of the League. With the exception of the defeat of Casey by Steen, the League had succeeded in electing every candidate it had endorsed; even their candidates for superintendent of public instruction and the Supreme Court, who were on a separate ballot without party designation, were elected. Lemke himself was in a strategic position within the League organization, and his record to this time would justify the assumption that he would exercise fully whatever power was granted to him by this position in the organization and by his influence with Townley, Wood, and Frazier.

Despite the narrow defeat of Charles Evans Hughes, which meant continued misfortune for Lemke's Mexican investments and loss of federal patronage in North Dakota, William Lemke had little time to brood. A new group of men who were largely untutored in government had been elected by the Nonpartisan League to the state legislature and to many state offices, and Lemke devoted much time and energy to guiding those who were new to public office. In his capacity as Townley's adviser, he moved quickly to a position where

* The defeat of Casey made certain that in North Dakota the Nonpartisan League would work as a faction seeking control of the Republican party.

in most instances A. C. Townley relied on his counsel. Lynn J. Frazier's nomination and election as governor had insured Lemke's position of leadership and control of the League.* A general recognition by the electorate that Lemke was the power behind the throne is apparent in the correspondence he received immediately following the election. From every direction came inquiries for jobs. Lemke's carefully phrased answers denied the power which the letters by implication attributed to him. Equally cautious were his predictions as to what would happen in the coming session of the legislature.[44]

Whether it was for love of power or for a more altruistic motive, Lemke's secret for success lay largely in a tireless capacity for work and a drive that sustained him through eighteen-hour days unbroken by the conviviality in which so many public figures find relaxation. Moreover, his vision and imagination, his capacity to dream great dreams, made Lemke the source of ideas for the League.† His political activity did not prevent him from giving much time and thought to policy matters and to proposed legislation. He sent inquiries regarding specific legislation and requests for suggestions to

* In an interview on January 14, 1951, Townley stated that Lemke had only a secondary role, that of adviser on legal matters. Townley's memory is that his own decisions were final. He placed no emphasis on the part that Lemke had in arriving at those decisions, nor did he recognize that Lemke's influence with Frazier was such that the latter's election gave Lemke much more influence that he otherwise would have had. Townley's chief power over Lemke came from the former's rule that the League could not endorse one of its own officers for state office. Townley admitted that Lemke was able by 1920 to circumvent this rule to run for office against Townley's wishes. Though continuing to assert that Lemke was just an employee, he admitted that his own (Townley's) inexperience caused him to permit advisers to ask for too much in the legislative session of 1917, a reference to Lemke influence. For the opinion of an anti-Leaguer, see Bruce, pp. 67–69. Supreme Court Justice Bruce was an instructor of Lemke during Lemke's last year at the University of North Dakota.

† In a letter to the author dated July 8, 1957, Mrs. Kathrine B. Tiffany, the widow of Neil C. Macdonald, stated that the best authority on the relationship of Frazier and Lemke would be Nelson Mason, who worked in Frazier's office. Mason wrote Lemke: "I have a clear recollection ... that your ideas, initiative and judgment was [sic] the general governing force. Lynn J., with all his good points, seldom initiated action. You on the other hand were always full of ideas, and devoted more time than you could really spare helping the Governor to get action under way" (Lemke Papers). The only interview the author has had where this point was discussed which did not confirm the impression given in Mason's letter is the interview with Townley himself. Bahmer describes Lemke as second only to Townley in his impact on the League's development (Bahmer, p. 451). He makes no statement that would accord Frazier influence in having a determining role on the kind of organization the League

each of the successful League candidates, to prominent Leaguers throughout the state, and to reference bureaus, libraries, and individuals throughout the country. Lemke had become the clearing house for the ideas to be considered for legislation; he had assembled a formidable body of information on probable legislative topics such as highway laws, local grain grading practices, insurance, landholding, agriculture, and state budgets. He had the material on hand, and his mastery of it was such that he stood ready to answer questions or to draft proposals. General recognition of the author of Nonpartisan League legislative proposals was apparent in the comments of one legislator, who stated, "Lemke would write the bills. 'Cross-eyed' Bowen would explain the bills and tell the farmers how to vote."[45] This situation was gratifying to Lemke, and he was ready to work long hours in order to strengthen his position within the League.

However, Lemke requested no advice and sought no ideas from North Dakotans who were not Leaguers.[46] Even when they were old friends and prominent persons such as Congressman Patrick D. Norton of the Third Congressional District, Lemke gave little information in his letters about his current legislative and League work. This secretive policy probably intensified the antagonism and suspicion of non-Leaguers and contributed to the difficulties the League later encountered; also, because Lemke spent much of his time doing legislative homework, where he could not be seen by others, he became not only a man of power but also one of mystery about whom legends grew.

The old Progressive group had split; the majority, including such men as Norton, refused to embrace the new movement. Eventually most of them were frightened by the rural radicals into an alliance with the right-wing Stalwarts. Only a few of the Progressive leaders

---

would be. Morlan emphasizes the role of Townley, but does concede that Lemke by 1919 had achieved a dominant position in North Dakota (Morlan, p. 250). In an interview in June, 1938, with George Shafer, attorney general of North Dakota from 1923 to 1929 and governor from 1929 to 1933, Shafer raised the question as to why Townley could create the League and in a short time lose control of it. He had known Townley when the latter was organizing for the Socialists before the advent of the League. Later, Schafer in a letter to the author, August 13, 1938, gave his own analysis: "While Townley was a genius in the field of promotional organization, I do not think that he was a smart political boss like McKenzie, and did not have the ability to maintain himself as the political leader of the League. His later activities indicate that his promotional instincts are his chief characteristics and that he lacks the talents necessary to a successful political boss."

such as Lemke, William Langer, and Thomas Hall moved into positions of prominence in the Nonpartisan League; many of them, such as Langer and Hall, would remain in the new movement for only a few years. The League program was more extensive than that of the Progressives; Leaguers advanced their proposals with more zeal; and League leaders such as Lemke were so unconcerned about the wishes of their former Progressive associates that the members of the latter group felt uneasy about the League. Many of them became leaders of League opposition. Some Progressives as well as most Stalwarts failed to understand that the terminal elevator proposal was designed not to destroy capitalism but to make it work advantageously for the farmer-entrepreneur. The Progressives had concerned themselves primarily with reforms designed to ensure honest government, and economic independence from the Twin Cities had not accompanied the political independence that Burke and his fellow liberals had won. Even such liberal Progressives as Usher L. Burdick and Asle J. Gronna were hesitant about identifying themselves with the Nonpartisan League.[47]

There were other calls on Lemke's time. He was the League's attorney. When farmers sought aid for their legal problems, their cases were turned over to Lemke. Although Lemke had accepted reimbursement fees whenever proffered, his fees in these cases were usually not on a contingent basis and were small. He was too alert not to know that low fees were strengthening his own political following. His own pioneer experiences and the difficult experiences his brothers and sisters were having in keeping their farms brought forth another side of the man who only a few years before had seemed a buccaneering promoter. Too, the constant contact in his work in Equity and the Nonpartisan League with those who were having a difficult time in keeping their farm homes had revealed a heretofore unnoticed sympathy for the underdog. Lemke's secretary recalled how difficult it was for Lemke "to say 'no' to someone who was 'down on his luck.' He was always dipping in his pocket to help someone who drifted into his office regardless of whether he was from North Dakota or not." But more than anything else, Lemke needed to feel that he was influential. It is doubtful if he would have given the same full measure of devotion to any cause in which his position was that of a private in the ranks. At the same time it is doubtful whether he recognized his own motivation, and he himself believed that his motives were altruistic.* His activities as a one-man legal aid society, his devotion to Nonpartisan League principles, and his investments in Mexico are three main reasons for his poor financial circumstances through most of his life, and for the very moderate circumstances in which he left his family at the time of his death. This was a source of embarrassment to his family and a concern to his creditors.[48]

Beginning in 1916 Lemke was a full-time employee of the League, earning a moderate salary; any services he gave League members or any work he did for the League was usually not on a fee basis. Few organizations have ever obtained legal services at such bargain rates. In effect they were receiving a one-hundred-twenty-hour week, and Lemke himself was not unsatisfied with the arrangement. Being at the center of power and influence and feeling that he was making progress toward the removal of society's ills were more satisfying rewards to Lemke than the larger fees he might have collected. Townley and the Nonpartisan League had made him a political factor in the state, a goal that had been Lemke's for a long time. It was not an unhappy Lemke who was now the focus of activity leading to the 1917 session of the legislature.

There were many decisions to be made. How was Frazier to be prepared for his new job? How were the legislators to be guided so that they could bring forth a constructive program? Who was to be the speaker of the lower chamber and who were to be committee chairmen? Most important of all, what means would be taken to amend North Dakota's constitution, a task that had to be accomplished before the League program of state ownership of marketing and credit facilities could be completed?

The difficult method of amending the constitution, which required

* The portrait of Lemke drawn by S. R. Maxwell, a former Leaguer who had become one of the League's severest critics, counterbalances perhaps more realistically the image of himself that Lemke at some times conveyed: "I have never seen Lemke flurried, and he has always treated me like a gentleman.... [He] is smooth, polite, and gentle. Bill is a good sport, a master hand in the great game of life. Bill is the cement that will hold the League together when Townley is discredited and forgotten. Lemke told me once at my home in St. Paul that he was never a socialist, but that he believes in social justice, and is willing to align himself with any movement directed at that object. He believes that is the object of the League, and was quite willing to take part in the kidnapping of the Republican party in North Dakota. At this conversation he said: 'Maxwell, there is no morality in the game of politics. It is simply a matter of beating the other fellow to it' " (Maxwell, p. 52).

approval by two successive legislatures and ratification by the people,
finally had been changed in 1914, when a constitutional amendment
had been passed which was thought to make amendment by initiated
measure possible. When an attempt was made to change the location
of the state capital from Bismarck to New Rockford by an initiated
constitutional measure, the state Supreme Court held in the fall of
1916 that the change in the method of amending the constitution was
not complete until implemented by legislative action.[49] The League
leaders were now facing a choice of methods which they might follow
in amending the constitution and in legalizing their contemplated
program. They could pass the legislation which the Supreme Court
had decreed in the New Rockford case to be necessary before the
constitution could be amended by initiative. Following that, they
could initiate their program of legislation in a special election called
for that purpose. Constitutional law, as developed in the United
States, would have sanctioned the legislature's convening a constitutional convention with the delegates to it chosen by vote of the electorate. Neither of these methods was adopted, and a course of procedure was taken which, in retrospect, seems to have been ill advised.
It was decided to rewrite the constitution of the state, have the legislature pass it, and then submit it to the people for ratification. The
League could depend on the vote of 81 of the 113 members of the
lower house; in the upper chamber, where there were holdover
members, it could count on only 20 votes, which were not enough to
give a majority. The fact that the League had been successful in
choosing three members of the Supreme Court and that it had made
such a clean sweep of the election encouraged League leaders to
believe they could mobilize public opinion so strongly that holdover
opposition members would feel compelled to support them. In addition it was the most rapid course of procedure they could adopt.

This last factor alarmed the conservative press. Hoping that time
would modify public opinion, conservatives argued against any action
that would be immediate. The Leaguers operated through a tight
caucus. Spending the entire session at Bismarck as an officer and
legal adviser of the League, Lemke drafted legislation, advised legislators, and worked on legislative strategy. As a confidant of Frazier
and chairman of the Republican party, he carried much greater
prestige than did the other League advisers. Moreover, Townley was
becoming increasingly dependent on Lemke. His creditors attempted

to attach League funds to satisfy his bonanza farming debts. Townley depended on Lemke to represent and protect him and the League treasury, and eventually Lemke advised Townley to plead bankruptcy and represented him in the bankruptcy action.[50] Lemke's willingness to work, his dynamic energy, his fiery caucus presentations, and his central position in the League headquarters made him a dominating figure.

It was probably Lemke more than Townley who was responsible for the decision to make the legislature a constitutional convention. Townley attributed his error to poor advice. It was typical of Lemke to drive hard, and Lemke told reporters: "One thing we want and will have is a constitutional convention. I am not ready to say how we will get it." Earlier in the same interview Lemke admitted that the League was eight votes short in the Senate but denied that the Equity convention during the first week in February was designed to bring pressure on the Senate. "We want to know where we are at first. By next week we hope to know and then I can tell you more about our plans. There will be news breaking very soon. There's no cause for you newsboys to worry."[51] This would indicate that the decision of which method of constitutional revision to attempt was delayed until shortly before the proposed revision of the constitution was actually introduced by Representative A. M. Hagen on January 13.

Repercussions were immediate and violent. Representative H. A. Mackoff from Stark County declared House Bill 44, as the proposal was known, "the greatest fraud and most colossal piece of grandstand play ever perpetrated on the public," adding that its author did not expect it to pass. J. F. T. O'Connor of Grand Forks emphasized the illegality of H.B. 44 and pointed out that the people had not intended the legislature to act as a constitutional convention. House members could do little but express their indignation and add amendments which the League leaders felt compelled to defeat. Representative A. G. Divet of Wahpeton was adept at proposing amendments which made League leaders appear unreasonable and even treasonable. He proposed that the new constitution provide for a debt limit of one million dollars. When that was defeated, he successively made proposals for limits of two, three, and then ten million dollars, only to be voted down each time by League leaders. More damaging was their opposition to his proposal to have the words "patriotism" and "morality" placed in the provision providing for public education.[52]

They had been omitted in the House Bill 44 proposed constitutional revision.* On January 27 House Bill 44 passed the lower house by a vote of 82 to 27 with four not voting.

In the Senate it was given a different reception. There it was referred to the Committee on State Affairs, where "William Lemke who is reported to have much to do with the framing of the new constitution addressed the . . . committee for an hour this morning in defense of the measure. . . . Mr. Lemke intimated that the house probably would pass the bill with certain amendments which were suggested, and he urged that the senate take immediate favorable action." The final Senate vote against House Bill 44 caused League leaders to assert that twenty-three political graves—those of those senators who would be up for election in 1918—had been dug by the defeat of constitutional revision.†[53]

Near the end of the session League opponents countered with Senate Bill 84, a proposal for an appropriation of $300,000 to build a terminal elevator. This was nearly a duplicate of the proposal in the 1915 legislature, the defeat of which had been the major argument used in selling Nonpartisan League memberships. What would have satisfied the farmers in 1915 was nothing in comparison to the League plans for 1917. League leaders quickly sensed the danger in S.B. 84. Its passage would assuage the farmer discontent which had made the rise of the League possible and make more difficult the forwarding of the extensive League reform program. Of all the opposition measures, this was the most difficult one to combat; it was difficult to convince longtime Equity members that they should not support the proposal for which they had fought for years. Lemke's feelings were unmistakable. He wrote that "it would have destroyed the

---

* The late Edward Erickson, who served as rural school supervisor under Neil C. Macdonald in the Department of Public Instruction, in an interview on October 20, 1956, stated that he felt this was a determining error on the League's part. A minor concession on phraseology would have prevented planting the seed of doubt regarding the patriotism of League leaders. He stated that he had pleaded with Macdonald to accept this change, but that the League leaders had been adamant. His explanation was that they felt minor concessions would lead to greater ones.

† The unconventional method of amendment that had been selected suggests the possibility that League leaders felt they could win regardless of legislative action. If the revision passed and was held constitutional, they would have gained their objective. If it failed, they would have been able to identify and defeat the conservatives responsible for blocking its passage.

whole League program. It was just what the enemy wanted." Lemke
thought he had the League legislators convinced of the necessity of
defeating the bill and left the last evening of the session. He was surprised by the vote and explained: "[I] left in a hurry that evening
after I thought that 84 was sure to be killed, and then to my surprise
learned next morning that it had passed."[54]

Most embarrassing was the position in which Governor Frazier was
placed by the passage of S.B. 84. He felt compelled to veto the bill
and gave an explanation in his veto message. Frazier stated that appropriations had been deliberately made so as to exceed revenue; that
the bill did not provide for a flour mill but for an elevator outside
the state; and that it was to be built from tax money rather than from
money obtained by the sale of bonds. The main objection—namely,
that the bill's passage would take the motive power from behind the
League program—was, of course, not mentioned in explanation of his
veto. The incident had its effect in turning some members against the
League. Feeling that the veto substantiated the charge of insincerity
leveled by the conservative press, they followed the lead of Theodore
G. Nelson of Dunn County, who was to become one of the key leaders
of League opposition in the years ahead.*

The battles over H.B. 44 and S.B. 84 were the major engagements,
but there had been constant skirmishes over other questions since
shortly after the League victory of the previous November. Almost
immediately thereafter Lemke had taken charge of a move to seat
the three League-sponsored judges, James E. Robinson, Luther B.
Birdzell, and Richard Grace, on December 1, 1916, instead of in
January, 1917. The issue was important to the League because the
time limit for a petition for a rehearing on a controversial bank case
expired during the month of December. The chief officer of the bank
involved had supporters in the League, and Lemke made a most
strenuous effort in his behalf. The effort to unseat the old court
failed, and the chief result of the incident was to intensify the efforts
of the opposition and provide them with another weapon with which
to combat the League.[55]

---

* At this time Nelson was just doubting and worrying; more considerate treatment might have resulted in neutralizing him. It was a fault of League leaders
that they would immediately classify all doubters as agents of "big biz" with
questionable motives. A stenographic error in Nelson's first name, which Lemke
did not note, was hardly calculated to assuage the feelings of this offended Equity
member (Theodore G. Nelson to William Lemke, March 23, 1917; William
Lemke to Peter G. Nelson, April 2, 1917; both Lemke Papers).

Another controversy revolved around the State Board of Regents, which had been established in 1915. On a technicality the League claimed that two members had not been legally appointed.\* Governor Frazier appointed new members to replace them and asked the institutions of higher learning to ignore the old board, which persisted in acting as the legally constituted body. Balked by Senate refusal to confirm his appointments, Frazier waited until the legislature adjourned and made interim appointments, for which Justice Bruce of the Supreme Court denounced him as another Oliver Cromwell. That Lemke's hand was in all these maneuvers seems clear from his correspondence and from the fact that one of the new appointees was his brother-in-law and former college friend Robert Muir.[56]

Much of Lemke's power came from his position as legal adviser. His decision was final on the articles of incorporation drawn up for League enterprises, and it was he who drew the papers in the important legal transactions of the League. His aggressiveness and the voice of authority with which he spoke may have hastened the subsequent revolt of Langer, Hall, and Carl Kositzky. Lemke's position was becoming clear to most observers as the session progressed. In view of the League legislation that was passed, Lemke must have continued the same ceaseless pace throughout the session. Numbered among Nonpartisan League accomplishments in the 1917 legislative session were a state grain grading system, proposed constitutional amendments regarding woman suffrage in some elections, exemption of farm improvements from taxation, a state bank deposit guarantee law, a nine-hour day for women, a Torrens land title registration law, regulation of railroads, and trebling of funds for rural education. When Lemke and the other leaders decided to pass a law removing the legal obstacles to amendment by initiated measure,[57] they met the opposition of the conservatives. Lemke made no attempt to conceal the violence of his feelings and, no doubt, knew that his vitriolic attacks helped win attention and consolidate a following within the League organization.†

\* The League claimed that Governor Hanna had appointed the board on March 2, 1915, two days before there was any law providing for establishment of such a board. The two members whose terms were to expire in July of 1917 were dismissed as a test case. The Supreme Court ruled in favor of those dismissed. The resignation of ex-Governor Frank White to serve with the National Guard and the expiration of the terms of two others enabled Frazier to gain unquestioned control of the board.

† But the appearance of anger he gave when thus aroused helped create the stereotype of a dangerous demagogue. It was for the moment a successful means

There were other issues coming before the legislature. Germany resumed unrestricted submarine warfare in February, 1917, while the legislature was in session. When resolutions regarding the crisis were forwarded to Lemke by Arthur Le Sueur and James Manahan for legislative consideration, Lemke wrote Le Sueur: "In regard to the resolutions, will state that I changed them some, so as not to make them offensive to the Germans"; and to Manahan: "Received . . . resolutions, which I modified somewhat. Did not feel like permitting you to take a slap at the Germans. Didn't you know that they were to make Ireland free?" [58]

Although "bitterness was brushed aside for the moment when jovial merrymaking accompanied adjournment," the issues had been set forth and the public was to have the final decision as to whether the constitutional changes could be made.[59] The work of the session could be summed up by saying that the League's aggressiveness and willingness to take advantage of legal technicalities to accomplish its purposes, for which Lemke must be assigned a major share of the responsibility, had been used by a resourceful, experienced opposition to create suspicions in the minds of the voters—suspicions which were to lead to future defeats. Some of the errors of the League resulted from the momentum of success. Carried away by their rapid rise to unprecedented power, the leaders were unable to exercise moderation or to resist the enthusiasm of those visionaries who had been attracted from other parts of the nation by the movement's success. Auxiliary enterprises not in the original League program were launched, and the presence of liberals and socialists from other states in the hotels and lobbies during the legislative session had added to the distrust and resentment felt by League opponents.

Almost automatically the League spread beyond the borders of the state. As the canvassing of North Dakota came to an end, it was as natural to the crews of salesmen and their directors who were working on commission to go to other states as it would have been for representatives of a commercial enterprise of any kind which had found it had a product it could sell. In August, 1916, one Minnesotan had written to Lemke: "I note the Non Partisan League is organizing rapidly in Minnesota. If I can be of any aid at any time, call on me." By the spring of 1917 it had been decided to establish a national headquarters and draw up bylaws for a Minnesota organization. This

---

of winning attention and gathering votes, but it was to become a handicap and a limiting factor in his career. Lemke failed to recognize many of the occasions which called for measured tones and carefully qualified statements.

development of the League's activities into more enterprises and
over a greater area had two effects. The numerous organizations were
difficult to watch, and the attention and energies of League leaders
were fragmented. Lemke himself had begun commuting between
Fargo and St. Paul in December, 1916, to make negotiations for rent-
ing a headquarters for the national organization of the Nonpartisan
League. As soon as the legislative session was over, he resumed the
work necessary to complete the transaction. From then until 1919 he
divided his time between the state headquarters at Fargo and the
national headquarters at St. Paul. His divided responsibilities caused
problems and he often had to postpone North Dakota work because
of his St. Paul commitments.[60]

His relationship with Townley in St. Paul was the same as in Fargo.
S. R. Maxwell wrote: "He stands closer to Townley than any other
man in the cabinet. His little den of an office adjoins the big office
of His Majesty with a connecting door. Townley always consults with
Lemke. They are wrapped up together in the same covering of
secrecy." But even at this distance Lemke continued to keep in close
touch with North Dakota affairs. Before leaving Bismarck, he had
been in consultation with Governor Frazier on most items, and he
continued to send letters of advice as to which college appropriations
to veto, who should be appointed game and fish commissioner, and
about the problems attendant upon removing recalcitrant board members.[61] His relations with other state officers carried the voice of authority. Although the League had rebelled against the Twin City rule of
Alexander McKenzie, League leader Lemke was now doing part of the
governing from the Twin Cities.

Lemke's plan to go to Mexico after the legislative session adjourned
was forgotten. He had nearly become a stranger in his own home,
and Mrs. Lemke complained that he was gone so much that his children did not know him. Always an intense person, he had become a
man of single purpose. As he later stated, the Nonpartisan League had
almost become his religion, and it was having an effect on his personality. His preoccupation caused him to fail to recognize close friends;
he was unable to keep his mind on the problems of driving an automobile. In 1917 he had taken his family by automobile to St. Paul
and while there he was involved in a serious accident in front of the
St. Paul Automobile Club building. Although he was able to prove
that the other driver was at fault, he must have had doubts about
his own responsibility, for he never drove again. When traveling by

car after 1917, he always provided himself with a driver. The same preoccupation with the business at hand made him indifferent to his personal appearance. This gave him a distinctiveness in dress which, though not pleasing to his family, became a legend among the farmer followers of the League and among those whose work brought them into contact with courtroom gossip. It is probable that his careless mode of attire, although at first accidental, later became a calculated measure to win votes. He disliked hats and wore an old-style cap which came to be his political trademark.[62] This indifference to dress and personal appearance added to the poor first impression he often gave of himself. In his home and on any social occasion, he conducted himself in a gracious, refined manner that many not knowing him better would not have expected.

New problems were soon to come to the Nonpartisan League and thus to Lemke. President Wilson, as Lemke had predicted he would, asked Congress to declare war upon Germany. On April 6 Congress acted upon the President's request. Almost simultaneously the news came that Congressman Henry T. Helgesen from the First Congressional District of North Dakota had died.* In the elections of 1916 the League had refused to campaign for national offices; its success in the campaigns of 1916 now led its officers to endorse a candidate to run for the vacancy caused by Helgesen's death. Lemke's position as state chairman of the Republican party placed him in a position to have influence on this decision as well as upon the choice of candidate. It was unfortunate for the League and for Lemke that the congressional vacancy occurred. Controlling the nomination and winning the election took time and energy that League leaders needed for the accomplishment of their program, and a contest at this time served to heighten the tension that had resulted from the debate on H.B. 44. The League leaders needed time in which to assess their position and make plans for the future. Instead, they were plunged into the middle of a heated political campaign that absorbed their energies, deepened antagonisms that existed between them and the conservatives, and gave their opponents an early opportunity to use the war issue against them.

* Lemke had used his influence with Helgesen to obtain an appointment to a military academy for a relative. Although the boy lived in the Twin Cities, Helgesen and Lemke arranged for him to obtain a North Dakota appointment by having his mail come to Fargo. This had occurred just a few weeks before Helgesen died. (H. T. Helgesen to William Lemke, February 8, 1917, Lemke Papers.)

# CHAPTER III

# High Tide

Congressman Henry T. Helgesen's death occurred just at the time when William Lemke had become prominent enough to be his logical successor. When Congressman Helgesen died, Congressman George M. Young wrote to Lemke: "If you have any idea of ever coming to Congress now is your time. . . . Come out squarely in favor of a united America back of the President in prosecution or conduct of the war." Not since his unfortunate determination to invest in Mexico had Lemke stood at such an apparent crossroads. There can be no doubt that he aspired to go to Congress. Had he known it would be sixteen years before he would be elected congressman, eleven of which would be in compulsory retirement from a public career—retirement that would have been permanent had it not been for the great depression—there is little doubt that his decision would have been to resign his position on the League executive committee in order to run in 1917. How logical his candidacy would have been at the time and how much support he would have had, even if Townley had disapproved, is indicated by the many letters he received. Former Minnesota Congressman James Manahan, who was at the heart of the movement at League headquarters, wrote: "I had a session with Townley this morning in which I strongly urged upon him the importance of . . . electing you to Congress. . . . I write . . . for fear . . . your characteristic modesty and backwardness might lead you to sidestep it." F. E. Packard, prominent in League circles at Bismarck, urged: "You are absolutely the man for this position. . . . We don't want a pussyfooter or anything of the sort at the present time in Washington but a fighter and a [sic] agitator who will get some advertising and make some impression." Robert Muir, Lemke's brother-in-law, hoped that Lemke would receive "Helgesen's job and then put [Senator] Gronna out when the time comes." Lemke was not the only possible candidate; Olger B. Burtness, a former Varsity Bachelor Club brother and a fellow Progressive and political aspirant, wrote to ask: "Are you intending to become a candidate?... I might state that I have been... considering becoming one."[1]

A. C. Townley, no doubt, was opposed to League endorsement of Lemke. He had steadfastly refused to run for office himself;* he felt that Fred B. Wood and Lemke should follow a similar policy to protect the League against the charge that its officers were self-seeking. Lemke's relationship with Wood and with other key Leaguers was such that it seems unlikely that Townley could have turned the League against Lemke if Lemke had resigned from his position in the League and announced his candidacy for Congress; it does seem probable that Townley could have insisted that Lemke give up his position on the executive committee of the League if Lemke insisted on becoming a candidate for Congress. Withdrawing from his key position was a price Lemke was reluctant to pay. In Congress he would lose his central position within the League and much of the power he then had. A zealot with political sense, he enjoyed his position as "political bishop," which gave full scope to his kingmaking abilities. His reluctance to give up this power made it easier for Townley and others to appeal to his loyalty and point out flatteringly how valuable he was to the League as an executive officer, at the same time making clear that he could not keep his present position in the League if he desired to become a candidate. Lemke wrote about the decision that "I and my friends... decided that I could render better service to the League here than in Washington." This seems an accurate reflection of the actual situation. He was a key man in the League[2] and had greater influence in its North Dakota branch than any other person.

Moreover, as though to complicate Lemke's career still further, during the summer of 1917 the Mexican situation seemed to be stabilizing. Lemke called a meeting of the Land Finance Company directors. Under the spell of his optimistic persuasion, they agreed to another assessment on the stockholders to pay the taxes and maintain title to their property. Only thus, Lemke argued, could the entire investment be saved. The fact that Lemke had put more of his own money into the company helped convince the directors of his sincerity,

* If League officers were to run for public office, Townley could have run himself. He regretted in later years not having gone to the Senate. His comment was: "If you give someone else the plums, the people come to listen to those who have the plums" (interview with A. C. Townley, January 14, 1951).

but it was more difficult to persuade the stockholders to pay. Lemke used the "carrot and stick" technique. He held out the promise of alluring gains while at the same time he hinted broadly at the sense of betrayal the other stockholders would feel toward any of their number who did not do their part by paying the assessments. The severity of tone of some of his letters fails to indicate any sense of self-reproach, and at times the letters sounded almost as though the stockholders had pushed Lemke into the project. The obvious implication was that to be fair to him, to themselves, and to their fellow investors, they were under an obligation to pay. Many of the stockholders, including Langer, as well as some who continued to regard Lemke as a close friend, remonstrated with him over the tone of the letters he sent. Many of them were ready to write off their losses, and others simply did not have the cash with which to pay the assessment. The correspondence with the stockholders and with Katze, Castellot, and Edward Musick* was enough to keep one office force busy. It was another serious drain on Lemke's time and energy. Particularly indicative of future trouble for the League were Lemke's letters to Langer.[3] It could not have been easy during these years for Langer to endure the fact that Lemke was so influential in the League. Nor was it easy for Langer to forget the $50,000 he and his family had lost because of investment in Lemke's company. It was irritating for him to receive letters from Lemke with the clear implication that those who failed to pay assessments were shirkers. What familiarity and cordiality there was between the two men was on the surface. Langer had been happy to have Lemke's assistance in obtaining the nomination for attorney general. His feelings toward Lemke were such, however, that they made it easier for him to break with the League when, for other reasons, he desired to do so.

Lemke was the logical prominent Leaguer to run as candidate for Congress. If it were not to be he, someone else had to be endorsed and elected or the position conceded to a League opponent. The actual selection was a surprise to those who were not in the inner circle of the League.[4] Although endorsement was made at a League meeting, it seems clear that Townley and Lemke were in a position to control the selection, and they decided on John M. Baer, a cartoonist for *The Leader* whom Townley had discovered at Beach and brought to Fargo to work for the Nonpartisan League. When farming at Beach, Townley

* Edward Musick was the manager or foreman of the Mexican properties of the Land Finance Company.

had learned that Baer was a man of very liberal views and that he had outstanding ability as a cartoonist. Baer was a Democrat who had been appointed by President Wilson to be postmaster at Beach. Townley had persuaded him to resign and devote his full time to drawing cartoons for League publications. Baer's success in drawing hard-hitting political cartoons had made him a major asset to the League.

At Fargo Baer and Lemke became acquainted; they found that they held like views on both domestic policies and foreign affairs and that there was a striking similarity in their backgrounds. Both were of German origin. The fathers of both had fought in the Civil War; Baer's father had indoctrinated his children with the same antipathy toward England as had Lemke's father.[5] In the short time they had been acquainted, Lemke had met and grown to like both Baer and his father, and he carried on an extensive correspondence with the latter, exchanging views on foreign affairs.

Meanwhile Baer was enjoying his work at Fargo, where he was able to make a living from what had formerly been an avocation; he had no more intention of becoming a candidate for Congress than did any working newspaperman. A League convention was called to decide whether to endorse a candidate and to select a nominee if the decision was in the affirmative.* While Baer was working at his easel one afternoon, Lemke stepped into his workroom and began talking about topics of international and national interest. After an extended conversation in which they found themselves in agreement on most questions, Lemke left and Baer returned to his work not realizing that he had been interviewed. Baer's own explanation of his nomination was that his "ideas on domestic and foreign policies were in harmony with Lemke's, and the idea of sending a cartoonist to Congress amused Townley." The decision to nominate Baer was made by the convention according to the practice begun in 1916 of discussing individual names written on a blackboard and then voting. Even after he had been endorsed at this convention, Baer was not informed that he was the candidate. On the evening following the convention, Baer and his wife chauffeured Townley and Lemke to a meeting at Casselton. They heard some jesting and laughing between Townley

* According to Morlan, fourteen possibilities were discussed for several hours. "Agreement was finally reached on John M. Baer" (Morlan, p. 130). It seems needless to point out that Baer's own account would indicate that the outcome of the discussion was not nearly so doubtful as Morlan's version would indicate.

and Lemke and later learned they were joking about how aristocratic it was to have a congressman for a chauffeur.[6] It was not until later that Baer learned of his selection. He was as surprised as any thirty-year-old cartoonist might have been.

There was no certainty as to how the election would be conducted. While primaries had been provided by statute to replace conventions for the regular elections, no provisions for primaries for special elections had been made. This problem was eventually solved when Attorney General Langer ruled that candidates must file by petition. In addition to Baer there were six other candidates, a fact which insured Baer's victory, for Baer had the League endorsement and the anti-League vote was split six ways. To unite the anti-League vote behind one of the six, the Republican national committeeman, Gunder Olson, assembled a convention which endorsed Olger B. Burtness and asked that the other candidates recognize Burtness as the official Republican candidate and consent to withdraw their own names.[7]

Burtness was himself behind this move, but he had not reckoned with his old university comrade. Lemke, as state chairman, convened the state executive committee of the Republican party. By a vote of ten to one the committee designated Baer as the official Republican candidate. This recommendation was then submitted to the county chairmen for approval or disapproval. The tabulation of county committeemen votes was Baer 112 and Burtness 57, with a few scattered votes for others. Apparent among the replies was a bitterness over the nomination of Baer as great as any expressed during the debate over revising the state constitution. Letters describing Baer as a Socialist, a Democrat, and a "Jim Jam Jems cartoonist" came to Lemke, and some of the correspondence included personal attacks upon Lemke marked by uncomplimentary epithets.[8]

Baer did an effective job of campaigning. As in the case of Frazier, Lemke had sensed the depth and capacity of the man. At first Baer depended on his cartoons, but he rapidly developed into an able campaigner and effective defender of the League program. He pointed out eloquently that the farmers' program was no more socialistic than many services urban residents expected of their municipal governments.[9]

This was the first campaign in which the loyalty issue played a major part. Both the United States' entrance into the war and Helgesen's death had come at a most inopportune time for Lemke and the League. While the League was successful in electing Baer and defeating Burtness, the campaign meant a further dispersion of the energy of League leaders and a heightening of the issues associated with the outbreak of the war. If, instead of nominating Baer, the League had chosen another long-time resident of the state and district, such as Frazier, it might have fared better. The fact that Baer was a recent arrival in North Dakota and had been in the First Congressional District only six months made him vulnerable to attack by rumor. It is possible that a candidate with a Scandinavian, English, or Scottish name might have been less susceptible to charges of disloyalty during the war hysteria.* Lemke's own background prevented him from sensing the dangers for the League that had been created by the war. His main fear was that the war would divert the attention of the people from the problems of social and economic reform, thus permitting the profiteers to gain at the expense of the country. Neither he nor Townley realized that the war, in addition to diminishing interest in reform, would also be the cudgel with which League leaders would be so battered that the League would never capture another state as it had North Dakota.

Meanwhile, League leaders regarded an election victory in Minnesota as the second step in their effort to make the League a nationwide movement. They hoped in 1918 to duplicate in Minnesota the initial success they had achieved in North Dakota in 1916. Just as in the latter state, they were planning to file candidates to run in the Republican primary. By this time Townley and Lemke were confidently expecting that the League would become a national movement supplanting or capturing one of the two older parties, and they were already thinking in terms of grooming Frazier for President.[10] To accomplish this it was essential that they carry Minnesota. Their candidate was Charles A. Lindbergh, and their failure to elect him broke the momentum of the League movement. It was the war issue and a religious issue† that defeated Lindbergh and stopped the League. Had it not been for the campaign to elect Baer, League leaders might

---

* Yet the name of Neil C. Macdonald and the fact that he had lived in North Dakota most of his life did not spare him from the most vicious attacks. Lynn J. Frazier, however, seemed to be much more immune to this type of campaign. Baer, as an individual, was more like Frazier and might have withstood the charges made against him better had he lived in the district longer.

† Lindbergh had favored a resolution to investigate some institutions of the Roman Catholic Church; this and the war issue defeated him (interview with John M. Baer, August 29, 1956).

have avoided the deep involvement with the war issue that contributed to Lindbergh's defeat.

The series of speeches Townley gave during the Baer campaign in North Dakota resulted in a press campaign which identified Townley as disloyal. These speeches were thoroughly covered in press reports in Minnesota and helped create the climate of opinion that heightened the tensions accompanying the public attitude toward the League in that state.[11] It was this emotionally charged situation which caused the forthcoming League-sponsored Producers' and Consumers' Conference to boomerang on the League. The war issue would have arisen and Lindbergh might have been defeated by it and by the religious issue in any case. But the war issue would not have come to the forefront so soon. It might have been well into 1918 before Townley was effectively tagged in the public mind as pro-German if his speeches during Baer's campaign had not given the League opponents an opportunity to use the issue immediately after the war began.

The speeches made by Townley in support of Baer gave the opposition their cue. Townley's and Lemke's plan was simple. By stressing elimination of profiteering and privilege in the conduct of the war, they hoped to construct a platform on which they could compel the President to stand. Failing in that, they hoped to have an issue that would make the League a national force and Frazier the President of the United States. Arguing that taxation of war profits could finance the war and make unnecessary the sale of liberty bonds, they were immediately charged with opposing the effort to market the bonds. From this it was only one step to identification with the cause of the Kaiser and treason.

During the campaign to elect Baer, the daily newspapers so persistently misquoted Townley that he was compelled to have a League stenographer on hand to take an exact record of what he said. Shortly before the election Townley was scheduled to appear in Fargo. The *Fargo Forum* expressed the hope that if the authorities did not put him in jail, there would be enough able-bodied men to prevent Townley from "repeating the offense." Newspapers in Minnesota and throughout the nation were quick to take their cue from these repercussions of the Baer-Burtness campaign. Baer won an overwhelming victory. He carried every county except Grand Forks and Ramsey and polled more votes than all other candidates combined. His total vote was 13,126; Burtness ran second with a total of 8,945 votes.[12]

Congress was in special session at the time of Baer's election. Although he was sworn in as a Republican, he employed D. H. Mc-Arthur, the Democratic candidate for governor in 1916, to be his secretary. This led to charges that the League had bargained with the Democrats to accomplish Baer's election. By the time of Baer's election and partly because of it, the League was regarded as an organization containing many leaders whose loyalty was open to question. Eastern newspapers reflected this suspicion. The *Boston Transcript* pointed out that North Dakota had the largest foreign-born population of any state in the nation and added: "We must therefore regard the newly elected Congressman from the first district of North Dakota, Mr. Baer, as the representative of a foreign influence in our Congress." Baer did not compile a radical record; in fact he actually voted against the seating of Victor Berger, the Socialist member from Wisconsin.[13]

Now that his native country was involved in the war, Lemke wanted to see her victorious over Germany. But at the same time, by all the powers vested in him, he was determined to see that the President would run the war so that there would be no advantage accruing to England from it.* He was determined that through Baer a start should be made to press President Wilson into taking measures that would benefit neither millionaires, banker profiteers, nor imperialistic Englishmen or Frenchmen. In his vision, the Nonpartisan League was to be not only an instrument of state and national political activity, but also the organization which was to mold the peace and bring a new world of economic justice—a world in which imperialist nations

* Not only at this time but through the period of World War II, he believed that the stronghold of those who start and run all wars was in the British Isles and France (William Lemke to A. F. Caldwell, September 21, 1939). His was the exaggerated nationalism of the second- and third-generation American. So marked is the development of this ultra-nationalism that later one of Lemke's most scholarly admirers sought to admonish him gently by quoting Mark Ingraham: "The man who neglects his family is despised. The family who shirks its duty is of no account. The town that brings disrepute upon the state is branded with shame. The state that will not cooperate with others is looked down upon with derision. But the nation often glories in its unmitigated sovereignty. This is not an old tradition; it is not at all in the tradition of Christian Europe; that tradition assumed that nations too had greater loyalties. Nationalism as against internal disunity, as against local self interest is of value. It substitutes a greater for a lesser loyalty. Nationalism held to as against the rights of humanity is the road to perdition. We must see that our loyalties are large enough. Today nothing short of loyalties to humanity is sufficient" (J. T. Salter, Professor of Political Science at the University of Wisconsin, to William Lemke, January 9, 1948, Lemke Papers).

would be rendered harmless because of the peace terms which the Nonpartisan League had caused the United States to advance. It was with this purpose in mind that the League demanded price control that would protect consumers.* Baer found Lemke constantly urging him on this point as well as pressing him to annoy President Wilson in any manner possible; but Baer often refused to carry out the latter requests from Lemke. Townley went to Washington in the fall of 1917 to advance arguments for price controls. Lemke and Lindbergh went there together, probably at a later date.[14] As representatives of a producer group, they found that in their efforts to protect consumers they had injured producers. Controls came in World War I but only on the basic staples produced by farmers. Retail prices soared, and the farmer found himself in a cost-price squeeze.†

It was with this motive of curbing the profits of the profiteers who, the League asserted, caused all wars, and of preventing them from starting future ones, that the League circulated during the summer and fall of 1917 a petition drawn by Lemke demanding that President Wilson lay down the terms of victory to prevent the despoiling of the world by victorious imperialists. According to Baer, eleven million signatures were secured for this petition to the President, who, to the surprise of some of the sponsors, proved very receptive. The points listed in the petition appealed to the President's idealism, and, in Baer's opinion, President Wilson saw in them an instrument with which he could appeal to the populations of Germany and Austria-Hungary. It was the opinion of former Representative Baer that the petition was instrumental in motivating Wilson to issue the statement of the Fourteen Points at the time when Communist publication of secret Allied treaties and Russian-German negotiations leading to Brest-Litovsk made some move necessary. Because ten of the Fourteen Points were roughly identical with those on the huge petition drawn up by Lemke, Baer thought it possible that one of the better-known documents of twentieth-century American history was in language and sense partly the work of William Lemke, who only two years previously had been an unknown Fargo attorney. While

---

* What was being requested was a form of price control that would operate on processors and manufacturers. There is a basic resemblance in this proposal to the OPA of World War II days, although it is certain that Leaguers were not thinking of the vast machinery of retail price control and rationing.

† Bruce cites how Gronna used this as campaign material in the election of 1920, blaming Townley for the ceiling on wheat (Bruce, p. 210).

hoping through President Wilson to modify wartime policies, Lemke still felt that the President was responsible for the disaster which had struck his Mexican properties. "He was always trying to get me to badger the President," Baer recalled.[15] This predisposition of Lemke against the President helped prevent the alliance between Democrats and the League which their mutual interest in social reform in addition to Republican disdain of the Nonpartisan League made logical.

Despite the savage attacks on the League, Townley and Lemke were taking the offensive. In order to influence the administration to control prices and prevent profiteering, they had the League sponsor a Producers' and Consumers' Conference for September, 1917. Held in St. Paul, it lasted three days and included speeches by Representatives Baer and Young and Senator Gronna of North Dakota, Senator William E. Borah of Idaho, and Representative Jeannette Rankin of Montana. Included also were speakers from the Department of Agriculture, Equity, and the National Public Ownership League. The speakers supported the war effort, asking only as did A. C. Townley in the keynote address that the price be fixed on the things sold to the consumer just as the price on wheat had been fixed. Resolutions were passed pledging "our lives, our fortunes, and our sacred honor to our country and our flag in this, OUR WAR."[16] Though the business meeting of the conference was adjourned, the members were invited to stay for the address to be given that evening, September 20, by Senator Robert M. La Follette.

La Follette had closeted himself in a room in the Frederick Hotel the day previously, preparing a speech to be given to the conference members. When Lemke and Manahan called for him at the hotel at about 6:30 the evening of the speech, he gave it to them to read. The incident is described in Belle and Fola La Follette's biography of La Follette: "But Manahan and Lemke, two men who usually had great courage, were afraid to have Bob deliver this speech that night." In this prepared address La Follette had planned to discuss the constitutional rights of American citizens to express their opinions freely and thus participate in shaping decisions as to how national problems should be solved. Lemke and Manahan realized that the opposition to the League had flooded their conference with undercover agents and newspapermen determined to discover something treasonable with which they could attack the League. Having brought the conference through without incident, their very success until now made them timid for fear that a last-minute incident might spoil all they had gained. La Follette offered to withdraw from the program, but Lemke and Manahan pleaded with him to talk extemporaneously for at least a few minutes, and La Follette consented. In their momentary caution they caused the very thing to happen which they had feared most. By the time they reached the auditorium they were reassured by the friendliness of the crowds, and so they told La Follette to go ahead with his original speech; but he had left it at the hotel and was unable to give it without the text at hand. La Follette was introduced by Frazier and gave a splendid address to which no exception was taken. He sketched the historical background of the struggle for representative government in the Northwest, recalling the struggle with the railroads, and emphasized that the Nonpartisan League was just a crop being harvested from the seed planted by the Grangers long ago. He then discussed the causes of the war, stating that they should have been weighed carefully. He laid particular stress on the circumstances surrounding the sailing of the *Lusitania*. In the latter part of his speech, he emphasized the necessity of financing the war from taxation rather than from borrowing. At the conclusion of the speech, Governor Frazier, who had presided at the meeting, rushed up to congratulate him and to say that there was not a single thing that La Follette had said to which the slightest objection could be made. In one exchange with a heckler, La Follette admitted: "We had grievance against Germany." This was reported in the press and carried by the Associated Press as: "We had no grievance against Germany."[17]

Helped through the surging crowds to a taxi by Representative Baer, the La Follettes had no idea of the repercussions the talk would have. It was eight months before the Associated Press admitted that the inclusion of the word "no" was an unfortunate error.[18] As unfortunate and unjust as the episode had been for La Follette, it was equally disastrous to the hopes of the Nonpartisan League. Coming immediately after the adverse publicity given Townley's speeches during the Baer-Burtness campaign, the error of the press in quoting La Follette gave Governor J. A. A. Burnquist of Minnesota the weapon he needed to defeat the League's attempt to capture Minnesota.

At the hands of the Minnesota press and of the Public Safety Commission, which Governor Burnquist had appointed in 1917, League leaders were submitted to what one writer has described as a "reign of terror." Because of his own German origin, his sympathy for Germany, and his suspicion of England, Lemke felt the full impact of this campaign. Prior to American entrance into the war, he had made no effort to conceal his feelings. From the time the United States entered the war, the tone of his talks and letters emphasized the theme of a just peace and an end to profiteering, and there were no more references to England being more guilty than Germany. Yet because of pre-April 6, 1917, remarks on the relative guilt of England and Germany, and his current expressions on profiteering and a just peace, the campaign on the loyalty issue, which had been begun during the Baer-Burtness campaign and which rose to lethal intensity after the Associated Press misquoted La Follette, injured Lemke and alarmed his friends.[19] Judge Robinson, his former law partner, wrote to him in July:

Now let me remind you of one thing. They are talking of you as the coming man. It seems you stand next to Townley. You are the chairman . . . of the Republican party . . . you are spoken of for Senator and . . . I know what not next. . . . The important suggestion I wish to make . . . is this: that you do get out and make some speeches or write some short articles showing as the fact is, that since war has been declared between this country and Germany, that you are a full-fledged American citizen and that you stand for America every time. I have often heard you express that sentiment that this is your country above every country and you cannot express it too strongly or too often.[20]

Robinson went on to observe that there was a popular suspicion that both Townley and Lemke were pro-German, adding that La Follette's "disloyal" speech at St. Paul had made the suspicion much more widely believed.

Strangely enough it was not the Wilson administration that gave the League trouble, but rather those political and occupational groups in each state that feared a League victory. The Wilson administration, dubious of the caliber and sincerity of its leaders, was worried about being identified with the League. Baer was able to arrange interviews for Townley with President Wilson, George Creel, and Herbert Hoover. When the situation in Minnesota reached a stage where speakers' lives were in danger and violence was being done in the name of the law without due process, Creel recognized the injustice and wrote to Wilson in the spring of 1918:

While I deeply resent this terrorism, we cannot afford an open break with the State Authorities. The League has been loyal absolutely and is loyal now, and the Safety Commission is willing to drive it into disloyalty in order to further its own political end.[21]

The type of terrorism to which Creel referred in Minnesota was not unknown in North Dakota. Lemke's brother wrote from Devils Lake that a pro-Nonpartisan League attorney of that city, because of his alleged pro-German sympathies, had been waylaid and assaulted in a manner that could have been fatal. Here as in Minnesota the persecution was on the local level, and the national administration had no part in it. Before the Associated Press admitted its error and under a persistent grilling by the Minnesota Public Safety Commission, Townley was reported to have admitted that La Follette's talk was seditious. Townley later maintained that what he had said under cross examination was misquoted; Lemke, it is true, never experienced a similar inquisition. However, simultaneously with Townley's reported desertion of La Follette, a League newspaper also disowned the senator. Lemke at no time wavered in his support of La Follette.[22]

By 1918 the League was active in thirteen states and a threat to those accustomed to govern.* Those thus threatened left no stone unturned to prevent the spread of the League. They were entrenched in the regional branches of the federal agencies such as the Federal Land Bank, which had been formed in 1916, and the emergency seed loan administration. The Land Bank used a technicality to withhold credit from North Dakota farmers, and Thorstein Veblen reported that the seed loan people regarded "the fortunes of war and the chances of famine . . . a secondary consideration." He included the regional representatives of the Department of Agriculture, the Department of Labor, and the Railway Administration in his indictment of those who were attacking the Nonpartisan League. Another writer observed: "Spearheading the campaign was the Public Safety Commission. . . . Topheavy with zealous Republicans, it encouraged summary action by local authorities to crush the League."[23]

Wood's confidence in Lemke and Townley's absorption in organizing activities enabled Lemke's decisions to prevail at League national headquarters with a minimum of friction. At the same time, while busy in the St. Paul office, Lemke was able by means of repeated trips and continual correspondence to keep control of the Fargo headquarters, and he was in constant touch with Frazier. There were two major problems ahead. The industrial program had to be enacted

---

* Colorado, Idaho, Iowa, Kansas, Minnesota, Montana, Nebraska, North Dakota, Oklahoma, South Dakota, Texas, Washington, and Wisconsin.

into law in North Dakota, and the Nonpartisan League needed to capture Minnesota. In North Dakota alone there were so many activities in which Lemke had his hand that even without the Minnesota campaign, there would have been many things to which Lemke could not attend. As legal adviser he was in close touch with the organization of every League newspaper, and one copy of the articles of incorporation and by-laws of each publishing corporation was filed with him. He signed accommodation notes to help start a League daily newspaper in Grand Forks. During 1918 it was part of his work to draft the initiated measures that were to enact the substance of House Bill 44. Others affiliated with the League were using their League position to wring credit from banks friendly to the League, particularly the Scandinavian-American Bank of Fargo. The League Exchange, the newspapers, the Service Bureau, and the consumers' stores constituted such a variety of enterprises that only the closest of supervision could have coordinated them and inspected them closely enough to prevent abuses from occurring. Lemke, the man who should have accomplished the necessary coordination and supervision, spent so much of his time in Minnesota during 1918 that he was unable to prevent these difficulties.

Lemke's time was taken up not only with the Minnesota election campaigns, but also with the time-consuming efforts to defend Townley and other League leaders against the charges of sedition. In the trial of Walter Thomas Mills, Lemke and the other defense attorneys were ingenious in their defense, demolishing the case of the prosecution. They were not so successful in defending Townley. Lemke's own description of the Mills case clearly depicts both the tactics of Nonpartisan League opponents and Lemke's resourcefulness as a defense attorney.

In regard to the Mills' case will say that he was arrested and indicted in Cass County, North Dakota, on a frame up and was tried, and four citizens of Fargo, who testified against him, so palpably committed perjury that Judge Amidon, at the close of the trial, directed a verdict of acquittal. These four parties all claimed that they had taken down a hundred words of Mills' speech, which were very different from the speech taken down by a court reporter. They insisted they were sure that they were correct and that they had not consulted together, and that they were competent to take a passage of a hundred words from a public address. We broke down this testimony by asking them to stand up and take down a hundred words read to them from the Scriptures, and not one of them got eight or ten words correct, although the passage was read to them three times.[24]

The judge refused Townley the right to introduce a letter from President Wilson lauding Townley for the great work he was doing in getting the farmers to produce. Townley was tried in Minnesota state courts rather than before Judge Amidon and he received a sentence of ninety days. The United States Supreme Court refused a writ of certiorari, and Townley was compelled to serve his sentence.[25]

The League was in control of North Dakota, however, and, contrary to the Minnesota situation, there was no Public Safety Commission with which the League had to contend. The freedom to call on Governor Frazier and the right to use the power of the state eased Lemke's task in that state. When the Federal Land Bank and other Twin City quasi-governmental agencies proved difficult, the League solved the situation in January, 1918, by calling a special session of the legislature. There were few difficulties in 1918 in winning in either the primary or the general elections in North Dakota, and the League experienced only one defeat. Neil C. Macdonald was not re-elected as state superintendent of public instruction, a reverse partly attributable to the "patriotism and morality" amendment to the state constitution offered in the 1917 legislature by A. G. Divet. Macdonald was aggressively promoting a fine program of rural education. In doing so he offended many citizens. His imperiousness of manner made it easier for an equally aggressive opponent to mobilize votes against him; the fact that his opponent was a woman made it possible to appeal to the women, who were at this time able to vote in elections involving school affairs. The fact that more town women than farm women voted helped bring defeat to Macdonald.

The triumph of the initiated laws in the November election meant that the North Dakota legislature was authorized to enact legislation establishing and inaugurating the industrial program of the Nonpartisan League.[26] This legislation had been drafted at League headquarters. Townley, Walter Thomas Mills, V. A. Day, W. G. Roylance, and Lemke are all credited with sharing jointly in their authorship. It is safe to assume that Townley did no desk work on the measures, and it seems unlikely that Mills did. Day was later an assistant of Lemke's in the attorney general's office; it would seem probable that at this time he worked under Lemke's direction. The only individual who could have been an author on an equal basis with Lemke was Roylance. The fact that all correspondence to or from Lemke, or between third parties, mentions Lemke as the author of the measures seems conclusive evidence that his was the directing hand. Max Eastman was in Bismarck for a few days during the legislative session, and Lemke told one Leaguer that Eastman also assisted in writing the laws.* The strategy of the League was to make the program work in North Dakota in order to convince the voters of other states that propaganda of League opponents was false. From this time forward, until the recall of the League Industrial Commission, Lemke's life was bound up in the establishment and defense of the North Dakota League industrial enterprises, which were the heart and soul of the League program.

Lemke was experiencing the most rewarding moment of his public life. Later, as the fortunes of the League began to ebb, his influence within the North Dakota organization was more direct and obvious, but after 1919 his was a defensive battle. In 1918 the League was on the march, and there was an air of confidence in its future that would never again exist. The first major blow fell in the Minnesota primary elections. Lindbergh and Lemke were friends of long standing, and Lemke fought hard to elect Lindbergh, but without success. This defeat was the first major reverse for Townley and the League; so essential was it that Minnesota not be lost that Lemke drew up the by-laws, suggested the name of Farmer-Labor, and filed the petitions for a third party to run against the two major parties in the November general election.†[27] No more successful in the fall election than in the primaries, Lemke returned to North Dakota; the Minnesota phase of his League career was in large part ended.

The defeat of Macdonald had been a serious loss. There were other losses not as clear but equally disastrous to Lemke's future. One of Lemke's fondest hopes was to make Melvin A. Brannon president of the University of North Dakota. Preoccupied with the Minnesota election, Lemke took only belated action to prevent the appointment of Thomas Kane; his hope of placing a liberal at the head of the University of North Dakota was gone. Lemke took an equal interest in combating the anti-Ladd influence of Thomas Cooper, the head of the extension service at the Agricultural College. Claiming that Cooper had interfered with former President John Worst, was then

---

* The *Bismarck Tribune* reported Max Eastman's stop in Bismarck in its February 11, 1919, issue; Herbert Swett informed the author that Lemke had spoken to him of Eastman's assistance.

† This party was kept alive and later it merged with the Democrats to become the Democratic Farmer-Labor party of Minnesota.

interfering with President E. F. Ladd, and was using the county agents under his direction as a conservative political machine, Lemke urged Frazier to take control and remove Cooper and other staff members of the college.[28]

Although he was state chairman of the Republican party, Lemke experienced very little difficulty with President Wilson and the Democratic administration, while receiving little or no cooperation from the Republican national party organization.[29] The warning was there in 1918 of more serious trouble in the future. When the time of the League's need arrived, the national organization of the Republican party was arrayed against it. The Republican party can hardly be blamed for not aiding an organization which showed clear indications of wanting to become a national party in its own right. But Lemke must certainly be held responsible for continuing to believe that he could obtain cooperation from the Republican national organization. It was a fatal error for the League not to give at least the appearance of being uncommitted.

The end of the year 1918 marked a change in Lemke's role. Gradually his part ceased to be solely that of kingmaker and director of affairs inside the Nonpartisan League. As the task of proving the soundness of the League's program came in 1919 to center in North Dakota, Townley was not always there to assume the burden. The vast organizational program of the National Nonpartisan League occupied his attention. While the state legislature was in session, Townley remained in the state; later he would come back from his travels from time to time when his services seemed most needed. The years of speaking and persecution had told on Townley; for a time he did not have as much to give as he had had in earlier years. When he was not in the state to take top billing at League rallies, it was often Lemke's name which was used to draw the crowds, and Lemke whose quips and sallies farmers quoted as they once had Townley's. But Lemke's preoccupation with the North Dakota League did mean that he was becoming less and less a guiding influence at national headquarters.

It was not that Lemke's power and influence over the North Dakota Nonpartisan League increased markedly during this period. These he had had from almost the beginning, at least since the nomination and election of Frazier. Rather, as the League's difficulties mounted and Townley was not there to meet them, Lemke's power became apparent as well as real.[30]

In retrospect it is not difficult to conclude that the Nonpartisan League as a national movement had been seriously injured in 1918 by the Minnesota persecution, but the fact that the tide had turned was, because of the North Dakota victory, not then as apparent. After the 1918 general election was over, Melvin A. Brannon wrote to William Lemke: "As near as I could determine, you had North Dakota well in your control. It is a mighty clever bit of work. I congratulate you on the marked success of your guidance." To Brannon and to Samuel Peterson, Lemke's former instructors, Lemke's attainments and present position of influence were matters of pride. He was some of the clay they had molded.[31]

The passage of the ten initiated measures in the general election of 1918 had seemed to remove the last roadblock to the accomplishment of the League program. This was the encouraging factor which caused Lemke and other League leaders to look upon 1919 not as a year of crisis but rather as the dawn of "A New Day in North Dakota," a title used for Nonpartisan League pamphlets in 1919 and a phrase repeated frequently by Nonpartisan League speakers. That it could have been everything they hoped for does not seem from this vantage point to have been impossible. All was not irretrievably lost. Cool heads, moderation, and restrained statements might yet have saved the League program in North Dakota. However, League leaders, including Lemke, failed to display those qualities during that time of stress.

In the face of the tactics of the opposition, the calmest leaders would have found moderation difficult. League opponents took advantage of the 1919 "Red scare" to distort and enlarge upon the background and activities of League leaders. They were so successful in this tactic that such organizations as church groups and the Women's Christian Temperance Union came to identify League leaders with the forces of intemperance and immorality. Yet one of the notable characteristics of leaders such as Lemke, Lynn J. Frazier, A. C. Townley, and William Langer was that they were temperate and not easily assailable on the matter of personal morals. Not one of the four drank or smoked. Frazier was so strict a Methodist that he eliminated the time-honored practice of having an inaugural ball when he took office as governor of North Dakota in 1917. As officials, they were all unusually strenuous in enforcing the laws against saloons and gambling establishments. In view of these facts it is easy to understand the bitterness of men such as Lemke when they found numbered among their opponents not only the law violators but also the organizations which advocated strict law enforcement.[32]

Another factor working against moderation was the mood and inclination of those with whom Lemke was associated. The League had gathered about it and had employed in one capacity or another liberals and some radicals from all over the nation—men who had seldom known the sobering responsibility of power and who, for the first time, were presented with the opportunity of putting their ideas into action. There were several who became well known in the state, such as Charles Edward Russell, Herbert E. Gaston, D. C. Coates, Joseph Gilbert, and Walter Thomas Mills. In addition there were many who were not as well known, such as Covington Hall, an itinerant poet and journalist from Louisiana who, more than any of the others, became a close personal friend of Lemke. Another group of doctrinaire reformers had been recruited by Townley from the ranks of the North Dakota Socialist party. A. E. Bowen, Henry G. Teigan, H. R. Martinson, Arthur Le Sueur, O. R. Thomason, D. C. Dorman, Leon Durocher, and L. L. Griffith were among those who either accompanied or followed Townley in his move from the Socialist party to the Nonpartisan League he was organizing.[33] These are some of the better known names; there were many others. It was the presence of some of these individuals which lent substance to the charges of Socialism directed at the League by its opponents, but actually they comprised only a small minority of the official hierarchy and were more closely identified with organization than with policy. From the Socialist point of view, the Nonpartisan League was too conservative.

Collectively in League circles those of this group who were not prominent were among those spoken of as "the crowd" or sometimes certain groups were identified as "the Lemke crowd" or "the Townley crowd." Many Leaguers admired Lemke because of his combative extremism and his forceful presentations, and their approval may have accentuated these characteristics in him. Whether Lemke was influenced by them or not, the very characteristics they admired were those which were his greatest weaknesses in his fight to save the League. Too, they effectively insulated Lemke from other more moderate groups within the League. As new Leaguers rose from the ranks and came to Bismarck, this inner circle attempted to convert each one to its point of view. Those whom they were unable to convince often found the channels of communication to the top echelon of the League closed to them and they themselves discredited. This situation at Bismarck and at League headquarters, in addition to the fact that it was usually the confirmed Leaguer that county organizations sent as delegate, insulated Lemke from the wavering members, that crucial middle-of-the-road group which held the balance of power. Earlier in the League's history, Lemke's own success in picking his university associates and other friends for key positions would have been jeopardized by antagonizing this inner circle.

Lemke's place in the League had not as yet been challenged. Recognizing his strategic position inside the League and the influence he had with Townley and Frazier, Lemke's subordinates were content to add to Lemke's power so long as his objections to their projects and ideas did not become insurmountable. Although Lemke later held that he had opposed projects such as the consumers' stores and the Service Bureau, there is no evidence in the Lemke correspondence at the time those enterprises were initiated to indicate that he conducted a fight against them. If he expressed disapproval, it was not so strongly stated as to injure him in the internal politics of the organization or to prevent him from taking an active part in these organizations once they were established.

While the League organization treated Lemke deferentially, it was not so gentle with many of the state officials whom the League had nominated and elected. These men were regarded as men who had been made by the League and who could be broken. How irritating this was to men such as Langer, Carl Kositzky, and Thomas Hall is revealed by a bitter two-page letter from Hall which denounced the "bunch of schemers who take every known leader who comes to town and wine and dine him so that he cannot get a true picture of the situation." He went on to say that he was a sincere believer in the League but that the Frazier administration was in a bad way even though Frazier was a "sincere fine man."[34] This inner circle whom Hall denounced did not know the meaning of moderation. To them anyone who doubted was a "trimmer" and a representative of "big business."

Humiliating as it must have been to Kositzky and Hall to hold positions of supposed power and to be treated as secondary to those such as Lemke and others who held no state office, it must have been even more galling for Langer. This cavalier treatment as well as his ambition and the bitterness he already felt toward Lemke over the Mexican investment meant that he would submit only as long as he was dependent on the League for political success. In anticipation of needing support from League legislators who could defy League leaders, Langer had carefully selected F. W. Mees and some of the other legislators from his home county of Morton.[35]

As League opposition became stronger, its leaders were constantly probing for spots of defection within the League. It was not successful in 1918 and might not have been in 1919 had the League leadership not gone beyond the League's original program. It was the abuses in these additions to their platform that caused Langer as attorney general to expose some of the practices indulged in by fringe Leaguers. Prior to this time, the consumers' stores and League newspapers had been organized with financing operations which left little margin for mistakes in management, and which were certain in many instances to result in loss. Banking operations had been undertaken in order to have financial institutions which would handle the postdated checks and other credit needs of the League and League enterprises. Individuals such as J. J. Hastings and T. Allan Box charged commissions when reorganizing banks, commissions which were not justified and which would not bear publicity. Many of the League banks had made larger loans than permitted by law to organizations affiliated with the League or controlled by Leaguers. Many of these loans were inadequately secured. Langer, Kositzky, and Hall became aware of the situation, and in February, 1919, Langer acted to expose the operations of Hastings and Box, forcing them to repay the money they had improperly reserved for themselves.[36] Hastings was dropped from all League associations, and the incident alerted League leaders to investigate further. They found their house was not in order and eventually severed all relationships with J. W. Brinton, who had been in charge of organizing League newspapers, and J. R. Waters, who was at first in charge of the Bank of North Dakota and later an officer of the United States Sisal Trust, a promotional development in Florida which was to raise the raw material for twine. Loans to this company, with which Townley had had some association, from the League-controlled Scandinavian-American Bank later constituted some of the major charges against League leaders. Although Brinton and Waters were not separated from the League organization until 1920, the scandals which were exposed in 1919 led to their removal.

League leaders did not feel critical of Langer's action in stopping the operations of Hastings and Box, but they did disapprove of the publicity which attended his action. The publicity was the important consequence. It pointed up weaknesses in the League and gave League opponents an indication as to whom they might find within the League who would be willing to bolt. The favorable comment in the opposition newspapers revealed to Langer the opportunity he had of becoming the candidate of the League opponents. This was the second time that Langer had exhibited independence. In the previous December, Frazier had supported Macdonald in a refusal to turn over the Department of Public Instruction because Minnie J. Nielson, it was alleged, lacked the qualifications to hold the office of superintendent. Langer defied Frazier and used the power of his office on behalf of Miss Nielson. The Supreme Court sustained Langer, and Miss Nielson was seated as superintendent of public instruction.[37] In retrospect it seems clear that Langer was ready to leave the League whenever mistakes or the extremism of its leadership made the organization vulnerable.

Townley and Arthur Le Sueur were the two other leading Leaguers consulting on the legislative program which was to begin the League industrial enterprises in North Dakota. One of the major points at issue was whether the Industrial Commission, which would run the state mill and elevator, state-owned bank or banks, a home building association, and other enterprises would be composed of an ex-officio commission consisting of the governor, attorney general, and commissioner of agriculture and labor, or whether it would be an independent board serving for staggered terms. The accepted version was that Townley favored an ex-officio board while Le Sueur favored an administrative agency. The dispute was settled by referring it to John Hagan, commissioner of agriculture and labor. Hagan decided for Townley's point of view, and Le Sueur resigned.[38]

Lemke's silence is significant. Had he been opposed, it can safely be assumed that his opposition would be a matter of record. Throughout his life he was consistent in maintaining that he had drafted the law, and there is no record of his disapproval of any portion of it after it was enacted. He was probably on Townley's side in this dispute, and it is probably more accurate to say that Townley was defending the point of view which Lemke had convinced him was the wisest. Referring the decision to Hagan was a stratagem worthy of either Townley or Lemke, it being reasonable to conclude that they would not hazard a decision on a matter about which they felt so strongly to a juror whose inclination they were unable to foretell. For Le Sueur the future was to be a vindication. The recall of the Industrial Commission in 1921 would wreck the League and would curtail further expansion of its program. Neither Lemke nor Townley could have suspected as late as February, 1919, that Langer was about to bolt. Most certainly if they had, they would not have made the attorney general one of the officials who served on the Industrial Commission.

The type of board which the League had chosen to run its state enterprises was only one mistake of the 1919 legislature for which Lemke must bear a heavy responsibility. Two newspaper bills were passed. One provided for an official newspaper in each county. The argument for this measure was plausible. Its supporters maintained that having one official paper would do away with the practice of printing legal notices in obscure papers to prevent their being noticed or read. The other bill provided that until the next election the official papers would be those selected by a state commission which was in turn to be appointed by the governor. This last measure meant that in every county it would be the League newspaper which would receive the income from official printing. Many of the League newspapers were newly organized, and passage of the bill meant that many non-League papers would have insufficient income to continue operation. Brinton, who managed the League bureau which serviced and controlled the League newspapers, was the Leaguer most persistent in urging passage of the newspaper bills. Arguing that otherwise many of the League papers would fail, he was able to persuade the leadership to support the measures. Once the League was committed to their support, Lemke used his influence to put the newspaper bills through the legislature. It was not easy to persuade some of the legislators to vote for the bills, and one observer described the vigorous activities of Townley, Lemke and Brinton in "hopping around back of the railing" as they lobbied to make certain that all League legislators were present when the roll was called.*39

* Lemke later stated that he had opposed these bills in the inner councils of the League and thus attempted to absolve himself of responsibility, and he later wrote bitterly: "I am not responsible for the work of crooks like Brinton and others who started the Service Bureau and got people into financial trouble in connection with it. I objected to the Service Bureau and to the Newspaper bill both during the Session of the Legislature and before" (William Lemke to Mrs. D. Larin, November 20, 1921, Lemke Papers). Allowing for his errors of memory, his statement can still be accepted at face value without adding to his stature. His position within the League caucus and his relationship with Townley and Frazier was such that he could have stopped the newspaper bills had he

By this time Lemke had gained a distinction as being unique among political leaders and lobbyists. Instead of spending his time in hotel lobbies and in convivially passing leisure time in hotel rooms and elsewhere, Lemke had established a routine that had become legendary. When not eating, sleeping, or appearing at such places as League caucuses or legislative corridors, he was in his own room or in some office working. When called before the caucus or a committee, he usually emerged directly from work and returned there when his part in the discussion had ended. He seemed to require little food and could work long days, often eating only one meal daily. In the small hours of the morning, he would be seen with the majority leader of each House and other key figures at a local restaurant. Unlike the others, Lemke would not order coffee but would eat cold cereal with "half and half"—half milk and half cream—while the legislative tactics for the next day were planned. From the session of 1917 until 1925, when the moderate Leaguers would take the control of the League machinery from Lemke's hands, this was to be his role—the undisputed architect of League legislative policy. The newspapers reflected the prevailing estimate of Lemke's influence. The *Bismarck Tribune* commented that the public utility tax bill had been "written by Roylance at the suggestion of Bishop Lemke," and referred to him as "William Lemke, Chairman of the Republican state central committee and the power behind the throne in the recent legislative session."[40]

The newspaper bills had been a serious error. A change that was made in the state's system of regulating its colleges and other institutions proved to be equally damaging to the League. There had been three boards: the state Board of Regents, which had been established in 1915; a state Board of Education; and a state Board of Control. The superintendent of public instruction served on the Board of Education, as did three members of his staff in ex-officio capacity. A new board resembling the old Board of Control, except that two of its members were ex-officio, was created, which absorbed the functions of the other three boards and which was empowered to employ executive officers who would assume many of the prerogatives

---

drawn the issue clearly and used all of his influence against them. The newspaper bills were an error which created bitter enemies and lost the League votes. Lemke did not make the fight against the bills that should have been made; there was no one other than he—besides Townley and Frazier—who could have halted Brinton's project. With power went a responsibility which Lemke failed to discharge.

formerly exercised by the superintendent of public instruction. The occupant of that office was an ex-officio member of the new board, but the governor was empowered to appoint three of the members; and a staunch Leaguer in the office of the commissioner of agriculture and labor was the remaining member. This meant that Minnie J. Nielson as state superintendent had lost much of the authority that had been heretofore associated with the office she held and that the new board, which was called the Board of Administration, could appoint Neil C. Macdonald to a position where he could exercise that authority. The measure was violently opposed by anti-Leaguers, who charged that it was being passed to nullify the incumbent anti-Leaguer's authority over the institutions of higher learning.[41] The charges would have had less effect had it not been for the introduction of the newspaper bills and the effort that Frazier, Townley, and Lemke had made at the beginning of the year to prevent Miss Nielson from taking office. As in the case of the newspaper bills and the insistence upon an ex-officio Industrial Commission, this measure became a potent weapon in the hands of the opposition and caused certain League members of the legislature to become restive during the sessions of the League caucus. There is no evidence at any point that Lemke tried to stop this bill, and his part in the effort to prevent Miss Nielson from assuming office indicated that he probably helped design the measure. It was another political mistake for which Lemke bore a major share of the responsibility. The law was not only a political error but, as its opponents charged and as events of the late 1930's confirmed, it had a substantive fault in exposing the state colleges to the hazards of gubernatorial tyranny.*

League leaders such as Lemke and Townley were out of touch with public sentiment or they would not have continued to urge measures which were not essential to the League program and which lost them important segments of votes. Within their own caucus, F. W. Mees, the man whom Langer had placed there, should have made them more careful. As Langer evidently had planned, Mees did not show the spirit of compromise necessary when outnumbered and outargued. Exasperated by the man's stubbornness, Townley silenced him with sarcasm and ridicule. Townley's verbal victory, won in a burst of temper, had its price. Mees and Langer held a conference,

* In 1938 the colleges were removed from the jurisdiction of the Board of Administration and were placed under that of the Board of Higher Education, over which the governor had less control (see Chapter Seven).

and other Morton County legislators learned that Langer was considering leaving the League.[42]

Langer's dissatisfaction with League leadership was carefully concealed. Just two weeks before the end of the legislative session in February, 1919, he attended a League rally and listened to Townley give a complimentary talk regarding Lemke's services. The *Bismarck Tribune* reported it as follows:

> Townley declared at a League rally that there had been in the service of the League for the last two years or two years and a half a native son of North Dakota who . . . possessed the qualities of Lincoln. He then went on to describe this farmer boy, born in poverty, born to years of struggle in his early youth but imbued with an ambition which carried him throgh [*sic*], which impelled him to seek more learning in letters and laws in the great universities of our country, and which brought him back, after his spurs were won, to see what could be done for his home state. Townley told how this man had served the League and the state for the paltry sum of $250. per month; how he had toiled fourteen and sixteen hours a day, and how he during the present session had been a center about which all the work of the legislature revolved. . . . Lemke was not in the hall. A delegation was dispatched to his room for him. Lemke was reluctant even after he reached the door of the big hall, and Langer then proved himself a good sportsman as well as a good athlete by literally picking up the lighter Bill and carrying him to the front of the room and dumping him on the stage. Then Lemke became oral, opening up with a story and finishing with an exhortation.[43]

Lemke had retired for the night and had been roused from bed to receive the ovation. The applause for him was equal to that given Frazier and surpassed only by that for Townley, and none of the other League incumbents received comparable ovations. The newspaper account mentioned how difficult the incident must have been for Langer and referred to his sportsmanship in carrying Lemke to the platform. However, the most significant thing about this episode is that within only a few weeks of Langer's withdrawal from the League, all appeared to be harmonious at a large League gathering.

Whether by pure accident or not, Langer was found in conference with Theodore G. Nelson, a leader of the League opposition. This was before Langer was ready to announce his defection. From that time on there was little misunderstanding of the true situation. For Langer there was no longer any virtue in waiting to state his position;[44] it was during this spring and summer that he and Thomas Hall and Carl Kositzky made their position clear. This was a serious blow to the League as three major offices—secretary of state, state auditor, and attorney general—had been lost to the opposition. They had not acted in collusion; Langer on one occasion had tried to put Hall in jail, and the two men were not on friendly terms. Hall later recalled that Langer's activities constituted a major reason for his own withdrawing from the League and that he had no idea Langer was going to bolt at the time he, Hall, had made up his mind to do so.

This was not the only indication of declining League strength. League opponents in the 1919 legislative session introduced bills which were difficult to oppose. One such measure was an "anti-Red Flag" law which forbade the carrying of a red or black flag in a parade, or any flag other than that of the United States or those of its allies. League leaders should have avoided opposing this measure, which, if passed, would probably have been declared unconstitutional when carried to the courts. The current hysteria was such that League opposition to the bill enabled opponents to convince many voters that the League was infiltrated with Bolsheviks. League leaders left themselves vulnerable to the same charge by opposing a bill to outlaw criminal syndicalism. The tactics of the opposition were changing. Gradually they were forging the weapons with which they would successfully hurl charges that the Nonpartisan League was nearly everything, ranging from the one extreme of anarchism to the other of communism. These charges took the place of the pro-German issue, which, now that the war was over, was no longer effective. Heretofore, the focal point of their attack had been Townley. As Townley's activity became less apparent, it began to point increasingly at Lemke. The wave of criticism directed at Lemke began in 1919 and became increasingly intense, reaching a peak during February, 1921, from which it did not recede until after the conclusion of the recall campaign.

The Independent Voters Association was the name taken by League opponents, and they become known as Independents or the IVA faction. Their newspaper, *The Independent,* was edited by the former Equity leader Theodore G. Nelson and Matt Johnson. At their first meeting in Grand Forks in 1917, they designated themselves the Lincoln Republican Club; the name was changed when they met in Minot in 1918 to avoid offending Democrats and to make it easy for League opponents to ignore party labels. A small group led by Olger B. Burtness and J. F. T. O'Connor in the lower house of the 1919 legislature were able to take advantage of being ignored in committee assignments, another instance of League leaders overreaching themselves. By immoderate use of their majority power, they made themselves appear to be tyrannical and gave the Independents the opportunity of appearing to be unjustly treated. Burtness and O'Connor were able antagonists and made the most of their psychological advantage.* By the end of the session, Burtness and O'Connor had won enough recruits among wavering Leaguers to prevent the League from applying the emergency clause to League legislation.[45]

Having prevented League laws from taking immediate effect, the Independents in March and April, 1919, circulated referendum petitions to refer the laws establishing the Industrial Commission, the state-owned bank, and the state newspaper commission. Other laws regarding the tax commissioner, the commissioner of immigration, and judicial districts were also referred, but they did not concern the heart of the League program. At the same time, the Independents attempted to initiate four measures, requesting that the vote on the referred measures be delayed long enough to make it legally possible to have the initiated measures voted upon at the same election as the referred measures. Lemke and Frazier agreed that having both the initiated and referred measures on the same ballot would force voters to decide which measures to vote for and which ones to vote against. By law ninety days had to elapse between the filing of initiated petitions and an election. The governor called the election on the referred measures for a date that came before this ninety-day period had passed. *The Independent* asserted: "No European monarch ever arrogated to himself more power than did Governor Frazier when he decreed what measures should be voted on at the . . . election. . . . He is as unfair as his ability permits him to be."[46]

In his book on the Nonpartisan League, Charles E. Russell stated: "The campaign preceding this referendum is likely to be remembered as the most strenuous in the history of the state." League leaders fought for those issues most vital to their program. National economic interests were now alerted to the League's program, and the Independents did not lack money or speakers to cover the state. The League countered with all of its resources, cutting short organizing activities elsewhere to save its program in the state where it had originated. The election on June 26 ended in a complete League victory, but with majorities not quite as great as those on the ten initiated measures of the previous November.[47] Errors in leadership,

* Myron W. Thatcher commented that "the one great weakness of the League was the manner in which the leaders threw themselves around and had top men calling the shots just a little bit too roughly. They herded the legislators up every night in the hotel here to brief them for the next day—and the people didn't like it" (Goldberg, p. 57).

delay, and the effect of constant opposition were beginning to diminish League strength.

League leadership had not waited for the election to take the initial steps necessary for establishment of the Bank of North Dakota, a state mill and elevator, and the Home Building Association, all of which were to be financed by the sale of approximately seventeen million dollars' worth of North Dakota bonds.[48] The confidence of League leaders—confidence that at times bordered on arrogance— during the 1919 legislative session had been predicated on the known fact that they had the votes necessary to authorize the bond issues. As soon as the industrial program became a fact, they reasoned, a grateful farmer electorate would maintain the League in power for the immediate future. The Independents reasoned similarly and, knowing that a successful industrial program would entrench the League and keep the Independents permanently out of control, they had no intention of permitting the industrial program to begin. They had two weapons at hand. They could attack the legality of the bond issues in the courts, and they could use their Eastern contacts to stop the sale of the bonds.

Perhaps it might be more accurate to say that the financial and marketing interests of the Twin Cities had their contacts in North Dakota to begin and guide opposition to the League. The status revolution in North Dakota that had accompanied the League's growth had left a large group of business and professional people without the influence on government to which they had been accustomed. This group was most anxious to defeat the League.* They were the natural allies of the marketing and financial interests of the Twin Cities, who had been exacting a heavy tribute from North Dakota farmers and who now found a strong government interfering with

* Anyone whose memory does not extend to that period in North Dakota history cannot fully comprehend the bitterness felt by business and professional groups toward those who had assumed the position of influence which had formerly belonged to them. Mrs. Gutzon Borglum depicts it graphically: "It was the first time in a controversy I had been associated with the side opposed by the socially elect and I was amazed at the epithets hurled at the Non Partisan Leaguers by otherwise respectable truthful members of society. Most frequently they were accused of advocating "free love" which considering the character of the candidates was ridiculous. . . . One story was of a meeting at which Mr. Lemke was scheduled to speak and at the last minute he asked Gutzon to go in his stead. Wholly unsuspecting Gutzon went and was deposited by the train in the midst of a mob who had come determined to do Bill physical injury. Luckily Gutzon can think quickly on his feet; he was able to capture the interest of the crowd" (undated memoir of Mrs. Gutzon Borglum, Borglum Papers).

their rich source of revenue. These League opponents within the state needed only to pass the word to those corporation attorneys representing Twin City interests who resided in the state, and no trips to the East by Independents were needed to initiate a nation-wide boycott of the bond sale.[49]

After Langer had defected, Lemke became the legal defender on whom the League relied to protect the legality of the industrial program in the courts. A suit was brought in the state courts alleging the illegality of the League program and was decided in favor of the League. An action was brought by Forty-two Taxpayers in Federal District Court, only to receive such a complete rebuke from Judge Charles F. Amidon that League members regarded the legal battle as ended. These victories had been won in May and April, 1919, making it possible throughout the summer to organize the Industrial Commission and to make the preliminary arrangements to begin the industrial program as soon as the sale of bonds was completed. No trouble on that score was anticipated by Leaguers now that the courts had held the bonds legal. On September 26, 1919, the sale of the first $2,000,000 worth of the bonds was announced. It was then that *The Independent* predicted that the sale would not be consummated, and by doing so revealed its own knowledge of the impending boycott.[50] Despite the resounding rebuke received in Federal District Court, the Forty-two Taxpayers (or possibly the corporations whose attorneys were representing these taxpayers) were, to the surprise of Leaguers, appealing to the United States Supreme Court. The prediction that the sale of the bonds would not be made proved correct. The underwriting company withdrew from the arrangement, and so effective was the boycott that it was to be two years before a sale of comparable proportions was made.

During the first eight months of this two-year period, financial centers could plead that the Forty-two Taxpayers' case created a doubt regarding the legality of the bonds. After May, 1920, when the United States Supreme Court unanimously upheld the legality of the bonds, there was no legal defense of the refusal to purchase the bonds. The financial interests used their control over the liquid sources of wealth for political purposes. The effect on Lemke was life-long. Naturally suspicious because of his heritage of "agrarian demonology," this confirmed him in everything he had ever read or heard about the money trust.

Other events had occurred during the summer months of 1919. Speaking squads sponsored by the Independents, who had enough money to make year-round campaigning possible, were traveling through the state. Hall, Kositzky, and Langer were doing everything within their power to weaken the League, and the speeches of Langer were particularly effective. Crisscrossing the state, giving dynamic lectures on the iniquities of League leaders with great emphasis on their financial peculations, Langer was most convincing not only to Independents but also to many Leaguers who began to doubt the integrity of their leaders. Here was the man who had been selected by Lemke to be the candidate for attorney general now denouncing the League leadership and asking to be sued for slander if he erred in his statements.*[51] To Lemke, a man of strong feelings, this was the most despicable thing that had ever happened to him.

While the opposition was utilizing every weapon that came to hand,† the League leaders, unaware of the future bond boycott, were proceeding with plans to begin the industrial program. When the appeal by the Forty-two Taxpayers to the United States Supreme Court interrupted their plans, League leaders were faced with the discouraging knowledge that, in the normal process of litigation, it would be two years before the Supreme Court would act upon the constitutionality of League legislation. Lemke advised Frazier to call a special session of the legislature to memorialize the Supreme Court to set the case forward on the calendar for immediate consideration. The Supreme Court acted favorably on this request and set the hearing on the case for the spring of 1920.

Although successful in petitioning the United States Supreme Court, the legislative session had other disastrous results for League leaders. League leaders sponsored laws that helped lend conviction to the charges of tyranny leveled at them by the Independents. These laws

* Langer's book *The Nonpartisan League: Its Birth, Activities and Leaders* (Mandan, North Dakota: Morton County Farmers Press, 1920) portrays the type of attack he made on the leaders of the League. Later when Langer returned to the League and captured control of it, this book was quoted to impair his political position. Copies of it mysteriously disappeared from libraries throughout the nation; even the Library of Congress had to borrow a copy from Senator Nye's secretary to have it microfilmed (interview with Margaret Rose, July 1, 1957).

† The author remembers as a small boy hearing one of these speakers devote most of his speech to the theme that one of the three varieties of Socialists believed in taking children from their mothers at the age of three weeks and having the state rear them. The implication of this speaker, sponsored by the Independents, was clear, i.e., a vote for the League might lead to this eventual result.

included some which were not part of the original League program,
such as one providing for a state sheriff, another making it possible
for farm women to vote by absentee ballot, an Anti-Liars law—a
sedition law which was designed to make League critics more cautious
about the charges they made—and a law creating a legislative committee with powers to investigate any state office. But the most
disastrous event of the special legislative session of 1919 was the dis-
covery by O. B. Burtness of books advocating free love, Socialism,
and sedition in the State Library Commission Building. Caught in
the emotionalism of the period, Burtness professed to believe that
the books he had found had been purchased during the period of
League rule and that they were being circulated to school children
in traveling libraries.* He had found the books by the merest chance
where they were stacked on boxes in which he assumed they were
to be mailed to schools. A five-man investigating committee, consisting
of three Leaguers and two Independents, presented a unanimous
report to the House. The books had never been sent to schools, and
there had been no plan to circulate them generally. The boxes on
which they happened to be stacked were being used as temporary
shelves. The most offensive book, one written by Ellen Key, was a
standard work in most libraries and was the last of a series of five,
four of which had been purchased before the League was in charge
of the state. Nevertheless, the head of the state Library Commission
was forced to resign.[52]

Burtness' accusations made the bond boycott more effective. The
League's attacks on Wall Street and Big Business were enough to
lessen the chances of marketing the North Dakota bonds; the charges

* S. A. Olsness, a Leaguer who was commissioner of insurance from 1917 to
1935, listed Langer's defection and the charges made by Burtness as the most
disastrous events in their effect on League fortunes. No other events, in his opinion, compared to these two in their irreparable impact upon the League and its
leaders. The fact that the head of the state Library Commission was compelled
to resign, even though the League was able to show that many of the books had
been purchased before he had accepted the position, indicates how effective the
charges were (interview with S. A. Olsness, June 8, 1938).

Burtness admitted that he had not fully checked the facts of library circulation
before speaking on the floor of the House, but he had become so concerned
about some of the people associated with the League that he felt his statements,
though later demonstrated to be not completely accurate, helped arouse the public
to a real danger. A fine, public-spirited person, he was obviously less proud than
he had once been regarding the incident, but he was reluctant to admit that he
had not been justified (interview with O. B. Burtness, June, 1938).

associated with the books Burtness had found gave the organization an even more unsavory reputation, for news stories had appeared regularly in New York and other Eastern newspapers about the sensational books. Despite the failure to market the bonds, however, a strategem of Lemke's made it possible to start the League program. A provision of the law establishing the Bank of North Dakota had

The proponents of the Bank of North Dakota, acting with the enthusiasm characteristic of supporters of a new program, were not exactly modest in their claims. It is the only institution of its kind in the nation, although there were some early nineteenth-century attempts in some of the southern and western states to establish similar institutions. See discussion on page 142.

required deposit in that bank of all public funds from the treasuries of school districts, townships, villages, cities, counties, and from that of the state. Lemke's device for opening the bank was to have the Bank of North Dakota issue two cashier's checks which amounted to a total of $2,000,000. The Industrial Commission issued state bonds in that amount and delivered them to the Bank of North Dakota in exchange for the cashier's checks. The checks were then endorsed back by the Industrial Commission to the Bank of North Dakota to become its capital.[53] Obviously the bank would not have been able to begin operations had it not been for the compulsory deposit of public funds. The legislature had created a Mill and Elevator Association, which was able to begin construction because of a loan of $1,000,000 it had obtained from the Bank of North Dakota. The association bought a flour mill at Drake to begin the program of milling while a large mill was being constructed at Grand Forks. The bank also lent $3,000,000 to farmers on real estate loans and redeposited $8,000,000 in banks throughout the state. Sufficient money was advanced to the Home Building Association to enable it to begin construction of homes.

To the consternation of League opponents who had expected the bond boycott to destroy the League program, League enterprises had been launched and were showing evidence of progress. The Independents had been aware that poor wheat crops and adverse economic conditions were crippling League finances and that banks controlled by, or friendly to, the League had extended themselves to the limit of their abilities to help the League. Since 1915 there had not been a good crop. Farmers had borrowed heavily to expand their operations during the war and had not been able to retire their obligations. The banking system had extended credit on the basis of inflated values, and many banks found the constant withdrawals of deposits by their hard-pressed patrons difficult to sustain. Banks which were friendly to the League had lent money to League enterprises with postdated checks as security. A substantial portion of this collateral was proving worthless. Redeposits from the Bank of North Dakota materially helped these institutions. This alleviated a condition on which the Independents had been counting to weaken the League.

As a member of the banking board, of the Industrial Commission, and—until March, 1919—a participant in League councils, Langer was in a position to know where League finances were weak. He knew that the Bank of North Dakota had made large redeposits in the

Scandinavian-American Bank of Fargo, which in turn had made some highly questionable loans to enterprises which had been started by League leaders or associates. As a member of the banking board, he cleverly managed to have the bank examiner, who was a League appointee and would do nothing to embarrass the League, sent out of the state to investigate other matters. While the examiner was gone, Langer in September, 1919, drew a resolution to investigate a small trust company reported to be in difficulty in Fargo. He worded the resolution loosely, empowering the deputy examiners to investigate any other necessary matters while in Fargo. Frazier was on the banking board, but he did not sense the ruse. When the Langer-directed deputies arrived in Fargo, they went directly to the Scandinavian-American Bank and did not visit the trust company which was their ostensible objective. Finding that sums of money in excess of the limits imposed by law had been lent to League enterprises, that the security consisted largely of postdated checks, and that these checks were not in possession of the bank, they declared the bank insolvent.[54]

So pivotal was this bank in the financing of League enterprises that this was nearly a fatal blow. The opposition press gave the story prominent coverage. Immediately Lemke took charge. He called the bank examiner back from Florida and had him apply to the state Supreme Court to be placed in charge of the bank. The Supreme Court granted the request, and re-examination by the examiner and a friendly audit company held that the lines of credit were actually to individual guarantors and that the postdated checks were ample security. Finding no faults serious enough to warrant closing the bank, the examiner successfully petitioned the Supreme Court for permission to reopen the institution. The North Dakota League state committee then called a mass meeting for October 21, 1919, in Fargo, at which time sufficient deposits were to be placed in the bank by members of the League to overcome the withdrawals which would result from the Langer raid. It had been a close call for the entire League financial structure, and only by strenuous and imaginative effort had Lemke saved the day and merited the "congratulations on the great work you did in rescuing the Fargo Bank" which came from the St. Paul office. What it had demanded of Lemke is clear from the next observation in the same communication: "can imagine the strain you have been under for several weeks."[55]

It was at this time that Lemke himself decided to take advantage of the Home Building Association. Under the plan ten or more citizens formed a home buyers' league. Each member was to deposit 20 per cent of the estimated cost of his house and pay the balance over a twenty- or thirty-year period. No farm home was to exceed $10,000 in cost, no town home over $5,000. When Mrs. Lemke protested that perhaps as a League official he should not borrow from the state, his reply was that "this was the way confidence in the League program could be demonstrated and others instructed as to how beneficial the League program could be."[56] He may have been sincere in this belief, but there were practical considerations as well. The Mexican debacle, coming just after he had married, had prevented him from building a home or displaying in this and other ways the business and professional success for which he had hoped. He was still living in a very modest manner, and the constant drain of his cash resources to pay Mexican taxes made it unlikely that he could build a house in the near future, at least not in the style and proportions he desired. He had neither the cash nor the credit, one or the other of which he needed before he could build a home.

A parallel situation in the 1930's was later to be used by officials of the Democratic party who exercised their rights as citizens to borrow through the HOLC and the FHA. Examined in this light, Lemke does not seem to have erred in using the facilities of the Home Building Association. He did err seriously in planning to violate the law by building a home with the borrowed money on which the original estimate of the cost was over $7,000 when the legal limit on the price of city houses built with money borrowed from the state was $5,000. Inflation, changes in plans, and inefficiency in the Home Building Association eventually increased the cost of the house to an amount over $20,000, and Lemke spent most of the rest of his life paying for it.

# CHAPTER IV

# Election and Recall

The winter and spring of 1920 were a time of worry and concern. The defection of William Langer, Thomas Hall, and Carl Kositzky in 1919 had been serious; the attacks of J. W. Brinton and James R. Waters on the Nonpartisan League in 1920, after they had been eliminated in "a long overdue 'house-cleaning,'" were telling blows that the League was in no condition to sustain. Brinton found that he could make money by attacking the League, and the daily papers publicized his charges. The *Grand Forks Herald* employed him to write a series of articles.[1] In the campaigns of 1920 and 1921 he not only continued his attacks but also testified in Bismarck against Lemke. In 1920 the League had to face three elections: the Presidential primary, the state primary, and the general election. The Forty-two Taxpayers' case against the League was to come before the United States Supreme Court in the spring of the same year. Only a man willing to dedicate his entire day to work could have played the many roles that were Lemke's. The defection of Langer had left Frazier with no one to whom he could entrust the legal work of the state; Lemke now had to perform work that had formerly been done by the attorney general's office, and Frazier finally appointed him a special assistant attorney general. Not wanting to depend on Langer to represent the state before the United States Supreme Court in the Forty-two Taxpayers' case, the Industrial Commission employed Lemke and Frederick A. Pike, a brilliant Twin City attorney. The Presidential primary election intervened before the case was called up and occupied much of Lemke's time.

One of Lemke's major objectives in the Presidential primary was the defeat of Gunder Olson for re-election. It was more than a matter of revenge for Olson's defeat of Lemke in the spring of 1916. Much more serious was the fact that for much of the time since that year, the Republican National Committee had treated Olson as though he were both national committeeman and state chairman. Because Olson represented the conservative wing of the North Dakota Republican party, Will Hays, the national Republican chairman, had often by-passed Lemke and dealt with Olson. To defeat Gunder Olson the League nominated Ole Olson of New Rockford, the only League candidate to file successfully, for Thomas Hall, the secretary of state, refused to permit Lemke to file the names of the other League candidates for them. Hall held that each candidate for delegate and elector should file individually. Hiram Johnson, the candidate the League favored, won the Presidential primary, but a blizzard on election day kept many farmers from the polls, enabling Gunder Olson to win re-election.[2] It was a serious defeat, for it made certain that the national Republican organization would cooperate with the Independents rather than with the League.

There were other results of the Presidential primary election which were to be the League's undoing. The League had risen to power on the principle that the will of the people should not be thwarted, and from the beginning it had been committed to the principles of direct government. To make government more responsive to the will of the people was its creed, and to prevent obstruction of that will it was anxious to initiate an amendment legalizing that progressive reform, the recall. This it did in March, 1920. As it turned out, neither side showed great political acumen. Lemke apparently believed that the creation of the Nonpartisan League had ended political instability for the immediate future. The League's success in North Dakota up to 1920 and his own isolation from borderline and wavering members prevented him from realizing how soon the League could meet defeat. No other reason can be advanced for the fostering by the League at this time of a constitutional amendment to legalize the recall. The conservatives were nearly as reluctant to accept the recall as the Leaguers were anxious to give it to them. The Independents were unaware of the extent to which mass media and money would enable them to influence popular government, and they were reluctant to see any measure adopted that would leave the government subject to the fluctuations of the popular mood.

The Independents were beginning to learn, however, that they could influence the voters. In the state primary in June they decided to use the League's weapon of direct legislation against the League program. Taking advantage of their enemies' tactical errors in the special session of 1919, the Independents circulated petitions to refer the three measures the League had passed which were not part of the original League program. Then, to test out the initiative, they filed petitions to initiate the law defeated by the League in the regular session of 1919 which prohibited the display of red or black flags.*

The Independents were having serious troubles of their own in deciding about their gubernatorial candidate. So effective had Langer's talks been that he was advanced as the candidate for governer who had the best chance of defeating Frazier. The fact that he had so recently been with those he was now attacking and that he still professed belief in the League program made many Independents prefer Ragnvold A. Nestos of Minot. Because his supporters contended that he could defeat Frazier and that no other candidate would be able to do so, Langer eventually won the endorsement on the Independent ticket.

Definitely on the defensive, the League delayed until May before endorsing its candidates. Lemke was devoting a major share of his time working with Pike on the United States Supreme Court test of the constitutionality of the League program. The Supreme Court granted only two hours to North Dakota to present its case, and Langer, still the legally elected attorney general of the state, had to be given precedence. Langer's two assistants agreed to divide the time equally with Lemke and Pike, but actually they took an hour and a half, leaving Lemke and Pike twenty-five minutes. Hastily Lemke yielded his time to Pike, who presented the case the two men had prepared. Supporting the Forty-two Taxpayers were some of the ablest corporation counsel in the state. The motive in bringing the case may only have been to delay the League program. If the Forty-two Taxpayers had any hope of a ruling from the court declaring the League laws unconstitutional, they were disappointed, for the court unanimously affirmed the legality of the Nonpartisan League industrial program. The League press exulted and maintained that the court had used the reasoning advanced by Lemke and Pike, that the people are sovereign in deciding what is a public purpose, rather than the more complex arguments advanced by Langer and his staff.[3]

Until now Lemke had been hailed as the center of power inside the League, as a political magician, and as an attorney sympathetic to the

---

* The three measures were the absentee voters' law, the state sheriff law, and the investigation committee law. All were referred by large majorities at election time, and the initiated measure regarding flags was passed by an equally large majority (North Dakota, *Blue Book, 1954*, p. 68).

underdog. Now he was cast in a new role. The League press gave him the credit for the legal victory; quickly he became the tribune of the people and was hailed by them as one of the ablest constitutional lawyers of the country. That the compliment was not entirely out of proportion was indicated by the increased attention paid him by the opposition. It must have been one of the more gratifying moments of Lemke's life as he received congratulations from his old mentor, M. A. Brannon: "You must be some prophet in order to have the Supreme Court of the United States do precisely what you indicated. . . . I send you my cordial congratulations."[4] Lemke was not the prophet that Brannon thought, for at that moment Lemke was certain that the bond boycott had been broken. He had no premonition that it would continue to be effective for another eighteen months. Now that the court case was over, he turned his attention to the League endorsements, for there were several difficult decisions still to be made.

There was no difficulty about the gubernatorial candidacy, for which Frazier was endorsed to oppose Langer, the Independent nominee; but the vacancies created by the defection of Langer, Kositzky, and Hall required study. League leaders were most concerned about the office of attorney general because the successful candidate for that office automatically became an ex-officio member of the all-powerful Industrial Commission, which controlled the League industrial enterprises. Langer's defection had left an administrative vacuum in the top echelon of the League, one that could be only partially filled by appointing Lemke as attorney for the Industrial Commission. The legal work of the state was devolving on Lemke; yet he was drawing his salary from the League rather than from the state treasury. League finances were declining, and the logic of the situation dictated that state work should be paid for from state funds. To arrange this, however, it was necessary to violate A. C. Townley's long-standing rule that no officer of the state or national Nonpartisan League should be a candidate for public office.

That this violation was now possible indicated Townley's waning hold on the organization. Still the spiritual and titular leader, his organizational activities had compelled him to leave day-to-day decisions to others; the many scandals that had descended upon the League reflected in part upon him and lessened the esteem in which he was held by the office bureaucracy. But it was Lemke's own ambition, the need for Lemke's services, and the serious condition of the League treasury that dictated Townley's action. Reluctantly, yet amiably, Townley consented to the move that he was no longer able to prevent.[5]

The most difficult problem for the League was the United States senatorial endorsement. The junior senator, Asle J. Gronna, was up for re-election. In Congress since 1905 and in the Senate since 1911, his affiliation with the Progressive movement as a disciple of Robert La Follette had not been sufficient to establish a working relationship between himself and the Nonpartisan League, a fact that would injure both Gronna and the League. Many liberal leaders looked upon the Nonpartisan League as a rival, and even LaFollette was concerned about merging the League with his own movement.[6] La Follette's concern made Gronna's attitude less surprising.

When League leaders first came to Washington, D.C., it was not as supplicants working for their own ends through Senator Gronna and asking his advice, but as men who knew the answers and wished to communicate directly with the President. Gronna had not been in agreement with Townley in the latter's willingness to agree to ceiling prices for wheat, and he felt that Townley was ready to concede on this point without sufficient assurance that there would be a ceiling on other prices. In Congress for ten years in his own right before the formation of the League, Gronna had his own following. Feeling that his greatest danger was from a conservative candidate, Gronna could not conceive of a Progressive nominated by the League who could defeat him. Here again Lemke might have bridged the gap except that the relationship between the two men had never been close. Gronna did not like Lemke, and Lemke felt that Gronna had betrayed Thomas Marshall by supporting Porter J. McCumber in 1910. The League directed Congressman John M. Baer to offer League endorsement to Gronna. The senator declined, stating that he disapproved of Townley's Socialist leanings. Expectation that the League was soon to fail and the realization that the Independents would endorse someone to oppose any League-supported candidate were undoubtedly factors influencing Gronna's decision.[7]

The Independents withheld endorsement from Gronna at their convention and endorsed no senatorial candidate. Later the Independents gave Gronna a post-convention endorsement.[8] If Gronna had accepted League support, it is reasonable to assume that the Independents would have nominated a candidate in an attempt to defeat him. They may have threatened him or he may have surmised that this was their plan. It seems probable that Gronna did not want the League's opposition, but that he was afraid to pay the price of Independent opposition that would result from League endorsement.

Gronna's refusal left the League in a dilemma. Their strong League candidates were needed in the state to fend off the thrust of the Independents. They solved their problem by endorsing Edwin F. Ladd, president of the Agricultural College. Had Gronna known that the League would endorse Ladd, Gronna might have capitulated and accepted League endorsement.[9] Ladd's research on the milling qualities of wheat and his exposure of the injustices in grain grading practices had in large measure created the indignant demand for a terminal elevator, the thwarting of which had caused the birth of the Nonpartisan League. No man was better known in North Dakota. In no way had Ladd been touched by the scandals swirling around the League. He was an ideal candidate to defeat Gronna and very possibly the only man in the state who could have done so in 1920. The selection of Ladd was a masterful bit of strategy which, by strengthening the League ticket, helped Frazier defeat Langer for the Republican gubernatorial nomination. Although there is no evidence that the selection of Ladd was Lemke's exclusive idea, Ladd's endorsement had the Lemke touch —it was the same type of thing he had done many times before. Lemke was a great admirer of Ladd, and it seems probable that the latter's nomination was the result of Lemke's generalship. There is no question that, at this time in 1920, it was Lemke who was running the North Dakota Nonpartisan League.

In June, 1920, the Independents had a formidable ticket for the state primary election. Besides Langer, whom they had endorsed for governor, they named Thomas Hall for secretary of state and Carl Kositzky for state auditor. They endorsed Asle J. Gronna for the United States Senate and Olger B. Burtness for the House seat held by John M. Baer. Minnie J. Nielson was re-endorsed for superintendent of public instruction. Other Independent candidates who worried the Leaguers were John Steen, who was running for state treasurer, and A. H. White and R. F. Gallagher, who were running against John Hagan and William Lemke for nomination for commissioner of agriculture and labor and attorney general, respectively.

The results of the primary election were not encouraging for the League. In the primary elections of 1916 and 1918, the League had suffered no defeats.* In 1920 Burtness defeated Baer, and both Hall

---

* Nielson had defeated Macdonald in the general election of 1918; Macdonald had had the most votes in the primary election of that year.

and Steen defeated their League opponents for the Republican nominations for secretary of state and state treasurer. As was expected, Nielson received the most votes for nomination as a candidate for state superintendent of public instruction. The contests for the Industrial Commission were close. Hagan received the largest majority, polling 10,949 more votes than White; Frazier's majority over Langer was 5,414, while Lemke ran far behind both Hagan and Frazier, barely winning his nomination with a majority of 2,414 votes. The greatest gain for the League was in Ladd's defeat of Gronna, a result which the League press emphasized in order to conceal the fact that the power of the League had been successfully challenged. There was some question as to whether the League elected Ladd or whether Ladd's name on the League guide cards saved Lemke and possibly Frazier from defeat. Ladd's name not only strengthened every candidate on the same ticket, but it also revived memories of the original issue on which the League had risen to power.

Failure of League leaders to exercise moderation and judgment during legislative sessions, the successful boycott of the bonds, the charges by Burtness, and the strength given to the Independents by Langer, Hall, and Kositzky were factors contributing to the diminution of League strength. Now that the primary was over, both factions prepared for the general election by supporting their successful nominees on the Republican ticket while refusing assistance to the successful candidates of the other faction. The Independents supported Democrats such as J. F. T. O'Connor, candidate for governor, while the League filed a slate of candidates to run against Burtness, Hall, and Steen, Independents who had won the Republican nomination.

Fully as ominous as their defeat of some of the League candidates was the success of the Independents in sponsoring direct legislation. The Independents had nominated only a few candidates, but they had carried their point on every measure they had initiated or referred. They reasoned correctly that what they had done with direct legislation in the primary, they could do again in the fall. They initiated additional measures, two of which were to prove disastrous for the League. One of these measures provided for an audit of the Bank of North Dakota. In 1919 Kositzky as state auditor had demanded the right to make such an audit and had been refused;[10] this gave the Independents an argument for passage of the measure. The other proposal permitted the withdrawal by political subdivisions of the state of their funds from the Bank of North Dakota. If passed, it would have the potential effect of removing the only resource that had financed the League industrial program when funds from bond sales were not forthcoming. If the measure providing for an audit passed, it threatened to expose the manipulations of League leaders in their efforts to solve the financial problems brought on by the mistakes and inefficiency of the administrators and by the financial instability of the period.

The League had one advantage as it faced the fall election. This was a Presidential election year, and all of the candidates it had succeeded in nominating would have the benefit of being in the Republican column, where they would profit from votes attracted by the Republican candidate, Warren G. Harding. League leaders such as Townley and Lemke erred, however, in threatening an economic boycott of businessmen, a tactic which probably hurt the League. Instead of defending themselves or ignoring the attacks made by Brinton and Waters, League newspapers counterattacked and exposed the past records of the two men with whom they had so recently been associated. This tactic, although characteristic of Lemke, was a mistake, for the League could scarcely criticize men who had so recently been leading employees without reflecting discredit upon itself. O'Connor had been associated with the effort to get the grain grading act declared unconstitutional, and the League used this argument in its campaign against him.[11]

While the Republican landslide saved Frazier and the other League candidates in the Republican column from defeat, it was not because Lemke had persuaded the national Republican organization to give the League candidates real support. Will Hays, the national chairman, knew that the League benefited from the Republican name and could reasonably feel that the League was taking unfair advantage of the Republican party. Even if this had not been so, it is probable that Lemke's unreasoning prejudice against Wilson would have prevented effective use of Nonpartisan League bargaining power. Republican leaders, if they were interested, could readily find out that an alliance between the League under Lemke's leadership and a Wilsonian Democratic party would be unlikely.

It was at this time that Gutzon Borglum, the famous sculptor who had dabbled in politics as a Bull Moose Progressive, became an active League campaigner. He was a colorful figure with an interesting background. Coming to Washington during the Theodore Roosevelt administration, he had moved in the circle that had access to the

President. In 1912 he was an active supporter of the Bull Moose movement; at the 1916 Republican convention he tried to bring about the
nomination of Major General Leonard Wood.* Essentially a romantic,
he could be depended on to take the part of those who seemed per-
secuted. In the 1820's he would have been with Byron, Drake, and
Halleck in Greece; during World War I he took the part of peoples
such as the Bohemians. He permitted a large number of the latter
to encamp and train on his estate and claimed to have written the
Declaration of Independence for Masaryk. In 1918 he embraced the
Nonpartisan League movement, coming to North Dakota with his
family to campaign for it. In 1920 he was a liberal without a cause.
Incorrectly he reasoned that by serving as an intermediary between
the League and the Republican party, he could liberalize the latter
and at the same time play a key role himself. He was sincere and
honest in his endeavor and did not intend to dupe League leaders,
as he proved in 1921, when he broke with President Harding because
he felt that the President had used him to deceive Lemke. Unwittingly
he served the Republicans by pacifying Lemke and the League, and
he obtained for the League in return such weak commitments that
Lemke should have recognized them for what they were.

Borglum's misunderstanding of the extent of the conservative
triumph over the Progressives within the power center of the Republican party by 1920 led him to believe that he could perpetuate the
Bull Moose Progressive wing by arranging for League support of the
Republican ticket in the seven states in which the League was most
active. As early as March, he wrote North Dakota Leaguers, and in
May and June he communicated with Will Hays and Warren G.
Harding, who was at that time senator from Ohio. When he was
unable to obtain endorsement of the League through these two men,
he refused to attend the Republican convention, going instead to
North Dakota to campaign for the League in the June primaries. He
again took the initiative in early August by writing to Senator John W.
Weeks and attempted to commit the Republicans not to support H. H.
Perry, the Democratic candidate for senator, against Ladd. Almost
simultaneously he wrote Lemke offering to serve as intermediary between the League and the Republican party. Lemke revealed the
weakness of his position or his own naiveté in accepting Borglum's

* In communications with Theodore Roosevelt, Borglum attributed any success
the support for Hughes would have to Roosevelt's failure to support Wood (Gutzon Borglum to Theodore Roosevelt, June 7, 1916, telegrams—Borglum papers).

offer by return mail without asking Borglum for supporting evidence of his ability to influence Republican policies. It was at this time that Lemke sought to see Will Hays and found him "otherwise engaged," and caused Borglum to comment that "Hays behaved as stupidly and as ungentlemanly as any man could."

Borglum felt that Hays's actions were so impolitic that it was safe to appeal to Harding. He felt that a direct appeal by himself to Wilson had persuaded the latter to recognize Czecho-Slovakia, thus putting an end to political colonialism in Europe, and now he thought he could end economic colonialism in the United States by going directly to Harding on behalf of the Nonpartisan League. Borglum was able to arrange a two-hour conference with Harding by using the plea that Hays's cavalier treatment of Lemke would cause four states to defect to the Democrats. On the basis of Lemke's letter, Borglum acted as the representative of the League and subsequently received from Harding a letter designed to assure Lemke that he was friendly to the principles of the League. Read by anyone not a party to the conference, the letter would have seemed the typical political gesture designed to conciliate without making any real commitments. Thin as Harding's assurance was, Borglum's desire to be successful in his project and Lemke's lack of an alternative made them both willing to be convinced. For a time Hays's office put on a deceptive appearance of cooperation, and there seems to be little doubt that Harding and Hays decided to conciliate Borglum and Lemke until it was too late for the League to rebel.[12] In the meantime Gunder Olson continued to serve in his capacity as intermediary between the Republicans and the Independents, causing Lemke to wire Hays:

Gunder Olson on the fence. Says he will have to get instructions from you. I advise you talk Turkey to him and instruct him imperatively to get busy and cooperate with the regular constituted Republican State Central Committee immediately. He claims he is neutral and will do nothing unless instructed by you. . . . Pretends not to know your attitude towards the regular constituted State Central Committee. He had better learn. . . . Advise prompt action in this matter or seven states will be lost to the party.[13]

By October, when it was too late to carry out the threat made in the wire, Lemke became afraid that he had been badly outmaneuvered. It was not enough, as both Lemke and Borglum found out in due time, to receive conciliatory letters and general assurances. They found out, too, that after the election they would not be able to ignore Will Hays, of whom Borglum had written that he had become "humble

and apologetic and willing to do anything and everything.... After
Tuesday we can forget him completely."[14]

It is a comment on Edwin F. Ladd's political astuteness and the
inadequacy of both Borglum and Lemke in this instance that neither
of the latter saw the situation as clearly as did the senator-elect. Both
before and after the election, it was evident to Ladd that the national
Republican organization was working with League opponents and
against the League.[15] It is possible that Lemke, too, understood the
situation but felt that public knowledge regarding it would harm the
League more than it would the Republicans and, for that reason,
concluded that the League should give an appearance of cooperation.
Whatever the explanation, the League had endorsed the Republican
ticket and would be ignored by the incoming Republican administration.

Earlier in the year Lemke had begun to receive smudged notes
which warned that Alexander McKenzie was back in Bismarck and
that shortly James R. Waters, J. W. Brinton, and L. A. Simpson
would give the League the same kind of trouble as had Langer,
Kositzky, and Hall. Brinton and Waters, who had been separated from
League activities, became most effective in the assistance they gave
the Independents. Brinton was especially aggressive both in this campaign and during the ensuing year. Waters had been in charge of the
Bank of North Dakota until replaced by Fred W. Cathro. Brinton
alleged that the change in management had been due to a promise
Lemke had made to Cathro. Brinton himself had been in charge of
organizing League newspapers.[16] One or the other had been on the
inside in many League deliberations and had witnessed the desperate
efforts of League leaders to save the Scandinavian-American Bank.

In May, 1920, Brinton had written to Governor Frazier and to A. C.
Townley, bitterly attacking Lemke. He blamed the Lemke machine
for the dismissal of Waters and for his own difficulties, and proclaimed
that he had been "forever discredited because of the ambition for
power of one man." He added: "I did not, nor did you, Governor,
enter this fight to make William Lemke the czar of North Dakota and
the state a plaything to satisfy his ambitions for power." Brinton complained to Frazier about the way Lemke, working with Cathro, had
managed to get complete control of the Bank of North Dakota, all of
the League enterprises, and the League newspapers. He pointed out
that under Lemke's directions, the Bank of North Dakota had rede-
posited $400,000 in what he described as the nearly insolvent Scan-

dinavian-American Bank and charged that Lemke controlled the
*Courier-News* and had it print articles favorable to himself and against
Brinton. Brinton was very bitter about the way Lemke ran the conventions. He maintained that the League convention of 1920 had been
under Lemke's complete control and that Lemke had accomplished
the endorsement of Ladd to get him out of the state so that Lemke
himself could control the flour mill and elevator. He further alleged
that Lemke had dictated his own endorsement for attorney general
and that his control of the convention was so complete that no one
unapproved by him could be endorsed. According to Brinton, "Bill
Langer [was] an amateur and Townley, in the most wild dream for
power that ever entered his head, [was] a young man without ambition in comparison."[17]

These charges, made throughout the 1920 campaign and repeated
again and again in the press during 1921, weakened the League and
transferred the blame for wrongdoing from Townley to Lemke. They
were made originally in the letter to Frazier and in a somewhat similar
one to Townley. But in the campaign during the late summer and fall
of 1920, they were exploited to the full by the Independent press.
Brinton and Waters had witnessed the closing and consequent reopening of the Scandinavian-American Bank in October, 1919. Bank
officials trying to save a shaky institution seldom present a pretty picture. Brinton charged that Lemke was in complete control of the bank,
and that he had used the bank as a conduit for state funds to reach
enterprises which were controlled by Townley and Lemke through
dummy corporations. Brinton's reports of the conversations between
Lemke and the other League leaders were not flattering to Lemke,
although Brinton did admit that he did not know whether Lemke's
interest in a loan to the National Nonpartisan League was a personal
one. During the campaign Langer charged Brinton with perjury and
announced that an acquittal for Brinton indicated that Lemke was
guilty of all the accusations. He then dared Lemke to appear in court
to prove that Brinton had falsified. This was in the midst of the
election campaign and Lemke had to weigh the relative disadvantage
of not appearing in court to defend himself against Brinton's charges
and the damage that would be done by exposure of the inadequately
secured loans to League enterprises and the votes that would be
lost by using campaign time to appear in a court case before an un-
friendly judge. In his own mind Lemke knew that what Brinton had
admitted to be true regarding the loan to the National Nonpartisan

League was true of the other loans to League enterprises.[18] They were
not loans for personal ventures of his own such as a loan to the Land
Finance Company would have been, but they were loans to companies
in which he was a director and legal adviser by virtue of his position
in the North Dakota Nonpartisan League.* What had been done had
been necessary to save the League program and was not unlike
maneuvers of many bank officials when trying to protect a struggling
institution.† There was this difference. Lemke was in a position to
channel state money from the Bank of North Dakota into the Scandinavian-American Bank, where it could be used to support shaky
League corporations. Banking at that time was conducted less strictly
than in the period which has followed the bank holiday crisis and
the inauguration of the regulatory practices adopted by the Federal
Deposit Insurance Corporation. Accommodation notes and unsecured
loans to bank officials were not at all uncommon and often went
unquestioned by examiners. It was not these things but the use of
deposits from the Bank of North Dakota that made Lemke's role a
questionable one.

The effect of these charges was to create enough doubt in the minds
of North Dakotans to assist the Independents in their efforts to initiate
laws requiring an audit of the Bank of North Dakota and the withdrawal of funds of political subdivisions from that institution. Lemke

* "I have not permitted myself to take part in any commercial venture since I
have begun working for the League" (William Lemke to W. M. Anderson, October 4, 1920, Lemke Papers). In an interview with H. A. Mackoff on July 7, 1957,
Mr. Mackoff stated that he knew of two specific instances which would substanti-
ate Lemke's statement. Mackoff was a member of the legislature in 1917. At the
beginning of the session he was considered friendly to the League, but he joined
the opposition and fought H.B. 44. He was an Independent and not an associate
of Lemke.

† ". . . I have to meet my payment at the Scandinavian American Bank for
money I borrowed for the Courier News, out of which those who handled the sale
of the Courier News are trying to jip me. I had intended to take this matter up
with you and Wood, and ascertain just why, or by whom this attempt is being
made. Surely after I worked for the League for over seven years, and while I
was supposed to be getting $3,000.00 a year, never got over $1500.00 on an average, I feel I had a reason to expect that the money I borrowed in 1920 and put
into the Courier News and on which I have been paying interest, and which I
know and can prove was on the books of the Courier News, should have been
paid back to me, even though I did not approve the sale. Dodson's explanation,
after having first admitted it was on the books, later on was that it was removed
from the books by somebody saying it was a donation. (William Lemke to A. C.
Townley, undated, Lemke Papers).

attempted to neutralize the effect of Brinton's charges by bringing
Walter Liggett, later well known as editor of *Plain Talk* and whose
murder in 1935 attracted nationwide attention, into the state. The
latter was acquainted with Brinton's newspaper operations, and he
attempted to show that Brinton had made commissions for himself
in organizing League newspapers, just as Hastings was alleged to
have done in organizing League banks, but Liggett had little effect
on the outcome. So effective was the Independent campaign that it
seems probable that Frazier and Lemke both would have been defeated if it had not been a Presidential election year. The issues of
inefficiency and corruption, coupled with those associated with the
charges of Socialism and Bolshevism, were pressed with vigor by the
Independents, whose available figures indicated that they themselves
had spent $130,000 in the primary; Borglum complained that much of
the money had come from a nationally famous salt company and other
large corporations. Despite everything the League could do, the charge
that it was associated with godless Communists was effective. The
Independents printed an expensive publication entitled *The Red
Flame* and distributed it free throughout the state. Its covers were
red and it portrayed such themes as liberty burning at the stake and
emphasized such sensational themes as "free love," "I.W.W. ism,"
"anarchism," and "bolshevism." League leaders were referred to as
"Comrade."[19]

Organizing the precinct committeemen to maintain control of the
state Republican committee took much of Lemke's time during the
Presidential election campaign; he was the coordinator and maker of
final decisions in political strategy and campaign tactics. He campaigned vigorously himself, writing many of his letters from the small
towns in the southwestern part of the state where he was speaking.
Townley was in the state only briefly, and Lemke was now the headline speaker for the League as well as its most effective one. Often
his speeches would last from one to two hours, and he would sustain
the interest of his audience for the entire period. His speeches, given
without benefit of amplifiers and public address systems, differed from
a typical harangue in that they were usually carefully prepared. He
roundly denounced bankers and big business and recited charges
against them, always in vague enough terms to avoid suits for slander.
He impugned the motives of all who opposed the League. His
speeches carried great emotional impact, and farmers left his meetings
convinced that the world was against them. He was adept at citing

sources and exhibiting documents, using the "I hold here in my hand" technique later so effective in the attacks made against the federal Department of State during the Truman administration. The listening farmers were convinced that Lemke had the documents in his brief-case which would support every charge and innuendo that he made. During this period of his career, his speeches urged political action; while they definitely resulted in setting one occupational group against another, they did not advocate violence or defiance of the law. They made the farmer believe that election of Nonpartisan League candidates would place the law on their side and that there was hope—that there was a way and that that way was through political action.[20] Many later remembered that Lemke gave them the courage to continue and that they eventually saved their farms.

J. F. T. O'Connor was the most effective opponent of the League candidates. Although he permitted the Independent organization to attack the League for radicalism in all of its various forms, his own speeches were moderate and non-vituperative, presenting a pleasing contrast to those of Lemke and most of the speeches made by other League candidates. It was an effective method; the threats of Townley and Lemke to boycott all businessmen who opposed the League contrasted unfavorably with the type of campaign O'Connor conducted. The *Nord Dakota Tidende*, a League paper printed in Norwegian, attempted to injure O'Connor by mentioning his Roman Catholicism. This tactic was immediately disavowed by the League daily, the *Fargo Courier-News*, which pointed out that some of the League founders were likewise Roman Catholics. The League was having its own troubles on this score. Faithful members of the Roman Catholic communion were receiving letters written in pen and ink asking how they could go to Mass and still vote for Socialists, and were advised to ask their confessors as to whether Roman Catholics could be Socialists. Apparently the League felt the silent hostility of many of the Roman Catholic clergy and the more vocal attacks of many members of the Protestant ministry. Lemke arranged for a Roman Catholic priest to speak for the League and insisted that Frazier attend the dedication of a Roman Catholic church at Warsaw. He urged the *Courier-News* to reprint articles from *The Congregationalist* and other Protestant church papers to prove that the churches were not against the League. Nevertheless, political use of the religious issue injured Lemke and others.[21]

Although able to elect Lemke and all of the candidates they had nominated in the primary, League leaders were unable to elect those who had been nominated in the third-party column to run against the Independent candidates who had won Republican nomination in the primary. The League could not elect candidates who were running in the third-party column even when they were incumbents because the Democrats withdrew from the contest. This indicates the extent of the League's dependence on the regular Republican voters. The League could not win in a two-way contest unless its candidates were in the Republican column. Still more unfortunate for the League was the passage of the Independent-sponsored initiated measures. The Independents had captured the lower house of the legislature by a vote of 57 to 56, an event which enabled them to take maximum advantage of the audit of the Bank of North Dakota.[22] From the standpoint of the Independents immediate use of the audit was vital, for Langer's and Kositzky's positions in the state offices until January meant that they could influence selection of the firm which would conduct the audit. By the narrow margin of one vote, the Independents were able to organize the state House of Representatives, to obtain the audit report which resulted from passage of the initiated measure, to create a House Audit Committee to examine the audit, and to conduct an investigation of the League administration. Under the best of circumstances this would have been a trying time for the newly elected attorney general. But Independent control of the House added to his troubles by denying him the necessary appropriations to discharge his duties effectively.

The critical situation that resulted from the withdrawal of funds from the Bank of North Dakota was made worse by the collapse of wheat prices at this time. In less than a month after the election, the price of wheat fell sixty cents a bushel. There was a general nation-wide contraction of credit which compelled the small banks to collect in order to protect their reserves in their correspondent banks. Farmers who had held their wheat with the hope of selling it at $3.00 a bushel were now faced with the prospect of selling it for less than $1.50. Unable to collect, banks saw their liquid assets disappear, and by November 27, fifteen banks had closed in North Dakota. The Bank of North Dakota might normally have stayed the deflation, but the initiated measure forced it to withdraw its own redeposits from rural banks, creating a panic situation. Cathro's hand had been forced immediately after the election as thirty-nine of the fifty-three county treasurers asked to withdraw their funds from the Bank of North Dakota and stopped making additional deposits.[23]

One more purpose of the Independents was accomplished. The industrial program, financed by the Bank of North Dakota, came to an abrupt halt. The state mill and elevator, which was under construction at Grand Forks, stood half-finished with no further work being attempted. The rural credits program ceased to make loans at the time they were needed most. The Home Building Association started no more homes. And the Bank of North Dakota ceased to honor its checks, giving them serial numbers to provide the order in which they would be paid when funds were available.[24] The campaign had been so bitter that the Independents, who had been directly involved in it, were not so concerned about these developments as were the bankers of the state. The situation of the Bank of North Dakota was more precarious than they knew, as it needed to accumulate funds to meet the note for $1,000,000 to the Merchants' Loan and Trust Company of Chicago, which would fall due on March 15, 1921. Because the amount of bonds given as security exceeded the loan by $200,000, failure to pay meant a financial loss to the state of major proportions.

The North Dakota Bankers Association felt that serious damage to the state's banking system was too high a price to pay for the destruction of the League, and it accordingly appointed a committee to meet with Frazier, Lemke, and Hagan, the members of the newly elected Industrial Commission, and offered to arrange for the sale of the state's bonds. Their offer was coupled with a demand that the Industrial Commission promise not to have the Bank of North Dakota function as a typical commercial bank. Other assurances which they stipulated as necessary before they arranged to market the bonds included promises not to expand the industrial program of the League or discriminate between banks in making redeposits. One ambiguous clause left them further room to bargain, for it would have committed the Industrial Commission to agree to any order which would make the bonds more marketable.[25]

This initial offer of the bankers was rejected by the Industrial Commission. There is some indication that there had been negotiations and meetings between Lemke and the bankers prior to the formal offer of the bankers' association. Possibly the indignant rejection by the Industrial Commission was due to a change in the position of the bankers during the interim between these meetings and the actual offer to the Industrial Commission. The Independents had no doubts as to which individual was responsible for the rejection of their offer. A typical conservative commentary during this controversy was given by one of the Supreme Court justices, who wrote that it was "William Lemke [who] was obdurate and still insisted that the state's industrial bonds could be sold and that the initiated measure which had repealed the act that required all the school district, municipal, and county taxes and moneys to be deposited in the Bank of North Dakota could again be submitted to the electorate."[26]

As the month of January wore on, the House Audit Committee hearings revealed favoritism and carelessness in the redeposit policy of the Bank of North Dakota. The exposures resulted in the closing of the Scandinavian-American Bank at Fargo and in a general weakening of the League position. Alarmed by the reports he heard, Townley returned from organizing League branches in neighboring states. He was more of a realist than Lemke and had less uncompromising tenacity in his personality. Willing to operate within the realm of the possible, he inquired why the Industrial Commission had not made a counteroffer to the bankers rather than to reject their offer flatly.*

As events developed, Townley appeared to have been justified in his criticism. But the situation had been changed by the time Townley arrived in late January by the revelations of the audit and the hearings of the House Audit Committee. The conservative bankers were no longer willing to purchase the bonds. By February it had become clear to them that their biggest political assets were the crippled Bank of North Dakota and the unfinished structures of the various League enterprises. Equally clearly they now realized that Townley had been replaced by Lemke as their arch enemy. Every corporation attorney for the railroads and utilities had come to recognize that Lemke was their greatest menace. Incorruptible and possessed with the drive and energy of a religious zealot, he had become their private monopoly enemy number one. In their reply to the offer which the League had sent at Townley's instigation, the bankers now demanded not only complete control of the Industrial Commission but the resignation of William Lemke as attorney general.[27] Hedging against the remote

* The response of the Industrial Commission, from the opening paragraph, which refers to the "attempt on the part of the financial interests, presumably Wall Street" to the last sentence, which reads: "Many men of influence and wealth outside of the state are seriously considering the purchase of these bonds just as soon as the present financial stringency passes." sounds as though it had been written by Lemke. The last sentence has the ring of desperate optimism encountered so often in his Land Finance Company correspondence. A copy of this response is in the Lemke Papers.

possibility that their offer might be accepted, they made certain that
if it were, they would eliminate Lemke, their most effective opponent.

Townley's counter offer might have been the one Lemke should
have made for the Industrial Commission in early January. Coming
as it did in early February, it was disastrous to League fortunes, revealing to the Independents that the League had been shaken and that
it no longer possessed the unity which had made it so formidable. By
offering to compromise to avoid disaster, Townley had acted too late
and paved the way for the very thing which he had sought to avert.*
While the effect of the League's refusal to the bankers' reply was to
reunite the League caucus, it was no longer possible for the League
to conceal its internal difficulties. Every effort was made to close
ranks. Townley became afraid that he might be subpoenaed by the
House Audit Committee, and he left the state hurriedly without keeping appointments that he had made. Lemke reasserted his leadership,
and every effort was made to emphasize that there was no dis-
harmony in League ranks. Nationwide publicity attempted to make
the most of League differences, and the *New York Times* reported:

A. C. Townley has been dethroned as a boss of the Nonpartisan League
in North Dakota and his early retirement as head of the national organization was said today by some of his friends to be a strong probability. William Lemke, long Townley's confidential attorney and right-hand man, has
seized the reins in North Dakota, where he was elected Attorney General
by the league organization last Fall. He defeated Townley in the League's
legislation caucus in Bismarck Monday night after a long and bitter debate.
Townley after the caucus, rushed down to the national headquarters in
Minneapolis, where he spent yesterday in conference with his supporters,
leaving again last night for Bismarck, where he was to resume his efforts
to dominate League affairs again. If Townley fails, it is likely he will resign
and abandon his national organization. The North Dakota League is still
the backbone of Townleyism, and without it his power would be seriously
curtailed. Lemke has been the actual boss in North Dakota for two years

---

* One of Lemke's friends later reminisced: "He [Townley] never had a clear
idea of the economic and political forces he was bucking and later on became
buffaloed, else he never would have made the gross blunder of coming into Bismarck over the protest of his best friends and following LeSueur with a demand
that 'we compromise.' He, more than any other man, is responsible for the recall
election and its outcome. But for him A. L. never would have dared to attempt
what he did and I.V.A.s would have hardly dared risk calling the election, but
that his actions tended to prove to them that our solidarity was badly shaken, and,
so they were encouraged to launch the recall" (C. Hall to William Lemke, April
23, 1923, Lemke Papers).

but has been supposed to be acting for Townley, who has turned over to Lemke control of the newspaper at Fargo, the organization of country newspapers and the store corporation.[28]

The political difference between Lemke and Townley, however, never became personal. There is no record of Lemke expressing at this time or later any resentment of Townley's action. Lemke felt that Townley was a genius but that he was, like many geniuses, sometimes irresponsible.[29] Later, when Townley seemed to have lost some quality or power he had once possessed, Lemke viewed him indulgently and always attempted to assist him when the latter was in difficulty. Disloyalty was not a trait of Lemke's. Townley, in the cynicism and regrets of old age, did criticize Lemke's judgment, just as he had in 1921; but he never impugned Lemke's motives or ability. At the time of the sale of the *Courier-News* in 1923, Townley disregarded Lemke's advice and placed the latter in an ambiguous position which weakened him politically; yet it never seemed to alter the relationship between the two men. They respected one another's motives, and no strained feelings resulted. But this did not lessen the fact that the Independents had been alerted to the internal difficulties within the League, and that stresses within the organization now developed that might not have appeared had Townley not come to the state at this time.

Increasing discontent within League ranks, stemming partly from the November defeats and partly from the successful efforts of Independent propagandists to separate the League members from their leaders, compelled the latter to reconsider the League's internal organization. In December a loyal friend and veteran Leaguer, R. H. Walker, had written to Lemke to warn him that all was not well.

Dear Bill, I had hoped to be able to have had a conference with you this trip, but am told you will not be back until after I am gone. In regard to your plan of reorganization I can see that there is quite an undercurrent amongst the farmers of dissatisfaction with the proposed method of selecting the Excutive [sic] Committee. I think it would be wise to call the delegates together at Bismarck either just before the session or early in the session and reorganize from the groundup and not from the Sky down. I am fully convinced that this must be done in a regular manner or there is grave danger that it will be done in an irregular manner. The farmers are just a little ugly and if you don't take the initiative in this I think it will be a tactical error.[30]

Lemke had replied to Walker indicating that he did not agree with those complaining but that plans were being made for a democratic election within the League organization of a new Executive Committee. Lemke warned that "unless great care is taken in the election of these men, a bunch of encompetents [sic] will be put in charge. Many farmers have recommended to me mere boys as Assistant Attorney General, when they should have known that these boys would have to face the greatest brains . . . before the Supreme Court of the United States in important cases."[31] Nevertheless, Lemke had been influenced by Walker's note, and in January he encouraged the League convention to nominate ten men from which the membership could select five as the new Executive Committee of the Nonpartisan League. The five elected were A. Liederbach; Ole Kaldor; Christ Levang; R. H. Walker, the writer of the letter; and Walter Maddock. At Walker's suggestion Lemke had acted soon enough in order to avoid loss of either prestige or power, and the League had agreed upon and was pursuing a program of no compromise, when Townley reappeared on the scene with his advocacy of a compromise.

After the five men had been chosen on the Executive Committee, Liederbach had promised Kaldor and Levang salaried jobs on the Nonpartisan League payroll in return for their votes for him as chairman. While surrendering control of the League Executive Committee, Lemke had kept control for Townley, Wood, and himself of the League enterprises such as the *Courier-News*. Although Lemke granted the new committee full authority to administer these enterprises, actual title and ultimate control still lay in the hands of the original three Executive Committee members. It was here that the difference between Townley and Lemke emboldened Liederbach, its new chairman. Despite the desperate nature of League finances, Liederbach placed Levang, Kaldor, and himself on the payroll at salaries of $250 a month each. Levang and Kaldor were given the titles of cashier and state organizer; Liederbach called himself state manager and, in that capacity, he now demanded that Townley, Lemke, and Wood surrender title to the League enterprises and especially to the League daily newspaper, the *Courier-News* of Fargo. There was no rupture at this time. Liederbach indicated that he did not want control but that he had merely assumed it to be logical in view of the change in the personnel of the state committee. Lemke was able to point out the legal difficulties in a transfer of title. No change was made, and apparently all remained harmonious. The staff members of the *Courier-News* disapproved of the salaries being paid the Liederbach triumvirate. The paper was suffering from an advertising boycott, and it badly needed League assistance. During the summer of 1921, a major dispute between the staff members and the committee erupted, and the internecine strife seriously handicapped the League during the recall campaign.[32]

In the period during which Liederbach assumed active direction of the League, the Independents were capitalizing on the sentiment and confusion created by the work of the House Audit Committee. During practically the entire course of the hearings, which continued for nearly forty-five days, Lemke was present to advise the bank employees and others who were being examined by the committee. He interrupted committee counsel constantly to advise those being examined. At every opportunity he demanded the right to cross-examine witnesses such as Brinton, but he was never accorded the privilege.[33]

As early as February 12, 1921, the Independents threatened a recall election, and the first recall petitions included the names of members of the Industrial Commission and the three League-endorsed members of the Supreme Court. The inclusion of the Supreme Court members was regarded by Leaguers as revenge by the Independents for the court's stand in the Scandinavian-American Bank case. During the time the petitions were being circulated, these judges, with the exception of Robinson, made a decision favorable to the Independents and inimical to the League. Promptly the recall petitions were called in and the names of all of the Supreme Court justices were taken off.[34]

The decision on which the judges had ruled in a manner pleasing to the Independents had been an important case for the Bank of North Dakota, which was at this time marshaling what resources it had to meet the $1,000,000 note to the Chicago bank. The Industrial Commission had ruled that withdrawals by governmental units could be made only for regular business and that wholesale withdrawals could not be made by county treasurers just to transfer the funds to private banks. Sargent County attached the funds. Lemke had been diverted from other activity by the case, which had taken much of his time, and to him the decision was "one of the crudest . . . that has ever been rendered in the history of the state." The indignation of the League press was violent. Lemke immediately applied for a rehearing of the decision and wrote the editor of the *Courier-News* to "lay off . . . the Supreme Court as I intend to make a motion for rehearing and if they stand pat after that, you will have my permission to open up on them full blast."[35] The rehearing was denied, and the financial situation of the state and that of the League and its enterprises was made even more desperate.

Lemke's optimism at this juncture inspires wonder. The telephones at League headquarters were disconnected because of unpaid bills. Many employees were being laid off, and others were going without salaries for months at a time. Neither the economic stringency nor the threat of a recall disturbed his outward equanimity. At the height of the House Audit Committee hearings, he wrote Borglum that "the enemy with its corrupt hand has overplayed the game [sic] reaction is setting in." As to the recall he was "satisfied that they will get the worst drubbing they ever got in case there is a recall." The most incredible comment, written just as League phones were being disconnected and the impact of the audit committee hearings was being felt, was to the Twin City headquarters of the League. "We are having a glorious time and are keeping on top. . . . Suppose you are just as hard up as we are."[36]

For a time there was some doubt within the Independent group as to whether there would be a recall. Seth Richardson, Fargo attorney and close friend of Lemke, wrote: "The recallers have had an attack of cold feet."[37] It was not long, however, until George Totten wrote from League headquarters at Fargo:

I have it on fairly reliable information that Two-Bit Nelson is going to be able to put over his recall proposition. He is trying very hard to do this and even the Forum seems to be letting up a little in their position to the recall election. I understand that recall petitions are now being circulated and that Two Bit declares that they have already secured over half the signatures necessary. He is using this as an arguement [sic] to show the sentiment for a recall.[38]

It was not long before doubt was removed. The Independents held a convention in Devils Lake on March 30 and 31, 1921, and nominated for governor R. A. Nestos, the man whom Langer had eliminated as a candidate of the Independents for governor in 1920; Sveinbjorn Johnson, a law partner of J. F. T. O'Connor, for Lemke's post as attorney general;[39] and someone whom the Independent executive committee would select later to run against John Hagan for commissioner of agriculture and labor. Joseph A. Kitchen of Sentinel Butte subsequently was selected for this candidacy. The three men against whom the Independents had filed recall petitions were, by virtue of their official positions, members of the Industrial Commission, and the reason given for recalling them was to provide efficient means of carrying out the industrial program of the League or at least to give it a probationary period under business management to determine if the enterprises were basically sound when directed by businessmen.

Despite the responsibilities he had undertaken and the duties and worries that accompanied them, Lemke made the seventeen months he served in the attorney general's department the most active in the history of that office. He justified to himself the tremendous energy he expended by his belief that the result would be a government which would truly protect the people from the Twin City and Wall Street interests, and he could not help but be conscious of the fact that he was creating a reputation that might be a future political asset. Never before or afterward did the office institute and prosecute vigorously more suits against the railroads and public utility interests than was done during the months Lemke was in office. He prosecuted a railroad tax case resulting in a payment of additional taxes into the state treasury, and H. G. Teigan wrote, "Attorney General Lemke won his suit against the railroads. . . . They paid into the State Treasury the sum of $1,399,000. . . . Langer . . . had practically agreed to compromise . . . and let them off." The railroads had never had a more able opponent or one more persistent and determined than Lemke. Without a board meeting, the chairman of the Board of Railroad Commissioners had approved a raise in railroad rates. Lemke obtained an order from the state Supreme Court restraining the railroads from putting increased rates into effect in intrastate commerce.[40] To buttress the legal position of the railroads and nullify the court action, the board chairman had his ruling approved by Samuel J. Aandahl, another member of the board. When Lemke again brought action, the case was taken to the Interstate Commerce Commission and the federal courts. A determining point was whether the Board of Railroad Commissioners had acted in legal session. Needed witnesses were in the East, and it was necessary that depositions be taken. This, and the fact that the railroads were plainly prepared to carry the case to the United States Supreme Court, made it necessary for North Dakota to retain an attorney in Washington, D. C., to cooperate with Lemke.

After correspondence with several attorneys, Lemke employed Karl K. Gartner for a fee of $2,000. By the time these arrangements had been made, Lemke had been elected and inaugurated attorney general, only to run into an unexpected obstacle. The general election of 1920 had resulted in an anti-League majority in the House of Representatives for the first time since 1915. That body passed a vote of censure of Lemke, charging him with past malfeasance and future intent to use all appropriations to enlarge an already huge political machine and refusing to appropriate money to take care of past deficiencies in the attorney general's office, and gave Lemke only $3,000 in addition to his own salary to run the office until July 1, 1921. Only the defection on one issue of John Halcrow of Pembina County from the Independent majority saved the appropriation for enforcement of North Dakota's prohibition law. Halcrow was threatened with reprisals by the leaders of the Independents, but he accepted Lemke's word that the funds would not be used for political purposes, a promise to which Lemke adhered by most actively enforcing North Dakota's prohibition law. Halcrow's defection gave a 57 to 56 majority to the League on this issue. When Halcrow refused to change, five other Independents joined him.[41]

No funds were appropriated from which legal counsel could be paid to fight the cases in Washington. Lemke used the columns of the *Courier-News* of Fargo and the other League papers to solicit funds with which to pay Gartner and other additional counsel. Misuse and misappropriation of this money, which came to be known as the "Lemke Fund," became one of the main charges against Lemke. Actually, the money was kept in a separate account and used for the purpose for which it had been solicited. No charges were ever pressed successfully against Lemke, and Gartner received large payments from the fund.＊

＊ Cases involving the conflicting jurisdictional claims of state and federal governments in regard to regulatory legislation became Gartner's special field, and he developed a large profitable practice and represented many other states. Later he represented North Dakota in defending against the attacks on the constitutionality of the League-sponsored grain grading legislation.

The decisions in these cases and in most other similar ones were in favor of federal jurisdiction and explain in part Lemke's later objections to Franklin D. Roosevelt's New Deal approach to the problem of regulating the economy. It was through state regulation and action that the League attempted to work. So often did state action intervene in an area where the federal government had enacted legislation that many of the League's key proposals were declared to be illegal by the federal courts. As one decision after another turned against them, both Gartner and Lemke became more ardent states' righters. Time after time it seemed that the relatively mild federal legislation on these subjects in effect protected big business; Lemke never could understand that the federal government in the hands of a party and President so desiring, such as Franklin D. Roosevelt at a later date, could be an ally of the states in efforts to regulate and restrain "Big Biz."

The electric light companies also felt the effect of Lemke's action, and in one case the Union Light, Heat, and Power Company of Fargo was compelled to refund money collected with higher rates illegally charged. Telephone and express companies found his hand against them too, for in Lemke the state had a fiery advocate who was determined that no corporation would take advantage of a natural monopoly position to extort unreasonable profits from its customers. For the state and for the customers of these corporations, Lemke's legal advice came at bargain rates.* The same kind of legal ability and activity bought in the market place could have been had only at a price many times the rather niggardly salary North Dakota paid its attorney general. The activity of his office was unusual; the failure of the legislators to appropriate the usual sums and the harassing conditions under which he was working indicate that his record as attorney general was due to the intensity of his application to his work and to a loyal and devoted staff. The Independents regarded him as an agitator motivated by personal ambition, and they charged that it was his desire for power and wealth which caused him to exploit the people and endanger the stability of the state. Lemke himself told others that the League program had become almost a religion with him, and his followers believed in his sincerity.[42]

Lemke was so certain that the record he was making would re-elect him and protect him against the recall that he was chiefly concerned about the initiated measures which the Independents had petitioned to have placed on the ballot. The Independents had placed five proposals on the ballot, passage of which would have prevented expansion of the League program and circumscribed the operation of that portion of it already begun. Lemke saw clearly that a personal victory accompanied by the passage of these initiated measures would be fatal to the League. Two additional laws initiated by the Independents proved beyond doubt that they understood fully the part that primary elections had in the success of the League. One bill

* Townley expressed his belief that the recall could have been prevented if Lemke had been willing to moderate his conduct of the office and speculated that the vigorous prosecution of cases against large corporations was the determining factor in the decision of the Independents to seek a recall election. In typical earthy humor he described the impossibility of restraining Lemke in his conduct of the office. He spoke in a critical vein and felt that it would have been better to have prevented the recall even if it had meant a diminution in the vigor with which suits were pressed against large corporations doing business in the state. (Interview with A. C. Townley, July 1, 1957.)

proposed the elimination of the party ballot and party labels in primary elections and further provided that the two highest candidates in the primary election would enter the general election in the fall. The second bill changed the date of the election of United States senators and representatives to March, a time different from those primaries for state offices. These candidates for Congress were to continue on a party ballot. It was also provided that in the general election there would be two ballots. One would name the candidates for state office; the other would list the candidates for Congress and, in Presidential years, for the electoral college. These ballots were both to be one-column, office-group ballots instead of the traditional party-column ballots common to one-party states. By the time of the recall campaign in October, Lemke understood that the two bills would completely remove one of the major reasons for League success and he opposed their adoption.* Had they passed, there would no longer have been a three-way split in the primaries, with the conservative Democrats segregated from the main contest between the Independents and the League. The separate ballots for state officials and the lack of party designation in the fall would have deprived the League of the support of the straight-ticket Republicans who heretofore had been the League's captive allies and who under the proposed law would become free to vote against the League without voting for someone wearing a Democratic label. Lemke apparently did not understand fully the dangers inherent in the recall movement until later in the year, but he did see that it would be unwise to confuse League voters by initiating a measure restoring compulsory deposit of public funds in the Bank of North Dakota. He stopped this by pointing out to state senator Bert F. Baker that it was easier to inform the voters to vote a straight "no" than to instruct them to pick and choose the laws for which they would vote negatively.[43]

Lemke and all of the League leaders were wary of the initiated laws. The catastrophe that had descended upon them as a consequence of the two initiated measures in the previous general election had made them fearful of direct legislation. This obsession characterized the entire League recall campaign. Often the viewpoint

* A copy of the pamphlet from which this information is taken is in the Lemke Papers and has Lemke's penciled notes in the margins detailing arguments against these measures. One of his comments was: "We have control of the Republican party now. Why change?" (North Dakota, *Publicity Pamphlet,* October 28, 1921, in Lemke Papers.)

was expressed both by Lemke and in communications from League headquarters that the Independents did not expect to elect their candidates but were simply trying to use them as stalking horses to initiate legislation limiting the League industrial program.[44] "Remember the initiated measures and do not be misled by them" became the key theme of the League campaign. It was not until September, about six weeks before the election, that Lemke seemed to contemplate the possibility of personal defeat for Frazier, Hagan, and himself.

Realization that sale of the bonds would start the stalled League industrial program and remove the monetary shortages that had revealed the difficulties in the various League enterprises caused Lemke to depend on finding a market for them. He felt that it could be done, and it was only when the election drew near with the bonds still unsold that he squarely faced the possibility that the recall would be successful. His plan was to find an alternative to the customary financial outlets through the use of labor unions, liberal organizations, and individuals sympathetic to the League. The sessions of the House Audit Committee had necessitated a hasty return from his second trip to the East in January, 1921, and had immobilized him in Bismarck. The Sargent County garnishment case prevented his return to the East until late in the spring. During this period of time Lemke employed Spurgeon O'Dell to go to New York, Boston, and other Eastern cities. O'Dell's instructions were to interview and to attempt to obtain the assistance of such prominent persons as Oswald Garrison Villard, Bernard Baruch, Hugh Johnson, William Lloyd Garrison, William Randolph Hearst, Roger Babson, and others. O'Dell spoke before labor groups and liberal organizations such as the Harvard Liberal Club and the Fabian Society. From there he went to New York interviewing bank bond departments and the normal financial outlets with the same discouraging results as Cathro's representatives had experienced before Lemke took charge of the bond sale. The banking houses pleaded that they were at the mercy of their customers, who were of the ultra-conservative type and who would not buy North Dakota bonds. Another key liberal employed by Lemke was Carl Thompson, secretary of the Public Ownership League of America; both Lemke and Frazier were officers of the Public Ownership League. For Thompson the sale of the bonds was a crusade, an opportunity to carry the message that the cities throughout the nation should own and operate those enterprises which were natural monopolies. Through his organization, advertisements were placed in magazines appealing to the public to rescue North Dakota from Wall Street by buying North Dakota 5 per cent bonds which were being refused by the financial community.[45]

George T. Webb, the man who finally sold the bonds, felt that Thompson's advertisements were increasing the antagonism of conservative financial interests and were destroying any possibility of selling the bonds. Lemke, to whom both Thompson and Webb appealed, advised Thompson to moderate the tone of his advertisements.[46] As soon as the legislature and the bank garnishment case permitted him, he left on a bond selling tour. Through most of April and May, Lemke was out of the state. He held meetings in many of the smaller cities of Iowa, Illinois, Indiana, and Ohio, and before returning, he visited Chicago, Cleveland, Boston, New York, Philadelphia, Washington, D.C., and many other cities in the East. Wherever he went, adverse newspaper stories often appeared in the front pages of the press just a few days before his arrival, and an interested Bostonian wrote: "I suspect that the *Boston Transcript* . . . has learned that you are soon to speak in Boston. Hence the enclosed article in their issue of last evening." Lemke was speaking to the Twentieth Century Club on this occasion.

Elsewhere, Leaguers and liberals noted the fight Lemke was making.* For a time he forgot his office in Bismarck, where a small but able staff held things together as well as they could. Lemke tried to interest Hearst but without success. Oswald Garrison Villard did his best to break the banker boycott. Henry Ford proved sympathetic but was having his own troubles with Wall Street at the time and lacked the liquidity to be of assistance. C. C. Daniels, brother of Wilson's Secretary of the Navy, tried to help by working through James Gerard, former ambassador to Germany. Lemke received his kindliest treatment from Bernard Baruch, who personally purchased $50,000 worth of the bonds; Borglum suspected that Baruch had Presidential ambitions and was engaged in winning the support of the Nonpartisan League. A banquet campaign was begun, but by May the total of all bond sales came to $350,000; when Lemke had to return to North Dakota for the recall election campaign, the total of bonds sold was $600,000—just a fraction of the millions the League leaders

* W. C. Zumach had suggested that Robert La Follette be asked to come to North Dakota to assist. H. G. Teigan replied to him: "I know that La Follette things [sic] well of Lempke [sic] and he surely cannot help but admire the latter for the splendid fight he is now making in North Dakota" (H. G. Teigan to W. C. Zumach, February 28, 1921, Teigan Papers).

had contemplated selling. Lemke himself was compelled to admit that the cost of the sales was far too high. He returned to North Dakota in June and then went East again in July in one more attempt to sell the bonds.[47] In August he returned to North Dakota to attend to office work and to begin plans for the recall campaign. In September, the campaign began formally. Ironically, Webb was able to arrange the sale of the bonds in early October, too late to save the members of the Industrial Commission from being recalled from office.

One complication developed that was related to the 1920 defeat of Gronna by Ladd. Frank White, governor of the state from 1901 to 1903, had run as a third candidate in the primary of June, 1920, and very probably had taken enough votes from Gronna to nominate Ladd. Subsequently, White had been appointed Treasurer of the United States to succeed John Burke, confirming in the minds of Independents their suspicions that McCumber had been the instigator of White's candidacy and that there had been an alliance between McCumber and the League to accomplish the defeat of Gronna and the election of Ladd. For a time White's name was used in an endorsement of the bonds until protests against using the position of Treasurer of the United States in this manner compelled withdrawing of his endorsement. Lemke received no cooperation from the administration in the sale of the bonds.[48]

The League had no patronage or assistance of any kind from the Harding administration in 1921. When a bill was put through to add an additional federal judge for North Dakota, Lemke selected Seth Richardson as the League's candidate. The conservative, Andrew Miller, received the appointment. Borglum complained to Harding that "not a suggestion or appointment Senator Ladd has made or asked has been granted. Senator Ladd says so. And Attorney-General Lemke says the same thing. . . . They say therefore, voting for Mr. Harding has been our ruin, our undoing." It was a severe disappointment for Lemke, who had asked, in return for the League's support of Harding, the control over the appointments of United States District Attorney, United States Marshal, and any federal judgeships should vacancies occur in the state.[49] The attitude of the national administration made it safe to assume that, if it were not an open ally of the recall movement, it was certainly not disposed to lift a finger to help the incumbent members of the Industrial Commission. Lemke, remembering bitterly his support of Harding in 1920, did not again support a Republican candidate for President until 1940.

Midsummer of 1921 was a period of discouragement for Lemke.

In early July, when Lemke was subpoenaed to appear in a perjury trial regarding charges Brinton had made against Lemke and others, Brinton was not convicted of perjury. The judge ruled that no evidence to indicate Brinton's past record for veracity could be introduced and that Brinton could not be punished so long as he thought what he said was true. The incident made it impossible for Lemke to keep a Fourth of July speaking engagement in Cavalier County or to be at home in Fargo when his family moved on July 8 into the new house which had been built with the aid of the Home Building Association. It was just at this time, too, that the feud between the regular staff members of the League newspapers and the Liederbach group of the executive committee broke into open warfare. On July 6, the *Fargo Courier-News* published an attack on the Liederbach faction of the executive committee. Before the paper could be distributed, a force of ten or twelve men under Liederbach's leadership entered the plant. The employees were ejected and the issue of the paper was destroyed. The paper had charged that Liederbach was hoarding the campaign money and advised sending the money to D. C. Poindexter, the state auditor. "Ultimately William Lemke served as peacemaker. . . . *The Courier-News* continued under the supervision of the majority members of the state committee." Perhaps it was this or Mrs. Lemke's wire: "Am moving today. Let me know when you will be home,"[50] that caused one of the few comments that reflected discouragement to creep into Lemke's correspondence:

The struggle has been a severe one and has at times exhausted our patience, but I can see the road clear to success, and hope that after a year or two more, I will be able to quietly go on with my own work and forget all about politics for the reason that it will not be necessary any longer as the movement will be so far along that it will succeed and it will not have so many enemies within a very short time.[51]

Lemke's hope was that the sale of the bonds and the successful inauguration of the League industrial program would diminish the opposition and permit him to solve his personal problems. These had been immensely complicated as a result of building the house into which his family had just moved. Too high in price to legally qualify for the provisions of the home building law, the house now cost nearly three times the original estimate, as a result of inflation and the additions asked for by the Lemkes and agreed to by the Home Building Association without either party fully realizing the price increases which would result. It first had been made a major issue during the general election campaign in 1920, and Lemke found it fruitless to assure inquiring voters that "this home is the size I gave in my talk at Marmarth, and that the State has loaned me $4,000., my wife putting in $3,000. and the balance being borrowed from I.V.A. bankers." He found it equally difficult to convince voters that this was a diversionary attack to keep their attention from "the $1,346,-250.85 I saved the state in freight rates . . . to say nothing about the $400,000 now being returned to the citizens of Fargo, Grank Forks, Minot [sic] in connection with the Union Light Heat & Power Company and the $360,000 Standard Oil taxes and $1,337,000 back railroad taxes saved to the state. As Mr. Shure, City Attorney of Fargo who is not a Leaguer said [sic] if those fools would pay me 1 per cent commission on what I have saved the State, then I wouldn't have to worry about my house."[52]

It is difficult to conceive the intensity of the attack on Lemke, against whom not one charge was ever successfully prosecuted. In Fargo free taxi service was available to take anyone from downtown Fargo on a tour to see the Lemke house, and a booth was maintained at the state fair at which any who so wished could obtain a free round trip to the new home the state had built for Lemke. Pictures of the house with a two-car garage were in every opposition paper in the state. Someone paid J. W. Brinton to cross and recross the state showing slides of the Lemke house and of the giant tractors standing idle on the project of the United States Sisal Trust in Florida. The newspapers fanned the flame of hate to a point where, in the fall of 1921, crowds surged around the Lemke home and hanged and burned him in effigy. It was a continuous campaign. The penitentiary was mentioned as a possibility for some who were now free. Farmers were constantly told that the League was responsible for the tightening of credit, an effective argument to men who needed additional funds or their mortgages renewed if they were not to lose their homes or their means of making a living. Long before the election, teams of speakers traveled through the state stressing the Red issue, a campaign device which proved particularly effective after Lemke had arrived in Devils Lake at the same time that a gathering of I.W.W.'s was there.[53]

In August Lemke made what was announced as an inspection trip of southwest North Dakota crop conditions; actually it was a campaign trip from which he returned very optimistic about the election outcome. There was one difference between this and the campaigns

of previous years: it was directed by the new Executive Committee
rather than by Lemke. Lemke's position, influence, and prestige were
such that the Executive Committee granted him every request and
acted upon his suggestions, and his authority was so generally
recognized that he felt free to make arrangements independently of
the committee, knowing that they would approve them; but the committee was doing the routing of speakers. This meant that the day-to-
day decisions, the evaluation of where speakers were needed and
would do the most good, the choice of issues, and the expenditures of
funds rested in the hands of A. Liederbach, Christ Levang, and Ole
Kaldor. During the course of the campaign, Walter Maddock wrote:
"Dislike bothering you with our state organization troubles and know
we should relieve you of all possible responsibility while you have
all the bigger things. . . . Yet I must confess we are not big enough
to handle the state organization without a lot of counsel from you."*54

Lemke always maintained and Cathro also asserted that if Lemke
had spent more time at headquarters and less on the campaign platform, the outcome would have been different, an allegation easier to
make than to prove. Cathro and Lemke most certainly did not mean
to imply that Lemke was an ineffective stump speaker. Now that
Townley had ceased to be active, Lemke was the best campaigner the
League had. The Lemke name could draw crowds better than any
other. It was hard to organize the giant gatherings of the early League days, and it was at this time that Lemke developed the technique
he used so successfully in later years in campaigning for Congress. He
would speak in from six to ten places a day. Local League members
would start the meetings before his arrival. Lemke spoke immediately
after he arrived and then, while someone else held the audience and
finished the meeting, he would be off to the next schoolhouse or town
hall for a repeat performance.† Roads were bad; he had to have a
driver or depend on local groups to deliver him to the next meeting.
But he had an amazing capacity for relaxation. After finishing a talk,
he would rest in the back seat of the waiting car. Covered with a

---

* Lemke and others frequently charged in later years that Liederbach had
husbanded the recall funds to keep the executive committee functioning in the
event the election was lost rather than spending it on winning the election.

† A typical Lemke campaign day started at Edgely at 10:30 A.M. After speaking there he went to Nortonville for an 11:30 meeting, then to Sydney at 2:00
P.M., Eldridge at 3:00 P.M., Windsor at 4:00 P.M., Cleveland at 4:30 P.M., and
Medina at 5:30 P.M. After a schedule such as this, he would speak at least once
and usually twice in the evening.

blanket or coat, he would relax until he reached the next destination. The rumpled condition of his clothes and the travel-weary appearance he presented added to rather than detracted from the political image he was creating. He was too much of a showman not to realize the value of staging, and he was certainly well aware of what he was doing. At the same time he gave guidance to the campaign despite the fact that he was away from headquarters and constantly traveling. There was a steady flow of letters to headquarters, to other speakers, and to his office in Bismarck. His staff there was very loyal and was both amazed and concerned at the risks he was taking with his health. One of his staff reported: "I succeeded in overtaking Mr. Lemke yesterday at Whitman, but I did not get away from him until this morning, for the reason that he wanted to take up a number of matters with me. . . . Mr. Lemke is in good condition, having good meetings and feeling fine."[55]

One reason Lemke was feeling fine was that news had just come through that Webb had succeeded in selling a large block of bonds to Spitzer, Rorick and Company of Toledo, Ohio. They had purchased a large enough consignment of the bonds to break the financial boycott.* Now the industrial program of the League could be started. League leaders were momentarily elated, but the sale had come too late to enable them to make sufficient political capital of it.

On October 18 the Independents executed a maneuver which may have been a determining factor in the most successful use of statewide recall election machinery in American history and the consequent removal from office of Lynn J. Frazier, William Lemke, and John Hagan. While passing through Jamestown just ten days before the election, Frazier was served with a restraining injunction which was so sweeping in its nature that it impeded continued functioning of the state government and made operation of the Bank of North Dakota impossible. The administration at Bismarck was immobilized.

At 2:00 A.M. a distress telephone call roused Lemke from his hotel room at Hatton. Lemke cancelled his campaign, roused his driver, and proceeded through the darkness along the prairie trails, arriving at Valley City, some seventy miles away, in time to board a train

* The terms of the sale had been favorable to the Toledo firm. Later the Nestos administration refused to deliver part of the bonds. The agreement was then renegotiated on more favorable terms to the state. Years later Spitzer, Rorick and Company successfully sued the state for non-fulfillment of contract (Hagen, p. 142).

to Bismarck.* On October 20, Lemke secured a writ from the state Supreme Court ordering Judge J. A. Coffey to certify the proceedings to the Supreme Court and directing that the restraining order be vacated until further order of the higher court. Although it was later testified by John Steen, a prominent Independent, that the assertions made to obtain the restraining order from the district court had been false, yet it had taken Lemke, Frazier, and a number of others out of the campaign for several days at a time most crucial to the League's success. While the entire attention of League headquarters was given to the problems of rescheduling and cancellation difficulties, the Independents again took the offensive. Many voters were confused by the incident and were thus more easily turned against the League. Former Governor Jacob Preus of Minnesota was brought into the state to tell how they had jailed League leaders in Minnesota. It was not until October 22, less than a week before the recall, that Lemke could again resume his campaign.[56]

The League had sought outside speakers too. Liederbach had left their scheduling to P. L. Aarhus. When the latter submitted the lists of speakers, routings, and other material, Lemke's letters indicated great dissatisfaction. For the first time his correspondence took on an urgent tone. Lemke himself arranged for W. H. "Coin" Harvey to come to the state, and he kept up a constant correspondence with Borglum in an effort to obtain speakers such as Burton Wheeler, Bert Cochrane, Dudley Field Malone, William Gibbs McAdoo, J. A. H. Hopkins, William Randolph Hearst, and Bernard Baruch, but he cautioned Ladd not to send Robert La Follette.† Borglum came, and Ladd arrived belatedly, as did Senator Henrik Shipstead of Minnesota.

---

* Neither this trip in the small hours of the morning nor Lemke's schedules can be fully appreciated by anyone who does not remember the roads and cars of 1921. High-center country roads made by pulling the dirt to a center ridge were the very best there were. There were no state highways, and travelers usually found their way from one destination to another by using directions based on landmarks such as schoolhouses, farm buildings, groves of trees, and fences. Only a driver thoroughly familiar with the country would be able to negotiate the seventy miles from Hatton to Valley City during the night over these roads, most of which were doubtless only prairie trails.

† In 1920 the League had defeated Gronna, who had been a close friend of La Follette. Gronna was working against the League in 1921, and Lemke was afraid of his influence on La Follette. Gronna died the following year, and the League secured La Follette's assistance in the general election campaign of 1922. The breach between Gronna and the League prevented the North Dakota branch of the League from taking advantage of the assistance the great Progressive could have given it in 1921.

Ladd had been pressed not to come by fellow senators who were concerned about his vote on a crucial issue; only after Borglum insisted and paid Ladd's railroad fare did he consent to come.[57]

Overconfidence partly explains this error and many others, while Liederbach's caution explains still more. Kaldor explained to Maddock that the latter's suggestion regarding sending the *Courier-News* to all League members could not be carried out for lack of funds. This was the only way in which the influence of the *Grand Forks Herald* could have been neutralized, and not doing it was a crucial error. The *Herald* was sent out in many areas of the state, to non-subscribers as well as to its customary audience. Because of McCumber's influence, the *Bismarck Tribune* opposed the recall.[58]

Many Leaguers contended that the forces opposed to enforcement of the liquor laws, particularly those centering in Minot, were the determining factor in bringing about the recall and in defeating the League. Whether the anti-Prohibition forces furnished the money that Leaguers alleged and, if they did, whether it went to the treasury of the Independents or into the pockets of some individual who was exploiting an opportunity for a "soft touch" is uncertain. Some facts stand out clearly. Lemke enforced the liquor laws vigorously and was proud of having done so. When he was defeated, prosecution of the liquor elements was immediately relaxed in Minot. C. L. Crum had been in charge of prosecuting criminal violators in Minot. He was immediately dismissed. Enforcement was returned to local and county officials, an action the significance of which was clear and which cannot be interpreted in a light favorable to the attorney general who succeeded Lemke nor to the IVA organization which had recalled him from office.[59]

Though opposed by many of the church groups and crusading "dry" organizations, Lemke did not seem to become bitter at this or at many of the other things that were occurring. It was during this period that the Varsity Bachelor Club saw fit to dismiss Lemke as Grand Bachelor, a position he had held from the time he had founded the organization. During the recent hectic times he had neglected the club, giving the members a valid excuse for their action. Nevertheless, the timing of his dismissal was one which might have made many men bitter. His conduct in defeat was admirable. Magnus Johnson and a Mr. Plumb were guests in Lemke's home on the night of the election. Notes scribbled as the reports came in have errors in computation that were caused possibly by concern and dismay. Yet Lemke viewed the result without bitterness, saving his strength to fight another day. He was enthusiastically certain that 1922 would see a League victory and a return to power.

There were other factors which make Lemke's optimism unrealistic. Liederbach's control of League machinery meant that there would not be unified support of Lemke in the spring of 1922. The organization would have to be won back from Liederbach first. A. C. Townley, who was spending ninety days in jail in Minnesota for his wartime sedition conviction, decided in 1922 to discard the League for a balance of power plan, and this further weakened the organization. Finally, the Independent candidates who were elected did not abandon the League program as N. C. Young wanted and Lemke expected them to do.* The margin of victory for the Independents ranged from between 5,000 and 6,000 for Nestos and Kitchen to nearly 7,000 for Johnson, Lemke's opponent. This would indicate that the house episode had hurt Lemke, for he trailed both Hagan and Frazier. The initiated measures were defeated by comparable margins. A shift of from two to three votes per precinct would have altered the result in every contest—both candidates and measures. One of the anomalies of the election was this rejection of the initiated measures which would have curtailed the League program. Nestos, Johnson, and Kitchen were given a mandate by the voters to continue the program the League had started at the same time that the Industrial Commission that supported the program was recalled. Either sincerity or political sense caused them to attempt to carry out that mandate. Had they done otherwise, Lemke's optimism would have been justified.

There were post-election problems that also required attention. Lemke had to appear in Washington in connection with the attack on the constitutionality of the grain grading laws. The money had to be raised so that he could pay the state for his house. No leader active during this period, League or Independent, took issue with the generally accepted conviction that the Lemke house was the cause of the League's defeat and the recall of the Industrial Commission. George Webb wrote to Borglum: "I know you will be interested in one item, and that is that a few of Mr. Lemke's friends, among whom

* Nestos later stressed his own resistance to great pressure from Young and others to terminate the industrial program. According to Nestos, Young argued that although there was a million dollars invested in the "dump" (the mill and elevator), in the long run the people could be brought to approve discontinuing it. To Nestos' argument that he was not going to break campaign promises, Young countered—according to Nestos—that it was all right to say some things in the heat of the campaign that sober, second thought would prove unwise to perform (interview with R. A. Nestos, May, 1938).

I number myself, came across with sufficient funds to clear up his house. Whether it will be sufficient to avoid further criticism only time can tell. As a friend of his, I knew you would be interested in this item."[60] Nearly a dozen of Lemke's friends had pooled their funds so that the state could be paid in full and Lemke relieved of the possibility of having to give up possession of his home.*

One serious problem which Lemke faced was what he should do with the "Lemke Fund"—the money he had raised by public subscription for the purpose of operating his office when the legislature had failed to provide him with the customary appropriations.[61] Lemke was reluctant to give it to Johnson, his successor in office; yet he could not keep it himself. For a time it was left in the custody of Fred Cathro, and eventually it was turned over to the state treasurer. The office of attorney general had to be transferred to Johnson. For a short ten- or fifteen-minute period, Lemke visited with his victorious opponent, who planned to do his utmost to prosecute Lemke on criminal indictments. Lemke then left and Sveinbjorn Johnson became the new attorney general of North Dakota.

Why the recall petitions were not challenged and the recall postponed until 1922 is difficult to explain. The regular elections would then have been so close in time that a recall would have been impractical. The decision was, no doubt, Lemke's.[62] It is probable that he planned on the successful sale of the bonds and felt that this would make a League victory certain. A defeat of the Independents in the recall would have destroyed their effectiveness for some elections in the future, and Lemke may have been influenced by this hope. He could not fully have realized early enough the electoral disadvantage to the League inherent in the lack of party columns on the recall ballot. He may have reasoned that an effort by the League to prevent the use of the reform they had sponsored just the previous year might weigh heavily against them in ensuing elections. There were duplications on the recall petitions, and Leaguers considered challenging the validity of the election in the courts. After the defeat and against Lemke's advice, some Leaguers attempted to do so. Lemke, who was

---

* The biggest creditor of Lemke at this time was H. G. Lykken. Others included Thomas Hennessey, I. P. Baker, Seth Richardson, George T. Webb, L. P. McAneney, Belle S. Roberts, Frank Telenga, M. Cook, J. A. Painter and J. Coghlan. Lemke agreed to pay 8 per cent interest from November 19, 1921. The loans were eventually refinanced through William J. Lane & Company. Lemke did not finish paying for the house until the mid-1940's, when he was past 65 years of age. Like the Land Finance Company, his house proved to be a life-long burden which interrupted the logical development of his career.

in Washington, D.C., conferring with Gartner on the grain grading case, counseled against the post-election court challenge, and the movement to do so made no further progress.[63]

An era in North Dakota history was closed and Lemke's ascent up the ladder of political fame was halted. A combination of circumstances, mistakes and misfortunes had conspired to interrupt his promising public career. It was not yet six years since Wood and Townley had called on him as he was recovering from typhus to ask him to play a major part in the movement they had under way; it was less than eight years since the Bingham case had first given him the forum and the issue with which to attract the attention of agrarian leaders. It would be nearly twelve years before he would again hold office. Every evidence indicates that had it not been for the great depression, his public career would have been ended.

But Lemke's public career in the years prior to the recall was not a loss for the state or for Lemke himself. North Dakota's institutions were modified and remain so today; its marketing, banking, and governmental institutions are more concerned with the general welfare because of Lemke's part in the Nonpartisan League. The Bank of North Dakota has performed many valuable services for North Dakota and its citizens. While doing this it earned, up to March 31, 1956, a gross profit of $17,204,955.53 and a net profit of $15,328,176.56. In addition, in one bond transaction alone the Bank of North Dakota saved the taxpayers of North Dakota a total of $5,880,027.14. The bank has made credit available to political subdivisions and to citizens when it would have been more expensive and difficult to obtain elsewhere. The indirect economic benefits of the North Dakota state mill and elevator may total millions of dollars. The actual profits the mill has made are small as compared to these indirect benefits resulting from its influence on marketing and grain grading practices.*[64] What Lemke had given to the League and to the state would not go totally unrewarded. His subsequent public career in Congress and as a Presidential candidate was built on the following and reputation he had gained in North Dakota from 1916 to 1921. But he would never be elected governor or United States senator. Lemke would resume his political career twelve years later, but it would continue to be one of personal disappointment. It had been a bitter year of trial, but equally trying years lay ahead.

* Current biennium transfers to the North Dakota treasury from bank and mill-elevator profits total $4,250,000.

# CHAPTER V

# Hold Fast—
# Until the Beast Is Finished

William Lemke's public career had been interrupted. The farm depression which began in 1921 and continued until 1940 later made it possible for him to return to public life. Otherwise, it seems probable that he would never again have been able to return to a prominent public position. His reputation had been damaged, and his type of political appeal did not win sufficient votes during prosperous years. The year of the recall, however, marked the beginning of a deflationary period as disastrous and prolonged as farmers had ever experienced. Since the nation as a whole was experiencing prosperity, national sympathy and governmental remedial action were not available to the farmer. The causes of the farm deflation lay in remote, complex factors which had increased the cost of production and contracted markets. Agrarian leaders, prone to be oversuspicious and to oversimplify, saw the cost-price squeeze as the result of a conspiracy. They saw clearly, as a later writer pointed out, that "a period of ruinous deflation such as the farmers experienced in 1920–21 necessitates immediate credit if the farmers are to survive as independent farmers."[1]

Victory in the 1922 election was absolutely essential if the headquarters of the North Dakota Nonpartisan League were to remain open. The same situation prevailed in the national headquarters of the League in St. Paul. As they surveyed the debris left by the victory of the Independents, Leaguers divided into two groups. One segment of the leadership was willing to moderate the League program and agree not to extend it further. They sensed the public mood and felt that this was the only approach which would return the League to power. Other leaders were in favor of a policy of no compromise. They wished to go ahead with the program of building homes, guaranteeing

143

bank deposits, and operating the mill and elevator and the Bank of North Dakota. They advocated expanding the program of rural credits and all other phases of the League program. They were especially concerned with regard to the nearly fifty laws which had been passed to give debtors, bank depositors, and consumers greater protection, especially during this period of deflation and hardship for North Dakota's farmers and economy.* William Lemke became the leader of the group which advocated expansion of the League program. He was determined that the League should "hold fast," and his advice was that the League should refer every law passed by the Independents.

Although Lemke wrote O. E. Lofthus that he did not plan "to give up the fight until the beast is finished," he first had to put his own financial affairs in order. The League had to be pushed into the background while he considered how to make a living. The firm of Robinson and Lemke had been dissolved in 1917, and the partner who had replaced Robinson in the firm died shortly after moving to Fargo. Lemke had continued to pay rent on the office; all other services, such as electricity and telephone, had been discontinued. For all practical purposes his law practice was dead. To add to the seriousness of the situation, he had purchased a house he could not afford to pay for or maintain and had borrowed from every possible source in order to keep possession of it. The agonizing postwar deflation experienced by the nation as a whole and the Wheat Belt in particular had made the situation even more difficult. The League debacle had left a mountain of unpaid obligations which had originally been secured by accommodation notes for which Lemke was one of the major signers. The Land Finance Company was threatened with confiscation and loss of all its assets unless money was forthcoming to pay taxes. Time and again, during the 1920's, his financial situation was such that it was a major problem for him to raise twenty-five dollars.[2] He was under the constant reproach of friends and relatives from whom he had borrowed or whom he had induced to invest in the Mexican land. Defending Townley, other Leaguers, and himself against the various charges of embezzlement, malfeasance of office,

---

* The inability of farmers to pay their debts resulted in the nearly complete collapse of the banking system of North Dakota. Not including bank closings prior to the recall election, there were 573 banks which failed between 1922 and 1933 in North Dakota (Koenker, p. 134).

and perjury was a further drain on his time, energies, and financial resources. His assets were few, and only election to Congress in 1932 rescued him from a desperate financial situation which threatened bankruptcy and the loss of his home.

The reputation and prominence he had achieved as an attorney was his chief asset, but its value was limited by the reluctance of conservative business institutions to employ him. Labor unions, debtor farmers, and cases against banks and insurance companies were his major source of income. Chief among the cases which brought him income and reputation was the Williams County bank case which he and Usher L. Burdick won in 1926. This victory compelled Eastern creditors to restore $380,000 in assets which they had transferred to Twin City and Eastern institutions just before the bank's failure.[3] The case brought both revenue and reputation to the attorneys involved, and it was rumored that both attorneys had rejected financial offers in order to continue prosecution of the case.[*] The treatment accorded the conservative banking interests in the Twin Cities was moderate compared to that which the same press had given League officials when they were trying to save the Scandinavian-American Bank. A different code operated when conservative Twin City bankers were involved. Lemke commented on one instance:

> When I was acting as attorney for Williams County . . . Jeffrey, who was Chairman of the Board of Directors of the First National of Minneapolis, was invited to give a speech at the Dakota Hotel. While he was making the speech I had the sheriff serve the summons and the complaint in the case on him so as to get jurisdiction. He . . . felt that it was an ungentlemanly act.[4]

Lemke perhaps remembered the summons served on Frazier in Jamestown just prior to the recall election or the procedure followed in the initial investigation of the Scandinavian-American Bank.

Two cases involving labor won Lemke the confidence of North Dakota unions. During the railroad strike of 1922 he was more successful than union attorneys from other states in obtaining federal court rulings favorable to labor. This was due partly to Judge Charles F. Amidon's liberal inclination. Later he successfully prosecuted a case against the Great Northern Railroad for the shooting and

---

[*] Usher L. Burdick recalled that offers to employ Lemke and himself came at this particular time and were refused (interview with Usher L. Burdick, October 30, 1954).

wounding of one of the strikers, Adolph Purpur of Grand Forks.*
Lemke handled the case on a contingent fee arrangement, and the
award of several thousand dollars was one of the few major strokes
of good fortune he experienced during the 1920's. These cases, combined with his League reputation, brought him many less remunera-
tive cases from debtors who were often unjustly treated by banks,
machine companies, and other business institutions. However, by
1925 Lemke's financial position had improved somewhat. Lemke was
able to refinance his mortgage and pay many of his friends. By one
means or another, he had discharged most of the various accommodation notes he had signed. He continued to pay on his debts just
what was necessary to satisfy his creditors, using the balance of his
income to prevent the Mexican government from confiscating the
property of the Land Finance Company. To prevent total confiscation
and loss of everything the stockholders had invested, title to the land
was transferred to Lemke.† Lemke became particularly bitter during
these years at the insurance companies, which seemed to him often
to be unjust both to policy holders and to the farmers whose mortgages they had purchased.‡ His legal reputation spread to other
states, and one Iowa Farmers Union leader, observing him in court
in 1924, noted "a capacity to reach for the jugular" and "a relentless
grip upon it once he had taken hold."[5]

During the twenties Lemke showed the same affinity for new commercial ideas conceived in terms of great future possibilities that he
had evidenced in years before the rise of the League. Not one to toy

* In this case Lemke again maneuvered cleverly to win. He feared that the
method of jury selection used in federal court would make up a panel of anti-
labor and conservative persons. To make certain that the railroads could not use
diverse citizenship as a reason for transferring the case from the Minnesota to
the federal courts, Lemke had Purpur move from Grand Forks, North Dakota, to
East Grand Forks, Minnesota.

† Upon his death in 1950 the expense of probating delayed settlement. The
investors, including the Lemke family, lost a sum that totaled approximately
$400,000, only partially reimbursed by the Mexican Claims Commission. For
them, as well as for Lemke, the entire episode was a tragedy.

‡ During the 1940's Ken Fitch would be a bitter opponent of Lemke, and he
probably prevented Lemke from being endorsed for the United States Senate in
1946. Lemke attributed Fitch's opposition to the influence of the liquor interests,
but Ole Gunvaldsen stated that it may have been due to "Lemke's . . . inauguration
of a number of laws that were applicable to insurance companies" (Ole Gunvaldsen to author, April 9, 1957).

with small enterprises, he readily embraced a major undertaking. Such was the New Way Harvester Company,* which he was certain would revolutionize the traditional process of binding and threshing throughout the Wheat Belt from Texas to northern Canada.[6] Like the Land Finance Company, the enterprise absorbed Lemke's enthusiasm, time, and capital without the returns that had been expected. Very moderate compensation from the Farmers Union was all that sustained him from 1930 to 1932, and his financial situation grew increasingly critical. The Farmers Union was having its own financial difficulties in the years from 1929 through 1932. All it could pay Lemke was a little above expenses which was hardly enough for the current operations of his home.

It had been a complex story and, for Lemke, a disheartening one that eventually brought him to the point where he would accept candidacy on the same ticket as William Langer, an eventuality which Lemke had regarded as impossible. Lemke had been certain that the recall defeat was temporary and that the League would regain power in 1922. This hope proved illusory except in the case of the United States senatorship; the League, because of the disagreement between McCumber and the Independents, was able to retain the advantage in the contest for senator that it had held in all election contests before the consolidation of League opposition into one organization. Partly because of Governor R. A. Nestos' policy of carrying out much of the League industrial program and partly due to the constant legal harassment of A. C. Townley, Lemke, and other League leaders, it was difficult in all other election contests for the League to make a convincing case to the voters. The League was further divided because A. A. Liederbach and his followers were willing to work with William Langer and Asle J. Gronna, a course of action that League extremists such as Lemke would not then contemplate. Gronna's Dakota friends made loans to Liederbach to enable him to continue publication of the *Courier-News*,[7] and during the winter of 1922 the editorial policies of the League's daily newspaper were

---

* The New Way Harvester cut the grain and fed it into a large circular drum. The drum stacked the grain into circular stacks the size of small hay stacks. It had the advantage of turning the heads into the center of the stack and thus protecting them from weathering. It eliminated the necessity of employing men to shock the grain. It never came into general use. The coming of the combine and adverse business conditions in the pre-depression years caused the company to disappear with little public notice. (William Lemke, jr., to author, February 28, 1963).

written with the intention of diminishing the influence of both Townley
and Lemke.

Lemke was determined in early 1922 to unseat the Liederbach
faction and to regain control of the League. He was particularly
angered by the failure of the *Courier-News* to defend itself against
a libel suit brought by Langer. In 1920 the League daily had accused
Langer of soliciting a slush fund. Langer alleged this was libelous
and brought suit against the paper and against Lemke as a co-
defendant. Lemke left for Mexico in the winter of 1922 believing he
had an understanding with the Liederbach faction to do nothing
without consulting Lemke's attorney, Vince A. Day. While he was
in Mexico, the *Courier-News* printed a full retraction written by
Langer, the effect of which, if believed by the readers, would have
been to discredit Townley and Lemke completely. Furious at what
had happened, Lemke prepared for the League convention to be
held in Fargo in the spring of 1922. He sent a letter explaining his
viewpoint to each county chairman to be read at each county convention. Lemke cited that he had always done the legal work of the
*Courier-News* without charge and that it was Liederbach, Ole Kaldor,
and P. L. Aarhus who were attacking him. At the state convention
the two men on the state committee who were loyal to Lemke, Walter
Maddock and R. H. Walker, argued for the election of a new state
committee. They offered to resign in the interest of harmony. At the
same time Townley offered to resign as president of the National
Nonpartisan League if it would end the schism. This placed the
Liederbach group in a position where they were compelled to resign
or appear responsible for League disunity. When they resigned, a new
committee was elected, and the Liederbach faction was no longer
in control.[8] The convention had been large and unwieldy, and it
had not been easy to accomplish this maneuver.

The convention had many problems in addition to Liederbach.
Besides changing its Executive Committee, it had to nominate state
officers, to decide whether to oppose Porter J. McCumber or not, and
to determine its relationship with Lemke and Townley. When Liederbach resigned, any chance that the convention might endorse Gronna
disappeared. Although Lemke had successfully defended himself
against the charges of the *Courier-News* and had assisted in ousting
Liederbach, he still was suffering from the effects of the recall campaign, particularly those which related to his home, and from the
feeling of many influential delegates that his extremism would

frighten middle-of-the-road voters. This prevented him from receiving the senatorial or any other nomination. Lemke himself was no problem to the convention; as long as he could overthrow the Liederbach faction and be certain that the candidates were strong believers in the League industrial program, he was willing to campaign vigorously even though he was not a nominee. Lemke's attitude is best described in his own words:

I do not know what part I will take in the campaign as there seems to be a feeling that the time has arrived for using the soft peddle [sic], and I know that I believe in a straight ahead on collission [sic], and it may be that those who are in charge of the campaign will not consider those the best tactics which will be perfectly agreeable to me.[9]

How to adjust to Townley's leadership was a more difficult matter. Having completed the jail sentence in Minnesota, A. C. Townley was attempting to resume leadership of League activities. He had come to the conclusion that the farmers, through their Nonpartisan League organization, should abandon the practice of acting as a political faction and follow the tactics of the Anti-Saloon League, i.e., throw the support of their organization to those party-nominated candidates and formulated platform planks which pleased them most. Originally Townley had not planned to have the League enter national politics, and the organization he had created had evolved into something nearer a political party than he may have intended. For this Lemke had been partly responsible. In 1922 Townley wanted to return to a plan which would place its emphasis on members who would pay dues. Titling his new theory the "balance of power" plan, Townley came to the state convention at Fargo prepared to put up a major fight for it. Lemke had stood united with Townley in the fight against Liederbach, but he was violently opposed to Townley's new plan of action.[10]

Again Gutzon Borglum entered the League picture and played a determining role. Angry at the failure of Harding to reward the League with patronage, and furious because he was convinced that the Republican high command had cooperated with the League's opponents, Borglum did all he could to prevent the adoption of the balance of power plan, urging nomination of a candidate to replace McCumber. His plea to Townley and his promise to raise campaign funds helped defeat the balance of power plan. Good as his word, he later raised thousands of dollars among Eastern liberals and forwarded the money to the League.[11]

With the balance of power plan defeated, the next problem was to choose candidates. Here again the Lemke extremist, or radical, wing of the party triumphed. With the exception of Lemke's own absence from the ticket, the convention's choice could not have suited him better. He was responsible for the selection of Lynn J. Frazier as a candidate, this time for the United States Senate seat held by Porter J. McCumber.[12] B. F. Baker, a close friend of Lemke's, was nominated for governor. Lemke's success in bringing about the nomination of his protégé and closest friend for senator made less painful the fact that but for the scandal about the Lemke house and the thin margin of defeat the preceding fall, Lemke himself might have been running for governor or senator. Lemke probably felt that he himself was better equipped to serve as senator than was Frazier; one redeeming feature from his viewpoint, however, was that he would have much to say about the conduct of the office should Frazier be elected.

In the interim between the convention and the election, Attorney General Sveinbjorn Johnson succeeded in having a grand jury return indictments against Lemke, Townley, and a number of others. These charged irregular and criminal conduct in the handling of the affairs of the Scandinavian-American Bank. Townley was first accused of having caused the embezzlement of $3,000 from the bank, a charge that was dismissed when it developed that the alleged item was a loan to the United States Sisal Trust which had been repaid three months after it had been borrowed. Lemke, Townley, and the others were then charged with conspiracy to redeposit Bank of North Dakota money in the Scandinavian-American Bank when the latter's insolvent condition was being concealed by their efforts. This charge was made just before the primaries, leaving the accused the doubtful alternatives of fighting the action and foregoing any part in the campaign, or postponing the actions until after the election. The latter course was adopted, although their effectiveness as campaigners was impaired because of the indictments against them. The same technique was followed by Johnson in the fall some six weeks before the general election. By this time, however, even lukewarm Leaguers began to suspect that there was more of persecution than prosecution in the treatment being accorded Lemke. Johnson had failed to gather the evidence necessary, although he had used many inducements to get J. J. Hastings to testify against them. The cases were finally dismissed

by Judge George M. McKenna in April, 1923, after having served one
of their purposes—the interruption of Lemke's career for a much
longer time than would have otherwise been the case.*[13]

With the exception of winning the Republican senatorial nomination
for Frazier, the primary election of 1922 was not a League success.
Frazier's victory was a real consolation to Lemke and ample reward
for Borglum, who in his anger at Harding and the Republicans now
set out to organize liberals for the purpose of purging the Senate
of all Republican conservatives. The Independents and the Democrats
had worked together closely, meanwhile, holding their conventions
at Jamestown.[14] A leading Independent, J. F. T. O'Connor, was the
Democratic nominee for United States senator. O'Connor's friends in
the Independent convention succeeded in preventing the endorsement
of McCumber; a number of them may have felt that it would be more
difficult for O'Connor to overcome McCumber than it would be to
defeat Frazier and therefore they voted in the primary to nominate
Frazier. Soon after the primary it became apparent to Leaguers that
O'Connor had a very good chance of defeating Frazier.

This presented Leaguers with a problem. If they advocated voting
Republican in the fall in order to elect Frazier, they would be supporting Governor R. A. Nestos, the Independent who had been nominated to succeed himself in the Republican primary. If they supported
the Democratic candidate for governor against Nestos, they ran the
risk of giving votes to O'Connor and defeating Frazier. Like the one-
party states of the Solid South, North Dakota had kept the party
column ballot instead of adopting the office group ballot as had
Minnesota and Montana. As a result, support of any one candidate in

---

* Newspapers in the East discredited Lemke, and the false rumor was circulated that Lemke had served in jail with Townley. The crucifying nature of the
prosecution is made plain in a private letter to Lemke from his attorney: "When
I resumed the practise of law about twenty years ago I highly resolved that I
would not try any lawsuit through the newspapers or on the street corners and
to date I have kept that resolve religiously, but I find that I am greatly tempted
now to 'take my pen in hand' and review this whole matter of the prosecutions
of these defendants. For general public information and in justice to the defendants some one who knows the facts and is capable of presenting them clearly
and intelligently ought to do this. I do not like to do this but I may feel that
I *must* do it." Lemke was less restrained, writing that he had been "double
crossed, deceived, tricked perhaps more than any other man in this state" (W. L.
Lauder to William Lemke, April 17, 1923; William Lemke to J. Sinclair, June 9,
1923; both Lemke Papers).

a party column brought votes to every candidate in the column to a much greater extent than would have been the case with the office group ballot.

The entire problem was considered by Leaguers at a post-primary convention. Lemke discovered that his status at this convention was nearly as great as it had been before the recall election. The willingness of Sveinbjorn Johnson to postpone Lemke's trial had now convinced Leaguers that the case against him was weak. The vigorous campaign he had waged for Frazier and the ticket, together with the unanimity that had resulted from the ouster of the Liederbach faction, had completely changed the attitude of League delegates toward him. In the spring meeting they had been willing to have him exert leadership behind the scenes, but they had been unwilling to endorse him. There were no further demands at the July meeting that Lemke or the League industrial program be "soft peddled." Unable in mid-July to determine exactly what course to pursue, but anxious that a vigorous policy be followed, the convention appointed a committee of fifteen to determine whether a third party ticket should be nominated and a candidate selected to run for governor against Nestos. The composition of the committee was such that the decision was really left to Lemke, and he had the option of becoming a candidate for governor if he were willing to make the race.[15] By running on a third party ticket, Lemke would be complying with the requirements of the North Dakota statute providing for the appearance of a new party on the primary ballot—a decision that would be of importance in later elections as well as in this one.

Lemke was very anxious to elect Frazier and to defeat O'Connor in the senatorial race. The thought of federal appointments going to the Independents—a certain result if O'Connor defeated Frazier—was abhorrent. If Frazier could win, the League would have two senators, both of whom would accept patronage advice from Lemke. In considering whether to run or not, Lemke probably felt he had a possibility of winning, and he was always optimistic once he was involved in a campaign. However, there was the obvious probability of defeat inherent in being in a new party column. Too, throughout 1922, he was being constantly harassed with indictments and prosecution for alleged malfeasance and corruption. Added to this was Lemke's own financial situation,* and the fact that Borglum was unwilling to supply

---

* Before the election was over Lemke wrote his brother Ben: "I will be in Cando and other parts of Towner County in about the middle of the month, and

funds for candidates other than Frazier in the fall election. But the determining considerations were his eagerness to see Frazier elected, the knowledge that he would be able to give Frazier more assistance than any other potential candidate, and his desire to give everything he had for what to him was a cause.

Lemke's primary objective was to defeat O'Connor. The charge was later made that religious prejudice had injured O'Connor.* Lemke did not attempt to arouse the religious prejudice against O'Connor that the Ku Klux Klan movement of that period would have made possible, but he found a vulnerable point in O'Connor's record that could be used with telling effect. The grain grading laws of North Dakota had been held unconstitutional the preceding February. Lemke remembered that O'Connor, as a private attorney, had been identified as one of the attorneys for the plaintiffs who had originally brought the suit questioning the constitutionality of the law. Lemke drafted a new law to replace the one declared unconstitutional, had petitions circulated, and succeeded in placing it on the 1922 general election ballot. By making it an election issue, Lemke had created an opportunity to discuss the issue and emphasize O'Connor's association with it.[16] More than any other campaign stratagem, that one elected Frazier and defeated O'Connor.

In spite of his serious financial difficulties, and although he was under criminal indictment, Lemke campaigned with the same complete forgetfulness of his own health and strength that was characteristic of his past campaigns. The strain told, and one of the few occasions occurred when frustration and anger caused him to demean himself publicly. Shortly before the election in a speech before the Eddy County courthouse in New Rockford, he had spoken at length on the number of false names such as those of children and even babies that had been included on the recall petitions. J. R. Hobbs of

---

will be completely broke at that time, and will need $150.00 for the campaign. Will ask you to kindly make arrangements to assist me to that extent when I see you during the campaign in Towner County" (William Lemke to Ben Lemke, October 1, 1922, Lemke Papers).

* This may have been the case in 1922. In 1920, however, the last time O'Connor had run, O'Connor had received the most votes of the three Independent candidates running for the Industrial Commission. Of the three League candidates running for the same position, John Hagan had received the most votes. If any conclusion could be drawn from that election, it was a disadvantage to be a Protestant; the two Roman Catholic candidates—one on each ticket— were the most successful candidates on their respective tickets.

Maddock spoke up from the crowd to say that "no babies voted in the recall election, and it was the election, not the petitions which put the N.P.L. out." According to the *Fargo Forum,* Lemke, white with rage, shouted: "You snipe, you rattlesnake, you rat, come up here, you snipe, come up here you rattlesnake."[17] Many times during the campaign he asserted that in 1919 he had been offered $150,000 to break with the League. He offered no proof, and his mere statement did not convince enough voters to enable him to defeat Nestos.

Only the League candidates who had been nominated in the June primary succeeded in the November election. This included Frazier, who won over O'Connor by a margin of just under 9,000 votes. His total vote was some 20,000 more than Lemke received. Lemke's total of 81,048 was insufficient to defeat Nestos, who polled 110,321. Still, Lemke's vote was very impressive for a third party candidate and there was little question that his candidacy had been a major factor in Frazier's success. The effectiveness of Lemke's grain grading law in defeating O'Connor was indicated by the total vote on the measure. There were 138,735 votes for the measure and only 44,406 against it. One ironic feature of the election was the opposition to Lemke of Warren Stone and some other ranking national labor leaders. As a result of the recall campaign Lemke was thoroughly discredited in the East. It is probable that Stone had met Lemke during the latter's bond selling campaign and had formed an unfavorable opinion of him. Stone was not at all evasive in his stand and wrote Lemke:

> The old crowd of the Non-Partisan League again got into power and put you on the ticket as Governor. It may be that the situation is so bad in Dakota that you can be elected. However, I doubt it very much and I think it is a mistake, if you will allow me to say so, for you to head the ticket in the State of North Dakota. I think all you will succeed in doing is ... defeat the election of Mr. Frazier.[18]

Stone added that no money and no campaigners would be given to what he regarded as a lost cause.

Of all the candidates labor should have favored, Lemke ranked at the top. Not only had he been a successful attorney for union labor in 1922, but his entire League record had been one which included the drafting of liberal labor legislation. Labor union locals in North Dakota in many instances disregarded the advice of their national leaders and supported Lemke. Other features of the campaign worthy of note included the statement later made by Lemke that the Republican National Committee spent $10,000 to elect O'Connor and to defeat Frazier, and that corporations and public utilities were very desirous of seeing Lemke's defeat. No stone had been left unturned by the daily press. Lemke maintained that his election would prove that his recall from office had been unjust and that his election as governor would vindicate him. The *Fargo Forum* ridiculed his desire for vindication, arguing in an editorial that "he will have an opportunity to secure it [vindication] before a jury in the criminal courts when his case comes to trial."[19]

The election of Frazier was gratifying to Lemke, as had been the many national contacts he himself had made during the year, including individuals with such varying backgrounds as Robert La Follette, Henry Ford, Mark Sullivan, and Upton Sinclair. Sinclair had obtained some of the material for *The Goosestep* from Lemke. The death of Gronna had paved the way for cooperation with La Follette, and the latter had, for the first time, come to North Dakota to campaign for the League.*

As interesting and important as these considerations may be, there was no way in which Lemke could ignore his own personal position. He had again neglected his law practice and had borrowed additional funds from close friends and relatives. He was a defeated candidate, practically penniless, and still under criminal indictment in the courts of the state. During the weeks after the election he devoted himself to the problem created by the accommodation paper on which he and so many other Leaguers were liable as a result of League financial disaster. The League caucus of the 1923 legislature employed him as their leader and legal adviser to combat A. G. Divet, who was serving in a similar capacity for the Independents. Although for the minority faction, this work kept him in the center of affairs and provided a moderate source of income. It was gratifying to Lemke to be where he could prevent damage to the industrial program and stop any alteration of the election laws.†

The legislative session ended with Lemke's prestige restored in

---

* La Follette's autobiography was one of the books which Lemke read on his 1922 trip to Mexico, and he regarded it as one of the most significant books he had read. There can be little doubt that La Follette's uncompromising steadfastness and high ideals of public service were influential factors in Lemke's life.

† The Independent majority did succeed in passing changes in the election laws similar to those which had been defeated at the time of the 1921 recall election; however, the League successfully referred them in 1924.

League circles. He was the hero of the League's senatorial victory of
the preceding year. In March, 1923, there was no reason to believe
that a resurgence of League political power would not result in his
return to public office. He was a leader of the regular Leaguers, whose
motto was "No retreat." Since the convention in March, 1922, these
Leaguers had been in control, and the other groups seeking to gain
ascendancy in the League had been discredited and for a time seemed
no longer to exist. While the criminal indictment still had not been
dismissed, it was not the source of concern or dismay it once had been
either to Lemke or his friends. Just a few weeks after the session, the
judge dismissed the charges. There was nothing to indicate that within
a short time Lemke himself would be discredited in the eyes of
many Leaguers and his leadership so weakened that the moderate
Leaguers would be able to capture the League organization.

The sale of the *Courier-News* was the event which ended Lemke's
dominance of the organization. There had been not only a conviction
among all Leaguers that the future of the League lay in keeping its
daily newspaper alive, but also an awareness of the precarious nature
of its finances. Suffering from an advertising boycott, the paper had
found it very difficult to obtain newsprint and to meet payrolls, and
there were rumors during the legislative session that the paper was
up for sale to avoid its capture by conservative creditors. A general
protest arose against the sale of the paper, as well as a demand that
it be turned over to the League. Townley, Lemke, and Wood held
title to the paper, as they had from the first. They were reluctant, as
they had been in 1921, to surrender the control to a League convention,where it might fall into the hands of the "pie counter brigade,"
"the pink tea crowd," and the "trimmers"—Lemke's favorite terms for
those Leaguers who, he judged, were more concerned about winning
elections than forwarding the League program. A League convention
was called for March 2 and 3, 1923, just at the close of the legislative
session. To forestall an ultimatum for transfer of title of the paper,
Lemke went before the convention and pledged that Townley, Wood,
and he himself would under no circumstances sell the *Courier-News*
without first giving the League, assembled in convention, opportunity
to assume control of the paper. Lemke's speech and pledge enabled
Herbert Swett, his close associate during the session, to move successfully that the ownership of the *Courier-News* should rest with Townley, Lemke, and Wood so long as the paper continued to stand for the

principles of the League.[20] The outcome was a disappointment to the moderates and particularly so to John Andrews, a staff member of the *Courier-News,* who blamed extremist Leaguers for the business troubles of the paper he was helping to edit. Lemke felt it necessary to give this assurance to prevent a controversy which would injure both the newspaper and the League.*

It was Lemke's inability to fulfill the pledge he had made that terminated his political domination of the League and enabled the moderates to seize control. For once Lemke was unable to restrain Townley and Wood. Convinced that the *Courier-News* could not be saved and concerned about its creditors, Townley determined to sell it and convinced Wood of the wisdom of doing so. Townley and Wood felt that if they did not act, the paper would fall into the hands of conservative creditors. If any news of the move reached the public, the sale of the paper would have been prevented by those creditors. Townley and Wood knew Lemke's opposition; knowing that Lemke would make a public fight out of the transaction, they moved quietly. Lemke was unaware until an hour or two before the sale was completed in the pre-dawn hours of April 18 that such a move was under way. Lemke took steps to obtain an injunction, but H. A. Paddock, who was handling the transaction for Townley, moved rapidly and completed the sale before Lemke could act.[21] On April 17 the paper appeared as usual; the edition for April 18 was printed but never mailed. Without notice to Leaguers or to subscribers, the *Courier-News* as a Nonpartisan League publication was terminated. Terminated also was Lemke's undisputed leadership of the North Dakota Nonpartisan League. Although Lemke had prevented the sale of the paper twice before and this sale had been made over his dis-

---

* Townley later said that Lemke had no right to make such a promise, and that neither Wood nor Townley had authorized him to do so. Townley contended that the *Courier-News* had to be sold to protect the men who had advanced money to the paper. One Leaguer, John Felver, had used trust funds, and if the paper could not be sold for sufficient funds to reimburse him, he would have been in serious legal difficulty. Lemke, according to Townley, was oblivious to these considerations and argued that if the paper were continued, it could be made profitable enough to meet the obligations to Felver and others. Townley very reasonably maintained that past experience indicated that Lemke was unrealistically optimistic, and the founder of the League denied any desire to kill the organization he had created. Some of his critics—but not Lemke—alleged that Townley did not want the League to continue if he himself could not control it (interview with A. C. Townley, July 1, 1957).

senting vote, his position was never clearly enough understood by all groups within the League for him to regain fully the power he had once held.*

The haste and secrecy surrounding the transaction made it easy to believe rumors. John Andrews and P. L. Aarhus immediately started a weekly paper known as *The Progressive,* whose political stock in trade was to capitalize on the suspicion and distrust of Lemke created by the sale of the *Courier-News,* always stressing Lemke's unqualified pledge that the League would be informed before any sale was consummated.[22] The Nonpartisan League existed as a faction of the Republican party until after Lemke's death, but the regulars— the old-guard, extremist, radical Leaguers of Lemke's type, who were committed to the expansion of the League industrial program—never again gained sufficient influence to control the League and win an election with it. When in ensuing years they controlled the nominations, they subsequently lost the elections. From this time forward it was either the moderate Leaguers, the Langer group, or a coalition of League factions which could use the League organization to win elections.

The timing of this loss of control was particularly unfortunate for Lemke, for it was only a short time later that the death of Edwin F. Ladd left a vacancy in the United States Senate for which Lemke would have been the most logical, almost the inevitable candidate of the League. But for the *Courier-News* episode, it is probable that Gerald P. Nye would not have been the League's choice to succeed Ladd. Lemke was again preoccupied with his own personal affairs. At the time he did not realize how much of a blow to his own political fortunes the sale of the *Courier-News* had been, and it was not until the loss of control of the 1924 League convention to the group backing Arthur G. Sorlie that he fully understood how completely he had been removed from a position of leadership. For the moment he continued his legal activities, and gradually worked toward disentanglement from the accommodation paper he had signed for the League and toward discharge from the criminal indictments still pending against him. He again engaged a partner, Harry

---

* Indicative of the relationship of the three men was the fact that no permanent ill feelings resulted. Lemke perhaps realized that he had erred in not keeping the others fully informed and in not being realistic about the financial situation of the *Courier-News.* Though momentarily angry at being by-passed, he later resumed friendly relations with Townley and Wood, who, living in the Twin Cities, were both out of touch with North Dakota and not fully aware of the compromising situation into which they were placing Lemke.

A. Weaver, stipulating that he must be one "who knows how to charge and collect . . . and who attends to details," as "those are my weak points as I see them." While Andrews charged in *The Progressive* that Lemke had sold the *Courier-News* because of jealousy of profits the paper was beginning to earn, Lemke did not believe that many Leaguers would take the charges seriously. When the League convened in October there was some disaffection, but Lemke was not alarmed until the press accounts which Andrews released gave those who were not in attendance an anti-Lemke interpretation of convention proceedings.[23]

Had Lemke taken vigorous steps in the latter months of 1923, he might successfully have combated the moderates who were seeking to dethrone him, or he could have used the third party created by the 1922 general election to make the Nonpartisan League a party in its own right. This would have left the moderates in control of only a portion of the League, with no possibility of defeating the Independents. Such a threat would have prevented the moderates from seizing the League machinery and nominating Sorlie. The main reason Lemke did not take the steps necessary to block the moderates was a patronage mirage that temporarily immobilized him politically.

Both Ladd and Frazier had permitted Lemke to handle their patronage decisions; they had recognized Lemke as leader of the League in North Dakota. It is not certain whether the idea originated with Lemke or Ladd, but in late October, 1923, Ladd recommended to President Calvin Coolidge that Lemke be appointed as ambassador to Mexico. The situation there had stabilized, and the United States had recognized the Obregon government. Lemke's knowledge of Mexican conditions, the fact that Lemke was on good terms with Obregon, having once been captured and protected by him, and Lemke's fluent use of the language, coupled with his close association with two Republican United States senators, all were cogent reasons advanced by Ladd. Coolidge's response to Ladd was not discouraging:

> Your letter of the first has been received. I note your cordial recommendation of Hon. William Lemke for appointment as Ambassador to Mexico. I have heard many fine things about him, and I am particularly glad to know of your high estimate of his qualifications. When the question of this appointment is before me, his name, you may be sure, will have careful consideration.[24]

The possibilities for recouping the losses sustained by the Land Finance Company were obvious; equally clear was the advisability that Lemke abandon activities which would point him out to the

President as a radical. Abstaining from his normal activities as leader of the League, he gave all of his energies to the campaign to obtain the ambassadorship. Combined with the disaffection created by the *Courier-News* sale, his inactivity practically gave the League organization to the new leadership.

Lemke's enemies in North Dakota did everything they could to prevent him from receiving the appointment. Although anxious for the ambassadorship, Lemke was inclined to think privately that his economic views would offend the business interests who backed the Coolidge administration. He expressed these doubts in a letter to Carl Thompson of the Public Ownership League:

> I will not personally make any bargain or agreement with any person, and if I go as Ambassador to Mexico will go unpledged and untied to do that which I think is best for our country. . . . I am more firmly converted to State ownership than ever before. . . . May state further to you, confidentially, that I do not believe that the President will be permitted to appoint me . . . let us make a test of it and see. . . .[25]

The Independents and the Andrews-Aarhus moderates in the League vied with one another in calling Coolidge's attention to Lemke's opposition to R. A. Nestos, the regular Republican nominee for governor, in the general election of 1922. It was to counteract this propaganda that Lemke stayed away from political activity in December, 1923, and January, 1924, going so far as to absent himself from the League convention in the latter month. His enemies not only succeeded in blocking his appointment but used the time when he was preoccupied with obtaining it to capture the League organization from him. It was the second time that the Mexican investment was to interfere with his leadership of the League. The Republicans were certainly correct in viewing Lemke's party regularity with suspicion. Not only had he run against the Republican nominee in 1922; he had also indicated as early as the summer of 1923 his willingness to support Henry Ford or William Gibbs McAdoo on the Democratic ticket in the event the Republicans nominated a conservative for President in 1924.

The moderates, anxious to find a winning candidate who would finance the 1924 campaign of the League, accepted Arthur G. Sorlie, a well-to-do businessman of Grand Forks, of whose willingness to finance the League they had been assured.[26] In Lemke's absence, his followers were not able to block Sorlie's nomination; reluctantly they accepted the nomination of Walter Maddock, the man whom Lemke and his followers had wanted as the gubernatorial candidate, for lieutenant governor. Shortly after the convention was adjourned,

Lemke realized that he had no chance of receiving an appointment of any kind from the Coolidge administration. It was too late; the League had nominated a candidate for governor who deemed Lemke so unimportant that he avoided him on many of the trips he made to Fargo during and after the campaign. Lemke considered the suggestion of many of his followers that the League file as a third party and leave the moderates high and dry in the Republican column. When he decided to try this tactic, the attorney general ruled that the law did not apply in this instance because the League was not a national party.[27]

The presence of Maddock and another loyal friend and radical Leaguer, Bert F. Baker, among the nominees finally brought Lemke into the campaign. Baker and Sorlie were in a serious auto accident early in May. Baker was killed and Sorlie hospitalized for several weeks.* Lemke campaigned vigorously for the ticket, hopeful that his efforts would be insufficient to nominate Sorlie. He revealed his true feelings to Covington Hall when he wrote: "I feel confident that unless the so-called League candidates are nominated in June that the trimmers will be swept out of the organization and a complete new line up [sic]. That will be the hour for us to strike." Political errors made by Nestos and the disintegration of the Independent organization gave Sorlie the advantage. The Independents had been held together by fear of the League. By its own success the Independent organization had weakened itself and lost major sources of revenue. Nestos had vetoed the appropriations for the Bottineau School of Forestry and for a bridge across the Missouri. These factors, plus the candidacy of I. J. Moe, which deprived Nestos of many Barnes County votes, permitted Sorlie to win by the narrow margin of 2,317 votes. The "trimmers" were swept into office; the hour to strike never arrived. Lemke was faced with the fact that the moderate Leaguers not only had won control of the League but had defeated the Independent candidate for the Republican nomination. Lemke had been ready with a third party slate which he had planned to file by petition after the elimination of Sorlie. He had drafted a set of initiated measures as campaign issues for the third party candidates to advocate.[28] When Sorlie was nominated, neither the third party candidates nor the measures were filed. There was nothing left for Lemke to do but to accept what had happened and to concentrate on supporting Robert La Follette in the latter's bid to defeat Coolidge.

* In later campaigns, Baker's widow, Berta, was elected to state office, serving in one or another of the major offices of the state until 1957.

Only an ambassadorial appointment could have caused Lemke to support another conservative Republican for President. To avoid splitting the liberal vote, he had advised La Follette to withdraw from the North Dakota Presidential primary in favor of Hiram Johnson. When Coolidge was nominated by the Republicans, Lemke did all he could to encourage North Dakota Democrats to support McAdoo. Choice of the New Yorker, John Davis, as a Democratic nominee destroyed any chance that party had of winning the farm belt, and Lemke gave his whole-hearted support to La Follette's third party candidacy. Sorlie, more conservative than the League which nominated him, hesitated to endorse La Follette; to compel him to do so, members of Lemke's faction of the League met in Jamestown and nominated Lemke to run for governor against Sorlie. The action had been taken without Lemke's prior consent, yet Lemke was greatly tempted to accept. Had the Democratic candidate for governor been a liberal, Lemke would have undertaken the campaign. Because Halvor Halvorson, the Democratic candidate, who probably would have been the beneficiary of his candidacy, was more opposed to the League industrial program than was Sorlie, Lemke declined the nomination.[29]

Had Lemke stayed in the race, North Dakota would probably have voted for La Follette instead of for Coolidge. Lemke had hoped to have employment from the national committee of the La Follette organization, but they refused him speaking engagements except in North Dakota and in border Minnesota communities because they were afraid he would frighten the small-businessmen from the La Follette camp. To Lemke this was a policy of timidity and a major explanation of La Follette's failure to carry more of the farm belt states. Lemke was capable of political maneuvers that took advantage of all the rules. Yet he was a firm believer in democratic principles. When some La Follette men who were electors on the Republican ballot threatened to stay on the ballot rather than to withdraw—a tactic the Dixiecrats followed in four states in 1948—Lemke was indignant. "The old gang may be able to play politics but the Progressives must play the game square," he wrote Ladd.[30] It was unthinkable to Lemke that North Dakotans were to be denied the chance to vote for Coolidge. Lemke was often ill-tempered, but he was not illiberal.

The 1925 legislature was the first since 1915 in which Lemke was not present as a prominent figure in the League caucus. For a decade he had been the League's mentor and director behind the scenes, a mixture of ability, eccentricity, and mystery, whose absence would make this an unusual session to the legislators, scarcely any of whom could remember when Lemke had not been a dominating feature of the legislative session. Ralph Ingerson, state senator and a Lemke devotee, tactfully informed Lemke that he had been dismissed from his customary role:

... The caucus has hired Mr. Crum and he is all right but in this line of work cannot hit your pace. However, we may get by. I hope you will be able to get down here, although a good many of the boys (almost all of whom are very friendly to you) believe you might be a disrupting influence if you should be retained by some of us who would like to make such a move. I am confident some money could be raised to take care of your expense and you could then stay with us a while, at least, without too great a sacrifice on your part. The rumor is current here that you will be here after you are through at Bowbells.[31]

Walter Maddock, lieutenant governor and another devoted Lemke follower, wrote that the "caucus paid you a fine tribute but voted not to engage your services for the Session . . . heard that Dave Hamilton got the floor and paid you one of the finest tributes one man could pay another."[32]

Lemke's loss of power came at a most unfortunate time for him. The opportunity that would have brought his career to full fruition lay just ahead. It was another link in the chain of frustration and disappointment for Lemke that events brought Gerald P. Nye, an obscure small-town newspaper publisher, into the public eye and made him one of the most prominent men in the United States. Nye, a native of Wisconsin, came from Iowa in 1916 to edit a small newspaper at Fryburg, North Dakota. In 1919 he moved to Cooperstown, a much larger community of about 1000 people. The first mention of his name in League papers was in 1921, and it in no way indicated that he was a Leaguer of consequence. He apparently won his first attention by his editorials condemning the sale of the *Courier-News*. Nye's first recognition came from the moderate Leaguers. They had nominated him in 1924 to oppose Thomas Hall for congressman from the second district as a reward for writing these editorials. He was defeated by Hall, a permanent favorite with North Dakota voters,*

---

* Hall had served continuously as a state officer since 1914. In office before the League began, he served both as a League candidate and again after breaking with the League until 1932 without suffering a defeat. He was elected Secretary of State in 1942 and continued the choice of the electorate for that office until his voluntary retirement in January of 1955.

for few Dakotans were familiar with Nye's name. Since the sale of the *Courier-News*, the League had tried to publish a small weekly, *The NonPartisan*, at Bismarck. John Bloom, a former publisher of a Democratic daily paper in Devils Lake, who had later been with the *Courier-News*, was the editor. When Bloom died during the legislative session of 1925, Nye wrote to Lemke asking for his assistance in securing the job as editor of the *NonPartisan*.

In his letter to Lemke, he apologized for the critical editorials in his paper, stating that Bloom had informed him of Lemke's true position at the time of the sale. Nye explained: "I visited with him [Bloom] often last week. My last visit, the day before he died, brought me first knowledge of the inside story of the night which witnessed the sale of the *Courier-News*. He told me then of your call to him over the phone and result of that talk in which more than two parties had their ear to the wire." Nye proved acceptable to all factions and assumed the editorship of the *NonPartisan*, a position which brought him close to Sorlie. He continued to published his own paper at Cooperstown and came on weekends to Bismarck, where he and his brother published the four-page weekly for the League.[33]

Just a few months after Nye assumed the editorship of the *NonPartisan*, Senator Ladd died on June 22, 1925. His passing was sudden and came only a few weeks after Robert La Follette's death. The only warning Lemke had received was a note from Frazier saying that Ladd had neuritis and would take some time to recover.[34] Frazier's message indicated that Ladd was seriously but not critically ill; the news of his death and the unexpected Senate vacancy was a shock to Lemke, who was now faced with the fact that Sorlie would appoint a United States senator, a contingency far worse than any Lemke had envisioned at the time of Sorlie's election.

Had Lemke and League leaders believed that Sorlie had the power to appoint a successor to Ladd, it is barely possible that they might have been able to influence his choice. If they had had their way, the appointment would have gone to Lemke. Certainly had any of the old, regular leaders such as Maddock been governor, Lemke would have been the choice. Roy Frazier, chairman of the League executive committee, sent out a call for a July convention, which was called with the determination of naming the man whom they would demand that Sorlie appoint. Before they convened, Lemke heard from Senator Frazier that there was a legal flaw in the governor's appointing power and that there was no possibility that any man the governor would appoint could be seated unless a special session of the legislature was called expressly to grant the governor the appointing power. A decision was postponed until July 22, at which time the group was to reconvene. In a trial poll Lemke had 25 more votes than Sorlie, his closest rival. Lemke had 38 votes out of 83, Sorlie had 13, and the rest of the votes were divided among a number of candidates. In the meantime Lemke studied the statutes and concluded that Senator Frazier's information was correct. Feeling that the nomination was worthless, the group granted the governor the right to appoint whom he wished, secretly hoping that he would resign and have the lieutenant governor succeed to the governor's chair and thus give Sorlie a worthless appointment to the Senate. So hopeful was Lemke that Sorlie might make this error that he wrote the lieutenant governor asking him to appoint John Pfeiffer as his secretary should he become governor.[35] If Sorlie called a special election, Lemke was considering becoming a candidate.

Sorlie followed neither of these courses. Senator George H. Moses of New Hampshire wrote Sorlie that he had polled a large number of the senators and was positive that no one appointed would be seated. He referred to the Senate refusal to seat Frank R. Glass of Alabama, and the similarity of the North Dakota legal situation to the one occupied by Alabama on that occasion. North Dakota laws authorized the governor to fill senatorial vacancies when senators were elected by the state legislature. The contention was that this law had been nullified by adoption of the seventeenth amendment to the federal Constitution, which provided for popular election of senators and that a 1917 statute referring to state officers did not include United State senators. Sorlie did not want either a special election or a special session of the legislature at this time. He had had too much trouble with the old-time Leaguers during the regular session to wish them back for a special meeting. Arguing that a special session or a special election would be too expensive, he did nothing until November 7. He then issued a call for a special election to be held the following June 30, the same day as the primary election. This made it obvious that he could then be a candidate for the Senate seat himself, as his term as governor would be drawing to a close. There was much criticism of this action, and Nye, the commuting editor of the weekly *NonPartisan,* had caustically criticized the governor's inaction and lamented the under-representation of North Dakota in the coming session of Congress. After the governor's November 7 announcement, he was equally critical, this time in the columns of his own newspaper, writing that "Sorlie has seriously fractured his pick and shovel insofar as concerns his personal status with the progressives of the state."

Nye's task as editor was to prepare the public for League policies. Advance news releases were sent to him. As a consequence Nye had forewarning of the governor's special election proclamation, for on November 6 he wrote to R. H. Walker and fourteen other Leaguers:

Certain political conditions now prevailing are causing me to receive many appeals to take the step that would bring fifteen or so of the prominent Leaguers of the state together for a meeting at an early date. After carefully weighing these appeals, I have decided that such a meeting would be of great aid in solving the present problem. For that reason I am taking upon myself the responsibility of asking you and others to be in Bismarck on Friday, November 13th, for a meeting which will be held in one of the rooms of the McKenzie Hotel. You can learn which room by inquiring for me at the desk.

Need I urge upon you the importance of this meeting, or are you fully appreciative of the condition which now prevails? I think you are. But I do want to urge upon you the importance of keeping this meeting unannounced publicly. We want, if possible, to get together and have this thing discussed without press-agenting. I am sure you will do your part in refraining from an announcement of the meeting. However, I want you to feel free to bring with you any Leaguer you may know to be interested at this time. We shall aim to hold the meeting at 2 o'clock in the afternoon. I hope you will find it possible to be here.[36]

Nye was not prominent enough to take such action on his own initiative. It seems difficult to believe that this meeting could have been called without the governor's foreknowledge and still obtain his amiable cooperation, as it did. Nye himself has stated that he did not believe the governor knew about the call, but that Frank Vogel had told him that it was all right to proceed with the meeting. Lemke believed that Vogel was maneuvering to have James H. Sinclair, representative from the Third Congressional District, appointed in order to make it possible for Vogel to become congressman from the third district.[37]

When they were gathered, Nye acted as spokesman, stating to the governor, who had consented to come down from the capital to the meeting, that the group felt an appointment should be made, and that the governor "could appoint any one of a half dozen and the whole crowd would rally." After some discussion Sorlie tore up some hotel stationery and made improvised ballots. He had each man present indicate his choice and went out alone to count them. Coming back to the room he said: "I am surprised and I will make an appointment in the morning." To Fred Graham of Ellendale he directed his next comment, "Judge, you come up." After leaving the room, "he stuck his head back in" and said to Nye: "Jerry, you come too." According to Nye, the entire group was of the opinion that night that the choice would be Judge Graham, and that the request for Nye's presence had come because it would be his task to break the news to League members through the columns of the *NonPartisan*.

On Saturday morning, November 14, 1925, C. C. Talbott, Lars Siljan, Graham, and Nye went to the capitol, and Nye and Graham went into the governor's office. Nye's first intimation that he might be the appointee came when the governor exacted a mutual pledge that each would support the other, whichever man received the appointment. Then he announced he was going to appoint Nye, telling him, "You don't have to get out of the way for me." This was a reference to the 1926 election, intended to be interpreted that Sorlie was not giving Nye a caretaker appointment to pave the way for Sorlie's election in 1926. The governor assured Nye that he would give him the necessary financial assistance, a promise he fulfilled. It is probable that Sorlie did not expect Nye to be seated and was merely attempting to avoid filling the vacancy until such time as he could be a candidate himself. In selecting Nye, he chose the man whom the valueless appointment would hurt least, excusing himself by thinking the sudden limelight would do an unknown more good than harm, so long as someone else provided the necessary financial assistance. When Walter Maddock succeeded to the governorship after Sorlie's death, he has been reported to have found the hotel meeting ballots in Sorlie's desk with a majority of the ballots in favor of Graham.[38]

Although apprised by R. H. Walker of the secret hotel meeting, Lemke made no move. Convinced that the appointment was worthless and feeling that he knew the governor's intentions, Lemke was confident that the radical Leaguers would select him (Lemke) when election time came. As for Sorlie, his Machiavellian scheme did not work—to his own surprise and to Lemke's. The political situation in the Senate, where the Republicans were endeavoring to discipline recalcitrant members from the Middle West, had endangered Coolidge's control of that body. All that was needed to permit politics to override previous precedents was an alliance of the western "maverick" senators with the Democrats. D. H. McArthur, a Democrat from Bottineau,

North Dakota, who had been secretary to both Baer and Ladd and who was anxious to become secretary to Nye, had negotiated with Southern Democrats and insurgent Republicans to arrange such an alliance. It was he who guided Nye through the difficult battle of confirmation which, after weeks of maneuvering, resulted in Nye's being seated by a vote of 41 to 39. This coup was fatal to Sorlie's plans as well as to Lemke's. It was an unexpectedly bitter blow to Lemke to see one of his critics, a moderate who had worked with Sorlie, seated in the choicest political chair in the power of the League to give. An unknown youngster had passed him by, and it was small consolation to know that Sorlie felt equally dismayed by the unexpected development.[39]

In his disappointment at the consequences of his failure to attend the 1924 League convention, Lemke resolved to avoid another such setback by being present at the 1926 convention. His plan was to attend and to propose that the League change its name to Farmer-Labor and file as a third party, as former Leaguers were then doing in Minnesota. If the League convention refused to adopt his suggestion, he planned to take his followers and form a third party. There seems little doubt that Lemke was thinking of the third party on a national scale, and that he gave his party the same name as its Minnesota counterpart for that reason. Strategy that would have been wise in 1924, with La Follette heading the third party ticket, was not necessarily useful in 1926. When the League convention rejected his proposal, he and his followers proceeded with their plans and filed as a third party in the primary to run in the fall election against the Republican and Democratic candidates. When Nye failed to keep an earlier commitment he had made to run on the third party ticket, Lemke accepted the nomination as Farmer-Labor candidate for senator. He had misjudged the temper of the electorate, and his third party excursion of 1926 was as unsuccessful as a similar attempt on a national scale was to be when he would run for President on the Union ticket in 1936. It was the nadir of Lemke's political fortunes. Lemke, who had captured 81,048 votes as the third party candidate for governor in 1922, now received a total of 4,977 votes for United States senator against Nye, the stripling newspaper editor who, but a little over a year before, had been petitioning for Lemke's assistance to obtain the part-time job of editing a struggling weekly for the League. The weeks of controversy about his being seated had made Nye's name a household word in the nation and in North Dakota, where he polled 107,291 votes to defeat Lemke by more than twenty to one.

Though still loyal to the Farmer-Labor third party, a project he did not abandon until 1928, Lemke was less active politically during the next year or so than he had been at any time since his emergence as a public figure in 1916. Even the severe defeat he had received and the failure of Frazier to support him publicly the preceding fall did not deter him from writing to men in other states for names that might be used to build a national third party movement. The Republicans needed the votes of Nye and Frazier and, following the election of 1926, they restored their patronage rights to them, making it more difficult for Lemke to arouse enthusiasm for his third party plans. Lemke alleged that an arrangement made by Nye, Graham, and Sorlie with Butler of the Republican National Committee, whereby the Republicans gave $10,000 to the League, was what had prevented the Leaguers from joining his Farmer-Labor party. He was particularly indignant at Nye. Frazier was skeptical of Lemke's plan for a third party. However, his term did not expire until 1928, and he did not need to declare himself. The situation was discouraging, and Lemke devoted less time to politics, giving most of his attention to the New Way Harvester Company. Moreover, an increasing number of farmers who were hopelessly in debt were seeking his legal assistance.[40]

While Lemke was absenting himself from the political arena, his friends and followers were humiliating one of his political enemies and permitting another to re-enter the League. Sorlie was being effectively handled by Lemke's old-time confederates in the state Senate. These men were increasingly aware that Sorlie was a Leaguer more by convenience than by conviction, and that Sorlie hoped the League would bring him further political advancement. His insincerity about the senatorial appointment and his attitude on a score of legislative items which governed the relations of vendor and vendee, creditor and debtor, and insurance companies and policy holders convinced them that he was an Independent in League clothing. Sorlie's position was further weakened because the League legislators who still remained in office were mainly Lemke's confederates; the moderate Leaguers had been defeated by Independents, and the latter group now controlled the Senate.

Sorlie had pledged to make the mill and elevator profitable, and the 1925 Independent-controlled legislature had obligingly given him sole control of the mill, making it impossible for him to shift the responsibility in the event that the mill showed a loss. In 1927 the Independents could think of no better way to punish Sorlie than to subject him to an investigation by the Lemke members of the Senate. Accordingly they created a mill investigating committee with David Hamilton and Lars Frederickson, two veteran Leaguers, as a majority of a three-man committee. It was an invitation to Hamilton and Frederickson to destroy Sorlie's political future, which they did with a vengeance, promptly bringing in a highly critical report of Sorlie's management of the mill.[41]

Through the spring and summer Sorlie squirmed under the effect of the report brought in by Leaguers, knowing that it was lessening any prospect he had of defeating Frazier for the United States Senate in 1928. To counteract the effect of the report, Sorlie called a special session of the legislature, intending to present dramatically a large check representing the profits of the mill. Like his maneuver in appointing Nye, his strategy boomeranged. The legislators were suspicious of Sorlie's accounting and were unimpressed by the check. Resenting having been called together for no other purpose, they passed by a vote of 80 to 30 in the lower house and of 43 to 6 in the state Senate a resolution highly critical of the governor for having called the session. Not a single legislator from either the League or the Independent faction stood up to speak in Sorlie's behalf. It was with pleasure that Lemke wrote Frazier that Sorlie was a "dead one" about whom they would no longer have to worry.[*42]

While Sorlie saw his own fortunes wrecked by the veteran Leaguers, Roy Frazier, who had maintained a harmonious working relation with both the moderate and radical Leaguers, was winning acceptance for Langer which would make the latter's return to the League possible. Langer had never been able to overcome the League ostracism he had experienced since 1919. Through the years since the recall, he had assisted some League leaders and candidates financially. Still, he was not able to attend League meetings or call himself a Leaguer. Because of Roy Frazier's legal difficulties,† Langer finally won his way back into the League in spite of the disapproval of Lemke and Lemke's

* Sorlie now knew that his only political future lay in obtaining a federal patronage appointment. He hoped to control the North Dakota Republican delegation at the 1928 Republican national nominating convention in Kansas City. Unable to obtain a favorite-son endorsement, he appeared committed to Lowden and subsequently made a belated and too apparent shift to support of Hoover. He died a few weeks after the convention, and Lieutenant Governor Walter Maddock served as governor during the remaining months of 1928.

† Roy Frazier was not a member of Lynn Frazier's family or known as a relative of Senator Frazier. They were from different areas of the state; other

close friends. Roy Frazier possessed a fiery disposition which had involved him in a legal predicament. Langer had assisted him and had used the opportunity to present his version of the 1919 rupture with the League. Roy Frazier became convinced that there had been a misunderstanding and that Langer had much to offer the League in campaigning ability and with financial contributions. He substituted Langer for Sorlie when the latter failed to appear for a scheduled speech at a League meeting in Powers Lake. Langer spoke very well and convinced Leaguers who heard him that his defection must either have been justified or else the result of a misunderstanding. Soon Roy Frazier had him speaking at other meetings, and fellow Leaguers became convinced that Langer should once again be permitted to become a member of the League and to be accepted as a delegate at League conventions.[43]

Langer's entrance through the back door of the League came at a time when Lemke's third party efforts had removed him from a position where he could prevent Langer's re-entry. When the League convention gathered in 1928, the assertion was made that Langer might be a major source of campaign funds if he were given a nomination. There could be no harm in it, Langer's proponents argued. It was unlikely that many League candidates would win in 1928 and Langer, because of his past defection, would be certain to trail the ticket and would have no chance of being elected. The convention accepted the argument, and Langer was nominated for his former position of attorney general against a newcomer in state politics, James Morris.

Lemke was increasingly subjected to arguments from Senator Frazier and other Leaguers for abandonment of the Farmer-Labor party. He had been on the sidelines urging on the radical Leaguers who were attacking Sorlie's record, and had been watching hopefully the national scene for signs that a third party movement might crystallize. His observations on the political scene were accurate. He had selected Calvin Coolidge as the Republican nominee but guessed immediately that his "I do not choose to run" statement would result in the selection of Herbert Hoover. Too, he was certain that Alfred E. Smith would be the Democratic nominee fully a year before their convention. Other than this, his only activity was to advise Senator Frazier of the mis-steps that he should avoid in order to be re-elected. One

---

than the fact that they were both members of the Nonpartisan League, they had little in common.

of the radical Leaguers kept Lemke informed of developments at the 1928 League convention, and he was delighted and surprised at the consequences of Sorlie's ill-advised special session. Leaguers of Lemke's own persuasion captured the convention from the moderates and adopted the original League industrial program. Moreover, they advocated an extension of public ownership of many natural monopolies and expansion of the Bank of North Dakota by establishment of branch banks. The only thing that disturbed Lemke was the nomination of Langer. Quickly he cautioned Senator Frazier not to "endorse Langer—they will read portions of his book in which he denounces you out loud to you." He advised Frazier to talk farm relief and the opposition, and he added that he would go to Bismarck to try to get things going smoothly.[44] Not to have accepted Langer, or for Lemke to have opposed him, now that he was on the ticket, would have endangered Senator Frazier's chance for re-election, a hazard Lemke wished to avoid at all costs.

The League's major success in 1928 was the March Presidential primary election of Fred Graham to the post of Republican national committeeman. By the time of the June primaries, however, the Independents under the leadership of their gubernatorial nominee, Attorney General George Shafer, had used the radical planks in the League platform to frighten the voters back into the Independent column. Painting pictures of the alleged excesses of the League during its heyday, they were so successful that with the exception of Frazier, Sinclair, and three other League candidates, all of whom were running for re-election, the Independents were victorious. Trailing even in the state legislature, the League never had been so weak. Clearly the voters preferred the moderate Leaguers to those of the Lemke variety.

The renomination of Frazier was the brightest spot in the dismal League picture when the death of Arthur G. Sorlie suddenly elevated Walter Maddock, one of Lemke's closest friends and political associates, to the governorship. New possibilities were suddenly opened to Lemke, the full implications of which he was quick to grasp. Maddock had originally been a Democrat, and it was probable that Alfred E. Smith, the Democratic nominee for President, would, because of farmer discontent, bid for the North Dakota vote. All that was needed was to have the Democratic gubernatorial nominee withdraw and to have Maddock selected by the Democratic state committee to take his place. Maddock might defeat Shafer for governor, giving the radical Leaguers control of the state, and if Smith were elected

President, it would mean federal patronage for the League. Lemke was the author of the political agreements which were drawn. Because the National Committee was anxious to carry the state for Smith, it was not difficult to persuade Fred L. Anderson, the Democratic gubernatorial nominee, to withdraw in favor of Maddock, nor was the national committee hesitant about investing money in the campaign, although they were somewhat fearful the Leaguers would work more vigorously for Maddock than they would for Smith. *

A Democratic representative to the League stated that the League could be expected to keep a foot in each camp and that Republican national committeeman Fred Graham, Gerald P. Nye and James H. Sinclair were actively campaigning for Herbert Hoover west of the river but would not be able to touch the German vote. Lemke's greatest disappointment was Senator Frazier's campaign for Hoover.[45] Also distressing to Lemke was the fact that North Dakota's party column ballot meant that votes won for Hoover would also in the aggregate add to Shafer's vote and subtract from Maddock's. Lemke and Maddock felt certain that had the League congressional delegation supported Smith and Maddock, Maddock would have been elected governor and Smith probably would have been North Dakota's choice for President.

The Prohibition question disturbed Lemke as it did Frazier. Lemke himself had come to see that Prohibition was not working and was ready for a modification of the laws when repeal came. In 1928 he tried to reassure the drys that only Congress could change the laws, and that Smith would enforce them until they were repealed. He promised the farmers that Smith was for the McNary-Haugen bill, an assurance not confirmed by a careful reading of Smith's speeches. Maintaining that the religious issue should not enter the campaign and that there was no desire of the clergy of any faith to restore the political situation which had existed in the Middle Ages, he bitterly lashed out at Hoover as a foreigner who had spent most of his life in China and England becoming a millionaire, and who was responsible for fixing a ruinously low ceiling on the price of wheat during World War I. Lemke had been criticized for not campaigning actively

* The alliance with the Leaguers was reported to the Democratic party: "Lemke's story of 100 men out in cars is not an accurate appraisal as they will be 75% for Maddock and 25% for Smith. No reflection on Lemke or committee—just human nature. Lemke is stronger than horse radish for Smith himself" (AWR—possibly A. W. Ricker—to Chester Davis, October 20, 1928, Lemke Papers. AWR was apparently a representative of the Democratic National Committee).

in the primaries.[46] No criticism could be made of his campaign for Smith and Maddock; he worked, spoke, and traveled with the same abandon and forgetfulness of himself as he had in the years from 1919 through 1922.

Though the election was lost, Lemke emerged from the campaign with enough prestige to resist two subsequent attempts to seize the League. One attempt was by Langer, who in the June primary had surprised all Leaguers by coming closer to winning nomination than any other nonincumbent, trailing James Morris, his opponent, by only 1769 votes. With the authority that came from vote-getting potential, Langer explained to a post-primary assemblage of Leaguers that only the lack of a newspaper had caused their defeat. Those assembled were impressed, and when Langer offered to use his own time and means to solicit funds and subscriptions to begin a newspaper, they authorized him to proceed.[47]

Lemke was astute enough to see where this would lead and began a counter-campaign to start a newspaper which would deal exclusively with political news and with the promotion of a farm relief bill. This legislative proposal, later known as the Frazier-Lemke bill, represented original, creative thinking and was Lemke's response to the plight of his many farmer-clients. This type of legislation would become his major preoccupation, but for the moment the newspaper was a device to complicate matters for Langer. Lemke did everything he could to make it difficult for Langer to capture the League organization through the medium of a newspaper. Lemke estimated that Langer sold about two thousand subscriptions at $10 each, but that he had heavy expenses for commissions to the salesmen, which diminished his net proceeds. When the October, 1929, crash made it impossible for Langer to continue, Langer had to refund some of the money; he needed control of the League organization if he were to refund all of it and not experience substantial loss himself. To accomplish this Langer brought forth a plan to reorganize the League on a pattern similar to Townley's original League proposal of 1915. Lemke was able to stop this, reporting that "the meeting of the N.P.L. at Bismarck did not turn out the way Langer expected. He tried to steal the organization but did not get away with it." A week later Lemke again wrote: "I am not interested in selling the remnants of the League to Langer.... I think Langer knows by this time that he cannot reorganize the League for Langer, nor for any underhanded purpose." Langer was having his own troubles with the newspaper subscription salesmen, and Lemke's opposition was too much for him to surmount at this time.[48]

Lemke had no sooner blocked Langer's ambitions before he was faced with an effort of Mayor Alfred T. Lynner of Fargo to capture the League as Sorlie had in 1924. Frantically Lemke mobilized his followers, writing that Lynner was an "IVA making a quiet hunt thinking he can pull a Sorlie stunt. His record as mayor here is reactionary." To Maddock, Lemke wrote that he had foiled Lynner in Cass County by pledging the delegates from that county to a farmer, adding that Lynner people were so confident that it frightened him. The Grand Forks Lemke followers were urged to endorse Tom Griffith, son of a pioneer Grand Forks merchant who had been a friend of Lemke's at college, because his friendliness to Frazier made him acceptable. As the situation grew more alarming, the tone of Lemke's letters became more urgent. To L. C. Miller he wrote: "For God's sake get some delegates from your county to the State convention that will be on the square. . . . There is another betrayal of the League which is even more rotten than the Sorlie betrayal. It originated in Washington. It is an attempt to put another I.V.A. who attended the recall convention . . . for governor."[49]

Lemke was successful in defeating Lynner and accomplishing the nomination of E. H. Brant. One delegate later wrote Lemke: "You have no doubt noticed you are again in the saddle as a result of . . . your work in the convention . . . restored your old prestige in North Dakota. . . . You made a very telling speech on the floor that put Brant over. I feel sorry that you did not allow yourself to be nominated for attorney general. If your name had been on the ticket with Brant, . . . you would have both won."[50] The selection of a congressional candidate for 1930 had been left to a Lemke-controlled committee, which unsuccessfully urged Lynner to accept the congressional nomination as a consolation prize.

As during the 1928 primary, the desperateness of Lemke's economic situation made it necessary for him to accept employment, this time for a Dickinson group which owned Wyoming oil interests. This work kept him from campaigning for Brant. The radicals, headed by Lemke and in control of the League, were repudiated at the polls. The Independents scored a quiet, confident, yet sweeping victory.* Moreover,

---

* In 1932, when Langer again moved toward a position of leadership in the League, Lemke and the radical Leaguers were thus not in an easily defensible position to protect their control from him or from other aspirants. They had had control in 1930 and had failed. They could not blame Liederbach, Sorlie, Langer, or any other group for their failure. The real reason for their defeat—that the political tide resulting from the economic crash had not as yet been set in motion— is more apparent in retrospect.

Lemke was increasingly preoccupied with his own debts and those of his relatives. Income from his legal practice, curtailed by the depression, was further depleted by the fact that the farmer-debtors who formed the greater part of his practice could not afford to pay for the legal services he gave them. The situation was critical before the stock market crash, and more and more he was inclined to devote the time he would ordinarily have given to the League to the formulation and advocacy of his federal bankruptcy and inflationary legislative proposals. The Farmers Union gave him some assistance. With Frazier's assistance, he was able to have his ideas incorporated into bills and introduced into Congress. When the hearing on the legislation was held, Lemke appeared before the Senate committee and was introduced by Frazier as the author of the legislation, who would testify in its behalf. The Farmers Union now came into the hands of John A. Simpson, who believed, as did Lemke, in monetary legislation.[51] Simpson employed Lemke to travel in other states, giving speeches about his ideas, which were then embodied in proposed legislation known as the Frazier bills; and Lemke appealed in each state for legislative enactment of a resolution memorializing Congress to enact his agrarian relief proposals.

Thus occupied, he did not take the necessary time to build his political fences in North Dakota. The 1928 campaign had ended his third party plan, and he had been ready to take his entire following into the North Dakota Democratic party, writing one friend: "No use trying to start a new party. We ought to be able to take over the Democratic party." He discussed with Democratic party officials the possibility of becoming a Democratic nominee for state office,[52] and only the threats from Langer and Lynner which, if successful, would have meant campaigning against the League name, brought him back into the North Dakota Republican campaign. Now, even in the Republican party, he found it impossible to fend off Langer.

Actually Lemke's strength came from his emotional and intellectual leadership and the confidence in him of key individuals throughout the state. When campaign time came, he usually was able to mobilize this following sufficiently well to control League conventions. During all of these years, he had asserted confidently that Langer would never gain leadership of the League. Lemke had neither expected nor wanted Langer readmitted, and he would never have permitted it had he not withdrawn temporarily from League activities in an attempt to form a third party. Now, in the years between 1930 and 1932, both

Langer and Lynner were diligently working toward winning the gubernatorial nomination for 1932.

When Lemke returned to the state in 1932 from his National Farmers Union speaking tours and attempted to assert his leadership in opposition to Langer and Lynner, as he had done successfully in 1930, he found that they had gained so much strength that it was impossible to nominate a ticket headed by an extremist leader of his own branch of the League. Upon the advice of Herbert Swett, one of his most faithful political associates, he decided to support T. H. H. Thoresen of Grand Forks, who was a member of the moderate group within the League.[53] Lemke's extremist faction had disintegrated, but it was able to give enough strength to Thoresen to discourage Lynner and cause the latter to withdraw. In return for Langer's promise of a congressional nomination, Lynner transferred those of his followers whom he could control to the support of Langer and against Thoresen. When Lemke accepted the advice of his supporters to seek the congressional nomination, Langer found it impossible to fulfill his commitment to Lynner.

Election of the permanent chairman of the League convention of 1932 was the first test of strength in the contest which would decide whether Lemke or Langer would control the organization. Lemke's followers supported Ole Olson of New Rockford, and Langer supported Oscar Erickson, who won by one vote. Despite this initial defeat, the Lemke forces persisted in their effort to nominate Thoresen for governor. A few delegates thought that Lynner would be the compromise candidate, and they continued to vote for him. There were eight ballots before Langer was finally chosen as gubernatorial candidate of the League. Lynner's support had dwindled on each succeeding ballot, and on the seventh, the convention was tied with forty votes for Langer, forty votes for Thoresen, and one vote for Lynner. The eighth ballot ended the tie; Langer emerged in control of the League, and the best Lemke could hope for was a place on the ticket. Despite an allegedly forged credential for Irwin B. Kruger that was reputed to have enabled Langer to win, Lemke had many reasons for remaining with the League organization even though Langer had won the gubernatorial nomination.[54]

Lemke's financial situation made it necessary for him to seek public office either through election or appointment. Had the League entered the Democratic primary, Lemke's problem would have been simplified, for he was actively engaged in supporting the candidacy of

Franklin D. Roosevelt in the latter's battle for the Democratic nomination, and he supported Roosevelt in the fall as he had Smith in 1928.
However, it would have been out of character and politically a
hazardous maneuver for him to oppose the Nonpartisan League,
especially after he had been outvoted in the convention. Unless he
accepted a nomination on the same ticket as Langer, his only hope of
public employment lay in a federal or state appointment, an uncertain
prospect in the job-hungry thirties.

If he permitted himself to be nominated for the United States
House of Representatives, the publicity he had won with his proposals
for revision of the federal bankruptcy laws and modification of national
monetary policies was almost certain to elect him and place him
where he felt certain he could quickly bring about their passage into
law. Reluctantly, Lemke recognized that he had no alternative and
accepted the place on the ticket which every candidate was glad to
accord him.

In the months just before the convention, Nye had won prominence
by an investigation of Ruth Hanna McCormick's campaign expenditures. Her alleged vow to defeat Nye had raised his political stock in
North Dakota to a point where in 1932 no candidate would have
considered trying to remove him from the League ticket. So voters
were treated to the strange spectacle of three headline candidates,
each representing different factions of the League, with little affection
for one another, on the same ticket. Gerald P. Nye, William Lemke,
and William Langer were linked together during the campaign, their
names on the same advertisements and billboards. Occasionally they
appeared on the same platforms. Nye's opponent was Governor Shafer;
Langer was opposed by Frank Hyland; Lemke and Sinclair were
opposing the two Independent incumbents, Thomas Hall and Olger B.
Burtness. Usher Burdick, who had been inactive politically since 1916,
had now become active in the Farm Holiday movement. Without
endorsement of either the Independents or the League, he ran for
Congress, filing his own name by petition.

The decision, so difficult because of the necessary compromise with
Langer, led to the second phase of Lemke's public career. It involved
what was to Lemke an unholy alliance. The relationship between
Langer and Lemke, considering their past enmity, was for over a year
remarkable in its cordiality. There was no open break between the
two men of which the public was aware until 1938. When Langer
sought to displace Nye in that year, Lemke made an open fight against

Langer; again, in 1940, Langer and Lemke were pitted against one another for the senatorship which Frazier held. But in 1932 they were allies on the Republican ticket and their immediate concern was the defeat of the Independents.

For the three years preceding 1932, Lemke had been thinking in national terms regarding the farm crisis. Although he was constantly drawing new bills for the North Dakota legislature which were designed to soften the effects of the law on debtors and to prevent creditors from capitalizing on the crisis, his major preoccupation for some time had been a national solution for what he recognized as a national problem. This did not violate Lemke's convictions regarding states' rights. He recognized that the federal Constitution expressly granted the central government control over both monetary and bankruptcy legislation. Lemke was certain that his solution of the farm problem would never be adopted unless Herbert Hoover was replaced by a Democratic President. His new career as congressman had roots in the political activities dealing with national problems and Presidential candidates. It was a new chapter in Lemke's life, representing an abrupt break from all that had transpired before.

# CHAPTER VI

# A True Friend and a Bitter Enemy

Proposals to alleviate the economic hardships of the farmer through action of the federal government were the central themes of Lemke's congressional campaign and of his congressional career in the 1930's. He repeatedly advanced and supported four basic proposals, three of which received serious consideration by Congress. Those bills known as the Frazier or as the Frazier-Lemke bills* and a Bank of the United States bill were conceived and written by William Lemke.

One Frazier-Lemke bill proposed a modification of the bankruptcy laws to make them more lenient toward those farmers whose debts so exceeded the current value of their property as to make their financial outlook hopeless. It provided for legal machinery in each county which would permit the appraisal of the property of a farmer who was heavily in debt. The federal courts were then to follow a bankruptcy procedure which would scale down the farmer's debts to a figure that would compare realistically with the value of his property. He would then be permitted to continue farming on the same land with the same equipment and chattels. If he succeeded in retiring his debts at the scaled-down figure set by the appraisers and the court, the property would again be his, and there would be no further encumbrances against it. This was the so-called Frazier-Lemke Bankruptcy Act, or more simply, the Bankruptcy Act, the only one of Lemke's four proposals to receive President Franklin D. Roosevelt's approval and to become law.

A second bill, the Frazier-Lemke refinance bill or the refinance measure, did not modify the bankruptcy laws but concerned lowering interest rates to farmers by governmental action. It provided for the refinancing of farm mortgages by a governmental farm credit agency.

* Frazier's contribution to these bills was his assistance in introducing them in Congress and in hastening their consideration. While they were known as the Frazier-Lemke bills, they were exclusively Lemke's in origin.

The farmer was to pay the agency 3 per cent annually. Half of this payment was to be interest and the other half was to apply on amortization of the loan. The farm credit agency was to sell bonds to obtain the funds necessary to carry out provisions of this measure. If these bonds did not prove marketable, the Federal Reserve Banks and the national banks were to invest their surplus funds in the bonds. If there were still insufficient funds, the Federal Reserve Banks were to issue Federal Reserve notes to purchase the bonds up to a total amount of $3,000,000,000. The purpose of the long-term loan feature was to make it possible for the farmer to discharge his indebtedness; the feature of the law authorizing the Federal Reserve Board to print paper money was intended to be inflationary. Higher prices were expected to result which would place the farmer in a better financial position.[1]

The proposal for a Bank of the United States never received serious consideration. The fourth measure offered by Lemke was a panacea known as the "cost of production" bill, or plan. It was the most radical of the proposed farm legislation and had originated in Iowa with E. E. Kennedy and Milo Reno.[2] Under its provisions, the government would fix prices on basic farm products. Under one version of the proposal, dealers and handlers of these farm commodities were to be licensed. They would then have to pay the fixed prices on the share of the crop that was sold in this country, the rest to be sold abroad for whatever it would bring. Under this plan there was to have been no production control, nor were there to be any marketing quotas. The farmer was to be able to grow all he wished and sell as much as he grew. This cost of production plan contrasted sharply with the domestic allotment plan, the major features of which were adopted by the Roosevelt administration, in that the latter provided for acreage control. Lemke abandoned the low tariff position he had once held; in this he was no different than the majority of agrarian leaders, who, before World War I and sometimes even during the 1920's, had been advocates of lower tariffs.

These proposals for farm relief had not suddenly mushroomed during the depression years of the 1930's. The farm depression had been practically continuous since the post-war depression of 1921. During the years from 1924 through 1928, almost all farm groups, including those which were in favor of the cost of production plan, had united behind George Peek and other leaders to bring about the passage of the McNary-Haugen bill.[3] This proposal had been enacted twice by Congress, and on both occasions it had been vetoed by President Coolidge. The bill included an equalization fee which was to have been levied on each unit of production. The plan called for a high domestic price on farm products with the proceeds from the equalization fee to be used to reimburse those who sold at a loss in foreign markets. After Coolidge's second veto, farm leaders advanced another proposal; under it the exporter would receive debentures equivalent to the difference in value between products sold on the domestic market and that sold abroad. These debentures were to have been accepted by the federal government in payment of tariff duties. However, it never passed Congress. Until the election of Herbert Hoover and the passage of the Agricultural Marketing Act of 1930, there had been near unanimity among farm leaders in the support of these bills, and Lemke had often participated in the regional meetings in the Twin Cities and elsewhere which had been called by farm organizations to formulate policies and mobilize sentiment for a farm relief program. During this period he had formed close friendships with many of the regional and national leaders of the Farmers Union.

The Agricultural Marketing Act of 1930 had appropriated $500,000,-000. This fund was administered by the Federal Farm Board, which attempted to work through cooperative marketing agencies to stabilize prices of farm products. The National Farmers Union was divided between the followers of Clarence Huff, president of the national organization, and John Simpson, president of the Oklahoma Farmers Union. The former favored cooperating with the Federal Farm Board; the latter felt that it was a futile measure and advocated the cost of production plan as well as monetary inflation. Lemke found himself the natural ally of Simpson and gave his support to him even though many of the Farmers Union leaders from North Dakota were supporters of Huff. In 1930 Simpson defeated Huff for the presidency of the National Farmers Union. During the period of Simpson's leadership of the Farmers Union, Lemke worked closely with that organization, assisting both in drafting and forwarding Farmers Union legislative proposals.[4]

Between the years 1929 and 1932, the nation-wide depression caused farm prices to fall far below those of the previous decade. In the 1920's they had been much lower in relation to the prices of commodities purchased by farmers than had been the case prior to World War I, and one of the insistent demands of the McNary-Haugen supporters had been for parity—a relationship between the prices of commodities purchased by the farmers and those he sold—which would be approximately equivalent to that prevailing in the years between 1909 and 1914. The average price received by the North Dakota farmer for wheat declined to sixty cents a bushel in 1930. This was just the beginning: in 1931 and 1932 it sank to forty-six and thirty-six cents respectively. Making the situation much worse was the fact that 1931 was a year of very poor yields.[5]

The critical nature of the situation gave rise in Iowa to a movement for a farm strike. It originated with Milo Reno and was known as the Farm Holiday movement. Usher L. Burdick became the key leader of this organization in North Dakota, but Lemke played an active part in it also, urging it to continue its activities in the spring of 1933 when the Farmers Holiday organization in many other states was waiting to see whether the new administration would enact a farm relief program which would be satisfactory to them. The situation in North Dakota was unbelievably bad; the total annual income of North Dakotans had dropped from $328,000,000 in 1929 to $165,000,000 in 1932 and went even lower to $137,000,000 in 1933. The average total cash income of all North Dakota farmers in the years from 1924 to 1928 had been $237,816,000. It sank to a low of $67,463,000 in 1932.[*6] After the federal government intervened, there were two periods when 48 per cent of the population of the state was on relief.[†] It is against this backdrop that Lemke's farm relief proposals, the conduct of his own campaign for Congress, and his support of Franklin D. Roosevelt,

---

[*] As early as 1927 Lemke had noted in a letter to Covington Hall that farmers were in a more desperate economic condition in North Dakota than they had been up until that time. His own observation was supplemented by letters he received. A letter which was forwarded to him commented that "conditions were almost unbelievable. The list of failures and loss of farms, insanity, illness, and general dwindling of population and business in the towns I know best passes adequate description" (William Lemke to Covington Hall, April 28, 1927; J. H. Greene to E. M. Williams, April 20, 1929; both Lemke Papers). This was an observation made in April of 1929, several months before the stock market crash ordinarily regarded as the beginning of the depression.

[†] The reality of conditions in terms of human lives is difficult to visualize. The author clearly remembers one farmer, successful enough to stay in good financial condition in the 1920's who, in 1932, wrote a relative in California that another five thousand bushels of wheat would ruin him. He eventually lost everything. It is true that he was a small-scale homesteader who had not made adjustment to tractor farming, but it was the fact that threshing the wheat and hauling it to town cost more than he could obtain for his grain and not lack of ability to raise good crops that destroyed him. He would have been better off if his crop had not come up and much better off if he had not planted any crop. One grim joke of the period was about the championship wrestler who broke his back attempting to lift fifty cents worth of oats.

first for the Democratic Presidential nomination and later for election as President, must be studied to be understood.

While close students of the economic situation were willing to concede that there had been serious errors in governmental policies that were in part responsible for the economic situation, they recognized, too, that the economic dislocation resulting from World War I and other complex and impersonal factors were involved in the agricultural depression of the 1920's and in the general economic collapse which began during the first year of Herbert Hoover's administration in October, 1929. Lemke did not fully understand the complex nature of the problem. For Lemke there was a devil behind every difficulty. This devil might live in St. Paul, Minneapolis, Wall Street, or among the international bankers of London, but wherever his residence, Lemke was certain that his tentacles reached into the Capitol at Washington and that his agents in North Dakota and other farm states were being well paid to block Lemke himself and his political associates. This oversimplification on his part led Lemke to believe that all that was needed to bring recovery and prosperity was to remove evil and selfish men from high places in both domestic and international politics.

From 1929 through 1937, Lemke's life was dedicated to the promotion of the bankruptcy and refinance plans as it once had been dedicated to the industrial program of the Nonpartisan League. Lemke, with the assistance of his brother Ben, who was a member of the lower house of the state legislature, persuaded the 1931 North Dakota Legislative Assembly to pass a resolution endorsing his legislative proposals and requesting Congress to pass them. He worked through Frazier in 1931, having Frazier introduce the bills and using Frazier's franking privilege to mail copies of the resolution passed by the North Dakota legislature to every state legislator in the nation. President Simpson of the National Farmers Union became a devotee of Lemke's ideas and made it possible for him to spend much of 1931 speaking in other states than North Dakota under the auspices of the Farmers Union.[7]

Lemke was willing to support any administration that would adopt his ideas and he did his best to convince President Hoover and his cabinet that these two measures would be long steps toward breaking the deflationary spiral. Gerald P. Nye, Lynn J. Frazier, and James H. Sinclair, having accepted Lemke's ideas, went in the fall of 1931 as a group to see Hoover, but they were informed that the Reconstruction Finance Corporation would indirectly approach the same problem and

bring relief. Senator McNary assisted in bringing Lemke's proposals
to the attention of Ogden Mills, Secretary of the Treasury, where they
received an equally unfavorable response. The chairman of the Federal Reserve Board and the Secretary of Agriculture both opposed
Lemke's proposals. Lemke even found it difficult to convince faithful
members of the farm bloc that his ideas were not dangerous and revolutionary. Nevertheless, the Senate subcommittee headed by Frazier
reported favorably on the refinance bill.[8]

The attitude of the Hoover administration made Lemke indignant,
and he related to his audiences in 1929 and during the four years
which followed how Charles A. Lindbergh, John M. Baer, and he
himself had pleaded with Hoover during World War I not to ruin
the farmers by setting low prices for wheat, only to encounter a wall
of indifference. Apparently Lemke regarded Alfred E. Smith's defeat
as final or he realized that Smith's endorsement of farm legislation in
1928 had not been all that Lemke had hoped at the time, for during
the years between 1929 and 1932, Lemke anxiously sought some other
Democrat, one who would support his own proposals. As early as
1930 he had selected Franklin D. Roosevelt as a possibility. He wrote
Burton K. Wheeler of his interest in the New York governor and
learned that Wheeler, too, was interested in Roosevelt but feared that
he would be hard to nominate, as "The power interests will fight Roosevelt tooth and toenail. . . . The idea of opposition will be that they
try to get delegations committed to different candidates in different
states. . . . They will seek to nominate Ritchie,* as they have apparently switched from Owen D. Young to Ritchie." Wheeler warned
that the conservatives would have "Alfalfa Bill" Murray, governor of
Oklahoma, file in North Dakota as a stalking horse for Ritchie. If it
had not been for the fact that the League was in danger of falling
into Langer's hands, both Lemke and Maddock would have joined the
Democratic party. With the Nonpartisan League in the hands of
Langer, the political future of any candidate for state office on the
Democratic ballot was dubious.† In January, 1932, Lemke's supporters
first urged him to run for Congress.[9]

The impossibility of running on the Democratic ticket because the
League, according to the view of one Minnesota Leaguer, continued

* Albert Ritchie, governor of Maryland.

† The fact that Maddock had run for governor on the Democratic ticket in
1928 had compelled the Lemke forces to abandon him for T. H. H. Thoresen
in their efforts to stop Langer in the 1932 League convention (Herbert Swett to
William Lemke, January 5, 1932, Lemke Papers).

to "pursue the old obsolete method of pretending to be Republican," did not deter Lemke from embracing the Roosevelt boom as his own and campaigning vigorously for him. Wheeler had convinced both Simpson and Lemke that Roosevelt would be sympathetic to some type of farm legislation. Fred McLean, manager of the Roosevelt pre-primary campaign and chairman of the North Dakota Democratic party, decided to depend on Lemke's influence in the Nonpartisan League and in the Farmers Union to make it possible for Roosevelt to defeat Murray. Lemke's correspondence with Wheeler had left uncertainty as to the type of farm legislation Roosevelt would support, and Lemke insisted on more definite information. McLean arranged for Lemke to visit Roosevelt.[10] This was at the time when Roosevelt, Louis Howe, James Farley, and Roosevelt's other advisers were making the necessary compromises to assure the required number of delegates for nomination.

The account of Lemke's visit, as recalled by Mrs. Lemke, indicated that Lemke was very favorably impressed.* When he showed his bankruptcy and refinance proposals to the future President, the latter listened closely, scanned the prepared material Lemke had brought with him, and said, "Yes, yes I am for all that." Roosevelt wrote a letter to Lemke that Lemke interpreted as an endorsement of the farm mortgage relief proposals, his interview with Roosevelt causing him to ignore phrases that made the endorsement a general statement and not an absolute commitment. When Herbert Swett called attention to some qualifying words in the Roosevelt letter, Lemke explained that he knew from his personal visit with Roosevelt where the governor stood and that he could be depended upon. Lemke believed he had a commission from the New York governor to make the necessary arrangements with the Farmers Union and with remnants of the Nonpartisan League to see that North Dakota, and the surrounding states as well, sent delegates to the national convention pledged to Roosevelt. During the 1932 campaign Lemke was regarded by the Roosevelt advisers as "the chief strategist of the Nonpartisan League in his state,"[11] and it seems reasonable to conclude that he had been treated solicitously during his visit with the Roosevelt family.

From Burton K. Wheeler, and from the Democrats who had represented Alfred E. Smith in 1928, the Roosevelt campaign managers

---

* While he was visiting with the governor, Mrs. Roosevelt came in to her husband's office to discuss what kind of food to serve one of the children, who was ill. Lemke was impressed by the homelike atmosphere and by Mrs. Roosevelt's graciousness. Whether the meeting with Mrs. Roosevelt was by design or not, Lemke came away with a very pleasant impression of the Roosevelt family.

learned that it was Lemke who had the most valuable contacts within North Dakota with both the Farmers Union and what remained of the Nonpartisan League. He became their key man in bringing League county leaders over to the support of Roosevelt. When Cornelius Vanderbilt, Jr., traveled to the state on behalf of the Roosevelt candidacy, it was with Lemke that he conducted negotiations.* When Lemke suggested that Wheeler be sent into the state to speak for the New York governor, Roosevelt's advisers requested Wheeler to do so; North Dakota Leaguers who remembered the 1924 ticket of La Follette and Wheeler responded favorably to his speech. At the convention of the League in February, 1932, and in the speech he gave before Farmers Union leaders, Lemke assured all who listened that they could depend upon Roosevelt—that he had talked with Roosevelt about farm legislation and knew from first-hand association that Roosevelt would support his farm proposals and other legislation favorable to farmers. He was in communication with Roosevelt, warning that the situation was precarious because of Murray's appeal and advising a public statement on the St. Lawrence Seaway and the Frazier bill.[12] Lemke felt certain he would have influence on farm policies when Roosevelt became President.

Although Roosevelt won over Murray all but one of North Dakota's ten delegates to the Democratic convention by a vote of 52,000 to 32,000, it had been done by accomplishing the transfer of voters who were normally Republican registrants into the Democratic column.†

* Vanderbilt later related: "All I can recall is that I went to see Bill Lembke [sic] at FDR's request. . . . Bill was very close to FDR in those early days before Moley and McIntyre got in there because Louie Howe liked him. . . . Farley . . . had no use for him. . . . I always felt Bill Lembke & Upton Sinclair were 'dedicated' men. I felt the 'palace court' around FDR sold them short. . . . I think Bill Lembke's [sic] foresight in those early days had everything to do with putting FDR in office" (Cornelius Vanderbilt, Jr., to author, June 25, 1957).

† Al Smith's suporters failed, because of snow blocking the roads, in a last-minute attempt to file petitions to place the names of delegates for Smith on the ballot, but Murray had proved to be a formidable opponent. He had campaigned in the state and the vote he received would have been sufficient to nominate him easily had Roosevelt not been the beneficiary of Farmers Union and Nonpartisan League support. Lemke had been invited to take a leading part in Murray's campaign. Murray, with his colorful nickname, unusual mannerisms, and distinctive dress, had created a rustic image of himself. His extreme views on agricultural and money problems were felt by many to be extremely appealing to North Dakotans (Friedel, p. 285; C. H. Hude, representative of the Murray campaign committee, to William Lemke, January 13, 1932, Lemke Papers; Farley, p. 97).

Less than 11,000 voters had registered as Democrats in March, 1928, and only 20,000 had been expected to register as Democrats in March, 1932. Just three months later, in June, 1932, most of North Dakota's voters had returned to the Republican column and there were only approximately 25,000 who registered as Democrats in the June primary in which candidates for state offices were nominated, a significant decline from the nearly 90,000 registrants in the March Democratic Presidential primary.

Murray's strength in North Dakota is indicated by the total of 32,000 votes he amassed in a state which customarily registered only 10,000 Democratic voters in the presidential preferential primary. Despite that strength, however, the Roosevelt managers were so confident that the arrangements they had made would enable Roosevelt to carry the state that they chose North Dakota as the place where he would announce his candidacy.* The results of the election clearly indicated that Roosevelt had strong support in North Dakota, and the hazards taken in choosing the state as his first battleground gave him a needed initial victory. It was convincing evidence of Roosevelt's vote-getting ability in the agricultural areas of the nation. Lemke was confident that through his work with Farmers Union and with the League he had increased Roosevelt's strength in those states, particularly in Minnesota, which had in convention chosen Roosevelt delegates on March 10, and in South Dakota, which elected delegates pledged to Roosevelt on May 3.[13]

It was during this same period that Lemke acceded to the endorsement of Langer as governor and accepted the congressional endorsement of the Nonpartisan League convention. North Dakota lost one representative in the reapportionment which followed the census of 1930. Its two representatives were until 1962 elected at large, for the legislature of 1931 had failed to redistrict the state. Sinclair and Lemke were the two League nominees for Republican endorsement to Congress, and they were opposed by the two Independent incumbents, Olger B. Burtness and Thomas Hall. Usher L. Burdick, whose Farm Holiday activities were making him again prominent, was a fifth Republican candidate for the two positions.

Langer, Lemke, and Nye were the headline names on the ticket. Nye's name usually held the featured position on billboard advertisements. As an incumbent who had won national prominence, he gave strength to the rest of the ticket. George Shafer, incumbent governor

* No record of Lemke's visit with Roosevelt is known to the staff of the Roosevelt Hyde Park library, attesting to the attendant secrecy.

and Independent nominee for the United States Senate, made a serious campaign error that injured his own candidacy and that of the entire Independent ticket. Instead of discussing his own stand on major issues, he concentrated on a defense of President Hoover.*

Langer and Lemke both conducted vigorous campaigns. Langer emphasized tax reduction and a termination of the nepotism and corruption which he alleged existed in the state government, while Lemke discussed the program of legislation for which he claimed he had Roosevelt's support.[14]

The wave of depression-born discontent brought an overwhelming majority for the Nonpartisan League. Not only did Nye, Langer, and Lemke win; every candidate nominated by the League was successful, and not a single Independent candidate for state office on the party ballot was nominated. Sinclair, a League congressman who had represented North Dakota since 1919, led Lemke by a vote of 99,625 to 89,822 for Lemke. The next highest candidate was Hall, who received 67,328 votes. Burtness received 62,810, and Burdick, who was endorsed neither by the Independents nor the League, received 39,688 votes. As there were two positions to be filled, both Sinclair and Lemke were Republican nominees.

June 29, 1932, the day of the primary election for state offices, was a significant day in Lemke's life, for Republican nomination was tantamount to election. Lemke's financial situation had been critical; now he was not only certain of being able to put forward legislation to help farmers save their homes, but he was also certain of an income that would keep him from losing his own home. The resumption of his public career came barely in time to save him from financial disaster.[15] Moreover, he had hope that in his new capacity, he could do something to salvage the investments of the Land Finance Company. To protect the stockholders, Lemke, with some assistance from Frazier, had been paying the taxes to the Mexican government in order to avoid losing their claim to the land in Mexico.

Victory was too important to both Lemke and Langer to permit their personal differences from jeopardizing the excellent chance both

* Former Governor Shafer later recalled that his support of Hoover had been pursued, despite the fact that it was politically unwise, as a matter of political conviction. This is at variance with another account, which stressed that the Republican National Committee was again intervening in a primary to assist the Independents and defeat the League and that in return for funds to finance the Independent campaign, the Republican National Committee insisted that Shafer campaign for Hoover (interview with George Shafer, June, 1938; interview with Harold Shaft, a prominent Independent, July, 1938).

candidates had of winning. Their distrust of one another seemed to lessen; after the election was over, Lemke was permitted by Langer to suggest names for some of the appointments. When Langer became seriously ill during the early part of 1933, Lemke took charge of the legislative caucus and worked closely with him, calling on him each day to collaborate on legislative policies and strategy.[16] To all outward appearances, the breach between the two men was healed.

Lemke campaigned vigorously; he was booked for ninety-nine scheduled speeches in the month of October alone. He openly campaigned for Roosevelt, not only criticizing Hoover but also advising his audiences to vote for the Democratic candidate. It is probable that all of the League candidates were opposed to Hoover's re-election; Nye and Sinclair bitterly criticized him in their speeches. Langer was for Roosevelt, but he devoted most of his campaign speeches to state issues. Langer was facing the most difficult contest of all League nominees in the fall election, and it would have been politically unwise for him unnecessarily to offend Republican voters.

The November election in North Dakota was a sweeping victory for the League candidates. Langer trailed the rest of the ticket, but still he won by a comfortable margin. Lemke polled fewer votes than Sinclair, but enough easily to defeat his nearest competitor; and there was no longer any doubt that he would be a member of Congress from North Dakota. Nye was the only candidate to approach in number of votes the total amassed by Roosevelt; the latter had a total of 178,350 to Hoover's 71,772. The League had not only carried every state office on a party ballot but had also won control of both houses of the legislature.[17]

When Lemke was elected to Congress, he rather naïvely expected to assist Roosevelt in making major alterations in the monetary system of the nation.* His own basic conviction was that all banking should be owned and controlled by the government. His greatest objection

---

* Lemke's monetary theories were completely at variance with those of the newly elected President. His correspondence and the dates of the books and pamphlets in his library indicate that he had become interested in monetary theory in the years between 1913 and 1915. He corresponded with W. H. (Coin) Harvey and brought the latter to North Dakota during the recall campaign in 1921. Charles A. Lindbergh had the most influence on Lemke in this field of thought. There were more books, pamphlets, and magazines in the Lemke library on monetary subjects than on any other. His interest from 1913 to the end of his life was constant. At no time did he cease to mention the subject in his letters; it became an obsession with him, and in 1938 he wrote a book entitled *You and Your Money* (Philadelphia: W. H. Dorrance, 1938).

to the systems in use was that bankers drew interest on money that they created. He was in favor of government ownership of the entire system and an increase in the amount of money in circulation. In his opinion, no group of private individuals should control the total supply of money or be in a position to profit from expanding or contracting that supply. His proposal for a Bank of the United States and his refinance measure represented his solutions to the banking and monetary problem. He had so confidently promised the voters what the election of Roosevelt would mean in terms of enactment of the bankruptcy and refinance measures, that as a new congressman he would have much explaining to do if the future President did not act as Lemke had assured his audiences he would. While the campaign was in progress, Roosevelt had collaborated with advisers such as Rexford G. Tugwell and Raymond Moley. Tugwell had gone to Chicago in June, 1932, to meet M. L. Wilson and had come back thoroughly convinced of the workability of the domestic allotment plan. Roosevelt then changed farm plans and no longer talked in terms of dumping agricultural surpluses abroad and inducing mild inflation as the solution to the farm problem. His speeches hinted at a new approach to the issue, but not broadly enough to convince Lemke that the candidate for the Presidency had changed his views. Contrary to Lemke's own opinion and that of his North Dakota political associates,[18] it would not be freshman congressmen like himself who would formulate the farm program, for Roosevelt had begun to gather a group of economists and others to advise him.

In December, 1932, Lemke did not realize how difficult would be the congressional career which lay ahead of him. He was advised to go to Washington and stay there in order to orient himself in the period between election and March 4.[19] He did engage W. O. Skeels, one of the younger men of the old League days, as his secretary, and went to Washington to testify on the refinance measure before the Senate Committee on Banking and Currency, but he did not heed the advice to stay. He returned to North Dakota, where he remained until early March.

The North Dakota situation was critical. There was little money in the state treasury. There was a completely new set of officials, and Governor Langer was reported to be too ill for a time to coordinate fully his new administration or guide the legislative program. The Farm Holiday movement was active, and crowds surged into Bismarck which so frightened the newspapers that their reports minimized the event.[20] Even veteran members of the League extremist faction were sobered by the unruliness which characterized delegations appearing before the state legislature. The League caucus voted to employ Lemke in the same capacity he had served in a number of sessions prior to 1925. Because of Langer's illness Lemke's responsibilities in the caucus were much greater than that in those sessions, and it was he upon whom League members depended to guide them through the session. The League legislative caucus of 1933 was not the disciplined body it had been in times past. The troubled legislators had many panaceas; they were not an easy group to lead. Through Langer they arranged to have Lemke appointed temporary assistant attorney general for the months of January and February at $240 per month, a welcome sum to Lemke, who would not be on the federal payroll until March. He had no work to do in the attorney general's office; his function was to draft legislation and act as legislative strategist for the League.

Before the session was over, Langer became well enough to assert leadership. When he did so, he took steps that completely alienated him from the other state officials. Citing the critical financial situation of the state government, he prevailed upon the legislature to enact a sales tax. Lemke, who did not have the responsibility to see that the state government continued to function, counseled against the sales tax. The bonds of the state were selling at a figure far below par. Langer corrected this situation by successfully encouraging the legislature to transfer funds from sources such as the tax on gasoline to the bond retirement fund. It was a measure which restored the state's credit and benefited greatly these persons who owned sizable blocks of bonds, particularly if they had acquired them during 1931 or 1932. The transfer of funds aroused vigorous criticism from many who alleged that the governor and other owners of North Dakota bonds had profited from their increase in value.[21] Although Lemke did not agree with some of the steps which Langer took, he recognized that Langer, as governor, had the right to formulate policy, and there was no rupture in the relationship between the two men at this time. He probably agreed with Langer's critics that the gasoline tax money should have been used for governmental operation purposes to remove the necessity of levying a sales tax. He made no public issue of it, however, and left for Washington.*

W. O. Skeels, his secretary, had become restive when Lemke stayed in Bismarck past the date when most of the congressmen had arrived

---

* It was during this session that Lemke assisted in passing the legislation establishing the International Peace Garden as a state park.

in Washington, and he wired Lemke that it was imperative that Lemke be there for the opening of the special session on March 7. Skeels recognized more clearly than did Lemke how important early acquaintanceships would be for Lemke in forwarding his legislative ideas and how much loss of power could result from the loss of seniority that came from being sworn into office after the other congressmen who were newly elected in the same year. Moreover, the news reports from the North Dakota legislature during January and February, 1933, had portrayed Lemke as a leader who was making extreme statements. In most other states the Farm Holiday movement and plans for a general strike withholding all farm products from the market had been held in abeyance while farmers bided their time to see what the Roosevelt administration would do. This was not the case in North Dakota. At Bismarck, under the leadership of Burdick and Lemke, a convention had been held during the legislative session of 1933 which urged farmers to organize councils of defense in each county to prevent foreclosures. Strong language typical of Lemke was included in the convention resolutions advising farmers to defy legal authority and "retire to . . . farms, and there barricade . . . to see the battle through until . . . cost of production [was received]."[22] This did not go unnoticed in the East by those holding councils on the farm problem. If they knew Lemke at all, they knew he was from North Dakota and possibly in part responsible. If they noticed him at all, it was as a man to appease rather than as a man to consult.

Perhaps Lemke's personality was such that nothing short of an actual position as policy maker for the administration would have satisfied his longing for influence. Denied this satisfaction, he became an inflexible legislator, known as much for his eccentricities as for any solid contributions he made. It seems reasonable to conclude that had Roosevelt and his advisers realized the extent of Lemke's opposition potential, they would have treated him with the same deference they were to give for many years to Nye, George Norris, Burton K. Wheeler, and other Northwestern liberals. Neither Frazier nor Lemke received similar consideration. The fact that Lemke was a man of fixed ideas and little flexibility might very justifiably have been used by the President as a valid reason for disqualifying him as an inner circle adviser. Roosevelt, by utilizing Lemke's knowledge of the farm situation and by adopting his bankruptcy proposal, might have made of him a firm ally. But as a freshman member of the lower house, he was one of many; the administration did not care whether he was disaffected or not. At this time, except for the inconvenience he caused, it hurt the administration very little to disregard him. It was Lemke's bitter recoil from this treatment—a recoil strong enough to cancel out his own achievements—that eventually aligned him with men who were anti-Semitic and associated with movements that some observers felt had the earmarks of incipient facism, a category in which Lemke did not belong, but a situation which his hatred of Roosevelt was to prevent him from recognizing or admitting.

It was unfortunate for Lemke's legislative career that he had not prolonged his post-election visit to Washington to observe the lame duck session as he had been advised to do. While he was immersed in the local problems of North Dakota at Bismarck, the stream of events had moved past him. Decisions had been made and policies formed that were irreversible. Lemke had been absent during the fluid, formative period of the new administration. By the time he arrived, the lines of communication among those who were to make the decisions had been opened, and Lemke's absence meant that he had not been included. In addition to Roosevelt's reliance on House leaders, Lemke's own depth and capacity were not apparent on first acquaintance. Although he could impress a rural audience in his capacity as agrarian orator and prairie rebel, he could not as readily impress a new Eastern acquaintance unless he had some time to visit with him. Let the new acquaintance ride with Lemke a half day on the train and he might come away feeling as if he had conversed with a man of ability; but a half hour taken from other busy tasks to visit with Lemke was not enough for the tense, preoccupied man who was Lemke to convey his real capability. "A skinny little guy with a puckering squint of a smile, and a casting director would type him for a hick," wrote Westbrook Pegler, adding, "[but] he went to Yale . . . and went around more colleges than an old-time tramp tackle and he is positively no yokel."[23] His appearance, plus a carelessness in dress, most noticeable during the years he lived in Washington before Mrs. Lemke and the family joined him there, was not one that would impress either the first or second echelon of the "brain trust" the President had recruited.*

When Lemke found himself completely outside the decision-making circle, his frustration and disappointment accentuated his habit of making over-strong statements that sometimes bordered on the abusive. He sincerely felt that Roosevelt was too conservative in his measures regarding money and banking and that the financiers themselves had

---

* Contrast between his graciousness of manner and carelessness of attire was noted by a college group (Interview with Mr. and Mrs. Harry Wienbergen).

too much influence on the President's policies. When he expressed this opinion, he did so in his usual colorful language, intensifying a stereotype of himself that nothing he would ever do could completely erase. To the economists, junior attorneys, and other officials of the Department of Agriculture, the Treasury Department, the Federal Reserve Board, as well as to those men clustered about the President in the executive office, Lemke was often thought of as a "madman from the sticks," one whom the excesses of democracy compelled more urbane public servants to endure. To them it was unfortunate that a demagogue such as they regarded Lemke to be should have such a hold on the voters of that area, and they deemed as unthinkable the possibility that Lemke truly had an intellectual contribution to make. The public image he had created, so valuable in getting elected, was his greatest obstacle in gaining influence in Washington.[24] Lemke was never able to penetrate this wall of contempt.

For a time Lemke vented his anger and frustration on the bureaucrats* and attempted to excuse Roosevelt. As the months wore on, he came closer to direct attacks on the President. Alarmed at the rift between Lemke and the administration, Walter Maddock wrote to Chester Davis in November, 1933:

I want to emphasize that it is very important that the President show Lemke some real consideration. He is deeply offended by the fact that Roosevelt has not allowd [sic] him to see him on some highly important matters. He must not forget that Lemke is a key man in this northwest area. He must take into consideration that he is a real "Evangelist" that appeals to the people in their present psychological attitude. He is absolutely honest and sincere and determined to carry on the battle as he sees it. He is a force in these northwest states and he will certainly be a force in Congress. Roosevelt has made a deep impression on him as has also Morgen-

---

* The existence of about fifty-five lawyers who had been recruited by Jerome Frank for the Department of Agriculture and who were more concerned with social reform than with raising farm prices caused Lemke to add the term "bureacrat" to his list of denunciatory epithets. A few of these lawyers were members of a Communist cell, a fact which Lemke came to realize and mention in his speeches. Too often he was careless in his remarks, and soon by implication most bureaucrats were "reds" or proponents of some foreign ideology (Young, p. 114). In his bitterness and carelessness he forgot that he had once been labeled as a bolshevik, a "wobbly," and a syndicalist. Extreme statements such as the one in which he later described the O.P.A. as an "Un-American child . . . put over by an official clique in Washington that think more of foreign institutions than our own" were frequently included in his speeches. Lemke no longer remembered that price control had been the object of the Nonpartisan League-sponsored Producers' and Consumers' Conference of 1917.

thau and a little attention will do wonders.... Cheap flattery will only disgust Lemke but at the same time he has a lot of pride ... and is quite easily offended. We expect to keep him in Congress for the next 20 years. He is a true friend and a bitter enemy....[25]

Davis wrote to Henry A. Wallace enclosing Maddock's letter, and the Secretary of Agriculture in turn wrote to Lemke, telling Lemke that he had heard fine reports about him, and asking that Lemke call on him.[26] Wallace's gesture was that and nothing more, and apparently the President never learned of Maddock's warning. Wallace had no intention of backing Lemke's proposals on farm indebtedness or of adopting Lemke's cost of production plan in lieu of the domestic allotment plan which provided for limitations on production which Wallace himself favored.

Lemke had been in Congress for eight months at the time that Maddock wrote to Davis in November. At first Lemke had been hopeful about the President's monetary policy. As the Congress opened during the banking crisis of 1933, Lemke watched with approval when Roosevelt opened up the "printing presses to print money." He regarded the President's economy bill as a mistake, commenting that "there is not enough money in circulation now." He waited patiently for the farm legislation, hoping each day to be called in for consultation. When the legislation came, Lemke was disappointed, for he did not believe in decreasing production. His first opportunity to speak came on March 11. He denounced Wall Street and suggested suspending interest on the bonded indebtedness of the United States for three years.[27]

Neither the opinion expressed nor the language used helped Lemke gain influence with the administration. Every incoming congressman is appraised by Washington observers and, if noticed at all, is soon assigned a stereotype. He is regarded as effective or ineffective, liberal or conservative, gradualist or extremist. Lemke did not change his pace. At a moment that called for restrained language, he spoke with campaign oratory. Statements that might have gone unnoticed if made while stump speaking could result only in his classification as an extremist by those informed Washingtonians who were appraising new congressmen. First impressions were damaging and it was not an auspicious start for the prairie rebel, who now needed the confidence of Washington officialdom in order to have any portion of his program accepted. Lemke's purpose was no doubt to arouse grass roots pressure for his proposals, and for that purpose impassioned oratory might accomplish much. In March, 1933, it was not needed, and Lemke's failure to adjust himself to the Washington scene was an initial error that made his future achievements more difficult.

The House of Representatives, with its strict discipline on debate and the tremendous power wielded by the Rules Committee and the officers of the majority party, was different than the free-wheeling Legislative Assembly of North Dakota. The "gag rule" was not for men of Lemke's stamp, and in late March, 1933, he grumbled that "so far I have been allowed to appear in it five times."[28] The United States Senate would have been a forum giving Lemke's talents full scope; in the House he was cramped and never completely happy. It was only gradually that he learned how to maneuver under the rules by which the House operated and became an influential member, despite the fact that he never served under a friendly Presidential administration.

The administration farm bills, with their emphasis on production control, were disappointing to Lemke, but they were the only farm bills that could reach the floor of the House. His own proposals were pigeonholed by committee chairmen. Under the rules of the House his activities were limited to running errands for his constituents and to voting for or against the New Deal legislative measures. He could not participate in debate except in rare instances and then only when and for the length of time the officers of the House decreed. It was a far different role from the one either he or his constituents had expected him to play, and, not realizing that he was a victim of his own miscalculation, he vigorously sought another. He asked George Webb to see if Bernard Baruch would obtain an interview with the President for him. Webb wrote to Baruch, stressing the fact that Lemke was in great part responsible for the unusually large vote polled for Roosevelt in North Dakota* and stating that "the administration does not seem to remember or appreciate . . . [this] fact."

---

* A comparison of South Dakota's vote to that of North Dakota in the 1932 election supports Webb's statement regarding the heavy vote for Roosevelt in North Dakota. Roosevelt's percentage of the vote cast for the two major candidates was 69.6 per cent in North Dakota as compared to 63.6 per cent in South Dakota. This is more remarkable when it is remembered that North Dakota voters elected a full slate of Republicans to state office when South Dakota was choosing Democrats for many major positions. These figures are from the general election; Roosevelt had been the beneficiary of a large migration of voters to the Democratic presidential preferential primary in North Dakota. (*Information Please Almanac, 1948* [Garden City, New York: Doubleday & Company, Inc. and Garden City Publishing Co., Inc., 1947], p. 133. Comparative election figures computed to the nearest tenth for North and South Dakota are taken from this source.)

Lemke was finally able to see the President and he returned to the House office building certain that administration leaders in the House would now hold hearings on Lemke's legislative proposals.[29] They did not do so, however.

After the special session adjourned in July, 1933, Lemke returned to Fargo. Here he found it necessary to explain to his supporters why the administration, which he had so positively declared would enact his proposals, was not doing so. Reports from farmers at this time convinced him that the Federal Land Bank and other government credit agencies were being unreasonably severe in their collection policies. There had been a rise in wheat prices between March and July, 1933; in July there was a sharp decline. Wheat producing states to the south of North Dakota had marketed a large proportion of their crop. Harvest was just beginning in North Dakota, and the effect of the price change was disastrous. Lemke attributed the lower prices to the Department of Agriculture, which had released figures on cost of production much lower than had been expected. His dismay at these figures and at what he regarded as the callousness of the federal credit agencies caused him to seek and obtain sponsorship from the Farmers Union for a speaking tour. That organization, under Simpson's leadership, arranged the meetings and provided the publicity. The purpose of the tour was to create a public demand for Lemke's legislative program. Throughout the first years of his congressional career, the Farmers Union purchased radio time for him. The letters which followed each radio talk were numerous, and one of his speeches resulted in requests for six thousand reprints[30] in addition to being printed in the Farmers Union magazine.

Lemke had decided to attempt to compel the United States House of Representatives to consider his bankruptcy measure, and this tour was the beginning of his campaign. The rules of the House permitted a representative to bring a bill to the floor regardless of the Rules Committee or chairman of the standing committee by obtaining the signatures of 145 representatives on a discharge petition. To obtain a sufficient number of signatures was difficult because representatives with bills of their own and favors they wished to ask hesitated to offend the Rules Committee and the powerful chairmen of the standing committees. It was a rare event and a minor miracle for a discharge petition to obtain the necessary names. Lemke had full confidence that once the bill was on the floor he could mobilize sufficient public sentiment to muster a respectable, if not a majority, vote. As long as the bill was in committee, he could not bring pressure to bear where it would be effective. The committee chairmen were men with great seniority which had come to them mainly through their election from "pocket borough" districts. So secure were they in their positions that they were immune to any pressure Lemke could bring. The only form of persuasion they respected was patronage from the White House, and that was being used to prevent passage of Lemke's proposals.

Lemke learned how to obtain free time from radio stations. He would mail transcriptions of his talks to small radio stations, and he frequently obtained time on national networks. After his return to Washington the Farmers Union continued to sponsor radio appearances for him, which helped bring pressure on individual congressmen. He felt compelled to continue this course of action in view of the fact that it was difficult to explain the intricate House rules to the public and to make clear to farmers what a discharge petition was. In the face of these obstacles, Lemke forced one representative after another to risk President Roosevelt's wrath and that of the House leaders. They knew it was safer to sign the petition than to refuse and face the resulting criticism of their constituents. Many urban representatives were convinced of the wisdom of the bill by Lemke's tireless persuasion and added their signatures; others signed so that Lemke would leave them alone. The administration was against him; the young attorneys in the government viewed him condescendingly; but many of the representatives who worked with him from day to day came to sense his unusual qualities and true merit, and this helped his cause.

Still reluctant to oppose the President, Lemke wanted to believe that advisers were responsible for the President's opposition to his program. He excused Roosevelt, writing: "I feel the President intends to make a record and to bring back prosperity. If he does not succeed in doing it, it is because of misinformation and misplaced confidence in his advisers." He wanted to believe he had not made a mistake in 1932 in supporting Roosevelt. "I am inclined to think that he is far more progressive than the reactionary Democratic machine. . . . I do not think that I made any mistake by falling in with Roosevelt and helping defeat Hoover."[31] But as Lemke intensified his efforts for the Frazier-Lemke proposals, it became more difficult for him to forgive President Roosevelt. Most despicable of all, it seemed to Lemke, was the administration's practice of waiting until he had almost enough signatures and then either promising favors or threatening reprisals to get representatives to withdraw their names from the discharge petition. Gradually he came to regard the President as a bitter enemy.

The long speaking tour and the many radio broadcasts he had given during the fall of 1933 made it easier for him to obtain signers for the discharge petition. By January 10, 1934, he had sixty-seven of the needed signatures. The Farmers Union again sponsored radio appearances for him, and a resulting groundswell of public opinion brought him additional signers. His son, William, Jr., was in law school in Washington but the rest of the Lemke family were in Fargo;* Lemke himself had no family life or social activity to distract him from his single objective of the moment. Night and day he worked, buttonholing congressmen in the Capitol, making appointments and telephone calls in the evening, writing letters to constituents of representatives he wished to influence. Whenever possible he traded votes and favors to obtain new signers. He had to obtain 145 signatures before the summer adjournment or face the North Dakota voters without any of the legislative accomplishments he had promised. On April 14, 1934, he was particularly successful in adding in one day eight more names to the petition only to find that Speaker Henry T. Rainey had applied pressure to have eight of those who had previously signed remove their names from the petition. His net gain had been nothing. He wrote Gutzon Borglum for assistance in bringing pressure on some of the Eastern representatives. Congress was scheduled to adjourn in mid-June, and the rule specified that a discharge petition must be filed seven legislative days before adjournment in order to bring a bill to the floor for consideration. By April 30 he had 132 signatures. On May 30 he was ready to admit the probability of defeat, but he persisted in his attempts.[32] He knew that House consideration of the measure would obtain for him more votes in the June primary than would his presence in North Dakota during the primary campaign.

In early June Lemke obtained the necessary signatures, but his elation was temporary. The administration had another parliamentary maneuver by which House consideration of the bankruptcy bill could be prevented. Instead of the customary adjournment at the end of

---

* Mrs. Lemke did not move permanently to Washington until Mary, the youngest of their three children, finished high school in 1936. William, Jr., the older of their two sons, kept bachelor quarters with his father while attending law school.

each day, the leaders had the House of Representatives recess each day to prevent the necessary seven legislative days from elapsing before adjournment. Lemke was able to bring enough pressure to bear on key members who were facing close election contests to force the administration to abandon this procedure. He was positive that the bill would pass if it came to the floor, and events proved him to be correct. Elatedly he had Skeels cancel his primary election campaign engagements. While the bill was through the House of Representatives, it still had to pass the Senate and from there return to conference committee. It had been the House and not the Senate which provided the major obstacle to the bankruptcy bill. The Senate at Frazier's urgings had held the necessary committee hearings. Although Senator Frazier was now in North Dakota campaigning for his third term, Lemke carefully watched and supervised the progress of the bill until it had passed both houses and had been sent to the White House for approval. It was President Roosevelt's turn to feel the anxious concern of debtor farmers who had been influenced by Lemke's persuasive radio talks and the urgings of the Farmers Union. Many congressmen had voted for it because it was politically embarrassing to do otherwise. The President was in a like situation. He was presented with a bill which he had tried to defeat by every means at his command without coming out publicly against it. Now, in spite of his efforts, he was confronted with the choice of signing or vetoing. If he signed, he would receive little credit for it; it had not been part of his New Deal program. If he vetoed it, he incurred the displeasure of the farm belt. It was with reluctance that he affixed his signature.[33]

Singlehandedly in his first term and almost within a year of his arrival, Lemke had accomplished an unprecedented feat. As a member of the minority and against administration wishes, he had brought about enactment of a major piece of legislation. For Lemke it was the greatest accomplishment of his congressional career. It was the only one of the four main proposals of his program to be enacted into law. C. C. Daniels, brother of the Secretary of the Navy during Wilson's administration, wrote: "For a grisly old fighter, you can't be beat."[34] Lemke's place in the agrarian hall of fame had been made secure.

Except for the passage of the Bankruptcy Act in June, 1934, Lemke's experience in Congress was a discouraging one. Nevertheless, he had set the pattern for the type of congressman he would be. Throughout his legislative career, his work was to be marked by a maximum of attention to public bills and only minor time spent with private bills.* This was significant, for it characterized him not as a builder of a machine but as a legislator concerned with the general welfare—the first but not the only quality necessary for the congressman who desires the role of statesman. If Lemke did not earn the right to be considered in the latter category, it was not because he was using his office as would a cheap ward-type politician. He was genuinely devoted to the public welfare and he had a high concept of the function of his office. The economic emergency again caused him to look upon himself as a kind of savior, a fact that had been noted in him by one of his contemporaries during the time when he was interested in the industrial program of the Nonpartisan League. He gave of himself so unsparingly that during his congressional years he barely managed to retire his debts and neither accumulated private means nor conserved his health and strength.

Lemke was now faced with the campaigns for renomination in the June primary and re-election in November. He had solved one problem by fulfilling one of his campaign promises. Events occurring in North Dakota since he had left presented him with another. Langer had completely alienated most of those who had been elected to office with him in 1932. With the exception of those who had been candidates for Congress, they were now opposing him. Despite the opposition among League leaders, Langer had taken effective steps to win the rank and file of the organization. He had declared a moratorium on farm foreclosures and had placed an embargo on wheat, and the sentiment created by these moves plus the use of state employees at League conventions enabled him to retain control of the League in spite of the defection of those who had been elected with him. These latter saw they could not keep control of the League convention. Citing what he alleged to be Langer's illegal tactics, the chairman of the Nonpartisan League Executive Committee called a second convention.[35] Thus, in 1934, there were two League conventions and there were two League slates running for the Republican nomination. The anti-Langer faction was hereafter known as the Rumper faction. Lemke and Frazier were able to avoid offending either faction and were nominated on both slates, although Frazier

---

* The absence of private bills and the preponderance of public bills among those Lemke introduced was unusual enough to elicit a comment regarding it from the archivist who helped the author study Lemke's legislative record.

had to explain to the Rumper convention that he had not authorized Langer to use his name at the county League conventions. The Langer convention refused to renominate Sinclair and gave congressional endorsement to Lemke and Burdick; the Rumpers renominated Lemke and Sinclair. These conventions were held at the time Lemke was carrying on the campaign to win signatures to the petition which brought passage of the Frazier-Lemke Bankruptcy Act—a proposal so popular that it made both Frazier and Lemke assets to fellow candidates on whatever guide card they were listed. The loyalties they still retained from past League associations made it hazardous for either League group to refuse to nominate them at this time.

By this time Langer's ambitions were apparent to Nye. Further success on the part of the governor might enable him to defeat Nye in 1938. From the beginning Lemke cautioned Frazier to stay out of the dispute, and he followed that policy himself. Actually Lemke and Langer had had a private disagreement in January, 1934, but both felt that they had more to lose than to gain from a public rupture.[36] Langer benefited from this, for he was eventually able to defeat Frazier and go to the United States Senate. Perhaps 1934 was not the politically opportune time to do so, but Lemke lost by delaying too long a public airing of his differences with Langer. His single-minded devotion to his congressional program and his desire to make certain of his own re-election occupied his time to the exclusion of all else.

What chance the Rumpers had of defeating Langer was removed by three factors: the refusal of Frazier and Lemke to break openly with Langer; the determination of the Independents to sponsor a ticket despite their total defeat of 1932; and the action of the federal government in bringing an indictment against Langer charging conspiracy and collusion to divert funds from relief appropriations.[37] No one factor was determining. The Independents split the anti-Langer vote, and the other two factors combined to create a situation which enabled Langer, who had trailed his own ticket in 1932, to discard that ticket and earn such a majority for re-election that he became the central pivot of North Dakota politics.

One of Langer's more unpopular actions had been to levy 5 per cent of the salaries of most state employees to finance a new newspaper, *The Leader.** If Langer had confined his levy to officers of the

---

* Employees were permitted to reimburse themselves by selling subscriptions to *The Leader.*

state who did not handle federal funds, he probably would not have been in serious legal trouble. But when Langer's representatives had called at the various offices in the state capitol, they had not overlooked the offices the state had established to dispense funds supplied by the Federal Emergency Relief Administration; funds had been obtained; and this was the basis for the federal government's indictment. Harry Hopkins had dismissed Langer as head of the relief administration on March 1, 1934. Harold Ickes, Secretary of the Interior, was actually behind the action; he was known to be determined that there be no diversion of funds appropriated for relief purposes, and North Dakota enemies of Langer—possibly with the encouragement of Senator Nye—are thought to have conveyed to Ickes the information about Langer's solicitation.[38]

Langer's trial and conviction coincided with the primary election political campaign, which made the episode appear to most North Dakotans as political persecution. His trial began on May 22, and the jury convicted him and four associates on June 17.[39] The primary election was on June 27, and Langer's attorneys successfully requested the judge to grant a stay of sentence until June 29; Langer campaigned vigorously in the period between June 17 and the election. Those who justified the verdict against Langer felt that it was worse for him to have tampered with relief appropriations than it was for political parties to levy their customary political assessments on postmasters and other officers. Langer's supporters felt that he was being legally "tarred and feathered"; speakers at Langer rallies spoke of him as a martyr and reminded their audiences of the crucifixion of Christ and the assassination of Lincoln. Milo Reno came to North Dakota to assist him. At public rallies for Langer, the mood of the people was almost reverential. As he entered a hall, the crowd would stand; there would follow cheering as great as North Dakota audiences possibly had ever given.* During this ten-day interim between Langer's conviction and the election, Lemke returned to the state.

Endorsed by both tickets and returning from his congressional victory, Lemke's popularity was such that he easily could have won without further campaigning. His relatives in Towner County were supporting Langer, and his brother Ben was running for the state Senate on the Langer ticket. Langer was praising Frazier and Lemke in his speeches. Lemke had accepted endorsement from the Langer

* The author attended the Langer rally at Cando and visited for a short time with Milo Reno on that occasion.

convention, and it would have been an invitation to political reprisal
to oppose Langer at election time. So long as he did not appear on
the same platform with Langer, he was able to avoid dangerous reprisals from the Rumper Leaguers. Nevertheless, he did speak in
Traill and neighboring counties in the days just before the primary.
He did not campaign with Langer, and he avoided the issues of personality and corruption which dominated the campaign for state office.
He devoted most of his time to a discussion of the need for money.
"We don't have enough money to do the work of money," was his
stock phrase during the campaign.[40]*

The election was an overwhelming victory for Lemke; he polled
72.11 per cent of the total vote cast in the Republican primary. Although he did not poll as large a percentage of the vote, Langer's
victory was more remarkable in that he did not have the advantage
of being nominated on two different slates. Langer was renominated
by a vote of 113,027 to nearly equal the combined votes of all other
candidates including the Rumper candidate, T. H. H. Thoresen, who
polled 47,380, the Independent candidate, James P. Cain, whose total
vote was 37,934 and Thomas Moodie, a Williston newspaperman, who
won the Democratic nomination by a vote of 30,796 to his opponent's
7,795. The election ended the congressional career of James Sinclair
and sent Usher Burdick to Congress to resume the public career
which had been interrupted some two decades earlier. Lemke did
not openly campaign for either Sinclair or Burdick, but he had not
been fond of Sinclair since the latter campaigned against Smith in
1928 and he desired Burdick to win. Burdick had assured Lemke
that he would take no offense if Lemke did not campaign for him
just so long as he did not campaign for Sinclair.[41]

The sequel to the primary nomination of Langer confronted Lemke
with other difficult decisions. Two days after the election Langer was
sentenced to eighteen months in federal prison, fined $10,000, and
automatically deprived of his civil rights. Lieutenant Governor Ole
Olson, who belonged to the Rumper faction, immediately claimed the
position as governor. The attorney general ruled that Langer's conviction was not final until his appeal to the Circuit Court of Appeals
had been heard, but on July 18 the Supreme Court overruled the

---

* Tracing the history of the monetary controversy since the time of the Civil
War, Lemke stressed the good fortune of the country that not all of the Civil
War greenbacks had been retired. His favorite device was to pass a dollar
bill around through the audience to show how many debts it could discharge
and come back to its original possessor in payment of a debt.

attorney general, and Langer was disqualified not only as governor but also for the nomination he had just received from the electorate at the June primary.[42]

For a time it was a question as to whether Langer or Ole Olson would act as governor. After the Supreme Court ruling, the adjutant general of the National Guard accepted orders from Olson, and Langer was compelled to give up his office, although he was permitted to reside in the governor's residence. Ole Gunvaldsen, United States Marshal for North Dakota, had called at Lemke's home and had asked him to assist in the legal maneuvers that resulted in Langer's removal; Lemke declined to assist, but Gunvaldsen knew that Lemke hoped they would succeed in removing Langer from office.[43] The Nonpartisan League had control of the Republican machinery; logically enough they substituted Mrs. Langer for her husband as the gubernatorial candidate of the Republicans to oppose Thomas Moodie, the Democratic candidate.

Charles C. Talbott, the president of the North Dakota Farmers Union, warned Lemke to leave the state and not return until after the fall election. He added that Milo Reno and E. E. Kennedy were taking personal credit for the passage of the Bankruptcy Act and were giving neither Lemke nor the Farmers Union as an organization the recognition that was their due.[44] Talbott was friendly to the cause of the Rumpers and knew that Lemke would offend many of that faction if he campaigned for the Langer ticket in the general election. The Bankruptcy Act was being challenged in federal court in Kentucky, and this gave Lemke a good excuse to leave the state. For a time he accepted Talbott's advice.

Attorney General P. O. Sathre appointed Lemke to a post as special assistant in his office. In that capacity Lemke went to Kentucky to help defend the constitutionality of the Bankruptcy Act. Before election day Lemke was back in the state, campaigning this time in the southwestern counties of North Dakota. Again he campaigned by himself, trying to reach as many communities of German origin as possible. The intensive campaign the Democrats were waging for Moodie may have been one of the reasons Lemke disregarded Talbott's advice. Those on the Langer ticket would have been offended had he not returned, and there was always the possibility that the coalition of Rumpers, Independents, and Democrats which had united behind Moodie might succeed in electing other Democrats than Moodie. It was unlikely but still possible that the Democrats might elect their two candidates for Congress. If Lemke had any such fears, they were groundless. Although Moodie defeated Mrs. Langer by a vote of 145,333 to 127,954, Lemke was an easy winner, polling 144,605, substantially more than Burdick, who received 114,844; and William D. Lynch and G. F. Lamb, the two Democratic candidates, who polled 85,771 and 79,338 votes respectively.[45]

Upon Lemke's return to Congress in January, 1935, his plan to attempt to pass the refinance measure by circulating a discharge petition encountered two obstacles. The experience of congressional leaders in the previous session caused them to revise the rules of the House. Instead of requiring 145 signatures on a discharge petition, the rules adopted by the Seventy-fourth Congress required 218 signatures. The second obstacle was a continuation of the legal assault upon the bankruptcy measure which had begun in the fall of 1934. In one Federal District Court after another the act was held unconstitutional. It was carried to the Federal Circuit Court of Appeals and from there to the United States Supreme Court. Lemke had cooperated with the attorneys who were defending the act, appearing in one court battle after another, and he took the leadership in preparing the case and pleading it before the Supreme Court. On May 27, 1935, the Supreme Court unanimously held the law unconstitutional, holding that it deprived creditors of property without due process of law.* Lemke appeared surprised at the decision of the court. The chief opposing counsel who succeeded in having the Bankruptcy Act declared unconstitutional was John W. Davis, Democratic candidate for President in 1924. Lemke charged later that the Associated Presidents of the Life Insurance Companies had paid Davis $60,000—a large sum of money in 1935—to prepare and plead the case against the bankruptcy measure. He also charged that the opposition to the bill had twice stolen it on its way through Congress. He was compelled to transfer much of the energy he had been exerting on behalf of the refinance bill in order to rewrite completely the bankruptcy measure. The revised act provided for a public sale at which the mortgagee could be permitted to bid and placed the property more fully within the discretion and control of the court. It also provided for a payment of a reasonable rent by the debtor,

---

* Charles and Mary Beard, in appraising the court's action, admitted that although the law had been loosely drawn and was not an official part of the administration's program, yet "it reflected the desperate plea of debtors for relief from the letter of the bond" (Beard, p. 262).

which the court was empowered to apply on taxes and upkeep. The court was also given authority to declare that the emergency period had elapsed whenever prosperity returned.[46] The rewritten bill went through Congress with greater dispatch than had the first bill. The original act had been declared unconstitutional in May; the revised act was passed in August. Lemke and the Farmers Union had done their work well, and there was little question about grass roots sentiment and its effect on farm-state congressmen who opposed the measure. August, 1935, was near the end of the first session of the Seventy-fourth Congress, and Lemke was compelled to wait until the second session, which began in January, 1936, to work for passage of the refinance measure.

The fight over the refinance measure had begun in 1934 and had run concurrently with that over the Bankruptcy Act. There was a significant difference in the outcome. Lemke never succeeded in obtaining passage of the refinance measure; his failure to do so caused him to make the major error of the second portion of his public career. Lemke had introduced the refinance measure during the Seventy-third Congress; it was not long before the administration had to decide whether to support or oppose the bill. Doggedly Lemke set out to obtain the signatures with the same methods he had used with the bankruptcy measure, devoting his every waking moment to the task. The administration was surprised at his success, and it was not long before he had nearly the necessary number of 218.[47]

The Post Office and Commerce departments both applied pressure on congressmen to take their names off the petition. The Department of Agriculture kept a list of the names Lemke had obtained on the discharge petition. Their attitude and that of the administration on the refinance bill had been determined in 1934. At that time Stephen Early had received a letter from radio station WSPA of Spartanburg, South Carolina, stating that Lemke had sent them recordings of speeches on his refinance bill. They inquired of Early whether the bill was one endorsed by the administration, and indicated that they would not otherwise use the recordings. Early forwarded the communication to the Department of Agriculture. There it was processed through the chain of command with one interesting memo from "MGE" attached, which termed Lemke's bill "a pipe dream." After the Department of Agriculture had deliberated over the provisions of the bill, Wallace wrote Early that the radio station was free to do as it wished, but that the bill did not represent administration policy.[48]

House leaders were particularly effective in getting names removed from the refinance bill discharge petition. To protect those representatives who did as they suggested from feeling Lemke's pressure through their constituents, they asserted that the names of those who signed the petition must remain secret and could not be made a matter of public information.* The climax of the refinance bill debate and its sequel, his Union party campaign, were not to come until the summer of 1936.

While Lemke was growing ever more bitter toward Roosevelt, North Dakota politics were taking a strange turn. Thomas Moodie, the newly elected governor who was both the only Democrat in office and also the only anti-Langer candidate to be elected, had been disqualified by a constitutional provision requiring five years of continuous residence in the state before being inaugurated as governor.† Moodie was a Williston newspaper man who had accepted employment in the Twin Cities, but within a few months he had returned to Williston. While in Minnesota he had registered to vote. The contention that Langer successfully advanced was that this registration was proof that Moodie had not been continuously a resident of North Dakota for five consecutive years prior to his inauguration. Langer reportedly telephoned Walter Welford, Pembina County farmer who had been elected lieutenant governor on the Langer ticket, and said: "I am going to make you governor of North Dakota." Action was brought against Moodie, and the fact that the Langer forces had control of the lower house and could bring impeachment charges against either Moodie or the judges meant that the court had to declare Moodie disqualified. Welford assumed the office of governor and shortly thereafter differed with Langer and joined the Rumpers, setting the stage for a Welford-Langer battle for the Republican gubernatorial nomination in June, 1936. During the interim, Langer's conviction had been set aside by the Federal Circuit Court of Appeals. He faced two more successive trials in Federal District Court which

---

* Such star-chamber proceedings outraged Lemke, but they did not destroy the sense of humor which was part of his platform effectiveness. Henry T. Rainey of Illinois, Speaker of the House from 1933, had before his death been particularly effective at getting names removed from the petition. Lemke quipped on the floor of the House that his project had run into a wet season, a "Rainey spell" (*Congressional Record*, 74th Cong. 2nd Sess., 1936, LXXX, Part 6, p. 6883). It was a lighter moment in an otherwise serious debate.

† Lemke and Frazier had not openly broken with Langer and were on the Langer League guidecards as well as on the guidecards of the Rumpers.

on both occasions resulted in hung juries. Langer filed an affidavit of prejudice against Andrew Miller, the federal judge for the North Dakota district. Federal Judge A. Lee Wyman from the South Dakota district presided at the last two trials.* The federal district attorney did not try to bring Langer to trial a fourth time; Langer was again free to enter the political arena.

From most of this Lemke was far removed. He was so deeply involved in battle with the administration that he had neither time nor attention for North Dakota politics. Too, nearly twenty suits against the revised bankruptcy measure had been instituted in various federal district courts, testing every facet of the law. Lemke aided in defending against these suits in every instance, participating in person whenever possible. For none of these services did he charge a fee, and his exasperation was increased by his conviction as to the unreasonable nature of the attacks on the law and the adverse rulings by many of the federal district judges, an opinion that was substantiated when the United States Supreme Court ruled unanimously in 1937 that the revised Bankruptcy Act was constitutional.

Incredible as it seemed to administration spokesmen who, as Lemke neared the goal of 218 signatures, stated they would have two names withdrawn for every one that Lemke had added, Lemke was able to obtain the necessary number of signatures to take the Frazier-Lemke refinance measure out of the hands of the standing committee and onto the floor of the House, avoiding the almost certain death it would have had at the hands of the Rules Committee. For the nervous dynamo of a man who for eight months had gone with little food and less sleep to bring the measure to the floor, this was his moment of triumph. As in 1934 with the bankruptcy measure, the months just before the election had made his grass roots pressure most effective. It was not an accident that it was exactly two years since his success with the discharge petition on the bankruptcy bill. Representatives did not want to go home to face their constituents in an election year and explain why they were opposed to permitting a vote on the measure. That the same pressure would insure its passage once it was on the floor, Lemke had not the slight-

---

* Later, at the hearings held to determine whether Langer would be disqualified from the United States Senate, it was charged that Langer had bribed Wyman's son during the trial. (Congress, Senate, Committee on Privileges and Elections, Hearings, Relative to a Protest to the Seating of William Langer, a Senator from the State of North Dakota, 77th Cong., 1st Sess., November 3 to 18, 1941, pp. 25-76.)

est doubt. He assumed that the battle was over when he had enough signatures, for 218 was a majority of the House.\*

On May 8 Representative John J. O'Connor admitted that the filing of the discharge petition meant that the Rules Committee could not prevent House consideration of the measure and pleaded with members to vote "nay" on Monday, May 11, when the House would vote whether to discharge the Rules Committee or not. Lemke had been certain of final victory when he had obtained the final signatures he needed. The vote of 145 to 134 to discharge the Rules Committee, which was changed to 220 to 153 after the "Yeas" and "Nays" had been called for, removed the last doubt in his mind as to final success. It was with pride and confidence that he stood up in the well of the House and addressed the Chair: "I call . . . motion no. 7 signed by 218 members of the House, to discharge the Committee on Rules from House Resolution 123," the resolution which provided for a special order and day on which no other bill than HR 2066, the Frazier-Lemke refinance bill, could be considered.[49]

It is probable that, just as was the first version of the Bankruptcy Act, the refinance measure was loosely drawn. One of its provisions certainly gave promise of difficulties to come. In an effort to right all of the wrongs incurred as a result of the agricultural depression, Lemke had included any farmer or member of that farmer's family who had lost his or her farm through indebtedness on mortgages foreclosed since 1921. During the debate he agreed to change the date to 1928. This provision had political appeal; it had elements of justice about it; but it would have been very complex to administer, and it would inevitably have affected the rights of third parties who were innocent holders of property which had gone through foreclosure proceedings. Another provision, for loans on farm livestock, weakened the bill, and Lemke was compelled to delete this during the course of the debate.[50]

The press and the financial world were frightened by the measure. The conservative *New York Times* attacked its inflationary features, calling it "one of the most extraordinary to be brought before this or any other session of Congress." After the bill was defeated, the *New York Times* expressed the relief of business interests, saying

\* This was not a safe assumption. Lemke had argued that the representatives should sign regardless of whether they were for or against the measure. His contention was that they should permit debate and a vote. Many signed the petition as a result of this argument and still had reservations as to how they would vote.

that "the enactment would have . . . forced private lenders out of the
farm mortgage business"[51]—a basic cause for the opposition. There
is serious doubt as to whether the inflationary feature was as dangerous as opponents of the bill thought. Demand deposits and currency
outside the banks had been increasing since 1933; the difference between the provisions of the refinance bill and the policy of the administration in increasing the money supply was a matter of method.
The administration was accomplishing a monetary increase by borrowing from commercial banks; Lemke proposed to have the administration issue more Federal Reserve notes.* The inflationary dangers
would have come only if, after a sample of inflation, the farmers and
other groups had asked for further currency inflation. If a similar
procedure had been followed for mortgages on urban housing and
other types of credit, basic damage to the monetary system of the
nation might have resulted. It is worth noting that the Congress had
in May, 1933, attached the Thomas amendment to the Agricultural
Adjustment Act. This amendment authorized the President to issue
three billion dollars in greenbacks; the refinance measure proposed by
Lemke made the issue of currency mandatory in the event the farm
loan bonds did not prove marketable, but only in this compulsory
feature did it differ from the provision attached to the Agricultural
Adjustment Act. Lemke pointed out on the floor that the government
was doing essentially the same thing with its Federal Farm Mortgage
Corporation Bank.

It was the fear of inflation that defeated the refinance measure. On
the first day of the debate Lemke denied the accuracy of a statement that the American Federation of Labor was opposed to the
bill. He said he knew it was not true because "the late Mr. Truax
got the statement from Mr. Green that neither he nor his organization
were fighting the Frazier-Lemke refinance bill; that they had no objection to it. That was in May, 1934, and it has not been repudiated
in writing. Mr. Green did give out a statement that he was against

---

* Representative Knute Hill, a Democrat from Washington, quoted Lewis W.
Douglas on this point: "There is no fundamental difference, says Lewis W.
Douglas, former Director of the Budget, between the issuance of new currency,
virtually greenback money, and the issuance of government bonds which represent more debt. . . . Therefore the former Director of the Budget sees no more
reason to become alarmed about . . . 'new money' . . . than about paying . . . with
baby bonds" (Congressional Record, 74th Cong. 2nd Sess., 1936, LXXX, Part
7, p. 7210). Douglas had been talking about a different issue, the payment of
the bonus, but the principle was the same.

inflation, but he knew enough to know, as I assume—I did not talk to him—that this bill is not inflation."[52] On the next day Joseph W. Bryns introduced a most telling point, a letter from William Green:

The executive council of the American Federation of Labor, which is now meeting here in Washington, gave special consideration to the provisions of the Frazier-Lemke Act. The council is in thorough accord with all practical legislation which has been advanced for the purpose of relieving the economic situation existing among farmers of the Nation. We wish to see them helped and assisted by the Federal Government. This fact was demonstrated when labor gave united support to the enactment of the processing tax which was embodied in the Agricultural Adjustment Act.

This executive council of the American Federation of Labor, however, is opposed to the Frazier-Lemke Act, largely because of the inflation feature of this proposed legislation.

Labor knows and understands that the proposal to print and circulate billions of currency as proposed in the Frazier-Lemke Act will very vitally affect the economic well-being and status of labor. We know quite well that when inflation of the kind and character embodied in the Frazier-Lemke Act is adopted commodity prices rise but wages stand still. We cannot subscribe to this sort of economic philosophy. Labor would suffer reduction in living standards, reduced buying power, and the problem of unemployment would become more acute. There are other features of the bill which are highly objectionable.

For this reason we call upon our friends in Congress to vote against the enactment of this legislation. We are confident that the best interests of the wage earners of the Nation would suffer very greatly if by any chance the Frazier-Lemke bill would be enacted into law.

We sincerely hope and trust that the Frazier-Lemke Act will be defeated. We rely upon the friends of labor to vote against this proposed inflation legislation.[53]

Lemke attempted to counter with a letter from A. P. Whitney, president of the Brotherhood of Railroad Trainmen, endorsing the Frazier-Lemke refinance bill and asking labor to support it. Representative Gardner R. Withrow of Wisconsin congratulated the American Federation of Labor for taking the same side as the Liberty League.[54] But nothing that could be said nor any letters that could be introduced could undo the harm done by the letter from Green.

The entire legislative day of May 12 was devoted to debate on the bill, and it was not until May 13 that a vote could be taken. Lemke was field marshal of the affirmative, yielding and apportioning the time fairly closely to prearranged plans. He was at his best, calmly trying to quiet the many rumors and what he alleged to be misinformation about the bill. Quietly he pointed out that it was not revolutionary but an extension of current governmental practices in issuing Federal Reserve notes based on commercial paper. The most effective floor attack against the bill was an emotionally charged speech by Representative David J. Lewis of Maryland. Stating that inflation followed World War I only in those countries which pursued unwise policies, sparing a nation such as England, he obviously had an effect on his auditors.* One of the members, knowing that Lemke disliked the man for whom he had campaigned for the Presidency in 1932, attempted to embarrass him by asking if he were not a "Roosevelt Republican." Lemke neatly sidestepped by replying that he was not a "Hoover Republican." A damaging point was scored by one member, who cited an advertisement in an Indiana newspaper to the effect that the bill provided for refinancing the entire farm indebtedness of eight billion dollars when actually it provided for the refinancing of only three billion. "Someone is misleading the public. The advocates of the bill know that the bill cannot and will not finance 'all' farm indebtedness. Either that, or they are not sincere when they say in the bill that the fund shall not exceed $3,000,-000,000." Sensing that he was losing votes, Lemke consented to amendments. Telling points had been made against him on the floor, but he knew that his defeat stemmed primarily from William Green's letter, which Roosevelt's congressional leaders had read into the record. Lemke claimed that Green had been called to the White House and that the President had pointed out to Green how adverse the inflationary effects of the bill would be for labor, and then had promised Green to have Congress write into law a provision setting minimum wages and maximum hours for all contractors engaged in work for the federal government.† On the final vote, the Frazier-Lemke refinance bill was defeated by a vote of 235 to 142.[55] It had been a floor debate such as occurs fairly often in the United States Senate but which rarely happens in the House of Representatives.

* According to W. O. Skeels, in an interview on August 30, 1956, this speech actually changed the minds of some representatives, something uncommon in congressional procedure, where most speeches are addressed to the constituents and not to fellow members.

† This was the Walsh-Healey Act, which was passed by the Congress the following August and signed by the President on August 30, 1936. In his interview of August 30, 1956, W. O. Skeels told the author of Lemke's claim that Green had been called to the White House.

As John J. O'Connor, chairman of the Rules Committee, was caustically commenting on Lemke and his tactics, Lemke himself with a few of his supporters withdrew to the corridors to discuss their overwhelming defeat. To Chairman O'Connor the result was a vindication of the committee system. Bitterly he complained: "As has been fairly clearly demonstrated in the debate here in the past two days . . . this bill is the greatest monstrosity which was ever presented to any legislature. . . . No legislature can conduct its business in town meeting. . . . About 13,000 bills have been introduced. . . . Only 400 will ever become public laws. . . . To bring on the floor of the House a bill just because it has a demagogic appeal . . . [is] a cruel dastardly deception [that] has been practiced on the farmer." Lemke blamed the defeat on the letter from William Green and on the fifty-eight "double-crossers" who signed the discharge petition but voted against the bill because the President sent bureaucratic lobbyists to the House to campaign against it.[56] Whether it was these lobbyists or William Green, Lemke knew that one man and one man alone had stood in his way—the man whom he, Lemke, felt that he had placed in the White House in 1932.

The *New York Times* commented editorially: "The House of Representatives has seldom done a better day's work or done more to restore confidence by a single vote, than when it beat this bill by a handsome margin."[57] A careful appraisal would seem to indicate that the *Times* was unfair in its conclusion. Much can be said in criticism of Lemke, but the refinance measure mobilized the credit resources of the government to redress the wrong done to the farmer by the drastic deflation. The bill possibly needed rewriting. The provision regarding livestock and the retroactive date of 1921 both seem unwise, but Lemke was willing during the floor debate to change both of these provisions. He understood the tragedy that had happened to the farmers; his measures were not revolutionary nor would they have undermined the economy. Lemke had constructive suggestions to offer the Roosevelt administration, and it was unfortunate that his suggestions did not have a more favorable hearing.

President Roosevelt now had a bitter enemy, more bitter in defeat than he would have been in victory—but he was in no position to injure the career of the President. In his disappointment and anger, Lemke seized the only allies available to hurt the President. He had nothing but contempt for Alfred M. Landon; he had had great assistance from Father Charles E. Coughlin in mobilizing the sentiment for the signing of the refinance measure discharge petition.* Lemke was ready for whatever weapon should come to hand, and Father Coughlin offered him the finances and the beginning of a party organization to run for President. His decision to accept this opportunity was a mistake that cost him heavily in money and reputation.

* Harold L. Ickes asserts that Father Coughlin's Washington representative demanded that the President support the Frazier-Lemke bill, failing which Father Coughlin would attack the President's policies on the radio (Ickes, p. 536).

# CHAPTER VII

# In Union There Was Weakness

To William Lemke, Franklin D. Roosevelt seemed to be a conservative President. He not only failed to support Lemke's inflationary measures, but he also failed to take full advantage of the inflationary Thomas amendment to the Agricultural Adjustment Act. Instead of having the federal government take over the banking system in 1933, he had shored up the private banking system by creating the Federal Deposit Insurance Corporation. His eyes blinded by disappointments, the accomplishments of the New Deal to Lemke were eclipsed by its failures. The power of the administrative employees in the Department of Agriculture especially embittered him. Many of them had no farm experience and had never won an election.[*] To Lemke these men seemed to be arguing about protocol and procedure when, in an economic sense, men were drowning.[†] With his customary zeal and faith in the easy perfectibility of society, he believed in cutting the Gordian knot by a few well-directed monetary measures.

There were other embittered reformers, most of whom had "single-shot" panaceas and all of whom were originally supporters of the President, but who were in 1936 estranged because of the latter's failure to adopt their ideas. Some of them had begun to adopt the

---

[*] George N. Peek relates an incident about one of the young attorneys who, not knowing that farmers speak of the wheat from which macaroni is made as durum, was very much concerned about the men who planted and grew the macaroni, i.e., the macaroni farmers (Fite, *George N. Peek and the Fight for Farm Parity,* p. 261).

[†] The author remembers a suicide by one farmer. It was not until copy of a note from Lemke to this farmer, found in the Lemke Papers while doing research, stating that the action of the federal judge would prevent implementation of the Frazier-Lemke Act in this farmer's instance that the author realized the relation between the invalidation of the Frazier-Lemke Act and the tragedy of an individual family. The timing of Lemke's letter leaves little doubt that the news regarding the court action was the immediate cause of the suicide.

217

symbolism, the ethnic hatreds, and the stage props that resembled the beginning of a fascist movement. Their dependence on the leadership principle and the authoritarian structure of their organizations heightened the suspicion that they might develop into movements which, if they gained power, would become one-party systems as in Italy, Spain, Russia, and Germany. There were a half-dozen of them. One centered in Louisiana, another in Michigan. Attacking the malefactors of wealth and promising "to make every man a king," Huey Long had become boss of Louisiana, crushing the political machine the misdeeds of which had helped make his rise possible. In the Senate to which he had come after serving as governor of Louisiana, he had supported the same measures as had Lemke. Lemke either did not realize or refused to recognize that there was a vast gulf setting him apart from Long and that their standards of personal rectitude and their convictions as to the proper operation of the democratic process were worlds apart.* When Huey Long was assassinated and it appeared that the Reverend Gerald L. K. Smith was assuming control over the Long machine, Lemke seemed to accept him as unreservedly as he had Long.[1] At least he was not hesitant about forming a political alliance with him.

The radio priest, Father Charles E. Coughlin of Royal Oak, Michigan, had started using the radio in the late 1920's in an effort to raise funds for his parish. Although he had originally confined his talks to religious subjects, he gradually turned to a discussion of politics and became a fervent advocate of Roosevelt's policies. Because the President refused to adopt the inflationary policies he was advocating, Coughlin turned against Roosevelt in early 1935, denouncing the President in vitriolic terms. By means of his radio talks, he had created an organization which he called the National Union for Social Justice. Like Long, he had an appeal to a following that was nationwide, and there was a definite tinge of anti-Semitism in the movement he led, which was especially apparent in heavily Catholic Massachusetts.[2] The two main centers of his strength were among members of the Roman Catholic communion in that state and, because of his

* To one of his very close friends who lived in Louisiana and who had written to Lemke warning him of Long's alleged fascist tendencies, Lemke replied: "I do not know anything about the Senator, excepting as I have seen him in action in the U.S. Senate. There he has always been a hundred per cent for the people, and a thousand per cent against Wall Street" (William Lemke to C. Hall, August 2, 1935, Lemke Papers).

eloquent appeals for inflation, among rural Protestants in the Middle West.

A third movement, which had none of the earmarks of fascism but which resembled the other two in the unilateral nature of its approach, was headed by a retired physician, Dr. Francis E. Townsend. Appalled by the tragedy dramatically portrayed for him by the spectacle of former middle-class elderly people rummaging in garbage cans for food and obviously without any means of support during their declining years, Townsend came forward with what seemed then to be a revolutionary plan for old age pensions which would provide an income of $200 per month for those over sixty-five years of age, to be paid from a 2 per cent transaction tax. The recipients of the pension were to spend it within thirty days. At first the movement had "a certain dignity and pathos" about it until it "formed an amalgam with [Long's] Share Our Wealth program." The "fanatical harangues and cynical methods" of the latter group modified the Townsend movement and "changed its tone."[3] Never as angry as its ally, it did assume some unfortunate aspects and eventually lost some of its respectability. Townsend's following, too, was nation-wide and consisted of clubs which were banded together into state organizations federated into a national movement.

These movements had affected public opinion, and they brought about or modified some of President Roosevelt's legislative proposals. The Townsend movement was responsible for hastening social security legislation; the pressure from Long's forces resulted in higher income taxes than would otherwise have been enacted; and Father Coughlin may have caused the President to take steps which it was hoped would prove reflationary. Roosevelt felt toward the proposals of these groups as he did toward those of Lemke, that they were too extreme and might weaken rather than strengthen the capitalistic system; and he probably shared the suspicion of some that both Long and Coughlin would prove a threat to the constitutional framework within which the United States traditionally operated.

The three movements were in touch with a substantial number of voters, but the leaders were deluded, as are so many leaders of organizations, into believing that they could deliver their followers in blocs. They were further deceived about their total strength by failing to realize that their memberships were duplicatory. No doubt there were many people who belonged to all three organizations, and a great many more who were members of at least two of them. Adding the memberships of the three groups together in computing the number of voters they influenced was one of the mistakes Lemke made.

Had Long lived, he would have been the logical candidate of a coalition of the three groups, although Father Coughlin might have sensed in time that an alliance with Long would be dangerous should the latter prove victorious. However, Long would have been a more effective Presidential candidate than Lemke was in 1936 in his attempt to deadlock the election and thus to leave the choice of President to the House of Representatives. There had been talk of a union of forces, and Long's death meant the necessity for finding a new candidate. Neither Smith nor Coughlin as clergymen were politically available, and Townsend was obviously not candidate material. To find a candidate who was available, it was necessary that Coughlin search among practicing politicians to find someone on whom they could agree and who in turn would accept endorsement. This last qualification was important. There were rumors, denied by the senator, that Senator Nye was approached.[4] But Nye refused to oppose Roosevelt in 1936. Inflationary Democrats, such as Elmer Thomas of Oklahoma, were from states where it was suicidal to run on any ticket other than the Democratic. The area of choice was narrow. The candidate would have to be a Republican now in office who was not dependent on either the Republican or the Democratic party for election and who was unwilling to support either Roosevelt or Landon. Lemke fit the pattern exactly, and the defeat of the refinance measure in May made him receptive in June, 1936, to such an offer.

Lemke's experience with the Nonpartisan League had led him to believe that a new party could mushroom nationally with a minimum of financial backing, as had the League in North Dakota.* His long experience had taught him that politics makes strange bedfellows, and that to be successful a politician had to accept support from those of whom he did not necessarily approve. He defended himself in one letter:

The fact that I may speak at Coughlin's or Long's meetings does not mean that I accept all of their ideas or ideals. But you surely know me

---

* Had Lemke been more realistic, he would have known the amount of money necessary for a campaign and would have insisted that his backers show ability to raise such a sum before he consented to run. Borah, when approached with a similar suggestion during the 1924 campaign, had estimated $3,000,000 as the minimum figure needed to start a new party on a sound basis (William E. Borah to Frank Knox, August 11, 1922, Borah Papers).

well enough to know that I am not afraid to speak with the devil, if necessary, and I have been on platforms with some speakers for whose views
I have not had the slightest respect, and which I did not hesitate to assail
at the first opportunity.[5]

But if Lemke had ever considered being a third party Presidential
candidate himself before, it had been as a nuisance candidate to
compel the two major parties to modify their stands on monetary
and agrarian issues.[6] When he actually accepted the Union party
candidacy, it was not with the thought of being a gadfly candidate,
but with the actual intention of capturing enough states to transfer
the election into the House of Representatives, an event which would
have given Lemke prestige and enormous bargaining power.

The defeat of the refinance bill set the stage. Wanting more than
anything else a national forum with which to reach the people and
sell his monetary views, he was tempted by the fact that such a forum
was what Townsend, Coughlin, and Smith had to offer. To Father
Coughlin he felt particularly indebted. The Michigan priest had
endorsed Lemke's refinance bill, had praised Lemke generously in
radio speeches, had given him the recognition denied by the administration, and had been extremely helpful in pressuring sufficient congressmen to get the discharge petition signed in the spring of 1936.
Coughlin and Lemke had occasionally corresponded, and it is probable that mutual friends carried messages of admiration back and
forth. Edward E. Kennedy, Lemke's strongest supporter within the
Farmers Union after Simpson's death in 1934, was of the same faith
as Coughlin and was in touch with him. Coughlin's Washington representative, Louis B. Ward, was Lemke's most available means of communication with the Michigan priest. An alliance between Coughlin
and Lemke was not difficult to forge, given Lemke's mood following
his May 13 defeat and Coughlin's lack of alternative candidates.

Between May 13 and June 19 the arrangements were made by
telephone and personal messengers. It was necessary that the four
parties most immediately concerned—Coughlin, Townsend, Smith,
and Lemke—have a meeting of minds and agree on concerted action.
Coughlin took the initiative and made the legal assistance available
to analyze the election laws. On June 8 he wrote to Lemke, whom
he thereby appointed as North Dakota state chairman of the new
party, sending a complete analysis of the election laws of the forty-
eight states and the steps necessary to get the party's candidates on the
ballot. This was a thorough study of the laws and very apparently had

been done by capable attorneys. A copy was probably sent to each
state chairman whom Coughlin had appointed. There was nothing
in this letter to indicate that Lemke was anything other than a state
chairman of the new party holding such position as an appointee of
Coughlin. In the letter there was one sentence that revealed a startling
difference between traditional American political machinery and the
methods by which Coughlin operated: "In due time telegrams will be
sent you containing the following information," that is, the names
of the candidates for President and Vice-President.[7]

Lemke's friends maintained that Coughlin promised more funds
than he gave, and the picture of money coming in hundreds of
thousands of dollars was attractive to a congressional candidate who
ordinarily borrowed on his life insurance to pay his campaign expenses.[8] The further assurance of votes in the millions from Coughlin,
Townsend, and Smith made Lemke feel fairly certain that these voters
combined with his own Nonpartisan League following would enable
him to carry at least North Dakota and perhaps some other states.
Lemke did not take into account that he himself spoke an "agrarian
tongue" and had an appeal limited to rural regions, and that votes
which could be won for state offices could not always be delivered
for President. Lemke had shown upon his arrival in Congress that he
lacked flexibility, a prime requisite in a candidate who must appeal
to various groups and regions of the nation. He was a regional figure,
not a national candidate.

On June 16 there was an announcement of an amalgamation of the
Townsend, Smith, Coughlin, and Lemke forces, and Lemke wrote
Thomas Charles O'Brien of Boston, Massachusetts, "I am happy that
you have consented, at my request, to seek the office of Vice-President
on the Union Party Ballot. We will stand and fall together on the
principles which are so dear to both of us." This seems a feeble
effort on Lemke's part to live up to the American tradition that the
Presidential candidate has the privilege of selecting his running mate.
There seems little doubt that Coughlin selected both Lemke and
O'Brien and that, in sending the wire, Lemke was deceiving himself
more than anyone else. Throughout the campaign the same staging
was necessary to attempt to prove that the Union party was in the
American political tradition. In August a nominating convention was
held, although Coughlin had nominated the candidates in June. Individuals interested in silver speculation may have recommended Lemke
to Coughlin, and it is possible that the choice of Lemke was first

seriously considered at a meeting on the estate of Francis P. Keelon.[9] News of Lemke's possible candidacy was a surprise to a public which never had heard his name suggested as a possible contender. Even in his home state, where he was well and favorably known, his candidacy was viewed as a move to worry the major parties, to force the New Deal to the left, or to extend the influence of the Hearst empire.

On June 18 Coughlin still professed uncertainty as to whom a third party might endorse. Lemke announced his candidacy on the following day. Almost simultaneously Coughlin endorsed him as eligible for support from the National Union for Social Justice, a transparent effort to conceal the prior arrangements that had been made between the two men. One wag quipped that it was the only convention that had ever been held in a telephone booth. Lemke, O'Brien, Coughlin, Francis P. Keelon of New York, and Martin Sweeney of Cleveland met at Great Barrington, Massachusetts, on Sunday, June 21. On June 23 Lemke conferred with Townsend and Smith. The following day he explained to his North Dakota constituents that he had "accepted the challenge of the reactionary elements of both the old parties [to] run for President of the United States on the Union party platform in accordance with the thousands of messages and requests I have received."[10]

Lemke then went to Michigan where he met with Father Coughlin and O'Brien in the rectory of Coughlin's church. After this meeting they announced a platform which endorsed a monetary and farm program similar to that which Lemke had been advocating, the probable inflationary nature of which had appealed to Coughlin and which had made possible an alliance between the two men.* The platform included planks calling for a central bank of issue and stipulated that the government would cease issuing interest-bearing bonds. It provided, too, for a farm aid bill that would include the cost of production formula, and it endorsed the Frazier-Lemke refinance bill. The Townsend pension plan was advocated, but there was no mention

---

* This was another example of staging comparable to the announcement of O'Brien's candidacy. Lemke's letter of June 16 offering the Vice Presidential nomination is evidence of prior arrangements, for he could not otherwise have so easily assumed that O'Brien would accept. Likewise the platform later announced scarcely differs from the statement originally given by Lemke. (*New York Times,* June 20, 1936.) It is safe to assume that just as there had been prior arrangement on the Vice Presidential candidacy, there also had been an earlier agreement on the nature of the platform.

of collective bargaining, a significant omission and one that lessened the appeal of the party to labor.[11] Although not expressly stated in the platform, the foreign policy of the leaders and the tone of the platform was definitely isolationist.

Lemke also spent some time at Cleveland, where later he was to appear at the Townsend and National Union for Social Justice meetings held there in July and August, respectively. After Usher L. Burdick had resigned from the chairmanship, which he had originally accepted, Lemke suggested the name of John Nystul of North Dakota for national campaign chairman; the suggestion was adopted and other North Dakotans such as Herbert Swett and former North Dakotans such as Louis P. McAneney became key figures in the party's campaign organization. Had the party succeeded, it might have evolved into the traditional American pattern with a channel available for authority to come from the precincts as had happened in the case of the Nonpartisan League.

The party had no reasonable hope of success unless, by some stroke of political fortune, the race between Roosevelt and Landon should be very close. In that event the capture of one state by Lemke would have given him great power in the House, where, if a deadlocked electoral college passed the decision to the House, each state would have one vote and North Dakota would have as much influence as New York. After Long's death, the Roosevelt administration had been able to woo the Long machine from Smith. The best chance for the Union party seemed to be in Lemke's carrying North Dakota and O'Brien's carrying his home state of Massachusetts, although there was some hope that the Progressive Wisconsin party organized by the two sons of La Follette and the Farmer-Labor party of Minnesota with Floyd Olson at its head might join with the new coalition. If there were any hope of the Union party's mushrooming into a significant movement, it lay in winning not only Philip La Follette and Floyd Olson but also key liberals such as Norris, Wheeler, Henrik Shipstead, and Frank Murphy. It had been a serious error on Lemke's part to accept the candidacy before the promised funds had been banked where they would be available; it was equally serious for him not to have made certain that the liberal wings of the two old parties would endorse his move. Had there been a genuine movement of liberals, Lemke would not have been the nominee, however, for there were many liberals who would have made far stronger candidates.

Members of Coughlin's group and the Townsendites caused Philip La Follette, his brother Senator Robert La Follette, Jr., and other leaders some difficulty. They stalled for time, pleading that they had agreed with the liberals of other states not to announce their decision until there had been a conference to decide on a course of action. The conference was held in late summer and as a result, Lemke received little support from any elected representatives, senators, or governors except that which came from Congressman Burdick and Senator Frazier of North Dakota. Even Nye refused to oppose President Roosevelt.* A further difficulty resulted from the legal provisions of many states, which made it impossible to get the Union party electoral candidates on the ballot in thirteen states.[12] In those states Townsend was compelled to advise his followers to vote for Landon.

Townsend was loyal to Lemke throughout, and his publications continued to support him, although the Townsend convention heard Lemke's address and significantly enough had then refused to endorse a third party ticket. The first rush of support to Lemke was short lived, and the volume of mail soon fell off sharply. Father Coughlin lost political face when he called President Roosevelt "a betrayer and liar," and this perhaps accounted in part for the later slackening in his support of the party he had begun. That he had hurt Lemke badly was clearly evident. On August 18, Lemke appeared before the National Union for Social Justice and met with better success than at the Townsend meeting. The members overwhelmingly ratified the candidate Father Coughlin had chosen. In a speech at this convention, Coughlin called the President an "anti-God," a statement for which he was rebuked by his own church and one which made Lemke strategists dubious as to the value of his support. Undeterred, Coughlin later spoke of bullets "when the ballot becomes useless." Smith's statements were likewise extreme, and he at one time called for 1,000,000 young men to bring about ballot reform by forcible measures.[13]

It was Lemke's hope that, if nothing else resulted, he would at least be able to salvage the party machinery for use in the 1940 campaign. Before the election was over, he ceased to have any personal association with Smith and told others that after election the Union party would be independent of Coughlin because the latter's interest would cease at that time. In one of Lemke's early Union party addresses, he said: "I am an optimist, though I know that truth is still on the

---

* Nye was reported to have joined George W. Norris and James Couzens in an endorsement of Roosevelt. (*Current History*, XLV [October, 1936], p. 9).

scaffold, and wrong is still on the throne. But I know behind that throne an enlightened public opinion is still shaping the destinies of this nation ... that in the end decency and righteousness will prevail." He was an optimist who gradually became disillusioned, for the money that had been promised was not forthcoming in anything like the

This cartoon in support of Lemke emphasizes that he was accessible to the people all over the nation and that he was not confining his speaking to large urban centers as were the candidates of the two traditional parties and the other third parties that had slates in the 1936 election.

anticipated amounts. Lemke found that the burden of setting up a national headquarters fell largely upon him and the men whom he could recruit. An effort was made to supplement the disappointing contributions by starting a national campaign for one-dollar memberships, but with meager results. Before the election was over Lemke had invested $7,000 of his own money, for which he was never reimbursed.[14]

There were other disappointing features. Even a politician whose life had been as rugged as Lemke's might notice the import of posters advertising a Union party political rally which featured a speech by Father Charles Coughlin and then, in much smaller print, mentioned that "William Lemke, Union Party candidate for President, will also speak." Father Coughlin promised to retire from the radio if he were unable to deliver the votes of the National Union for Social Justice, a promise that he kept for a time. The nomination of O'Brien brought nothing to the ticket. The man was unknown nationally and had held no high elective office in his home state. His nomination brought no Roman Catholics to the support of the party not already attracted there by Coughlin's leadership. The large farm organizations supported Roosevelt despite Kennedy's determined efforts to hold them for Lemke. Kennedy charged that the farm leaders had been bribed by patronage jobs from the administration. Because Kennedy's policies were not in accord with those of the Farmers Union majority, he lost his position with that organization. He maintained that the other farm leaders sold out to Roosevelt and that part of Roosevelt's price was the dismissal of Kennedy.[15] Lemke's only appeal was agrarian, and that was in large part nullified by the leaders of the other major farm organizations, who remained loyal to Roosevelt. Passage of the social security bill had mollified many of Townsend's followers, though the doctor, irate at the treatment accorded him by a congressional committee in May, 1936, loyally supported Lemke.

Most discouraging of all was the argument that to vote for the Union party was to throw a vote away. With a candidate that would appeal only to one or two segments of the electorate; with one of those segments offended by Coughlin's stand on labor; with the farm leaders against him; with business groups supporting Landon; and with the leading liberal, progressive leaders of the nation supporting Roosevelt almost to a man, there were only fringe elements left for Lemke, and his candidacy appeared pathetic. It was a discouraging, disheartening experience, and it was made the more so by the necessity of keeping up a confident appearance and by the concern about the effect of his candidacy on his chance of being re-elected Representative from North Dakota. Through September Lemke still clung to the hope that he might be a factor in the election, and friends of Lemke remember statements he made that indicate he may still have been deceiving himself as to the status of his candidacy. More probably he was maintaining the traditional optimism expected of

political candidates. Meanwhile Lemke at times found audiences even
in the farm belt unreceptive. Undeterred, he continued the course
he had begun. The A.A.A. he denounced as "a national lunacy" and
Wallace as "the greatest vandal in history."[16]

By the end of a tour to the Pacific Coast which started at Kankakee,
Illinois, on October 14, it had become clear that Lemke's campaign
was lagging and that he would do better to devote his efforts toward
being re-elected representative from North Dakota. This was doubly
important because Lemke had not only not retired the debt he had
incurred for his home but had borrowed more money during the
campaign. The congressional position had saved Lemke from financial
disaster; to have lost it before the depression had ended and to
be left with an additional burden of debt, assumed during the campaign, would have been a major catastrophe to Lemke and his family.
Sensing this, Herbert Swett, one of Lemke's most devoted followers, called Mrs. Lemke and told her he thought it important "to
see that we still have a Congressman Lemke." They agreed that it was
vital that Lemke give several radio talks in North Dakota before the
election, but this was difficult because there was neither money nor
credit available. By means of a stratagem Swett borrowed the money
from a Valley City bank, cashing the draft before the banker awoke
to what poor security there would have been for the loan had Lemke
been defeated.* With the money Swett had borrowed, Lemke was
able to deliver four radio talks on a state-wide network. In an attempt
to win the Midwest corn, dairy, and wheat areas, he continued his
bitter attacks on administration farm policies and advocated his own
measures and the cost of production formula. There was little restraint
in his criticism of an administration which he alleged was "continuing
this insane policy in the midst of hunger, misery, want and rags. . . .
There is an overproduction of just one thing, and that is an overproduction of ignorance."[17] Everywhere in the farm area he promised
to put an end to eviction for debt.

It was apparent to Lemke followers that the Democratic party
leadership did not appreciate his attacks on the New Deal. He attacked the President personally, stating that "If all the insurance
companies and mortgage holders are doing as well as President
Roosevelt, there will be no homes left. They will all have been looted

* The banker did try to stop payment on the draft, but Swett had cashed it
immediately.

either by the government or mortgage holders." He further charged
that the President was bringing foreign corn right into the heart of
the agricultural area "to drive down the price," and then added that
"when President Roosevelt gets the river fixed up, we can get this
foreign farm produce delivered right at your door here in Minneapolis.[18]

It was not surprising that the Democratic organization launched
a campaign to defeat Lemke for Congress in North Dakota. Despite
this threat and the fact that his campaign headquarters was without
funds and he himself without further personal resources upon which to
draw, he had returned to Eastern states, speaking there and in Midwest states such as Indiana, areas which there was little realistic
hope of carrying. Lemke neatly parried the Democratic argument that
he was running for two jobs and therefore was not being honest with
his constitutents. "Some of my so-called friends ... even suggest that
I am running for two offices. ... I am not running for President. The
Union Party electors are running for Presidential electors. ... I am
running as a Nonpartisan candidate for Congress on the Republican
ticket. ... I want to be there to help elect myself President. ... [Do]
not ... forget Usher L. Burdick. ... When this election is thrown into
the House I also want him there to help elect the Union Party candidates."[19]

Lemke was re-elected to Congress, but the Union candidates for
elector received only 12.8 per cent of the votes of his home state and
less than a million nationally, hardly more than the total vote for
Norman Thomas in 1932. It was appallingly less than he had hoped,
and he never ceased to try to explain it. In no other state did he
receive as high a percentage of the total vote as in North Dakota.
He ran nearly as well in some large cities, receiving 12 per cent of
the vote in Cincinnati, 11 per cent in St. Paul, 9 per cent in Dubuque,
and 8 per cent in Boston. He polled a big vote in Stearns County,
Minnesota, where he was born and the county which Samuel Lubell
termed the "classic isolationist county in the whole United States." His
largest vote was in Ohio, where he received 132,212; Massachusetts
was next with 118,639; Illinois gave him 89,439; Michigan and Minnesota added 75,795 and 74,296 respectively to his total, while Penn-
sylvania and Wisconsin, the other two states in which he had sizable
totals, gave him 67,467 and 60,297. These seven states and North
Dakota, where he polled 36,708 votes, provided him with a total of

654,853 votes. This was 73.42 per cent of the total of 891,886 votes that
he received. The other twenty-seven states in which he was on the
ballot gave him less than 26 per cent of his total vote.*

Lemke was apparently weakest in northeastern North Dakota, in his
home county of Cass, and in a number of counties in southwestern

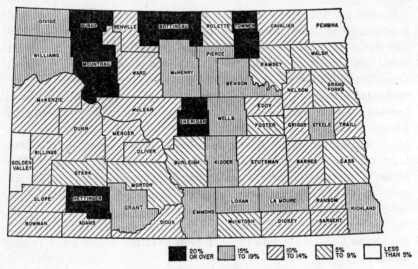

FIG. 2.—1936, Union Party Vote

North Dakota. One county in the central part of the state, and
Rolette County, on the Canadian border, gave him a very light vote.
His heaviest vote came in Burke County, where he polled 29.88 per
cent of the vote. Two other northwestern counties, one southwestern,
one centrally located, and Towner—the county where he lived as a
boy—gave him more than 20 per cent of their votes. Lemke's vote was
greatest in those counties where he had leaders who were able to hold

---

* Samuel Lubell ascribes the national vote concentration to religious and
ethnic factors. His studies revealed that except for North Dakota, Lemke's vote
was greatest in the states, cities, and wards which had high concentrations of
voters who were German or Irish Roman Catholics. He does not believe that
was true of North Dakota during the election of 1936, and a study of North
Dakota counties in which Lemke polled the greatest votes does not indicate
that ethnic or religious factors weighed heavily in that state (Lubell, pp.
142–144). Owing to various party labels, the figure given for Lemke's total vote
varies slightly. The total used here includes those cast for the Union, Royal Oak,
Independent, Third, and National Union for Social Justice parties (*Information
Please Almanac*, 1948 [Garden City: Doubleday and Co., 1947] p. 134).

a following for him or in other counties where the organization of one or both of the major parties was weak. There is certainly no indication that he received a preponderance of the German Roman Catholic vote in North Dakota.

An unfavorable press, which played up the attacks on Lemke's integrity made at the time of the recall campaign, and unfavorable headlines of magazine articles did much to lessen his chances. His personal appearance did not conform with the urbanity and polish that Americans had come to expect in their Presidents. The effect of the campaign on Lemke's national reputation was disastrous. The same extremism, inflexibility, tendency to exaggerate, and propensity for invective which had helped exclude him from Roosevelt's circle of advisers left an even more unfavorable impression because of the political company he was keeping. His finer qualities were completely obscured so far as the national electorate was concerned. The fact that by election time he had become genuinely concerned about re-election to Congress meant that he was not too depressed by the result, and his overwhelming re-election to Congress did much to ease the disappointment. Lemke received 131,117 votes for Congress to lead Burdick, who received 115,913. The two Democratic candidates, Henry Holt and Jess Nygaard, received 100,609 and 89,722 respectively.[20]

The Union party episode was not over. Lemke was determined to keep the party alive, and national headquarters were maintained in Chicago for two years. Lemke unrealistically hoped it would survive the unfortunate circumstances under which it had been born and would become a major party. This presented problems in each state, for the party machinery lay subject to capture by whoever wished to seize the opportunity. In North Dakota in 1938 Langer filed dummies on the Union party ticket to prevent the organization from being used against him in the campaign for state offices. From Illinois came information, which Lemke refused to believe, that the party was being used by Nazi groups. From many of his Union party supporters came anti-Semitic material that was abhorrent to Lemke. Angrily he wrote that the material he had just received trying to prove that the Jews had kidnapped the Lindbergh baby "is fit for the waste basket and not worthy of that," and he condemned the Silver Shirts or any group that attacked people because "of their race or religion." In letters to Rabbi Stephen S. Wise and to an editor of a Jewish daily he consented to serve as a sponsor of the American Jewish Congress and he endorsed Zionism, stating that Palestine should be given prime consideration as a haven for Jewish refugees, although in his letter to the latter he was almost prescient about Jewish-Arab friction. He wrote to one constituent that "no one regrets the persecution of the Jews or of any other people more than I do. I am also very sorry that in our own country there is an undercurrent against the Jews. I have repeatedly taken the position that in this nation all are entitled to equal protection and equal rights. It seems that many of our people are forgetting that there is no room for European hatreds in the United States of America."[21]

Although Lemke maintained contact with Father Coughlin and through him received some help in his 1940 campaign against Langer, he had been disillusioned by the priest's failure to give the financial help which he had thought was forthcoming, and also by Coughlin's repudiation and subsequent approval of Mayor James Curley of Boston. About the latter he wrote: "I do not know how a lepard [sic] could change its spots so quickly in two years. If Curley was as bad as they told us in 1936, he certainly did not become an angel by 1938." Meanwhile the Union party organization functioned despite the failure of Coughlin to give assistance. Meetings at which collections were taken, together with membership fees, kept a skeleton organization alive. Nystul recommended that it be dissolved in the fall of 1938. Lemke was reluctant, and it was only after a trip to Ohio in the spring of 1939 that he was willing to see the organization dissolved.[22]

Lemke's association with the Union party resulted in a change in his relation with House Democrats who had previously regarded him as a Republican "maverick," more Democratic than Republican except in party label. This had enabled him to marshal many Democratic votes for his agrarian measures despite opposition from the executive branch. Previously he had received assistance from the Farmers Union in influencing Congress, but most of that organization had supported Roosevelt, and those few leaders who had supported Lemke lost influence and position in the organization. The disillusionment of Democratic congressmen and his own inability to depend on the Farmers Union for as extensive assistance as in the past meant that Lemke was no longer the effective leader of an agrarian bloc that he had once been.

The Union party's greatest damage to Lemke, however, was to create a political situation in North Dakota which in 1940 would enable Langer to eliminate both Frazier and Lemke from Congress. In 1934 the political situation was not opportune for Lemke to have an open rupture with Langer. However, in 1936 Lemke could have prevented Langer from regaining the political strength he had lost since 1934. If Lemke had openly opposed Langer in 1936, Walter Welford would have been returned to the governor's chair and Langer would not have had a chance to rebuild his political organization.* Langer had barely held it together until 1936; it would have been much more difficult for him to maintain his organization until 1938 had he not been elected governor. The Union party was the determining factor in Lemke's failure to campaign openly for Welford in 1936. The Union party incident was a weakness in the second phase of Lemke's public career as the Lemke house had been in the first. The politically fatal result for Frazier and for Lemke was not apparent until 1940; actually Lemke never appeared stronger in North Dakota than in the years between 1937 and 1939. He could jokingly remark at the annual North Dakota dinner held in Washington in February, 1937, that he had intended to have this party in the White House.[23] North Dakotans had never had a Presidential candidate before and they were as much flattered as chagrined at Lemke's political misadventure.

Besides, a change was taking place in Lemke that made him more acceptable to the conservatives who had once fanned the flames of hate against him. His attacks on New Deal bureaucrats during the 1936 campaign made him a favorite of many conservative North Dakotans who differed with him only in preferring a return to Hoover policies rather than an adoption of Lemke's proposals. These latter would have been abhorrent to them. However, there was no possi-

---

* Welford had bested Langer for the Republican nomination in the June primary of 1936 by a vote of 90,788 to 90,093. Langer then filed as a third party candidate in the fall of that year, polling 99,750 votes to 95,697 for Welford and 80,726 for John Moses, the Democratic candidate. Instead of assisting Welford as he should have, Lemke was also in a third party column and assisted Langer, thus injuring Welford. Langer's vote was only a little over 36 per cent of the total, and his plurality of 4,053 meant that a switch of less than one vote per precinct from Welford to Langer was enough to result in the election of the latter, a shift which North Dakota's party column ballot facilitated. There were usually between 2200 and 2500 precincts in North Dakota. Every vote that switches counts twice, for it is subtracted from one candidate and added to the other. The Union party ticket would not have injured Welford so much if North Dakota had used an office group ballot. (North Dakota Secretary of State, Compilation of State and National Election Returns [1930-1944]).

bility that Lemke's ideas would be adopted; therefore, he was not dangerous as was Roosevelt, whose ideas were being translated into reality. Lemke and such men as Will Stern of Fargo could safely ignore their differences because neither one was in a position to put his ideas into effect, and in their aversion to almost everything Rooseveltian they spoke the same language. L. B. Hanna congratulated Lemke on his opposition to Roosevelt; this was the reopening of an alliance that had been terminated by the rise of the Nonpartisan League. Yet Lemke had not abandoned his radical ideas. In 1938 he published a book on money which was an up-to-date version of books by W. H. (Coin) Harvey and the senior Lindbergh.[24] Lemke corresponded with Harvey until the time of the latter's death in 1936, and he believed as strongly as he ever had that monetary measures such as his Bank of the United States and the Frazier-Lemke refinance measures, as well as government control of all credit facilities, would have made Roosevelt's strong central government with its consequent diminution of states' rights unnecessary. The fact that there was no possibility that Lemke would ever realize his program was not the only condition that made him acceptable to North Dakota conservatives. Langer's return in 1936 had completely removed the latter group from power, and at the time any opponent of Langer's became automatically an ally of theirs.

One other event occurring in early 1937 made conservatives even more confident that Lemke was becoming one of them. So embittered had Lemke been by the use of the labor vote to defeat his refinance bill that he was ready for any opportunity to embarrass the President. When, early in 1937, the President proposed to reform the organization of the United States Supreme Court, Lemke abandoned his previous ideas on legislation by judicial usurpation and participated in the attack on the President's proposal. At different times in the past, Lemke had supported proposals that would limit the power of the courts, and in 1936, after the first Frazier-Lemke bankruptcy measure had been declared unconstitutional and the second one was being so declared by one district court after another, he had attacked the Supreme Court in radio speeches which contained statements such as this:

The judges are just as much bound by the Constitution as is Congress and the President. Their violating the Constitution in the name of the Constitution will not longer be tolerated by Congress nor the people. . . . They know that the power of the Court is not to amend but only to expound the Constitution.... No Court should read limitations into the Constitution that do not exist. It should avoid judicial legislation, and leave Congress free to act.... Our Constitution is a masterpiece of fundamental legislation.... They made it elastic. They realized ... that the nation would grow.... They had no intention of putting hobble-skirts on Congress, and hindering Progress.[25]

Such comments in 1936 make very surprising and contradictory his violent attacks on Roosevelt's proposed modification of the United States Supreme Court in 1937 and his assertion that "no honest man could quarrel with the decision of the Court in more than ten to fifteen cases" during the entire history of the nation. He should have been aware of the contrast with his previous position, for he finished the speech with a paragraph starting with the words, "Our Constitution is a masterpiece of fundamental legislation" which was apparently taken word for word from the final portion of the speech he had given a year earlier.[26] Unless it is conceded that his purpose was to sway the court in its action on the second Frazier-Lemke bankruptcy bill, it is difficult to avoid the conclusion that he was influenced by the animus he felt toward the President.

It was at this time that Lemke appeared before the United States Supreme Court to defend the second Frazier-Lemke bankruptcy bill. Flatteringly, he told the court that he realized that their function was to guide the legislators in the drafting of future legislation, and that in drawing up the second bill he had been scrupulously careful to make the changes they had suggested. The Supreme Court was under attack from President Roosevelt and from the halls of Congress. These were kind words, and the language of the act indicated that Lemke had tried to overcome their objections. They unanimously upheld the second Frazier-Lemke bankruptcy act as being constitutional, an unusual consensus in that period of judicial controversy. Though inconsistent with Lemke's life-long convictions, his change in attitude between 1936 and 1937 had forwarded his program. One of the officers of the court remembered particularly the effectiveness of Lemke's plea on this case and commented that for any case in which Lemke was interested, he would as soon have Lemke plead as any lawyer who had appeared before the Supreme Court in his time.[27]

A second change in Lemke's congressional career that occurred between 1937 and 1939 was more consistent with his life-long convictions than was his reversal in his attitude toward the judiciary. With the exception of his views on Mexico, he was and always had been

an isolationist. So convinced from boyhood had he been of the iniquity
of the British Empire and the danger it held for the world position
of the United States that no other menace such as Hitler, Mussolini,
Stalin, or the Japanese emperor compared in his mind with the British as a threat to world peace and to the safety of the United States.
Actually, if these rising empires had destroyed the British Empire,
Lemke would have viewed it as an event enhancing the safety of the
United States and the peace of the world. Though his German origin
predisposed him to such opinions as these—as did the Irish origin of
other Americans—many who were neither Irish nor German by an-
cestry held similar views. Nye, Frazier, and Burdick were equally
isolationist. Ethnic factors coincided with "hostility to Eastern business interests, concern for economic advantage [improperly accruing
to Eastern industrial and financial interests], and fear lest war's
alarums impede the cause of social justice." The antipathy acquired from his father made it easier for Lemke to join Nye in denun-
ciations of the thefts and wrongs of the British Empire. When the
King and Queen of England visited in the White House in 1939,
Lemke grew vehement, exclaiming: "The executive seems to have lost
its head," and he declared that not even the King and Queen in the
White House would "induce Congress to again permit one man to
mix us up with the European insanity and thievery."[28]

His distrust of the President caused him to modify his stand on
armaments. Lemke never had been a pacifist; he was instead a na-
tionalist who believed in strong military defenses and who was opposed to disarmament. During his first term in Congress he wrote:
"I do not feel that one nation alone should disarm. . . . The way that
Japan treated China about two years ago, and is treating her now,
should be sufficient lesson to us that the defenceless [sic] are not
spared by militaristic nations . . . and I feel either Russia or the United
States will have to defend itself against the agressions [sic] of Japan
in the next five years."* In 1939 his views had changed; he was
critical because Congress had just appropriated an additional $1,600,-
000 for the navy. In one of his newsletters he commented that "that
$1,600,000 used to make our people again self supporting would have

* It is interesting to note that in 1934 Lemke's fear was of Japan and not
Russia, an attitude that he and many other isolationists forgot when at a later
date they criticized President Roosevelt for not foreseeing in these early years
of the New Deal that Russia was a threat to the United States.

shown real intelligence. In addition to this we appropriated millions upon millions for airplanes and army equipment. This in spite of the fact that a former chief of staff warned us that what we needed was national defense, not equipment for foreign aggression. He [the former chief of staff] said that what we needed was roads and transportation facilities." In the early 1930's, when practically all liberals with the exception of the President were advocates of disarmament, Lemke's had been one of the voices crying the need of national defense; but later, when large numbers of liberals were abandoning the isolationism which had resulted from World War I disillusionment,[29] Lemke had not only become more isolationist but was also opposing the strong armament policy he had once supported. This, too, was a change that would make him more acceptable to those conservatives who would later be influenced by the America First movement of Robert Wood of Chicago.

One thing that Lemke never fully understood was the effect of bank lending upon the volume of money. Apparently he did not realize that deficit financing by the government, with the balance between outgo and income borrowed from banks, would increase the quantity of circulating medium. He did vigorously support measures, such as the Federal Housing Administration, which insured creditors against loss. Measures such as these did increase bank lending and had a reflationary result. One thing Lemke felt that he understood about these programs was that banks drew interest not on money they had invested but rather on money they had created. This latter function of creating money, Lemke felt, rightfully belonged to the government. In the tradition of Jefferson and Jackson, he argued against private ownership of the facilities that create money, carefully explaining that his proposed Bank of the United States differed from the one Jackson attacked in that he was proposing a government-owned bank as contrasted with Nicholas Biddle's Bank of the United States, which was largely privately owned and controlled. It was not the radicalism of President Roosevelt that angered Lemke, but the fact that instead of "driving the money-changers from the temple,"[30] he was, in Lemke's view, enriching them by permitting them to manufacture money and draw interest on that which they had created. Lemke was consistent in his position on this issue throughout his public career, and in his last session in Congress at the time of his death in 1950, he was still introducing and supporting his bill for a Bank of the United States to be established and operated on the principles governing the Bank of North Dakota.

During his congressional career the bills Lemke introduced included proposals to outlaw vivisection, or to prohibit vaccination in the District of Columbia, or to postalize railway rates. His office was a hospitable one for any proponent of an idea which was so novel it could not get a hearing elsewhere. Usually Lemke would draw up a bill embodying the new proposal and introduce it. Some of these bills had greater respectability than others, such as his legislation to foster frequency modulation broadcasting or the proposal to establish an international university staffed largely by those associated in one way or another with the embassies and legations of other countries. This latter was as non-isolationistic a proposal as could be imagined, and Lemke would have been severely critical if the President had come forward with a similar plan. Lemke accepted the idea from an elderly gentleman who called at Lemke's office.[31] These bills seldom received much consideration except from Lemke himself. They constitute an unimportant part of his career except that many of them reveal weaknesses; it is proposals such as some of these that caused many reporters to speak of him as a "crackpot." Lemke's reputation was deservedly impaired by his readiness to sponsor sensational proposals that were not practical or which had been insufficiently studied.

During his second term in Congress, from 1935 to 1937, he began introducing bills which foreshadowed the character his congressional career would take when he returned to Congress after his 1940 defeat by Langer. The dominant interest of his last years in Congress was in the use and conservation of natural resources. His first interest in legislation of this type was a consequence of the drought years and resulted in a proposal in 1935 to impound, conserve, and make use of all unappropriated waters of the eastern slope of the Rocky Mountains. Legislation such as this, which was concerned with the problems of the interior, natural resources, Indian reservations, national parks, and land use, later became a major interest and modified the single-minded preoccupation with monetary and credit problems that characterized the earlier portion of his congressional career.

Meanwhile Lemke ran into political problems in North Dakota resulting from his failure to assist Welford in defeating Langer in November, 1936, problems that took much of the happiness and satisfaction from the rest of his public career. It was the political machine

built in 1937 and 1938 during his second term as governor that eventually elevated William Langer to the Senate. Nye's Senate position
was saved from Langer in 1938 only by an alliance with the Democrats and by a long and difficult campaign by Lemke. Langer had
been intensely popular in 1934 at the time of his trial, but the attitude of the public had changed before 1936; his election to the
governorship in that year was in a three-cornered race and by less
than a majority vote. He did not approach a majority of the vote of
the electorate after 1934 until 1946, and it was not until 1952 that
he again won a victory at the polls comparable to the one he had
won in June, 1934. His victories between 1934 and 1946 were won
in three-way contests. During the years between 1938 and 1946, the
issues which were debated in North Dakota political campaigns were
mainly state issues and revolved about Langer's conduct of his office
as governor. This made it possible for his opponents to form organizations which included those elements of the League who were still
identified with Lemke—Rumpers—and those who had formerly been
Independents but, until 1944, did not usually have an organization
of their own. Between 1934 and 1944 the Republican primary was
fought between this coalition and the Langer Nonpartisan League.
In 1944 the conservatives again assumed the initiative by forming an
organization somewhat similar to the Independent Voters Association.
The latter group had not waged a campaign since its overwhelming
defeat in 1934; the new group which replaced it in 1944 was known
as the Republican Organizing Committee and was referred to as the
ROC. The issue of Langer's conduct of his office became so intense
that the coalition against him broadened in the general elections
between 1938 and 1944 to include Democrats. A disturbed situation
in the North Dakota Agricultural College, where in 1937 a number
of faculty members had been abruptly dismissed, was attributed to
Langer by his opponents, and the institution was disciplined by the
North Central Association of Colleges and Secondary Schools. Public
reaction to this resulted in the passage of an initiated measure in 1938
creating a Board of Higher Education which was less directly under
the control of the governor than the Board of Administration. The
proposal for the new board was endorsed by the North Dakota Education Association after having been presented to that group by Ole
Gunvaldsen, one of Lemke's key supporters in the state, and it is
safe to assume that Lemke was fully aware of what was happening

and that he approved of the proposed change. It is possible that he
may have suggested some of the provisions of the new act.* It was
a tempestuous period in the state's history in which charges of corruption in the sale of bonds by some counties and other charges of
"kickbacks" were leveled at Langer.[32]

By 1938 Lemke was so thoroughly aroused by the alleged conditions, which he felt were true, and so dismayed because the old-
time Leaguers stubbornly were staying with Langer, that he decided
to openly oppose Langer. It was obvious by then that Langer intended to unseat Nye and enter the Senate. Although Nye and Lemke
had never been close, Nye's need of Lemke's assistance and Lemke's
determination to expose and end Langer's career caused them to draw
together and a Nye-Lemke-Frazier coalition became a central factor
in the anti-Langer forces then gathering. It drew to its support the
conservatives who had once been Independents and who now felt
less antagonistic to the three old-time Leaguers. At the same time
Lemke and Frazier still had a League following that stemmed from
the time when they had been central figures of that organization.
Many Leaguers who voted for Langer for governor continued to vote
for Nye, Frazier, and Lemke for Congress. The test that strained their
divided loyalties came when Langer ran unsuccessfully against Nye
in the June primary of 1938 and again equally unsuccessfully in the
general election of the same year; and it came again in 1940, when he
successfully ran against and defeated both Frazier in the June primary and Lemke in the November general election.

In the spring of 1938 the League endorsed Langer for Nye's seat
in the Senate and Burdick and Lemke for Congress. Lemke refused to
support Langer against Nye. The League then nominated Henry G.
Owen to run against Lemke. The anti-Langer coalition was willing
to nominate Lemke, but he refused to accept any offer which made
it necessary for him to campaign against Burdick, who was still on
the Langer ticket. Charles F. Kelsch and Sievert W. Thompson then
became anti-Langer candidates for Congress, and Lemke was left
without a ticket on which to run. He decided to conduct his own campaign with headquarters "in a room that cost us thirty dollars a

* The author was present at the meeting of the Legislative Assembly of the
North Dakota Education Association in October, 1937, when Gunvaldsen presented the plan. The North Dakota Agricultural College at Fargo is now known
as The North Dakota State University of Agriculture and Applied Sciences. The
University of North Dakota is at Grand Forks. Both institutions, as well as the
other state colleges, were affected by this initiated measure.

month, with one man in charge and one stenographer. I gave three radio talks and made fifty speeches, averaging two or three a day.... Even my friends were surprised that I could go into that campaign without any organization, without guide cards and singlehandedly win two to one and eliminate a corrupt system at the same time." The corrupt system Lemke alleged existed was Langer's, for Lemke had campaigned not so much for himself as for Nye and against Langer.* He polled 83,113 votes for a substantial victory over Owen, who received 51,922 votes and Kelsch, who received 37,502. He trailed Burdick, who had the advantage of being nominated on the League ticket. Burdick received 93,119 votes, and Burdick and Lemke received the two nominations. Lemke's voice had been the decisive one that it had not been in 1936, for there was little question that he had won the nomination for Nye, who defeated Langer by only 5,151 votes.[33]

Langer was not defeated that easily. He filed as a third party candidate in the fall, using the same device that had been so successful against Welford in 1936. Again Lemke made a great personal sacrifice to elect Nye and defeat Langer. As one of the two Republican nominees, he had organization support and was on the guide cards for the fall campaign. Able to win without that support in June, he would not have had to give a single talk to be certain of election in the fall. Lemke saw clearly that failure to campaign might mean a victory for Langer, and he worked as hard to defeat him as if it were he himself rather than Nye who was opposing Langer.

To defeat Langer, it was necessary to avoid what had happened when the Democratic candidate for governor† had put on a vigorous campaign in the fall of 1936. By doing so, he had taken so many

---

* Written just before the primary election, a letter of the author's indicates the role Lemke was playing. "I may be a sad-appearing prophet. If the trend which I indicate has occurred, its two main causes are... Nye's effective radio voice and Wm. Lemke's stump speaking. Nye has a radio voice second to few. Wm. Lemke is so closely associated with the old Nonpartisan League in the days when it was a radical party with an industrial program that he is respected by farmers as being one of their best friends. It was a political error of Langer's to break with Lemke if he could avoid it. Most people believe and Lemke's own story would seem to indicate that Lemke's refusal to support Langer forced Langer to drop Lemke" (author to E. M. Sait, June 25, 1938).

† "As far as State offices are concerned, the Democratic party in this State [North Dakota] is hardly more significant than the Republican party in Mississippi" (Talbot, p. 5).

votes from Welford that he had elected Langer. To prevent this from recurring, it was necessary to offer the Democrats something valuable enough to persuade them to restrain their own senatorial candidate, for the only chance of defeating Langer lay in not dividing the anti-Langer vote. The Democratic organization was ready to bargain. The national Democratic organization was greatly dissatisfied with the Democratic party in North Dakota. In a decade when most states had elected many Democrats to office, it had been able to elect only one, and he had been disqualified immediately, an event which reflected on the alertness of the party leadership. The national Democratic organization had been disappointed with the party in North Dakota and served notice on H. H. Perry, Collector of Internal Revenue, that in 1938 the party would have to do better in North Dakota or there would be a new Collector of Internal Revenue.[34]

Aware of this situation, Nye and Lemke agreed that the anti-Langer coalition would support John Moses for governor. The latter was a conservative Democrat and a candidate whom conservative Republicans could accept. The bargain to re-elect Nye in 1938 must have been acceptable both to Roosevelt and to the national Democratic organization, for although Nye had opposed Roosevelt on the Supreme Court issue, he had not been otherwise at serious cross purposes with the President. In return the Democrats did not have Jess J. Nygaard, their candidate for senator, campaign vigorously. These arrangements made more certain that the anti-Langer vote would not be divided, and Nye was able to defeat Langer again in the fall election. Langer's opponents attempted to make corruption the central issue of the campaign, while Langer emphasized old age assistance. Langer gained less than might be expected from use of this latter issue because Dr. Townsend came to the state and gave a speech endorsing Nye. The actual vote was Nye, 131,907; Langer, 112,007; and Nygaard, 19,244. The figures clearly showed that had Nygaard campaigned more vigorously, Nye's election would have been jeopardized.[35]

The coalition had been successful in defeating Langer and electing Moses, and Lemke felt certain that his rival would never again return to public life; he was sure that finally, and irrevocably, Langer was through. Thus it could and would have been, had the coalition not fallen apart. The fault of the Nye-Lemke-Frazier-conservative Republican alliance was that it was loosely held together, becoming a working alliance only at election time and then only if Langer's figure loomed on the political horizon. The three members of Congress were in Washington with no national patronage to dispense, and Governor Moses gave most of his patronage to Democrats instead of to those Lemke Leaguers who had helped elect him. In many instances, he retained Langer appointees. Lemke was too far away to alter the situation, although he did fly to Bismarck on one occasion in an attempt to do so. There was a further weakness in the coalition in that among the younger members of the group there were those who had political ambitions of their own. Noteworthy among these was Thomas Whelan. Often the coalition acted as two groups, the Regular Republicans and the Progressive Republicans. Lemke's habit of leaving politics until election time and conscientiously concentrating on his duties as congressman invited difficulty.[36]

The denouement came in 1940. Though defeated and out of office, Langer continued active and circulated petitions for an old age pension law which necessitated a special election in 1939. Though his proposal was defeated, Langer had endeared himself to another bloc of voters. There was a general feeling, however, that Langer's political power had been destroyed, and when the anti-Langer factions met at Jamestown on March 27, 1940, it was not with the same feeling of urgency that had prevailed in 1938, when Langer was governor. A. C. Townley's activities in this convention may have affected its outcome. He had been impressed with the political strength of Lemke during the 1938 campaign and was in close touch with Leaguers who had worked hard for Lemke and against Langer in that year. These Leaguers, at Lemke's urging, had campaigned vigorously for the election of John Moses and the defeat of John Hagan, Langer's candidate for governor in 1938. They felt that they were entitled to political jobs from Moses in 1939. Instead, Moses had appointed Democrats and kept on Langer appointees, leaving many of these Lemke Leaguers without the spoils of office. They wrote to Lemke many times, and Lemke had written to Moses on their behalf, but few of them had received serious consideration. Their discontent and Lemke's popularity caused them to decide to nominate Lemke for governor in 1940 to oppose Moses. Their argument was that if Frazier ran for the Senate and Lemke for the governorship, the conservatives would have to join them, for to do otherwise, they argued, would invite defeat. Led by Townley, they constituted the Progressive Republican organization. Townley and Charles E. Joyce led a delegation to see Lemke at Washington on March 13, and Lemke seriously considered their proposal.[37] Lemke finally agreed to run under certain conditions, and gave Joyce this letter:

I am not a candidate for Governor. I do not want the job. I much prefer to continue my work here in Congress. The only condition under which I would consent to become a candidate for Governor, would be to prevent the corrupt political machine that we put out of power two years ago from coming back again.

Never again shall we tolerate a political system that extracts part of the monthly salary of state employees, or that exacts kick-backs from those who deal financially with the state.

Under no circumstances would I become a candidate for Governor for the purpose of giving jobs to job-seekers. Our state is in a dreadful financial condition, and whoever is Governor must have the full confidence and cooperation of all the people. Our finances and in fact the very life of some of our people must be readjusted.

This cannot be accomplished by the restoration of the Langer machine. That machine does not represent the heart or the conscience of the Nonpartisan League—the farmers—nor of the business or professional men and women of our state. I find no fault with the Moses administration. I also feel that the Republicans can find many persons who can defeat the Langer machine other than myself. In this I shall be guided by the judgment of my friends with whom I had the pleasure of cooperating with two years ago when we routed the Langer machine. If at your next meeting the parties who attended the Jamestown and Bismarck conventions, together with others, feel that it is necessary for me to become the candidate for Governor I shall of course accept their judgment as final.[38]

The Jamestown and Bismarck meetings referred to had been called by the Progressive Republican group, which was now pleading with Lemke to run for governor. The qualifying phrase in Lemke's letter was "together with others." It is safe to assume that Lemke meant that the Regular Republicans must participate in the request that he run. He gave some evidence of taking his candidacy seriously and appointed Joyce to be his campaign manager for what Joyce felt certain was the race for governor. Frazier, according to Townley and Joyce, had consented to go along with the plan. In the meantime numerous factors caused Lemke to reconsider. He and his family had grown accustomed to Washington life; his secretary, W. O. Skeels, had no desire to live in Bismarck; many of his friends called on him and advised him against running; it is probable that he felt less certainty of election as a candidate for governor than he did as a candidate for re-election to Congress. Moses was proving to be a popular governor. The Regular Republicans had called a meeting at Jamestown for March 27 at the same time the Townley-Joyce Progressive Republican group was meeting there, in the same building. When Frazier was told on the telephone by the latter group that they were nominating him for senator, he declined to accept their nomination. Townley, Joyce, and their group realized then that this meant their plans to nominate Lemke for governor were not going to be acceptable to Lemke. They disbanded the Progressive Republican meeting, and many of their delegates became delegates to the Regular Republican convention, for none of the anti-Langer conventions depended strongly on credential committees. Calls were issued for the meetings, and those who came were often acknowledged to be delegates. The Progressive Republicans were "in a momentary state of pique"; in the Regular Republican convention they helped to defeat Frazier, a fact which they later regretted. The Progressive Republican group made up the central core of the Rumper and anti-Langer Leaguers; yet in their resentment at Frazier and Lemke, they helped send Langer to the Senate. Townley wanted the conservatives to refuse endorsement of both Frazier and Lemke, which he felt would insure defeat of the Republican ticket.[39]

Many of the conservative Regular Republicans were restive. They had welcomed allies such as Lemke and Frazier when Langer was in power. Now that he had been eliminated, the two congressmen appeared disagreeably radical. The hostility of Frazier and Lemke to creditors generally and to insurance companies and banks in particular, which had been forgotten in 1938, again seemed important. One conservative, L. L. Twitchell, understood Townley's intention of defeating the entire ticket. Remembering Lemke's successful campaign in 1938, he urged the convention not to refuse endorsement to Lemke, explaining that without Lemke they had no chance to elect a single candidate. Just as had the 1934 Independent convention, so some of these conservatives reasoned that they could win by splitting the vote of the League between the Rumpers and the Langer Leaguers. Just as had the Independents in 1934, they succeeded in splitting the anti-Langer vote and insuring Langer's election. The convention had delegates of many economic views. There were near-Socialists, progressives, and moderate liberals who had joined the Regular Republican group when their own Progressive Republican group failed to persuade Frazier and Lemke to accept endorsement from them. The conservatives were divided among those who wanted to nominate Frazier and Lemke and those who felt that the latter were too radical and too isolationist.

It was this latter group which Townley urged to nominate Thomas Whelan for senator. Townley worked with Jack Williams, a prominent member of the American Legion, and directed the strategy to bring about Whelan's nomination. The first move was to nominate the state candidates before naming the congressional slate. Townley convinced Williams and Whelan that Whelan had a chance for the nomination. There is no evidence that Whelan and Langer had an understanding with one another prior to this convention. This was the spring of 1940, when Hitler was on the march, and there was growing sentiment among many of the conservatives in support of Roosevelt's opposition to isolationism. Whelan was a member of a partnership in St. Thomas, North Dakota, which had indicated its feelings about the European situation by pinning a label on each sack of potatoes they handled which read "To Hell With Hitler." Whelan, like many other conservatives, was not an isolationist. The next step in the strategy was to demand a prior pledge from Frazier that he would support the entire ticket before tendering nomination to him. They knew that Frazier would be fearful of a situation in which he would either have to repudiate a promise or oppose Lemke. They insisted that a wire communicating their demand be sent by Gunvaldsen to Frazier. Gunvaldsen recalled that the text of the wire was "Unified committee assures your nomination in convention. It becomes essential that they have your support of ticket that will be nominated before endorsing you." It was Gunvaldsen's hope that Frazier would not answer or would delay answering, giving his supporters time to handle the convention. When Frazier replied stating that he would appreciate the nomination but could not pledge prior support to a ticket before it was nominated, Franklin Page, Jack Williams and other conservatives were able to persuade the convention that Frazier's reply disqualified him from convention support, and the nomination of Whelan resulted. Robert Larson, Frazier's secretary, was possibly responsible for sending the wire. If so, he was influenced by the fears of Lemke's secretary, W. O. Skeels, that a pledge by Frazier might be used against Lemke.*40

To Lemke the result was an unbelievable disaster, and Moses, who

---

* In an interview on August 30, 1956, W. O. Skeels stated that he may have influenced Robert Larson to urge this type of reply. He did not explain why Lemke and Frazier would not formulate a matter of such important policy.

had been sincere in his opposition to Langer, wired Lemke in April that the situation was "too horrible to contemplate." Nevertheless, the men around Moses were relieved that Lemke was not nominated as a candidate to oppose Moses for governor. Lemke felt that the major sacrifice he had made in 1938 had been thrown away. He had helped the conservatives defeat Langer in 1938, but in spite of this they had created a political situation in 1940 that made it possible for Langer to benefit from "a three-cornered fight." Frazier and Lemke called a small group together at Fargo on Sunday, April 21. This group pledged its support to Frazier in his campaign for the Republican nomination in the June primary. His two opponents were Whelan, who had been nominated by the anti-Langer Republicans, and Langer, who was the nominee of the Nonpartisan League. They nominated Lemke for Congress and made no other nominations for any other office. At this meeting Joyce was very critical of Lemke for not accepting the gubernatorial nomination, but Lemke defended himself by maintaining that the conditions he had outlined in his letter of March 13 had not been met.[41]

The anti-Langer coalition had been broken. Lemke refused to support Walter Welford, who had been nominated for congress by the Regular Republicans, and continued to support Burdick, who was on the Langer ticket. Moreover, he campaigned actively for Frazier and against Whelan. The Regular Republicans attempted to punish Lemke by refusing to include him on their guide cards and in their advertising. This failure of conservatives to realize their need of the anti-Langer Leaguers to defeat Langer was the secret of Langer's success and the reason for the end of Frazier's career and the anticlimactic nature of the rest of Lemke's public career.

Lemke was easily renominated for Congress in the June primary, polling 80,203, approximately 3,000 more votes than Burdick, who received 77,276. In the four-man race for the two nominations, James Gronna and Walter Welford received respectively 58,457 and 45,051 votes. Frazier was not so fortunate. Running on a platform of party regularity—an implied repudiation of the 1938 bargain with Moses—Whelan attacked Langer and ignored Frazier. Langer likewise gave no attention to Frazier and directed his criticism at Whelan. The European war affected the election. France surrendered immediately before and the air attack on England was beginning at the time of the primary. President Roosevelt had come before Congress in May and had asked for a two-ocean navy and armament appropriations such as had never been contemplated, making much of the fact that his previous requests for arms had been

defeated by Senate isolationists. This, in addition to the fact that
Whelan was from Frazier's home county, helped to take votes away
from Frazier and give them to Whelan. Langer again triumphed in
a three-cornered race, netting 61,538 votes out of a total of 152,250
votes cast for the three Senate contestants. This was 40.41 per cent
of the vote cast for senator in the Republican column and 33.45 per
cent of the total vote cast for both Republican and Democratic
candidates for senator.[42]

Langer had been defeated twice, in the primaries of 1936 and again
in 1938, only to run for the same office in the fall elections. To prevent a similar maneuver on Langer's part in any future election, the
1939 legislature had passed a law making a candidate ineligible to
run in the fall election for an office for which he had been defeated
in the primaries. Designed to handicap Langer, it now appeared to
make it impossible for Frazier to file as a third party candidate in
the fall of 1940. A later interpretation held that this law did not apply
to congressional races. In 1940 the prevailing interpretation, and the
one that Frazier accepted, was that it did. Unless the Langer opposition were to agree to support a Democrat, someone other than Frazier
would have to be nominated as a candidate without major party
designation. Former Independents such as Burtness and Stern were
genuinely alarmed, knowing that only the strongest candidate could
run as a third-party candidate and defeat Langer.

There was no question about who that strongest candidate was. At
the same time that Frazier was being defeated and in spite of the
war feeling, Lemke, without the support of any faction, had led the
field of congressional candidates. That each of the other candidates
had run with the full backing of an organized faction only to trail
Lemke was an indication of tremendous political strength in any
Lemke candidacy. Moses was under obligation to Lemke, and Lemke
felt that he could trust the governor's assurances that he would do
everything within his power to support him in a bid for the senatorship, and Lemke assumed it would be within the power of
Moses to have Charles Vogel, the Democratic candidate for senator,
restrained as Nygaard had been in 1938.[43] Lemke felt certain that he
could obtain most of the Frazier and Whelan votes. No other candidate was conceded a chance to win in the third party column, and
Lemke was confronted with the alternative of supporting Langer or
the Democratic nominee; to give Roosevelt another Democratic senator to support his foreign policy was an unpleasant alternative to
Lemke. Besides Moses there were many Cass County conservatives,

such as Walter Stockwell and Robert Haggard, as well as men such as Burtness of Grand Forks, who were pressing Lemke to enter the contest for the United States Senate seat.

In the last analysis, it was not pressure that caused Lemke to run but the drawing power of the opportunity that appeared before him and seemed within his grasp. He was an aggressive legislator and knew what he could accomplish if given the scope of the United States Senate in which to work. For the first time since 1925 what seemed to him as the logical fruition of his public career appeared possible. Another concern for both Moses and Lemke was that Langer's candidate for governor might defeat Moses unless Lemke attracted votes away from the Republican column instead of to the Republican column, as he would if he remained a Republican congressional nominee.

Lemke had many warnings from friends that he might be making a fatal error in giving up a certain position for one that was uncertain. One wrote that public opinion was changing on foreign policy rather rapidly, implying that Lemke would find himself less popular in November than he had been in June. Another warned him that he should stay away from war talk, as the great majority of the people believed in preparedness and were in sympathy with England; and another pointed out that the conservatives were urging him to resign from the congressional race to create a congressional post into which they could place a conservative. A group of Lemke supporters had met on July 11, at Jamestown, but had not acted because of uncertainty about the wisest course to pursue and because some Langer representatives had intruded themselves. They finally signed a call for a meeting at Devils Lake to occur on the same day as the meeting of the Republican state central committee, and they strongly urged that Lemke come to the meeting. Lemke did not attend but again he put his trust in his friends, writing that John Miklethun's group, Joe LePire's group, and S. B. Ellsworth's group were meeting on July 23. "I am sure that Mr. Langer will not be permitted to plant any of his men in any of these groups because each group knows its own, ... however, I would appreciate it if you and Charlie and others ... would go to the meeting." The story of the Devils Lake convention carried in the *Bismarck Tribune* revealed no suspicion that Whelan would not support Lemke. It was generally assumed that all anti-Langer, Regular Republican conservatives would support Lemke as opposed to Langer and Vogel.[44]

The Lemke supporters met on the ground floor of the Devils Lake

Memorial Building while the Langer group, who were in control of the party machinery, met upstairs. There, to the surprise of many and most certainly to Lemke, Langer threw his support for chairman

LEMKE IS ALWAYS RIGHT!

In the fall of 1940 William Lemke gave up certain re-election to the House of Representatives to file as an independent candidate in a third-party column against William Langer, who was the Republican nominee, and Charles Vogel, who was the Democratic nominee, for the United States Senate seat held by Lynn J. Frazier.

to a conservative, none other than the recently defeated senatorial candidate, Thomas Whelan. The latter congratulated Langer on his victory and rumors circulated that in order to defeat Frazier, Langer had financed Whelan's campaign and that now Whelan would support Langer for the Senate on the plea of living up to party regularity.* Lemke could not believe it. "Yes, I understand that Whelan congratulated Langer but that, of course, is the usual courtesy. I do not know what he will do, but I know that most of his [Whelan's] followers now insist that I become a candidate, and these inform me that Whelan will have to fall in line or else he will himself be through in the state." Part of Lemke's decision depended on whether Joseph Martin of the Republican National Committee would help with campaign funds, and he was depending on Nye to attend to this source of help.[45]

There were other factors that Lemke neglected to consider. Moses had been able to control the senatorial campaign in 1938, when it was not a Presidential election year. For a number of reasons, it would not be as easily done in 1940. First, many of the voters voting for Roosevelt for President would again, by virtue of North Dakota's party column ballot, stay in the Democratic column to vote a straight ticket. Second, it was less likely that the national party organization, in a Presidential year, would agree to the first candidate listed below the Presidential electors becoming a captive candidate. A third factor was that in 1938 Nye, who had refused to oppose Roosevelt in 1936, was the Republican senatorial candidate while Lemke, who had attempted to defeat Roosevelt in 1936, was the candidate asking assistance from the Democratic organization. It was expecting more than the logic of the situation would suggest to believe that Roosevelt's political advisers would assist Lemke to become a member of the United States Senate. Lemke set doubts aside, withdrew his name as Republican candidate for Representative, and filed in the third party column for Senator. President Roosevelt's experience with Lemke could conceivably cause him to prefer either Langer or Charles Vogel. Lemke would have to defeat the Democratic candidate, Charles Vogel, and the Republican candidate, William Langer.

It became apparent immediately that Vogel, unlike Nygaard in

* These rumors were revived during Truman's administration, when Democratic President Truman acted upon Republican Senator Langer's recommendation that Thomas Whelan be appointed ambassador to Nicaragua. Langer had previously voted with the Democrats on a committee that killed an investigation of the defeat of Representative Slaughter of Missouri in the primary election of 1946.

1938, was going to wage a vigorous campaign for the senatorship. He began a full-scale program on his own behalf with every evidence of backing from the national committee. Lemke concluded that Langer had gone East and made his own arrangements with the Democratic national committee to have Vogel do this.[46] The Lemke family and close Lemke supporters believed that Vogel was urged to defy the arrangement Moses had made and that Vogel had been promised a patronage plum. Later when Vogel received a federal judgeship, it confirmed them in their belief. However, the appointment was a logical one, and it does not seem that it would have been necessary to promise a candidate a federal appointment in order to persuade him to campaign for an office for which he was a candidate.

Moses did his utmost to live up to his agreement with Lemke, and relations between Vogel and Moses were always strained thereafter. Vogel felt that Moses was doublecrossing him by supporting Lemke. It was Vogel's contention that he was standing for Roosevelt's domestic and foreign policies, and that Moses was weakening the President's chance of carrying North Dakota in order that he himself might be re-elected governor of the state. There were differences in political conviction separating Vogel from Lemke and Langer while the only issues separating Lemke and Langer were Langer's record as governor—which Lemke and his supporters called "Langerism"— and one of personalities. Lemke and Langer agreed on foreign and domestic policy.

The only study that has been made of Moses' career defends his conduct in this campaign; if he believed in the foreign policies followed by Roosevelt, his 1940 record needs defense, for he was following a policy which assisted Lemke in his attempt to be elected senator, and Lemke as senator would have made it more difficult for the President to forward his policy of aid and encouragement to the nations which were in danger of being defeated by Germany. Vogel could not be blamed for resenting Moses' policy. During the campaign Lemke showed his customary inflexibility and inability to change pace. His hatred of Roosevelt was such that it was impossible for him to abstain from attacking the President, although his supporters asked him to stop because of the votes he was losing. Lemke continued support of Wendell Willkie and ignored a caution from Gunvaldsen that he had said "enough good words for Willkie. Leave him out except in generalities."[47]

The hints that Whelan would support Langer proved to be correct.

Under the guise of party regularity, specious because it was being used for a highly irregular Republican, Whelan gave an all-out effort on behalf of Langer. He had great influence in his home county of Pembina and in the northeastern counties of the state, and he was effective in American Legion circles throughout the state. This was especially true among those who did not like Lemke's arguments against Roosevelt's armament proposals. North Dakotans who favored Lemke's stand on national defense and foreign policy could vote for the same policies by supporting Langer. While the state might still be isolationist, there was a growing number of voters who were changing their minds on this vital issue in this pre-Pearl Harbor year. This was particularly noticeable in northeastern North Dakota, where Vogel came within 121 votes of carrying Grand Forks County, and where he did carry Pembina, Walsh, Nelson, and Foster counties. The *Grand Forks Herald,* because of the influence of its political columnist, William B. Allen, refused to support Lemke, and this may have affected the vote in all of the above counties except Foster. Some of Lemke's key supporters, still indignant with Moses about patronage decisions, transferred their support to Jack A. Patterson, Langer's candidate for governor. Although Moses was not offended, some of his followers were, and they decided to vote for Vogel.[48]

The total number of votes cast in the election was 288,776. Of these, 280,775 voted for President; 274,565 for governor; and only 264,101 for senator. As the senatorial position on the ballot was next below that of President and above that of governor, there should have been as many votes for senator as for governor. Possibly some voters refused to vote against either Langer or Lemke and abstained from voting as a solution to the problem of deciding between these men in the senatorial race. Lemke later felt that some election boards, which were completely dominated by Langer men in certain localities, ignored the votes in the third party column and that a recount would have shown Lemke victorious. However, Lemke did not awaken to the discrepancy in vote totals in time to petition legally for a recount. The final result was Langer, 100,847; Lemke, 92,593; and Vogel, 69,847. Vogel's vote was over 50,000 greater than Nygaard's had been in 1938, and this is the explanation of Langer's defeat of Lemke in 1940 when he had been unable to defeat Nye in 1938. Again Langer had won with less than a majority vote. His total vote was 34.85 per cent of the total vote cast as compared to 32.06 and 24.18 respectively cast for Lemke and Vogel. A Communist party candidate received approximately one-half of 1 per cent of the vote and between 8 and 9 per cent of the voters either failed to vote in the senatorial contest or their votes were not counted if they did.[49]

Except for the northern portion of the Red River Valley, where Vogel was most successful, Lemke carried the entire eastern tier of counties in North Dakota. He carried scattered counties in the rest

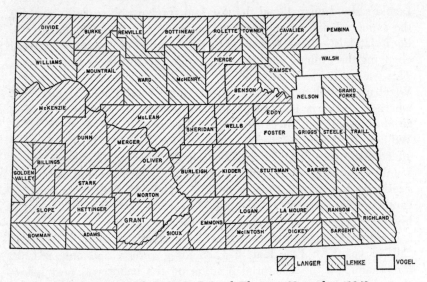

FIG. 3.—Senatorial Contest, General Election, November, 1940

of the state and polled a strong vote in many of the counties with large urban centers. A special issue of *Labor* was published by the railway labor unions in support of Lemke. The daily papers, the influence of the railroad labor vote,[50] and the preponderance of urban conservatives in the Republican column in those centers probably explains Lemke's vote in the large towns. Langer benefited from Willkie's strength in the state. The latter carried thirty-seven counties as compared to Roosevelt's sixteen. Of the thirty counties that Langer carried, twenty-five were counties which had been won by Willkie. Vogel's four counties were all counties that had been carried by Roosevelt. Lemke won in nineteen counties. Seven of these had been won by Roosevelt, and twelve by Willkie. Lemke was able to carry a number of counties in which Willkie had a majority, but Langer was able to carry only a few of those which Roosevelt had won. When there was a choice between Langer and Lemke, the counties known

by North Dakota politicians as the German counties were inclined to
choose Langer. Thus Langer won in territory where Lemke was
usually strong, and Lemke gained many votes in the Red River Valley
and in some of the larger towns because of conservative support that
was not customarily his.

Lemke never again attempted to be elected governor or senator. He was sixty-two years of age and would be sixty-eight when

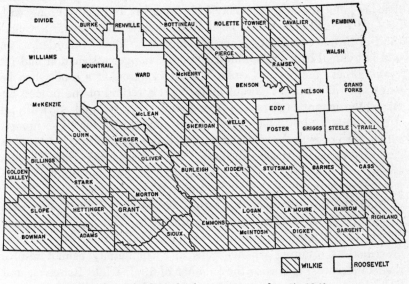

FIG. 4.—Presidential Election, November 5, 1940

Langer came up for re-election in 1946. The realization that his time
of opportunity had passed saddened him. An endorsement of Langer
by Burdick, printed at the last minute in the Farmers Union paper,
which later was alleged to have been mailed to the newspaper over
Burdick's forged signature, may have determined the election against
Lemke. Burdick's position had been difficult. He was bound by close
ties of friendship with Lemke and yet he was a candidate of the
Langer Nonpartisan League. Langer was not one to allow someone
on his guide card to oppose him or even to give him lukewarm
endorsement, and Lemke had representatives at the Burdick meetings
to report on Burdick statements which might influence the senatorial
contest. The allegedly forged newspaper item appeared in the Langer
Senate hearings as one of the exhibits attempting to prove Langer's

unfitness for office. A further factor injuring Lemke was an attack he had made on the American Medical Association, denouncing it as a monopoly that was abusing its position of power. Langer made use of this and cited further the anti-vaccination and anti-vivisection legislation Lemke had introduced. This strategy of Langer's lost Lemke a large portion of the support of an influential occupational group.[51]

The defeat had come at the moment when Lemke was achieving greater esteem from his congressional colleagues. His files indicate that his influence in the Seventy-fifth Congress and his standing with his fellow congressmen had been much greater than in the Seventy-third or Seventy-fourth Congresses. He was no longer regarded as an odd individual or a single-minded fanatic. Longer association had revealed other qualities in Lemke. He left Congress at a time when he was in the midst of a vigorous fight to get a refund of the processing tax which manufacturers had levied under the original Agricultural Adjustment Act but which it had been unnecessary for these processors to turn over to the government when the Agricultural Adjustment Act was declared unconstitutional. He lost seniority rights in the House and also the sense of continuity that comes from uninterrupted contact with pending legislation and fellow members.

From the standpoint of the nation, his absence from Congress in the period from 1941 to 1943 was fortunate. The nation was very clearly in the political condition of stasis that Arnold Toynbee has described as resulting when groups in a community cannot resolve their differences. It was in the summer of 1941, while Roosevelt and Churchill were meeting on the *Prince of Wales,* that the House voted by the narrow margin of one vote to extend the draft.* Had Lemke been in the House, it would have been more difficult to obtain that one-vote margin. Had he been in the Senate, the President would have had a more determined and effective opponent, and Lemke would have been effective in the debate against Lend-Lease. Langer's opinions on these issues were identical with those of Lemke, but Langer was new on the national scene. The influence of a freshman member of Congress—though seldom great—was diminished by an attempt to remove him from the Senate. Until December, 1941, Langer

---

* The vote was 203 to 202 (Link, *The American Epoch,* p. 490). Very possibly there were other votes which might have switched had it been necessary. Lemke's ability to influence others in situations such as this, however, would have made the situation more difficult for the administration if it had been he rather than Robertson serving as one of North Dakota's representatives.

was under investigation by a Senate committee. He was in no position to embarrass or to oppose effectively the administration on any issue. The fact that Lemke would have been such a problem for the administration was, from the President's point of view, ample justification for the money that had been spent in 1940 to establish a separate headquarters in Fargo to support the Democratic congressional candidates.[52] This was true even though it resulted in the election of Langer. By the time Lemke returned to Congress, Pearl Harbor had occurred and the time had passed when his stand on armaments or on foreign policy would be a matter of serious concern to the President.

Lemke emerged from his 1940 defeat a changed man. From this time forward his public life was a way of making a living; elements of his agrarian program persisted, but in the future he was not dreaming great dreams so much as building a typical legislative program that would please the people of North Dakota. His friends remarked that he had become more mellow; in reality he had come to recognize and accept that life was not going to bring him much for which he had hoped. His underlying convictions remained—belief in progressive legislation such as the initiative, referendum, recall, direct election, and primary elections; transfer of the control of credit from the banks to the government; preservation of the independence of the states in their relationship to the federal government; of absolute freedom from all entangling alliances in the relation of that federal government with the rest of the world; and sympathy for the underprivileged of his own country. The difference was that Lemke no longer felt any degree of certainty that he could do anything about it. Government from now on was an occupation and a way of making a living. He performed the tasks of that occupation, hoping that while he was making certain of his own livelihood, he could still make some contributions to the general welfare. It is in this sense that the remaining years of Lemke's public career seem anticlimactic.

# CHAPTER VIII

# A Purposeful Life

The nature of William Lemke's work during the two years he was out of Congress between 1941 and 1943 differed little from that which he had been pursuing as a congressman. He had in Congress divided his time between serving as a spokesman for agriculture and attempting to prevent the involvement of the United States in world affairs. While carrying out the first function, he had been disturbed by the judicial obstruction of legislation that Congress had passed. He now made it his career to help farmers wherever judges or government employees stood between the farmer and the benefits of congressional legislation. In his home state and throughout the nation, he was engaged by one attorney after another to assist in representing insolvent farmers who, because of judicial interpretation, could not obtain benefits from the Frazier-Lemke Bankruptcy Act.*

Lemke now began to see at first hand the benefits of the legislation he had conceived and single-handedly put through Congress. Not only had it provided a method of relief for a farmer who found that deflation had made his debts insurmountable, but it had also forced considerate treatment of debtors by creditors in many instances where the act was not used. In one county it was reported to Lemke that thirty-two farms had been foreclosed upon by the Federal Land Bank that winter, but that the foreclosures had immediately ceased when the Supreme Court declared the Frazier-Lemke Bankruptcy Act consti-

---

* In addition to the many cases involving the Frazier-Lemke Bankruptcy Act litigation, Lemke represented those who were challenging the constitutionality of wheat penalties imposed under provisions of the New Deal agricultural legislation. Although the outcome was not favorable to Lemke's clients, the decision is among those considered significant during recent decades (*Wickard* v. *Filburn* (1942) 317 U.S. Ill., 63 S. Ct. 82, 87 L. ed. 122. U.S. Supreme Court). He was very active on behalf of groups of farmers in Ohio, assisting them in taking advantage of the provisions of the Frazier-Lemke Act, and he was employed to handle condemnation cases in Kankakee, Illinois, and Omaha, Nebraska.

tutional. It was the gun behind the door which, though not fired, still by its presence contributed to the safety of the household. Not only had the creditors become more considerate, but the interest rates of all government lending agencies had been lowered and the entire structure of the many governmental agricultural credit bureaus had been consolidated into the Farm Credit Administration, actions that Lemke's decade-long compaign had expedited. One of the interesting results of Lemke's efforts was that farmers who had been saved as a result of Lemke's legislative influence prospered and often became wealthy in the inflationary period that ensued. Many of these possessed short memories and soon became unsympathetic to other less fortunate farmers.* The selfishness of some of those who had been assisted was disheartening and disappointing to agrarian leaders such as Lemke. Because of the Bankruptcy Act, Lemke's political strength in North Dakota had remained undiminished despite a quarrel and near break with the Farmers Union leadership in 1939 over whether a cost of production farm plan should be substituted for the Roosevelt-Wallace program. Charles Robertson, the Bismarck businessman whom Langer had selected to run for Congress in 1940, when Lemke withdrew to run for the Senate, found this strength unassailable in 1942. When Lemke decided to return to Congress in 1942, he was able to defeat Robertson. Lemke won, though campaigning with very little organization support, and though Robertson had Langer's support as well as that of Senator Robert Taft and other powerful national Republican leaders.[1]

Before his return to Congress, Lemke busied himself not only with battles for agrarian debtors but also with efforts to assist the opponents of Lend-Lease. Lemke felt that Governor John Moses would like to assist him in some way, and he waited hopefully. Seeing that it was politically impossible for Moses to give him an appointment in the state government, and appalled at Roosevelt's proposals for giving aid to nations who were victims of aggression, Lemke projected a plan early in 1941 which he called "My America" program. Its central theme was that internal reform and not foreign aid was the United

* The liberal credit terms during a deflationary period enabled some farmers to become financially independent in the ensuing years. They consequently had the advantage that economists describe as "internal financing," meaning they could expand their holdings without having to pay interest charges to others. Oftentimes they interpreted their new competitive advantage to be due to managerial ability, and had little sympathy for those who were in the same economic situation they had been when rescued by liberal governmental credit policies.

States' best defense. Lemke included in its platform a Bank of the United States, a cost of production agricultural plank, and the other reforms that had been his favorite projects through the years. To support "My America," Lemke hoped to have 1,000 isolationists contribute $100 each. With these funds he planned to create an organization which with speakers, radio time, and pamphlets could mobilize the sentiment necessary to stop Roosevelt's foreign aid program. Edward A. Rumely introduced Lemke to Frank Gannett, a newspaper publisher, who furnished some funds. However, it was assistance from Robert Wood that enabled Lemke to continue on a lecture tour through the Middle West during the summer and fall of 1941. "My America" was dropped as Lemke saw he could work toward the same objective by speaking for Wood's America First movement.[2]

Before Pearl Harbor, it was Lemke's hope to elect enough isolationist congressmen in the 1942 election to block Roosevelt in the latter's effort to give aid to those nations which were attacked by Germany and her allies. Pearl Harbor interrupted his lecture series and brought an abrupt end to America First. Soon after Pearl Harbor, Lemke wrote to Robert Wood:

Since I saw you a lot of water has passed under the bridge. We are now at war. In fact we have two wars. We have the Japs to whip abroad, and we are going to do it, and we also have the Japs to whip at home. The Jap at home is more dangerous to our liberty than the one abroad. We must not surrender our liberties while we are fighting a war. Liberties once surrendered are seldom if ever returned.[3]

Probably it is the deep suspicion held by Lemke regarding President Roosevelt that is referred to in the cryptic reference to the Japanese at home. A letter from a loyal North Dakota supporter mentioned a fear that Roosevelt would use the war as an excuse not to hold congressional elections in 1942. In the letter to Wood quoted above, there is no reference to the fact that the nation was also at war with Italy and Germany. Though Hitler's treatment of the Jews was revolting to Lemke, he felt that Germany's actions toward other countries were more defensible than England's and that they paled into insignificance as compared to England's conquests of other lands. He could speak of Halifax, Chamberlain, Churchill, Stalin, and Hitler in the same breath as jointly responsible for the slaughter of four million youths. Lemke still felt that the real responsibility at that time for starting all wars and running them lay in the British Isles and France. He wrote once that Roosevelt wanted to amend the laws governing neutrality because of the marriage of his son to a Du Pont. Lemke believed that Lend-Lease had been Roosevelt's device to assist the "most cruel and brutal attempt in all history . . . to deliberately starve half of Europe in order to knuckle to Great Britain's desire." As had all isolationists and many others, Lemke had assumed that the United States was secure against attack. In Lemke's view fear of Hitler was just a political red herring to divert attention away from social reform. "The truth is," he wrote to B. T. Holloway, "you need not be afraid. Hitler will not get us. That stuff is just doped out by politicians for home consumption. Please don't fall for it. . . . [The] map of Eurpoc [*sic*] . . . will continue to change until they have intelligence enough to form the United States of Europe." And Lemke asserted that "our leading army officials feel that other nations than Germany, Italy, and Japan are our natural enemies."[4] For Lemke the war was the result of a conspiracy, and this was the message he had carried across the nation until Pearl Harbor abruptly brought his activities to a halt.

In the meantime, the Langer removal hearings had been proceeding in the Senate. The charges, which were brought by Dakotans who alleged that they were fully acquainted with Langer's record, almost prevented Langer from keeping his Senate seat. Many of the charges were the same as those made by Lemke in the campaigns of 1938 and 1940. The Senate appointed a committee to hear the charges, and Langer, though permitted to act as senator, did so only tentatively pending the outcome of the investigation. The major charges involved "kickbacks" in the sale of bonds and in other transactions during Langer's term as governor of North Dakota. A prison inmate who took care of the governor's yard was alleged to have found large sums of cash in Langer's home. There were also charges of bribery in connection with the conspiracy trials, and accusations of irregularities in the practice of law.[5]

Lemke was in communication with the investigating committee from the first. He advised the committee counsel to interview Charles Verry, Ole Gunvaldsen, James Mulloy, and Governor Moses. Lemke added that he had known long ago that "Mr. Langer not only [was] dishonest but insane as well. Yet he is shrewd and cunning, but he does not know right from wrong. If there ever was a Dr. Jekyll and Mr. Hyde, here is one." The course of the hearing held in Washington during 1941 indicated that Langer might be removed as the committee examined the evidence and reacted very unfavorably toward Langer. There was speculation about who would succeed Langer if the Senate refused to seat him. At first many of Lemke's friends assumed that Lemke, as the second highest contestant in the election, would automatically become senator if Langer were unseated. Examination of legal precedents indicated that Moses would have the appointing power, and Lemke's friends were hopeful that Moses would violate all precedent and appoint him, even though Moses was a member of the opposite major party. Lemke himself believed that Moses might do so, as unlikely as this appears in retrospect. The National Committee of the Democratic party, as well as members of his party within the state, would have made it very difficult for Moses to appoint Lemke. Until the hearing was over, little was said about this possibility for fear of alarming Senate Democrats and causing them to vote to seat Langer.[6] To Senate Democratic leaders who had observed Lemke in the House, he was an irreconcilable who would have made their position more difficult, and they would have been less likely to unseat Langer if it had meant the seating of Lemke in his place.

Controversy regarding the Land Finance Company entered into the hearings. The committee confronted Langer with $25,000 in unexplained income which Langer stated was payment for an interest in stock of the Land Finance Company. Lemke immediately pointed out that the stock was so worthless that no one would pay thousands of dollars for it, and that furthermore Langer no longer had the stock to sell. Langer's explanation was that after he had sold an interest in the stock for cash, he was unable to make delivery because he did not know where the stock was. Lemke contended that Langer had surrendered the stock to the company in the early 1920's in return for an option on part of the company's land. Lemke had possession of the stock, and Langer had failed to exercise his option. Langer later sued for return of the stock, but the courts ruled that Langer's rights under the contract for options were no longer legally valid. John Gray, North Dakota state tax commissioner, filed suit for unpaid income taxes, and Langer had to pay taxes on some of the income that the committee had questioned.[7]

Lemke was elated when the committee voted in December, 1941, thirteen to three, against the permanent seating of Langer in the Senate. His optimism was premature, however. Pearl Harbor had just occurred, diverting the attention of the Senate and the nation from the committee's report. The feeling of the Republicans was that Langer would be preferable to a Democrat; Senator George Norris was afraid of setting a precedent that might be unjustly used against others and did not play the leading role in the fight against Langer that Lemke had anticipated; certain Southern senators, notably Ellison D. Smith of South Carolina, felt that one could not indict an entire state. The final vote in the Senate to seat Langer was 52 to 30.[8]

Although Gerald P. Nye had been anxious to see Langer refused admittance to the United States Senate and had worked quietly with Lemke and the committee, he did not wish to give the North Dakota public the impression that the Senate hearings were a private vendetta. Publicly he played the part of a neutral, disinterested observer, content to let the committee and the Senate determine the outcome. Although Lemke fully understood Nye's position and did not condemn it, he felt certain that if Nye had thrown his full influence into the fight, Langer would not have been seated. Nye's defense of his action was that as a senator from Langer's state, he was bound by propriety and custom to follow the course that he did.[9] He made a major miscalculation if his own safety in the next election influenced his decision, for he was defeated for re-election in 1944 by John Moses.

When Langer was seated, Lemke knew that it was necessary for him to defeat Charles Robertson, the man who had replaced him in the House of Representatives, or retire from public life. Lemke's reputation as an agrarian spokesman made it possible for him in 1942 to wage a successful campaign to return to Congress. It was not an easy task. Lemke had hoped that the Langer hearings held by the Senate Committee on Privileges and Elections would discredit any candidate associated with him and make it easy to defeat Robertson. Actually, many North Dakotans tended to discount the Senate hearings regarding Langer. They remembered that a Circuit Court of Appeals had nullified the action of a Federal District Court which had convicted Langer, and they now hesitated to believe any charges brought against him. In early 1942, a number of Lemke's followers urged him to run for governor, but he declined to do so.[10] He was reluctant to run against Moses, who was politically stronger than ever. Lemke filed in the Republican primary for nomination to run for his former position in the House of Representatives. He and W. M. Smart were running against Usher L. Burdick and Robertson.

This was the spring after Pearl Harbor, and the election campaign was not the center of attention it had been in former years. The anti-Langer coalition had a full ticket in the field but had very little success in an election characterized by a small vote. There were 135,273 votes cast for governor as compared to 175,482 and 214,908 in 1940 and 1938 respectively. The small vote seems to have been a disadvantage for Lemke, and he very narrowly escaped defeat. Burdick received 60,668 votes, almost exactly 10,000 more than Lemke, who polled a total of 50,666 to defeat Robertson by less than 2,000 votes. Robertson's total was 48,717, and Smart, Lemke's running-mate on the ticket, received 26,040 votes. Robertson filed against Lemke and Burdick in the November general election, and Lemke was more successful than in June, although in this election he still proved to be a much weaker candidate than Burdick. Burdick received 85,936 votes as compared to Lemke's 65,905. Robertson led the two Democratic candidates, receiving 48,472. The *Fargo Forum* argued that Langer's support of Robertson weakened his candidacy.

Not the least interesting phase of the election . . . was Mr. Langer's return to the state and his attempt to put the clincher on Mr. Lemke. Not a single candidate on the League ticket wanted Mr. Langer back in North Dakota. Neither did Mr. Robertson. They all felt that they could have been better off without him. . . . How many votes Senator Langer lost for Charley Robertson is guess. . . . The thing that happened, of course, was Senator Langer's bitter personality talk of Saturday night. It lost hundreds of votes for Mr. Robertson in Fargo. It turned the same hundreds of voters to Mr. Lemke, whom they do not love. . . . Sickest man in North Dakota on the night of that broadcast was Robertson. Even he knew the speech spelled doom for him.[11]

The two Democrats polled 47,972 and 31,547 for fourth and fifth place respectively in the five-man race for the two congressional positions. In the 1942 elections, many of the conservatives were encouraged by national leaders such as Senator Robert Taft to support Robertson and oppose Lemke. While still victorious, Lemke was incensed and warned Nye that the latter's plans for 1944 would not succeed. "I will never again permit myself to be double crossed the way I was in this election. I am through with fair weather friends, who are with me when I don't need them, but who will knife me when I need them. They will do the same to you. . . . I found them out in time. If I get time I will pay my respects to Taft some time this week." Lemke's supporters told him that Langer was bitterly disappointed at his failure to defeat Lemke. One supporter wrote: "Oh boy you should have seen Bill and Robertson about midnight of Nov. 3rd. They were so downhearted that they looked as though they had been torpedoed."[12]

It was two years after Lemke's return to Congress before he again had a program and a measure of influence such as he had had in the last Congress before his withdrawal from the House of Representatives in 1940. Loss of seniority and change in the personnel of the membership were two reasons; a third was a modification in the nature of the nation's problems. Lemke had been the advocate of those whom the depression had hurt and whose wounds had not been treated to their satisfaction by the New Deal. He was the nervous, quick-voiced prairie protester against deflation. Congress now faced the problem of inflation, and Lemke's former program had lost its appeal. The men who had formerly been debtor farmers were now prosperous capitalists, protesting because the OPA and government regulations limited their business activity. In these years from 1943 to 1947, Lemke was the voice of protest against those regulations. Although his own sons joined the military service and he was proud of their service records, he felt that the draft bore unfairly on the farmer. To him the OPA was the "illegitimate child of foreign ideologies."[13] The world had changed, but Lemke's propensity for robust speech that appealed to the folk humor of his prairie constituents had not. He also made himself champion of veterans' legislation, claiming to have written the North Dakota Adjusted Compensation law after World War I. It was a popular issue, a fact that he sensed, and it helped him win elections. He was a liberal of another day whose panacea for government ills had been in political reform. Time and again Lemke spoke for and introduced bills which provide for a national initiative and referendum, direct election of the President,* limitation of the President's term of office, and elimination of gerrymandering. Although these reforms did not strike a popular response, Lemke introduced some of them in each session of Congress.

Lemke was now nearly seventy years of age. His home was paid for in 1945. The children had grown up and left home; and he and Mrs. Lemke now lived by themselves in Washington. The two boys, William and Robert, had attended law school in Washington; later they

---

* It is possible that Lemke did not realize the extent to which direct election of the President would have weakened the political power of the agrarian sections of the nation. Had it been adopted, it might have resembled the recall in North Dakota, a reform which Lemke had helped sponsor but which had weakened him politically.

served overseas in the armed forces. Both of them married and had
families of their own. Subsequently they secured positions with the
federal government. Mary, the youngest of the three children, attended Principia, a Christian Science school in Elsah, Illinois. She
married Robert Ely and became a permanent resident of Missouri.
These were the sunset years of Lemke's life. He was content to serve
in his capacity as a member of the House of Representatives. Re-election was usually not too difficult, and these were not arduous years for
him. He adjusted himself to the changes taking place in North Dakota
politics from 1944 until the year of his death in 1950, and he felt fairly
certain that he could hold his position in Congress against all chal-
lengers.

In North Dakota a significant political change was taking place.
In 1944, the Republican Organizing Committee nominated Fred J.
Aandahl, a former state senator from Barnes County, for the governorship. Usher L. Burdick withdrew from the race for United States representative to be a candidate against Nye, the ROC nominee for the
Republican United States senatorial nomination. Lemke and Milton
R. Young, a state senator from LaMoure County, were endorsed by
the ROC to be candidates for the Republican nomination as congressional candidates; their opponents were the Langer League nominees
Charles Robertson and Ralph Beede. Lemke and Robertson won
the Republican nominations, receiving respectively 55,777 and 43,592
votes; Young very nearly defeated Robertson by obtaining 41,248
votes, while Beede trailed with 29,712. A heavy rain in northwestern North Dakota influenced the result of the election, in
which the ROC had been remarkably successful. Some polling
places in counties where the Langer following held a preponderance
of voter support were unable to open because of the near torrential
downpour, an act of nature that withheld a seat in the United States
Senate from Usher L. Burdick some sixteen years before his son,
Quentin, was to be elected United States Senator. Both Aandahl and
Nye won Republican nomination by defeating Alvin Strutz and Burdick, the League nominees for governor and senator. One feature of
the senatorial race had been the nomination of Lynn U. Stambaugh,
a Fargo attorney who had been a national commander of the American
Legion. The Nye-Lemke faction felt certain that his candidacy was
arranged by Langer at the instigation of the Democrats. They contended that the purpose of Stambaugh's candidacy was to take enough
Republican votes from Nye to defeat him. The strategy failed, perhaps

because large numbers of Democrats took advantage of the secrecy provided by the consolidated ballot* and voted in the Republican column for Nye. The Democratic registration sank from a normal of over 25,000 to 14,650. This combined with the heavy rainfall in Bottineau and neighboring counties to deprive Burdick of the nomination. Democrats were relieved because they felt it would be easier for John Moses, the Democratic nominee for senator, to defeat Nye than it would have been for him to defeat either Burdick or Stambaugh. Nye had a small margin, winning by a vote of 38,191 to Stambaugh's 37,219 and Burdick's 35,687. A. C. Townley had entered as a nuisance candidate and received approximately 1,300 votes, many of which would probably have otherwise gone to Burdick.

The key battle in the fall election for the senatorship was between Nye, Moses, and Stambaugh. After having been eliminated in the Republican primary, Stambaugh had filed as an independent candidate in the fall. Lemke was certain of election himself but campaigned vigorously for the ROC ticket, and more especially for Nye. Aandahl, son of one of the original League endorsees in the election of 1916, was elected governor, to assume the post Moses had held since 1938, and Moses defeated Nye and Stambaugh for United States senator. After his defeat for the senatorial nomination in the primary, Burdick had filed for representative in a third party column on the November ballot. Lemke led all other congressional candidates, receiving 101,007 votes; Robertson was the other successful nominee, obtaining a total of 91,425. Burdick ran a poor fifth, receiving only 39,888 votes. The

* The consolidated ballot prints the name of candidates in primary elections on the same ballot regardless of their affiliation in the Republican, Democratic, or a third party. It was a ballot reform adopted in the 1930's by the Republican legislature to protect the voter from alleged intimidation by the Franklin Roosevelt administration. It was argued that voters would hesitate to ask for a Republican ballot because of fear of reprisal. The legislature of 1947, stating that too many voters were confused and spoiled their ballots, discontinued the use of the consolidated ballot. Democrats contended that spoiled ballots had not disturbed the Republican-controlled legislature until the election of the 80th Congress led Republican leaders to believe they would regain control of the national government in the 1948 election. It was the contention of the Democrats that these were typical devices by which a dominant party protected its privileged position in a one-party state. The consolidated ballot has the advantage of preserving the secret ballot and the disadvantage of permitting opposition party members to help select candidates when there is a contest in one party and not in the other. In 1962 the Democrats of North Dakota supported a successful effort to initiate a measure restoring the consolidated ballot.

two Democratic candidates, Halvor Halvorson and J. R. Kennedy, received 56,699 and 45,308 votes respectively. Only four Langer Leaguers were victorious; two of these were long-time incumbents.[14]

The campaign was an easy one for Lemke. The ROC had been uncertain of its strength and was glad to have Lemke on its guide card. The contrast in this respect with 1942 was a pleasant one. The campaign against Nye had been revolting to Lemke, for it was an example of the same type of opposition from which he had suffered in 1942 and which he had predicted would affect Nye. Lemke felt Nye's defeat had been "the rottenest and one of the most contemptible campaigns I have gone through," although he admitted that the senator's marital difficulty had affected the votes of many women.[*15] That Lemke campaigned for the ticket is indicated by a letter he received from Milton Young:

I would like to thank you from the bottom of my heart for the good work that you have done in this campaign for all of us. You have been true blue and have had tremendous influence over the state. Nels [Johnson] tells me that in all your talks that you have done your best for all the candidates, never mentioning a word for yourself. I believe, Bill, this is one of the things that makes you so popular over North Dakota. This, and the fact that you have continually, through all the years, fought the battle of the under dog.[16]

"I have never seen a man put on a more unselfish campaign as you have this last month," Nels Johnson, successful candidate for attorney general, wrote to Lemke.[17]

Lemke was the logical ROC candidate for senator against Langer in 1946, and he felt that the organization owed him the endorsement for his services to the conservative, anti-Langer group in the elections of 1938, 1940, and 1944. Lemke felt, too, that the national Republican organization was indebted to him for carrying North Dakota for Wendell Willkie in 1940 and for Thomas Dewey in 1944.[†] Roosevelt's gain over 1940 is perhaps explained by the senatorial candidacy of Moses. The position of senator is immediately below that of Presidential electors. On North Dakota's party column ballot, many voters were

* Nye was divorced in March, 1940, and married Marguerite Johnson in December of that year. Nye's endorsement of a brand of cigarettes offended many.

† The keynote of Lemke's campaigns among the farmers during those two campaigns had been bureaucratic bungling and the administration's foreign policies. The Republicans had carried the state by winning from six to seven votes a precinct in 1940, but the campaign of 1944 had been more closely contested. It is possible that Lemke had influenced the totals, but hardly probable to a sufficient extent to account for the Republican victories.

attracted to the Democratic column by Moses. Once there, some of them voted for Presidential electors in the same column. In 1946, despite the fact that Lemke was both the most effective and the most deserving candidate, the anti-Langer conservatives repeated their error of 1940 and nominated a conservative to run against Langer. Langer's position had been weakened by the Senate hearings, but the intervening years had given him ample time to mend political fences, and his influence as senator had enabled him to win new followers. Aware of the original impact of the hearings, the anti-Langer conservatives decided that they could defeat Langer with one of their own. Actually their only chance of defeating Langer lay in utilizing anti-Langer Leaguers who, with the reputation they had won as Leaguers, could attract League votes from Langer. By adding their votes to the votes of the conservatives, Langer could be attacked most successfully.

Following his traditional policy, Lemke remained in Washington during the endorsing conventions. Nor is there any correspondence indicating that he sought the senatorial nomination, although his subsequent letters plainly indicate his disappointment when the ROC convention endorsed Joseph B. Bridston of Grand Forks. Ken Fitch, an ROC member, was opposed to Lemke and did much to injure his chance of receiving the nomination.[18] Bridston himself was so convinced that North Dakota people had changed their minds on the question of isolation that he felt certain of Langer's defeat. Although the ROC convention endorsed Lemke for renomination to the House of Representatives, he was furious at what he considered to be the ingratitude of the ROC, and issued a statement:

While I welcome and appreciate the support and endorsement of my friends, yet whatever office I finally decide to seek will be without asking endorsement from any political faction. The primary election is the people's convention and is going to be my convention. I want my name placed before the Republican voters solely on my record of service in Congress.[19]

This was the election which chose the Eightieth Congress. Lemke, along with other Republicans, capitalized on the confusion they had created by terminating the Office of Price Administration. There were no significant issues between Langer and Lemke other than Langer's record. Lemke, for a moment, considered filing for the senatorial position without ROC endorsement. His friends and his own better judgment advised him to file for renomination to the lower house. Refusing to accept the proffered endorsement or any assistance from the ROC, Lemke managed his own June primary campaign, emerging from the election with over 2,000 more votes than Robertson, his League-endorsed opponent and his nearest rival.* The other candidates were not close contestants. As Lemke had anticipated, Bridston was no match for Langer, leaving the electorate a choice between Langer, who had an option on a Senate seat which he held until his death in 1959, and P. W. Lanier, Jr., the Democratic candidate. For a time Lemke contemplated making a three-way fight in the November general election, but the memory of the defeat he had suffered in a similar maneuver in 1940 was too vivid. His friends counseled against being "Langerized" as Frazier, Nye, and Burdick had been.[20] Many of Lemke's supporters disliked Langer so intensely that they were anxious to keep a two-way race in order to defeat him. Langer was re-elected, polling a majority of all votes cast for senator—the first time he had succeeded in obtaining a comparable vote since June, 1934.

It was an agonizing experience for Lemke. He was certain that he could have defeated Langer had his conservative allies given him a chance for a two-way fight for the nomination. Langer was eight years younger than Lemke, and though not knowing he had only one more election left, Lemke was realistic enough to know he would probably never be a member of the United States Senate. Lemke's generation was leaving the scene. Lynn J. Frazier died in 1947, and one by one Lemke's brothers and sisters were succumbing to ill health and old age.

The accomplishments of the remaining three and one-half years of Lemke's life are a testimonial to its purposefulness, to his high concept of public trust, and to his dedication to the public good. As a member of the Public Lands Committee in the House of Representatives, he went on a tour of the North Dakota Badlands area, much of which had been purchased as submarginal land by the federal government.

* Robertson replaced Lemke for one term and was then defeated in 1942. After a one-term absence from Congress, he succeeded Burdick when the latter withdrew from the House race to run against Nye in 1944. Robertson remained in Congress for two terms, but was defeated by Burdick in 1948. Burdick remained in Congress until 1959, when he was succeeded by his son, Quentin, the first Democrat in North Dakota history to be elected to the House of Representatives. Quentin Burdick was elected to the United States Senate in 1960 replacing Norman Brunsdale who had been appointed to fill the vacancy caused by the death of Senator Langer. Nye was unable in 1946 to defeat Milton Young, whom Aandahl appointed to the Senate to take the seat left vacant by the death of John Moses.

He had seen the Badlands many times, but on this occasion he was forcefully impressed by the effect of the area on the committee chairman, J. Hardin Peterson of Florida. Peterson, in his capacity as chairman, had seen most of the national parks and scenic areas in the country. Lemke concluded that if the scenic properties of the area impressed Peterson so vividly, North Dakota had missed an opportunity for national recognition.[21] He seized on a suggestion by local residents that the area be made into a national park dedicated to Theodore Roosevelt, who had once ranched in the area. It did not disturb Lemke that he himself had never been an admirer of Roosevelt; the latter had won recognition as one of the more famous Presidents of the United States, and Lemke was willing to forward the project in Roosevelt's memory if, in so doing, he could thus best work to preserve a fine recreational area and assist his state in utilizing its resources to the full. Too, Lemke the politician must have recognized that the establishment of the park would enhance his own reputation.

Once he had decided that the idea was practicable, he advanced it with the same energy that had been characteristic of his every project. He enlisted the cooperation of Russell Reid, Superintendent of the State Historical Society, but had less success with the Fish and Wildlife Service and the National Parks Service. The former bureau wished to utilize the area as a game preserve, and the latter did not desire an additional national park in this area. This did not deter Lemke, nor did protests from some of the local residents. Informing them that they were wrong, he proceeded with efforts to pass legislation creating a national memorial park. When continued objection prevented passage of the measure in the House, Lemke asked the chairman of the Rules Committee for a decision that would permit the bill to come to the floor of the House. He used all of his influence in Congress and wrote citizens in Eastern states to bring pressure on their representatives and senators. Although the resistance to his efforts was not as intense, there was little difference between the determination he was now showing and that which he had evidenced with the Frazier-Lemke Bankruptcy Act. In the summer of 1946 he secured passage of the bill in the House. Both Langer and Young were in North Dakota vigorously prosecuting their respective senatorial campaigns, and it was necessary for Lemke to spend time on the Senate side of the Capitol to make certain that the bill was not defeated there. The bill was passed unanimously. Lemke was elated

at his accomplishment. But again the men in the administrative departments blocked his purposes. They presented the case against the bill
so effectively to President Truman that the bill was vetoed. Truman
gave as his reasons: (1) that the scenic qualities were not outstanding
enough; (2) that Theodore Roosevelt had not actually lived within
the boundaries of the proposed park; and (3) that the land titles
were to be examined by the Department of the Interior rather than
by the Department of Justice.[22]

Just as when the United States Supreme Court had declared the
Bankruptcy Act unconstitutional, so now the President's message was
for Lemke a call to action. Lemke rewrote his park bill, revising its
provisions, insofar as possible, to please the President. He guided
it through Congress a second time, and this time President Truman
signed it into law. Although a suggestion for such a park had been
made twenty-five years earlier, it was generally recognized that Lemke
was responsible for the enactment of the law and establishment of
the park. The newsletter with a newspaper format published by the
Greater North Dakota Association commented:

The bill creating the park was put through almost single handedly by
Congressman William Lemke, during the past two sessions. . . . It was the
work of Congressman Lemke during the past four years which brought
a national park to North Dakota.[23]

Lemke had utilized to advantage the prestige and influence that
came to him as committee member and subcommittee chairman; Democratic victories in the congressional elections of 1948 were soon to deprive him of his chairmanship, but he had made the most of the two
years when his own party was in control of Congress.* He had used his
influence not only on behalf of the park but also to forward legislation on irrigation and reclamation. The drought of the 1930's had
made him determined that no opportunity be lost to fortify the state
against another such disaster.

Yet as anxious as he was to see these projects undertaken, the end
did not justify the means in Lemke's view if the Indians of North
Dakota were dispossessed of tribal lands without measures being
taken to enable them to adjust to their misfortune. His memories
extended to the years of his boyhood on the Towner County Lemke
farm, when Indians had frequently visited and occasionally worked
for his father. This may have made him more sympathetic to them.
He was willing to halt projects such as Garrison Dam until such time

* At a June 4, 1949, site ceremony, Lemke made the official presentation of the
park.

as the Indians were given the compensation which Lemke deemed
fair and wise. Lemke showed similar consideration for the Navajo
and Osage Indians as well as for the residents of remote Pacific out-
posts. The Indians "look upon you as one of the greatest friends they
have ever had, and I agree fully," was typical of comments he received.[24]

One of the major controversies revolving around the conservation
projects was the height of the water level behind Garrison Dam. If
it were raised to 1850 feet above sea level, dikes would be needed
to protect part of the city of Williston. With Representative Burdick
of that city, Lemke worked for an amendment which would permit
only an 1830-foot water level, and as long as he was in Congress,
his and Burdick's joint efforts were enough to insure that dikes would
not be needed at Williston.[25] Businessmen of that city became some
of Lemke's key supporters, on whom he could depend for campaign
funds and full support. As the campaign strength that was his legacy
from the days of the Nonpartisan League was diminishing, he was
building new bases of support by the various measures he undertook.

Among other suggestions which won his support was one promoted
by G. S. Sessions of Alaska, which asked Congress to pass a bill
increasing the amount of land that veterans could homestead. Sessions
maintained that 160 acres was insufficient to attract settlers. Lemke
adopted his suggestion and vigorously advocated it. Lemke believed
in statehood for Hawaii and Alaska and showed here the same expan-
sionist fervor that he had once displayed toward Latin America. As
a small child he had accompanied his parents on the crest of a land
boom that carried them into Dakota territory, and new country where
the land lay open had an appeal for him. Sessions aroused Lemke's
interest, and it was not long before the latter was planning a hunt-
ing expedition to Alaska. With scarcely any support from other congressmen, he guided the bill encountering determined opposition from
commercial interests who preferred to have the area open for leasing
and large-scale operations rather than for homesteading. The Forest
Service was opposed to the measure but was unable to defeat the bill.
In 1950, less than a week before he died, Lemke succeeded in having
the Alaska bill passed by the House.[26] Had he lived, it seems probable
that it would have been passed by the Senate and enacted into law.
The Alaska bill died with its sponsor. It was Lemke's conviction
that its passage would cause a large migration to Alaska and that
such a population movement would be the nation's best national
defense of that area. If Lemke had lived another year, statehood for

the United States' northernmost territory might have been hastened.

The change in Lemke during the Eightieth Congress in 1947 and 1948 revealed the differences between him and the conservatives with whom he had been allied by mutual dislike of Roosevelt. He repeatedly told Republican leaders that they were being too reactionary and were forfeiting their advantage for the 1948 election. During the campaign he cautioned them again. "It would be foolish for us to close our eyes and make ourselves believe that Truman has not been making headway.... At present there are many farmers who will vote for Truman on the agricultural issue.... It is all right to be optimistic in public announcements, but... Truman is no pushover in the middle west."[27] The Republican party farm program was as far from Lemke's cost of production farm plank as it was from Truman's farm plan. Lemke's choice for Republican nominee had been General Douglas MacArthur. The latter's nationalistic approach appealed to Lemke as it did to other former isolationists. Despite his disapproval of Thomas Dewey and disappointment at his nomination, Lemke campaigned vigorously for him and won this commendation from the Republican state chairman:

> William Lemke did an outstanding service... in the campaign... in behalf of Dewey, Warren.... It so happens this year that Mr. Lemke... would not have had to campaign a day so far as his own election was concerned.... But he put on a vigorous campaign speaking every day in small towns and large in all parts of our state.[28]

Strangely, he felt more kindly to Truman than to any previous President, although he opposed much of Truman's program and political philosophy. Truman's personality appealed to Lemke. The former's forthrightness was preferable to Roosevelt's adroitness or Dewey's indefiniteness, and he was not as disappointed at the outcome as he had been with the re-election of Roosevelt in 1940 and again in 1944.[29]

Lemke's own election had presented no problem. Angered when the ROC endorsed Robertson as his running mate and at the personal attacks of Ken Fitch, he wrote to the ROC headquarters that he would not campaign for a single one of their endorsees in the primary but would stay in Congress to get needed legislation passed and save his campaigning until the fall election. He cited bills that were before the Congress which would enlarge Theodore Roosevelt National Memorial Park and would grant appropriations for the Missouri-Souris Diversion and Buford-Trenton projects. He also mentioned legislation introduced by Senator Young for Red River Valley flood control.[30] Burdick now saw his opportunity to return to Congress. When the League had supported Robertson in 1946, Burdick was afraid of being defeated by Lemke and Robertson for the two congressional posts. Now that the League had ceased to support Robertson, Burdick again became their candidate. He felt certain, and was not mistaken, that he could rely on Lemke to help defeat Robertson. Burdick succeeded, for Leaguers did not support Robertson when he was not on the League guide card. Lemke could depend on old League loyalties to bring him the votes of many Leaguers even when he himself was not on any guide card. Robertson received votes of very few Leaguers after transferring from the League slate to the ROC ticket.

It had been the plan for the House Subcommittee on Insular Affairs to make an inspection trip to the Pacific immediately following the 1948 election, but plans were changed and the trip was postponed a year. In late 1949, seven representatives, including Lemke, left on the trip that had been planned for a year earlier. It took them through Hawaii, most of the island groups in the new trusteeship area, and Guam, Samoa, the Philippines, Formosa, Korea, and Japan. It was a long tedious journey made harder by many hearings which Lemke conscientiously attended and patiently sat through.* He was appalled at what he regarded as the wastefulness of the armed services and disgusted with the policies of the Department of State; and he was particularly concerned about the problem of Formosa. He felt that more vigorous measures should be taken to assist Chiang Kai-Shek. He was true to the post–World War II pattern of evolution experi-

* "I was with Mr. Lemke [on] . . . a . . . tour down to American Samoa, through the Marshall and Caroline Islands and then up to Guam. . . . Few [of the committee members] were willing to take the trip. . . . Despite his advanced years . . . He sat for hours through hearings in American Samoa when the temperature was running close to 90. One afternoon he drove through a driving rain without any protection to attend a small meeting at Mokil, an island many of you may never have heard of. His clothing was soaking wet, but he remained throughout the meeting to hear what the natives had to say. He sat for days listening to the people of Guam tell their story. Throughout the Pacific islands, Kwajalein and Majero in the Marshall Islands, Kusaie, Mokil, Panape, and Truk in the Caroline Islands, American Samoa, Guam and Hawaii the people will grieve the loss of this man. . . . He had sympathy. . . . He understood. . . . I know of no finer manifestation of unselfishness in public service" (speech of Joseph Rider Farrington, the delegate from Hawaii, *Congressional Record*, 81st Cong. 2nd Sess., May 31, 1950, p. 7982). The hunger he witnessed in Korea in 1949 so affected him that it made him sleepless at night and unable to enjoy his meals (interview with Mrs. William Lemke, June 3, 1951).

enced by most isolationists. In favor of withdrawal from Europe and
opposed to NATO and the Marshall and Point Four plans, he was
very unexplainably opposed to any proposal for a diminution of
American influence in the Far East. General Douglas MacArthur,
Supreme Allied Commander in Japan refused to see any of the
seven Representatives except Lemke. To Lemke this was a matter of
pride; there was a blind spot in his liberalism that did not recognize
the anomaly of an appointed member of the executive branch of the
government refusing to see the elected representatives of the people.
Similar treatment by the members of a bureau of any other department of the government would have angered him. As did most of
those who interviewed MacArthur, Lemke came away a greater admirer of the general than he had been before, and he was especially
flattered that the general had given him an hour and a half of his
time, a commentary on Lemke's failure to see clearly the significant
difference between MacArthur's attitude toward the civilian branch
of the government and that of General George Washington.[31]

Lemke returned a tired man. His family noticed that on picnics,
short climbs fatigued him.[32] But his absence had left work to be
done. There was no possibility of taking the vacation he needed so
badly, for the second session of the Eighty-first Congress had begun,
and the Alaska bill, the bill to protect the Fort Berthold Indians, and
an extension of the Frazier-Lemke Bankruptcy Act needed careful
guidance if they were not to be caught in the legislative log jam at
the end of the session. On May 24, his three major bills passed the
House. This enabled him to return to North Dakota, where for the
first time since 1942 he faced a difficult problem in being re-elected.
The ROC governor, Fred Aandahl, had served three terms and had
been endorsed by the ROC as Lemke's running mate for Congress.
He had been a popular governor, and his name was familiar to every
voter. If he were successful, either Burdick or Lemke would be defeated.

Lemke was scheduled to give the opening radio address of his
campaign on the evening of Memorial Day. The big house into which
the Lemkes had moved in 1921 stood empty and the flower garden
was not planted. Lemke had been proud of his unusual flowers. In
the years he himself could not return, he had always arranged with
a neighbor to plant several hundred bulbs. The house might be empty
most of the summer, but the flowers were there to greet the Lemkes
when they arrived home in the fall after Congress had adjourned.

Lemke had never found relaxation easy and he often sought relief from tension by changing his type of work. His speech for the evening radio address was written, and with all of the enthusiasm he felt for his favorite hobby, he spent the day setting out bulbs and doing the necessary spading. Eating lightly as was his custom and scarcely stopping for lunch, he finished in time to return to the Powers Hotel for his evening meal. He collapsed just as he stepped to the clerk's desk to ask for the key to his room, and he died in a taxi on the way to the hospital. The strain of the Far Eastern trip with no rest before resuming his labors in Congress had not left him the energy for a rugged political campaign. Apparently he had had no warning that the end was near, and the over-exertion in his garden at unaccustomed labor had been too much. He passed away as suddenly as had his father at the land sale in the Towner County courthouse forty-nine years earlier. Services were held in the Christian Science Church and burial was in Fargo. In late summer, when his family returned to open the Fargo home, they had the poignant experience of seeing in full bloom the flowers Lemke had planted on the day of his death.

Lemke's life had been notable for its dedication to that in which he believed. His public career had been marked by continued public confidence over a period of decades, yet he had never been granted the governorship or one of the senatorial posts. There were typical things about him; yet he did not fit any type. He had been one of the most distinctive figures in North Dakota, and the state would not always be so fortunate in having devoted and able leadership such as he provided. No attorney general surpassed him in devotion to duty or accomplishments. No congressman was more effective in obtaining things for his home state than Lemke was during the Eightieth and Eighty-first Congressional sessions. Less visible are the permanent governmental changes such as the Bank of North Dakota, the state mill and elevator, and the state insurance program. Because of his work, provisions protecting the weak and unfortunate were imbedded in countless provisions of the laws of the state. That these provisions, as all laws sometimes do, have occasionally protected the unworthy does not lessen their value or cheapen the motives of the man who wrote them. Throughout the nation tens of thousands of citizens owned their homes and their businesses because Lemke had lived and served as a state official and as a congressman from North Dakota.[33] He would have been an outstanding governor. Although he would have aroused the opposition of those whom he disturbed and might eventually have been defeated, he would have left a structure of state government which would have been modified for the better. He missed some of the main chances, and perhaps it was just as well. He served where he could serve best, and his influence was not confined to his own state. His misunderstanding of international relations and his theories about the causes of war would not have made him as adequate a national leader as those whom he often criticized.

In his entire public career, there was nothing sordid, mean, or cheap. When the issue was drawn, he was always on the side of justice. He had courage and the optimism that came from the conviction that somehow right would triumph, and he usually never hesitated to act forthrightly when basic issues presented themselves. At no time did he profit at the state's expense, and his errors were those of judgment. He was unjustly maligned as few men have been in the state's history.

There were many eulogies, but fittingly enough, just two weeks before he died, the Public Lands Committee received a resolution from the Fort Berthold Reservation Tribal Council. It was presented at a regular meeting of the committee with all members, including Lemke, present. The committee had been called into session by the chairman so that the resolution might be accepted by unanimous vote. The resolution read:

[The Fort Berthold Reservation Tribal Council] further adopts a resolution as a monument to Congressman William Lemke who so courageously sponsored . . . and valiantly fought for such enactment [Public Law Number 437, 81st Congress] and further, as permanent evidence of this appreciation, the Tribal Business Council hereby authorizes construction and establishment of a monument at an appropriate place on the residual reservation in honor of the said Honorable William Lemke, Congressman at large from North Dakota.[34]

With the resolution were letters from Lemke's colleagues on the committee who took the occasion to add expressions of their appreciation of his work. Lemke was obviously touched and he spoke briefly in appreciation, but he added that monuments were reserved for the dead, and he hoped to be around a long time unless he were defeated in the coming election. His life had been so full of disappointments that it seemed most fitting that he should have had this recognition during his lifetime from some of those whom he had helped.

There will never be another prairie rebel such as Lemke was, for he was a product of the frontier and his roots were deep in all the agrarian movements of the past. Had he lived longer, there were things he would have accomplished that have not since been done. Yet he had served his mission for his time. North Dakota was changing, and those who had known pioneer conditions and who understood Lemke's language were becoming fewer. It was their confidence in him that had elevated him to public position and permitted him to have a public career. He was a rebel, a "zealot with political acumen," but he had a constructive program that had made his life a purposeful one and that had caused him to compile a record as one of North Dakota's more distinguished sons.

# Notes

## I. PRAIRIE HERITAGE

1. Richard Hofstadter, *The Age of Reform from Bryan to F. D. R.* (New York: Knopf, 1955), pp. 60–81. The phrases "agrarian myth" and "agrarian demonology," commonly used to describe the language and feelings of farmers toward an idyllic past that had been destroyed by distant conspiracies, were popularized, if not originated, by Hofstadter in this study.

2. United States, Department of Commerce, *Twelfth Census of the United States, 1900, Population,* Vol. I, Parts 1 and 2; Harold E. Briggs, *Frontiers of the Northwest: A History of the Upper Missouri Valley* (New York: D. Appleton Century, 1940), p. 93.

3. Robert E. Bahmer, "The Economic and Political Background of the Non-partisan League" (unpublished Ph.D. dissertation, University of Minnesota, 1941), pp. 79–81.

4. Interview with Charles E. Blackorby, William Lemke's teacher in the seventh and eighth grades and son of another farmer in the area settled by the Lemkes, September 14, 1955. Glenn L. Brudvig, "The Farmers Alliance and Populist Movement in North Dakota, 1884–1894" (unpublished Master's thesis, University of North Dakota, 1956), p. 165.

5. C. L. Sulzberger, *New York Times,* October 31, 1956.

6. *Cando Record,* September 7, 1933. Information is from the obituary of Mrs. Frederick Lemke, Sr.; interview with Mrs. William Lemke, June 3, 1951.

7. Interview with Mrs. William Lemke, June 3, 1951; with Charles E. Blackorby, September 14, 1955; with Mrs. Fred Lemke, Jr., August 24, 1957.

8. Charles E. Blackorby to author, October 4, 1957.

9. *Cando Record,* September 7, 1933; interview with Mrs. Henry Lemke, June 1, 1955; Charles E. Blackorby to author, October 4, 1955.

10. Interview with Mrs. William Lemke, June 3, 1951; H. C. Middaugh to President Calvin Coolidge, December 1, 1923; William Lemke to Frances Bolek, September 24, 1941, both William Lemke Papers, Orin G. Libby Historical Manuscripts Collection, University of North Dakota Library, Grand Forks, North Dakota, hereafter referred to as Lemke Papers.

11. *Bismarck Tribune,* March 6, 1901; North Dakota Legislative Assembly, *Journal of the House of the Seventh Session of the North Dakota Legislative Assembly* (Bismarck, 1901), p. 908.

12. Charles E. Blackorby to author, October 4, 1955; J. J. Kehoe to Federal Land Bank, December 28, 1934, Lemke Papers.

13. Charles E. Blackorby to author, October 4, 1955.

14. Interview with Charles E. Blackorby, September 14, 1955.

15. Louis G. Geiger, *University of the Northern Plains* (Grand Forks: University of North Dakota, 1958), p. 132.

16. Kathrine B. Tiffany to author, January 31, 1957.

17. *Ibid.*

18. Interviews with Earl Duell, May 29, 1954; with Vernon McCutchan, May 1, 1957; with Brigadier General Frank Richards, August 25, 1956, all members of either the Varsity Bachelor Club or its successor, Phi Delta Theta; M. Beatrice Johnstone to author, July 4, 1951.

19. Paul Griffith to William Lemke, December 20, 1909, Lemke Papers.

20. University of North Dakota Faculty Minutes, 8 June, 1901, p. 255.

21. Record in Office of Registrar, University of North Dakota; interview with Mrs. William Lemke, June 3, 1951.

22. *The Student*, the University periodical, November, 1902 (quotation); Andrew A. Bruce, *The Non-Partisan League* (New York: Macmillan, 1921), p. 66.

23. Samuel Peterson, *Democracy and Government* (New York: Knopf, 1919).

24. Paul Griffith to William Lemke, February 1, Lemke Papers; Charles N. Glaab, "John Burke and the North Dakota Progressive Movement, 1906–12" (unpublished Master's thesis, University of North Dakota, 1952); Glaab, "The Revolution of 1906—North Dakota versus McKenzie," *The North Dakota Quarterly*, XXV (Fall, 1956), p. 102.

25. Kathrine B. Tiffany to author, January 31, 1957.

26. Interview with Mrs. William Lemke, June 3, 1951; Marie L. Stoll, Registrar of Georgetown University Law Center, to author, November 13, 1956.

27. Elsa Wolf, Registrar of Yale University Law School, to author, December 12, 1956; Dean Henry Wade Rogers to President William H. Taft, July 26, 1911, copy in Lemke Papers. "Mr. Lemke made a good record when in the Law School."; William Lemke to Edward M. Nolan, April 19, 1939, Lemke Papers; interview with Mrs. William Lemke, June 3, 1951.

28. Interview with C. C. Converse, September 11, 1956.

29. Interview with Mrs. William Lemke, June 3, 1951.

30. Interview with Mrs. William Lemke, June 3, 1951; Bruce, pp. 170–184; many of Robinson's letters are extant in the Lemke Papers.

31. Copies of *The Common Good* are among the Lemke Papers.

32. Interview with Mrs. William Lemke, June 3, 1951.

33. Interview with Mrs. William Lemke, June 3, 1951, concerning Lemke's purchase of land for a few cents per acre; interview with Judge Gudmundur Grimson of the North Dakota Supreme Court, one of the investors in the Land Finance Company, July 1, 1954.

34. Land Finance Company to Frederick Anderson, February 23, 1914; William Lemke to Marcia Bisbee, a former University of North Dakota instructor who invested in the Land Finance Company and went to Mexico as a colonist, November 30, 1913; statement of company; all Lemke Papers.

35. Interview with Earl Duell, May 29, 1954.

36. M. B. Katze to William Lemke, October 13, 1908, Lemke Papers; William Lemke to William Langer, September 24, 1909, Lemke Papers. "Please send me your write up about Mexico at once if you can. We are getting out a special

number of *The Common Good*, describing the west coast of Mexico and want your article for it."

37. Luis Para y Pardo, *De Porfirio Diaz a Francisco Madero* (New York: Polyglot Publishing and Commercial, 1912), pp. 81–87, trans. by Benjamin Keen in *Readings in Latin American Civilization, 1492 to the Present* (Boston: Houghton Mifflin, 1955), p. 352; William Lemke to J. E. Davis, October 13, 1909, Lemke Papers, a letter requesting a loan and describing his financial situation; interview with Earl Duell, May 29, 1954.

38. William Lemke to *American Magazine*, October 20, 1909 (quotation); William Lemke to Frank Langer, November 17, 1909; both Lemke Papers.

39. Mrs. William Lemke to author, January 8, 1957.

40. *Loc. cit.*

41. Interviews with Earl Duell, May 29, 1954; with Mrs. William Lemke, June 3, 1951; with Usher L. Burdick, October 29, 1954.

42. Alfred B. Thomas, *Latin America: A History* (New York: Macmillan, 1956), p. 667.

43. William Lemke to Senator A. B. Fall, February 23, 1915; to W. M. Schufeldt, October 15, 1915; to J. E. Robinson, February 25, 1914; to T. T. Lindsay, November 11, 1913; all Lemke Papers.

44. William Lemke to C. W. Salie, January 12, 1915 (quotation); to C. W. Westergard, March 30, 1916; both Lemke Papers.

45. William Lemke to Father F. C. Kelly, April 6 and August 8, 1916, Lemke Papers; Austin F. MacDonald, *Latin American Politics and Government* (New York: Crowell, 1954), p. 215; William Lemke, *Crimes Against Mexico* (Minneapolis: Great West Printing Co., 1915), *passim;* W. M. Anderson to William Lemke, July 5, 1916; William Lemke to Joseph Blatchford, August 17, 1915; both Lemke Papers; *The Searchlight* (Fargo, North Dakota), September 11, 1915.

46. Interview with Mrs. William Lemke, June 3, 1951; H. N. Tucker to Mrs. William Lemke, January 29, 1916, Lemke Papers; William Lemke to José Castellot, February 7, 1915, Lemke Papers, "I am bankrupt . . . for the time being."

47. William Lemke to Woodrow Wilson, April 22, 1914. The carbon copy of this letter and the form memo are in Mrs. William Lemke's possession.

48. Interview with Mrs. William Lemke, June 3, 1951; Webster Merrifield to William Lemke, January 15 and February 18, 1909, Lemke Papers; William Lemke to Kathrine B. Macdonald, June 3, 1912, Lemke Papers. Lemke wrote to accept the invitation to act as toastmaster. Mrs. Macdonald, the wife of Neil C. Macdonald, later state superintendent of public instruction, remarried after Mr. Macdonald's death and is the Kathrine B. Tiffany elsewhere cited; interview with Vernon L. McCutchan, May 1, 1957. McCutchan, a member of the Varsity Bachelor Club, remembers Lemke as visiting frequently.

49. William Lemke to J. M. Anderson, October 20, 1909, Lemke Papers; *The Searchlight*, March 26 and April 9, 1910.

50. Interview with H. L. Walster, June 18, 1957. The late Mr. Walster was Dean Emeritus of North Dakota Agricultural College; H. L. Walster to author, June 27, 1957; H. L. Walster, "History of the North Dakota Agricultural College" (MS in preparation at the time of his death) (quotation).

51. Interview with A. C. Townley, January 14, 1951.

52. *The State of North Dakota ex rel Henry J. Linde v. The Equity Cooperative*

*Exchange; T. F. McCue v. Cooperators' Herald* (briefs of both among Lemke Papers).

53. *Cooperators' Herald,* January 30, 1914; *Fargo Courier-News,* February 7, 1914.

54. *Cooperators' Herald,* February 6, 1914; *Fargo Courier-News,* February 12 and March 4, 1914; William Lemke to L. B. Hanna, April 15, 1914; L. B. Hanna to William Lemke, May 26 and October 21, 1914; all Lemke Papers; *Fargo Courier-News,* February 8, 1914.

55. Robert P. Wilkins, "North Dakota and the European War, 1914–17: A Study in Public Opinion" (unpublished Ph.D. dissertation, West Virginia University, 1954), p. 64; Brudvig, pp. 204–206; William Lemke to H. D. Munn, February 11, 1915, Lemke Papers.

56. William Lemke to John A. Johnson, February 7, 1914, Lemke Papers.


## II. INSIDE THE NPL

1. Glenn Brudvig, "The Farmers Alliance and Populist Movement in North Dakota (1884–1894)" (unpublished Master's thesis, University of North Dakota, 1956), p. 178; Gilbert Cooke, "The North Dakota State Mill and Elevator," *Journal of Political Economy* XLVI (February, 1938), p. 24; Robert Bahmer "The Economic and Political Background of the Nonpartisan League" (unpublished Ph.D. dissertation, University of Minnesota, 1941), p. 367; Cooke, *Journal of Political Economy,* p. 24; Andrew A. Bruce, *The Non-Partisan League* (New York: Macmillan, 1921), p. 57. These percentages were computed from voting figures given by Bruce.

2. North Dakota, Session Laws, 1913, Chapter 179, p. 435

3. North Dakota Legislative Assembly, Journal of the House of the Fourteenth Session of the North Dakota Legislative Assembly (Bismarck, 1915) pp. 187–188.

4. Theodore Saloutos and John D. Hicks, *Agricultural Discontent in the Middle West, 1900–1939* (Madison: University of Wisconsin, 1951), p. 150.

5. Interviews with Luther A. Bratten, July, 1944; with Charles C. Converse, September 11, 1956; Paul R. Fossum, *The Agrarian Movement in North Dakota* (Baltimore: Johns Hopkins, 1925), pp. 91–93.

6. Alvin S. Tostlebe, *The Bank of North Dakota: An Experiment in Agrarian Banking* (Columbia University Publications: Studies in History, Economics and Public Law, Vol. CXIV, No. 1 [New York: Longmans Green, 1924]), p. 31; Paul Studenski and Herman E. Kroos, *Financial History of the United States* (New York: McGraw-Hill, 1952), p. 282; William Lemke to George Fifer, January 14, 1915, William Lemke Papers, Orin G. Libby Historical Manuscripts Collection, University of North Dakota, hereafter referred to as Lemke Papers.

7. Bahmer, pp. 408–409; interview with A. C. Townley, January 14, 1951.

8. Jackson Putnam, "The Socialist Party in North Dakota, 1902–1918" (unpublished Master's thesis, University of North Dakota, 1956), pp. 95, 150, 174.

9. Putnam, p. 151; Usher L. Burdick, *History of Farmers Political Action in North Dakota* (Baltimore: Wirth Brothers, 1944), p. 81; Bahmer, p. 451; interview with A. C. Townley, January 14, 1951.

10. Bruce, p. 69.

11. Mrs. William Lemke to author, February 18, 1957.

12. Robert P. Wilkins, "North Dakota and the European War, 1914-1917; A Study in Public Opinion" (unpublished Ph.D. dissertation, West Virginia University, 1954), p. 64; Bahmer, p. 461; Robert M. Morlan, *Political Prairie Fire* (Minneapolis: University of Minnesota, 1955), pp. 48-51; William Lemke to William Langer, November 1, 1915, Lemke Papers. Lemke mentioned to Langer that Burtness knew of the League but that he did not realize how strong it was.

13. *Cooperators' Herald,* March 17, 1916; Dorr Carroll to William Lemke, October 19, 1916, Lemke Papers.

14. Morlan, p. 57; interview with W. B. Allen, political analyst of the *Grand Forks Herald,* February 13, 1957. Morlan emphasized the ability of the headquarters personnel to make out good cases for the favored candidates; it was Allen's belief that Lemke had many political talents but that the primary source of his success lay in his ability to control conventions, an explanation of his later failures when as a Congressman he was unable or unwilling to absent himself from Washington to attend conventions in North Dakota.

15. Interview with A. C. Townley, July 1, 1957; Carl C. Taylor, *The Farmers Movement, 1620-1920* (New York: American Book Co., 1953), pp. 436-437.

16. William Lemke to William Langer, November 1, 1915, Lemke Papers.

17. Victor Wardrope to William Lemke, April 1, 1916, Lemke Papers.

18. O. B. Burtness to William Lemke, April 2, 1916; Victor Wardrope to William Lemke, April 1 and April 13, 1916 (quotations); *Cooperators' Herald,* April 28, 1916.

19. William Lemke to J. M. Anderson, May 2 and 9, 1916; J. M. Anderson to William Lemke, May 8 and May 10, 1916; all Lemke Papers.

20. Interview with Herbert Swett, August 11, 1956; William Lemke to Lynn J. Frazier, April 23, 1917. Lemke advised Frazier to make a good speech because the White House was looming ahead. There are a number of such references by Lemke to Frazier in the Lemke Papers; Taylor, p. 462. Taylor quotes Lemke as having told him in an interview on November 28, 1940 that if World War I had not intervened, the League would have spread over the nation and would "have elected Lynn Frazier President of the United States."; *New York Times,* January 12, 1947 (obituary reference to interruption of Frazier's training to be a doctor).

21. Interview with W. O. Skeels, August 30, 1956; with A. C. Townley, January 14, 1951.

22. D. C. Coates to W. E. Borah, May 13, 1916, William E. Borah Papers, Manuscripts Division, Library of Congress, Washington, D.C., a discussion of plans for the special train and a request that Borah campaign for Frazier.

23. Robert T. Muir, June 24, 1916; William G. Owens, July 1, 1916; Congressman P. D. Norton, July 3, 1916; all to William Lemke, Lemke Papers.

24. Herbert E. Gaston, *The Non-Partisan League* (New York: Harcourt Brace, 1920), p. 125.

25. William Lemke to Percy Abbey, August 20, 1916, Lemke Papers. Lemke's letter was written just after the full extent of the wheat crop failure of 1916 had become apparent.

26. K. S. Ramsett to William Lemke, September 9, 1916, Lemke Papers.

27. Wilkins, pp. 218, 222-223.

28. William Lemke to A. T. Hert, September 18, 1916; unsigned letter to

John Eversman, October 2, 1916, both Lemke Papers. Eversman was an officer at Republican national headquarters.

29. H. E. More to W. C. Coates, October 17, 1916; J. J. Lee to William Lemke, September 25, 1916; Senator Porter J. McCumber, October 19, 1916; George M. Young, Representative from the Second Congressional District, October 22, 1916; both to William Lemke; all Lemke Papers.

30. William Lemke to Ben Lemke, November 2, 1916, Lemke Papers.

31. W. Purcell to Senator Thomas Walsh, September 4, 1916, Thomas Walsh Papers, Manuscripts Division, Library of Congress, Washington, D.C., hereafter referred to as Walsh Papers. "When Mr. Hughes made his speech at Fargo. . . . he made more friends for Wilson than Mr. Wilson had in the state before Hughes came into it." This letter was from a prominent North Dakota Democrat to a United States senator from Montana; Edward A. Rumely, "There Is No Vision," an editorial clipping from an unidentified magazine dated July 16, 1917, Gutzon Borglum Papers, Manuscripts Division, Library of Congress, Washington, D.C.; Wilkins, pp. 206, 329; William Lemke to J. R. Walker, November 28, 1916, Lemke Papers.

32. Victor Wardrope to William Lemke, June 5, 1915; Ben Lemke to William Lemke, June 7, 1916; William Lemke to Herman Lemke, December 3, 1916, Lemke Papers.

33. J. E. Robinson to William Lemke, February 8, 1918; Ray McKaig to William Lemke, December 7, 1934; both Lemke Papers; Carl Wittke, *The German Language Press in America* (Lexington: University of Kentucky, 1957) p. 256. The German press regarded "He Kept Us Out of War" as a "seductive appeal" and countered with "Peace with Hughes with Wilson War."

34. G. D. Mann, October 19, 1916 (quotation); W. M. Anderson, October 25, 1916; Henry Albrecht, October 13, 1916 (quotation); all to William Lemke; William Lemke to Fred Stanley, October 7, 1916; to N. Y. Morgan, October 16, 1916; to O. A. Spillum, October 17, 1916; all Lemke Papers.

35. William Lemke to J. R. Walker, November 28, 1916, Lemke Papers.

36. Wilkins, pp. 226–227; R. J. Hughes to author, July 26, 1938. Hughes, who was one of McCumber's closest advisers, emphatically denied that any arrangement existed between McCumber and the League. Hughes may not have told all he knew. However, such an arrangement could have been made through McKenzie without Hughes' knowledge and possibly without McCumber being fully informed. It is difficult to see any advantage accruing to Townley, and this argues that Hughes was correct in his statement that no arrangement existed.

37. Wilkins, pp. 221, 229; R. A. Nestos, November 6, 1916; Usher L. Burdick, October 25, 1916; both to William Lemke; William Lemke to Frank P. Woods, October 15, 1916; William Langer to William Lemke, October 12, 1916; Harry M. Case to William Lemke, October 25, 1916; William Lemke to Alf O. Nelson, October 12, 1916, "Will state that Frazier and McCumber are not touring together. . . . More effective work can be done by them speaking separately."; Henry M. Case to William Lemke, October 21, 1916; all letters Lemke Papers.

38. Ray McKaig to William Lemke, December 7, 1934; A. T. Hert to William Lemke, wire, 8:00 P. M., November 8, 1916; National Republican Headquarters to William Lemke, November 11, 1916; all Lemke Papers.

39. Wilkins, p. 246; William Lemke to Karl Farup, November 11, 1916, Lemke Papers.

40. North Dakota Secretary of State, *Blue Book*, 1913, pp. 262–264. The differences between the election return figures of 1912 and 1916 portray the problem that Lemke failed to solve.

41. William Lemke to K. S. Ramsett, November 2, 1916; to Ben Lemke, November 2, 1916, both Lemke Papers; Earl Duell to author, July 6, 1957.

42. Morlan, p. 85; interview with John Steen in June of 1938. Steen emphasized his use of this situation.

43. Wilkins, pp. 206, 243; Usher L. Burdick to William Lemke, October 25, 1916, Lemke Papers.

44. See correspondence for 1916 and 1917 in Lemke Papers.

45. See League Headquarters correspondence in Lemke Papers; Ray Goldberg, *The Nonpartisan League in North Dakota* (Fargo: Midwest Printing and Lithographing Company, 1948), p. 56. Herbert A. Mackoff, a Dickinson attorney and a member of the 1917 legislature who had declined an offer to affiliate with the League caucus is quoted by Goldberg.

46. See Lemke's correspondence of the weeks before the meeting of the 1917 legislature, Lemke Papers.

47. Morlan, p. 72; Gaston, p. 103.

48. Alex E. Gedistad to William Lemke, October 12, 1914, "I got your name from Mr. Ben Goldman. I will kindly ask you . . . [to] help me . . . get my land back"; also C. W. Sherwin to E. H. Behrns, October 14, 1915; William Lemke to C. W. Sherwin, November 1 and 8, 1915; all Lemke Papers.

49. Bruce, p. 171.

50. See *Grand Forks Herald*, December 30, 1916; William Lemke to A. C. Townley, March 18, 1917, Lemke Papers.

51. Interview with A. C. Townley, January 14, 1951; *Bismarck Tribune*, January 6 and 13, 1917 (quotations).

52. *Ibid.*, January 26, 1917 (quotation); Alice Johnson, "The Public Career of J. F. T. O'Connor" (unpublished Master's thesis, University of North Dakota, 1956), pp. 24–33; *Bismarck Tribune*, January 24, 1917.

53. *Bismarck Tribune*, January 30 and 31, 1917.

54. William Lemke to D. C. Coates, April 26, 1917, Lemke Papers.

55. William Lemke to Carl Jorgenson, state treasurer, December 16, 1916, Lemke Papers. The letter instructs Jorgenson not to pay Fisk, Goss, and Burke, the outgoing judges for December. I am writing as attorney for Robinson, Birdzell and Grace.; Bruce pp. 195–196; William Lemke to John Steen, December 16, 1916, Lemke Papers.

56. Bruce, p. 114; William Lemke to William Langer, March 16, 1917, Lemke Papers.

57. See William Lemke to Thomas Hall, October 18, 1916; W. L. Nuessle to William Lemke, July 22, 1917, both Lemke Papers; Morlan, pp. 106–107.

58. William Lemke to Arthur Le Sueur, February 24, 1917; to James Manahan, February 24, 1917; both Lemke Papers.

59. Alice J. Johnson, pp. 32–33.

60. Benjamin Drake to William Lemke, August 24, 1916; William Lemke to A. C. Townley, March 18, and 20, 1917 (the letter of March 18 accompanied by

a copy of the lease of the third floor of the Gilfallan Building in St. Paul); William Lemke to B. H. O'Laughlin, April 27, 1917; all Lemke Papers.

61. S. R. Maxwell, *The Non-Partisan League from the Inside* (St. Paul, 1918), p. 52 (quotation); Lynn J. Frazier to William Lemke, March 18, 1917; William Lemke to Lynn J. Frazier, March 11, 14, 16, and 18, 1917; to William Langer, March 16, 1917; to S. A. Olsness, March 15, 1917; all Lemke Papers.

62. Interview with Mrs. William Lemke, June 3, 1951; *Washington Post,* December 13, 1939.


III. HIGH TIDE

1. George M. Young to William Lemke, April 11, 1917, William Lemke Papers, Orin G. Libby Collection, University of North Dakota Library, Grand Forks, North Dakota, hereafter referred to as the Lemke Papers (quotation); see William Lemke to Victor Wardrope, October 21, 1909, Lemke Papers, for an indication of Lemke's political ambition; James Manahan, April 16, 1917; F. E. Packard, April 21, 1917; Robert T. Muir, April 21, 1917; O. B. Burtness, April 25, 1917; all to William Lemke, Lemke Papers (all quotations).

2. F. B. Wood to William Lemke, November 7, 1923: "I have the most love and respect for old Bill Lemke of any man outside of my family." William Lemke to Carl Nelson, June 11, 1917 (quotation); both Lemke Papers; Robert M. Morlan, *Political Prairie Fire* (Minneapolis: University of Minnesota, 1955), p. 85. Morlan, who is reluctant to assign Lemke as major a role as do Bahmer and Bruce, concedes that Lemke was a key figure in the League.

3. William Lemke to William Langer, November 4 and December 26, 1917; Lemke Papers. Langer was one of the larger investors in the scheme and the correspondence is typical.

4. Carl Nelson to William Lemke, June 6, 1917, Lemke Papers.

5. J. M. Baer, Senior, to William Lemke, March 23, 1917, Lemke Papers.

6. Information and quotation in this paragraph are from interview with former Congressman John M. Baer, August 29, 1956.

7. William Lemke to L. A. Simpson, June 19, 1917, Lemke Papers.

8. These vote tabulations are in the records which were kept by Lemke as state chairman of the Republican party, and are included among the Lemke Papers. Morlan, p. 131, states that Lemke was "one of the chief backers of Baer."; P. O. Thorson to addressee, a circular letter dated June 25, 1917; J. E. Lee to William Lemke, undated (quotation); unsigned note to William Lemke, undated; all Lemke Papers.

9. J. M. Baer to William Lemke, undated, Lemke Papers.

10. William Lemke to Lynn J. Frazier, March 23, 1917, Lemke Papers.

11. Morlan, pp. 138–140. Morlan's account of the use of the war issue is vivid, thorough, and of great assistance in understanding this period.

12. *Loc. cit.;* Fargo Forum, June 9, 1917, as quoted in Morlan, p. 139; see also Herbert E. Gaston, *The Non-Partisan League* (New York: Harcourt Brace, 1920), p. 179; Morlan, p. 132.

13. *Loc. cit.* (quotation); interview with John M. Baer, August 29, 1956.

14. Interview with John M. Baer, August 29, 1956; Charles Edward Russell, *The Story of the Nonpartisan League* (New York: Harper and Brothers, 1920), p. 243; interview with Mrs. William Lemke, June 3, 1951.

15. Information and quotation in this paragraph are from interview with John M. Baer, August 29, 1956.

16. Morlan, p. 143.

17. Information and quotations in this paragraph are from Belle C. La Follette and Fola La Follette, *Robert M. La Follette, June 14, 1855–June 18, 1925* (New York: Macmillan, 1953), II, 761–772.

18. John M. Baer to author, March 5, 1957; La Follette, pp. 882–883.

19. Morlan, pp. 152–182 (quotation); James M. Manahan, *Trials of a Lawyer* (Minneapolis: privately printed, 1933). No understanding of the full meaning of this episode can be obtained without reading Manahan's account; William Lemke to Henry Lemke, July 12, 1918, Lemke Papers.

20. J. E. Robinson to William Lemke, February 8, 1918, Lemke Papers.

21. George Creel to Woodrow Wilson, April 2, 1918, Woodrow Wilson Papers, Manuscripts Division, Library of Congress, Washington, D.C.

22. Fred Lemke to William Lemke, December 11, 1918, Lemke Papers; Morlan, p. 145; William Lemke to Robert La Follette, November 18, 1918, Lemke Papers.

23. Gaston, p. 275; Joseph Dorfman, *Thorstein Veblen and His America* (New York: Viking, 1935), p. 384 (quotation); George H. Mayer, *The Political Career of Floyd B. Olson* (Minneapolis: University of Minnesota, 1951), p. 21 (quotation).

24. William Lemke to Mary D. Brite, October 21, 1929, Lemke Papers.

25. *Loc. cit.*

26. P. O. Sathre to John Hagan, October 6, 1950, letter in Mrs. William Lemke's possession; H. G. Teigan to Judson King, February 28, 1917, National Nonpartisan League Papers, Minnesota Historical Society, St. Paul, Minnesota; Theodore Saloutos and John D. Hicks, *Agricultural Discontent in the Middle West, 1900–1939* (Madison: University of Wisconsin, 1951), p. 192.

27. William Lemke to H. G. Teigan, November 12, 1923, Henry G. Teigan Papers, Minnesota Historical Society, St. Paul, Minnesota, hereafter referred to as Teigan Papers.

28. William Lemke to R. T. Muir, January 14, 1918 and October 31, 1917; to Lynn J. Frazier, October 31, 1917; all Lemke Papers.

29. William Lemke to George N. Young, October 1, 1918; to Will Hayes, September 2, 1918; both Lemke Papers.

30. Gaston, pp. 243, 247; Morlan, p. 250.

31. M. A. Brannon to William Lemke, November 22, 1918 (quotation); December 30, 1918; both Lemke Papers.

32. Interview with Herbert Swett, May 10, 1956; with W. O. Skeels, August 30, 1956.

33. Jackson Putnam, "The Socialist Party in North Dakota, 1902–1918" (unpublished Master's thesis, University of North Dakota, 1956), pp. 174–191.

34. Thomas Hall to O. T. Rischoff, January 13, 1918, Teigan Papers. Hall had recently been humiliated at the hands of some of those whom he bitterly described in this letter.

35. William Langer, *The Nonpartisan League: Its Birth, Activities and Leaders* (Mandan, North Dakota: Morton County Farmers Press, 1920), p. 129.

36. Morlan, pp. 241–243; Gaston, pp. 304–305.

37. Kathrine B. Tiffany to author, July 8, 1957.

38. Morlan, p. 230.

39. Langer, p. 54. Langer assigned responsibility to Brinton, thus agreeing with Lemke (see footnote p. 90), a significant concurrence of opinion leaving little doubt as to Brinton's role; Joseph M. Mader, "The Political Influence of the Nonpartisan League on the Press of North Dakota" (unpublished Master's thesis, University of Minnesota, 1937), p. 38.

40. Interview with Herbert Swett, September 10, 1955; *Bismarck Tribune,* February 21 and March 7, 1919 (quotations).

41. North Dakota, Session Laws, 1919, Chapter 71, pp. 85–87; Morlan pp. 225, 234.

42. Morlan, p. 228; W. Caddell to A. C. Townley, March 5, 1919.

43. *Bismarck Tribune,* February 13, 1919.

44. *The Goat* [a League publication], May–June, 1920, p. 22, editorial; Nelson A. Mason to William Lemke, May 14, 1942, Lemke Papers.

45. Interview with O. B. Burtness, July, 1937.

46. Lynn J. Frazier to William Lemke, May 15, 1919, Lemke Papers; *The Independent,* May 15, 1919 (quotation).

47. Russell, p. 283 (quotation); 287–292.

48. Saloutos and Hicks, p. 201.

49. Spurgeon O'Dell to William Lemke, December 30, 1920, Lemke Papers.

50. Russell, pp. 295–296; *Fargo Courier-News,* September 26, 1919; *The Independent,* October 2, 1919.

51. Langer, p. 28.

52. Morlan, p. 272.

53. E. C. Blackorby, "Political Factional Strife in North Dakota from 1920 to 1932" (unpublished Master's thesis, University of North Dakota, 1938), p. 19.

54. Gaston, pp. 303–310; Alvin S. Tostlebe, *The Bank of North Dakota: An Experiment in Agrarian Banking* (Columbia University Publications: Studies in History, Economics and Public Law, Vol. CXIV, No. 1 [New York: Longmans Green, 1924]), pp. 96–103.

55. Oliver S. Morris to William Lemke, October 24, 1919, Lemke Papers.

56. Interview with Mrs. William Lemke, September 3, 1951.

## IV. ELECTION AND RECALL

1. Robert M. Morlan, *Political Prairie Fire* (Minneapolis: University of Minnesota, 1955), p. 299.

2. *Ibid.,* p. 285.

3. Morlan, p. 291; *Green* v. *Frazier,* 253 U. S. 233 (1920).

4. *Non-Partisan Leader,* June 21, 1920; M. A. Brannon to William Lemke, June 2, 1920 (quotation), William Lemke Papers, Orin G. Libby Historical Manuscripts Collection, University of North Dakota Library, Grand Forks, North Dakota, hereafter referred to as Lemke Papers.

5. Interview with A. C. Townley, January 14, 1951. Townley recalled the

pleasantries and joking indulged in by Wood to make Lemke's endorsement more palatable to Townley.

6. Theodore Saloutos and John D. Hicks, *Agricultural Discontent in the Middle West, 1900–1939* (Madison: University of Wisconsin, 1951), p. 211.

7. Andrew A. Bruce, *The Non-Partisan League* (New York: Macmillan, 1921), p. 210; William W. Phillips, "The Growth of a Progressive, Asle J. Gronna" (unpublished Master's thesis, University of North Dakota, 1952), p. 176; interview with John M. Baer, August 29, 1956; John M. Baer to author, March 5, 1957.

8. Phillips, p. 181.

9. *Ibid.*, p. 179.

10. E. C. Blackorby, "Political Factional Strife in North Dakota from 1920 to 1932" (unpublished Master's thesis, University of North Dakota, 1938), p. 28.

11. Alice J. Johnson, "The Public Career of J. F. T. O'Connor" (unpublished Master's thesis, University of North Dakota, 1956), pp. 66–69.

12. Gutzon Borglum to F. W. Cathro, March 27, 1920; to Warren G. Harding, June 17, 1920; Warren G. Harding to Will Hays, May 26, 1920; Warren G. Harding to Gutzon Borglum, June 8, 1920; Gutzon Borglum to Hiram Johnson, June 5, 1920; J. M. Baer to Gutzon Borglum, July 26, 1920; Gutzon Borglum to Senator John W. Weeks, August 10, 1920, all Gutzon Borglum Papers, Manuscripts Division, Library of Congress, Washington, D.C., hereafter referred to as Borglum Papers; Gutzon Borglum to William Lemke, August 7, 1920; William Lemke to Gutzon Borglum, August 10, 1920; both Lemke Papers; Gutzon Borglum to Senator Miles Poindexter, August 31, 1920 (quotations); Gutzon Borglum to Coleman DuPont, May 17, 1930; to Warren G. Harding, rough copy undated, 1920; Warren G. Harding to Gutzon Borglum, August 27, 1920; Gutzon Borglum to Will Hayes, September 14, 1920; all Borglum Papers.

13. William Lemke to Will Hays, September 4, 1920 (telegram), Lemke Papers.

14. See correspondence for October, 1920, to or from Gutzon Borglum, Borglum Papers: and to or from William Lemke, Lemke Papers; Gutzon Borglum to William Lemke, October 27, 1920, Lemke Papers (quotation).

15. Edwin F. Ladd to Gutzon Borglum, October 23 and November 12, 1920, both Borglum Papers.

16. Unsigned, undated notes to William Lemke, Lemke Papers. These notes were typewritten and then smeared to prevent identification of the typewriter; North Dakota Legislative Assembly, *Journal of the House of the Seventeenth Session of the North Dakota Legislative Assembly*, p. 1203, hereafter referred to as *House Journal, 17th Session;* Joseph M. Mader, "The Political Influence of the Non-Partisan League on the Press of North Dakota" (unpublished Master's thesis, University of Minnesota, 1937), p. 28.

17. *House Journal, 17th Session*, pp. 1205–1211; quotations from pp. 1211, 1208.

18. Morlan, p. 299; *House Journal, 17th Session*, pp. 1061, 1211; William Langer to William Lemke, August 20, 1920 (telegram), Lemke Papers.

19. Treadwell Twitchell, Sveinbjorn Johnson, and Theodore G. Nelson to key Independents, August 3, 1920, Lemke Papers; Gutzon Borglum to Mrs. Haviland H. Lund, September 7, 1921, Borglum Papers; Lawrence Todd to William Lemke, four letters dated September 16, 17, 21, and 25, 1920, all Lemke Papers; Morlan, pp. 266–268.

20. Lemke's letters directing the campaign are among the Lemke Papers.

They leave no room for doubt as to who was in charge; see Adam Lefor to William Lemke, July 14, 1921, Lemke Papers; various interviews with Mr. and Mrs. Herbert Swett, 1955, 56, 57.

21. Alice J. Johnson, p. 66; James Quinn to Howard Wood, November 15, 1920; George A. Totten to William Lemke, January 24, 1921; William Lemke to R. M. McClintock, October 19, 1920; S. M. Aasboe to William Lemke, October 4, 1920, all Lemke Papers.

22. Morlan, p. 304.

23. Blackorby, pp. 31–36.

24. E. Bruce Hagen, "The North Dakota State Mill and Elevator Association: History, Organization, Administration and Operation" (unpublished Master's thesis, University of North Dakota, 1955), passim; Blackorby, p. 34.

25. Bruce, p. 233.

26. Ed Pierce to William Lemke, undated but between December 7 and December 14, 1920, Lemke Papers; Bruce, p. 237.

27. Blackorby, p. 37; interview with R. A. Nestos, May, 1938; Bruce, p. 237.

28. *New York Times,* February 10, 1921.

29. Mrs. William Lemke to author, February 18, 1957.

30. R. H. Walker to William Lemke, December 24, 1920, Lemke Papers.

31. William Lemke to R. H. Walker, December 28, 1920, Lemke Papers.

32. Morlan, p. 319; A. Liederbach to A. C. Townley, April 3, 1921; William Lemke to George Totten, June 30, 1921; both Lemke Papers. The second letter was an attempt to prevent the dispute from breaking into open warfare.

33. *House Journal, 17th Session,* pp. 901–1484.

34. Interview with S. A. Olsness, June 7, 1938; Lynn J. Frazier to author, May 11, 1938.

35. William Lemke to C. W. Reichert, March 22, 1921; to R. M. McClintock, March 19, 1921; both Lemke Papers.

36. William Lemke to Gutzon Borglum, February 18, 1921; to J. E. Gressel, May 18, 1921; to John Thompson, January 31, 1921, all Lemke Papers.

37. Seth Richardson to William Lemke, March 17, 1921, Lemke Papers.

38. George Totten to William Lemke, March 22, 1921, Lemke Papers.

39. C. K. Gummerson to William Lemke, March 31, 1921 (telegram), Lemke Papers.

40. H. G. Teigan to C. O. Parsons, February 4, 1921, Henry G. Teigan Papers, Minnesota Historical Society, St. Paul, Minnesota (quotation); W. A. Anderson to J. A. Van Wagenen, April 11, 1921, Lemke Papers.

41. Karl Knox Gartner to William Lemke, March 2, 1921; William Lemke to J. R. Burton, March 7, 1921; both Lemke Papers; interview with John Halcrow, February 14, 1953; F. L. Watkins to J. C. Miller, March 9, 1921, Lemke Papers; John Halcrow to author, January 31, 1951.

42. William Lemke to O. E. Lofthus, May 28, 1923.

43. William Lemke to B. F. Baker, March 2, 1921, Lemke Papers.

44. E. F. Ladd to William Lemke, July 3, 1921; P. L. Aarhus to O. T. Carlson, October 8, 1921; A. A. Liederbach to Olaf Ericson, April 22, 1921; all Lemke Papers.

45. Spurgeon O'Dell to William Lemke, January 15, 1921; Carl Thompson to members of Public Ownership League of America, *Newsletter,* February 1921; both Lemke papers.

46. William Lemke to John Baer, January 5, 1927; Harold Wheeler to Carl Thompson, June 3, 1921; Carl Thompson to George Webb, July 9, 1921; all Lemke Papers.

47. J. V. Dittemore to William Lemke, April 7, 1921 (quotation); W. A. Anderson to Mrs. W. J. Rademacher, May 20, 1921; Oswald Garrison Villard to William Rutter, undated; C. C. Daniels to William Lemke, May 4, 1921; George T. Webb to Bernard Baruch, March 12, 1935; William Lemke to Carl Thompson, September 29, 1921; William Lemke to F. B. Wood, July 18, 1921; all Lemke Papers; Gutzon Borglum to Mrs. Haviland H. Lund, May 7, 1921, Borglum Papers.

48. W. A. Anderson to Frank White, June 10, 1921, Lemke Papers; Benjamin C. Marsh to Henry C. Wallace, April 20, 1921; memo from F. C. C. to Henry C. Wallace, April 21, 1921; both Department of Agriculture Papers, National Archives, Washington, D.C.

49. Gutzon Borglum to Warren G. Harding, undated rough draft, Borglum Papers (quotation); William Lemke to Gutzon Borglum, November 13, 1920, Lemke Papers.

50. Morlan, p. 319 (quotation); Mrs. William Lemke to William Lemke, July 8, 1921 (telegram), Lemke Papers.

51. William Lemke to W. W. Liggett, undated but apparently in July, 1921, Lemke Papers.

52. William Lemke to Henry O'Connell, September 20, 1921; to E. M. Crosby, September 30, 1921; both Lemke Papers.

53. Morlan, p. 324; Blackorby, p. 50; interview with a Lemke neighbor who witnessed the incident; *Grand Forks Herald,* October 16 and September 8, 1921.

54. *Farmer Labor State Record* to county newspapers, a news release dated July 22, 1921; Walter Maddock to William Lemke, May 16, 1921; both Lemke Papers.

55. F. W. Cathro to Gutzon Borglum, April 18, 1922, Borglum Papers; William Lemke to Ralph Ingerson, September 25, 1921, Lemke Papers; interview with Herbert Swett, September, 1955; George K. Foster to someone at Bismarck, October 12, 1921, Lemke Papers (quotation).

56. P. L. Aarhus to Walter Welford, October 20, 1921, Lemke Papers; Morlan, pp. 325–326; William Lemke to Fred Argast, October 21, 1921, Lemke Papers.

57. William Lemke to P. L. Aarhus, September 6 and 7, 1921; William Lemke to Gutzon Borglum, September 25, 1921; to E. F. Ladd, August 22, 1921; all Lemke Papers. Most of the names are mentioned in Lemke's letter to Borglum; others are mentioned elsewhere; Edwin F. Ladd to Gutzon Borglum, October 15, 1921, Borglum Papers.

58. Ole Kaldor to Walter Maddock, October 11, 1921, Lemke Papers.

59. Interview with W. O. Skeels, August 30, 1956; William Lemke to H. S. Saunders, September 20, 1928; Sveinbjorn Johnson to C. L. Crum, November 24, 1921 (telegram); both Lemke Papers.

60. George T. Webb to Gutzon Borglum, November 25, 1921, Borglum Papers.

61. F. W. Cathro to William Lemke, August 1, 1924, Lemke Papers.

62. P. L. Aarhus to A. A. Liederbach, December 1, 1921, Lemke Papers.

63. William Lemke to Gutzon Borglum, November 15, 1921, Lemke Papers.

64. Kenneth C. Johnson, "The Bank of North Dakota, an Analysis of Its Value" (unpublished Master's thesis, University of North Dakota, 1957), pp. 34–38; Hagen, *passim.*

V. HOLD FAST—UNTIL THE BEAST IS FINISHED

1. Arthur M. Schlesinger, Jr., *The Age of Roosevelt: The Crisis of the Old Order* (Boston: Houghton Mifflin, 1957), p. 20. Schlesinger describes even La Follette as being guilty of "ruthless simplicities"; Arthur S. Link, "The Federal Reserve Policy and the Agricultural Depression of 1920–21," *Agricultural History*, XX (July, 1946), p. 166 (quotation).

2. William Lemke to L. C. Miller, January 3, 1924; to Ralph Ingerson, December 15, 1922; to O. E. Lofthus, May 28, 1923; to Belle Roberts, September 1, 1923; all William Lemke Papers, Orin G. Libby Historical Manuscripts Collection, University of North Dakota Library, Grand Forks, North Dakota, hereafter referred to as Lemke Papers.

3. *William County Farmers Press*, May 13, 1926.

4. William Lemke to C. J. Murphy, April 21, 1939, Lemke Papers.

5. Interview with E. E. Kennedy, August 31, 1956.

6. William Lemke to John Hinkle, March 6, 1927, Lemke Papers.

7. William Lemke to E. F. Ladd, May 14, 1922, Lemke Papers.

8. William Lemke to county chairmen, March 14, 1922, Lemke Papers; Robert M. Morlan, *Political Prairie Fire* (Minneapolis: University of Minnesota, 1955), p. 340.

9. William Lemke to M. J. Murray, April 25, 1922, Lemke Papers.

10. William Lemke to F. Genetzkey, May 2, 1922; to F. W. Cathro, February 24, 1922; both Lemke Papers.

11. A. C. Townley to Gutzon Borglum, March 26, 1922, Gutzon Borglum Papers, Manuscripts Division, Library of Congress, Washington, D.C., hereafter referred to as Borglum Papers; Gutzon Borglum to Joseph Coghlan, March 21, 1922 (telegram); Gutzon Borglum to William Lemke, March 27, 1922 (telegram); S. T. (probably Stephen Ter Horst) to Gutzon Borglum, May 25, 1922; all Lemke Papers; Gutzon Borglum to Mrs. Henry Goddard Leach, May 22, 1922, Borglum Papers.

12. E. C. Blackorby, "Political Factional Strife in North Dakota from 1920 to 1932" (unpublished Master's thesis, University of North Dakota, 1938), p. 63.

13. Blackorby, p. 67; Morlan, pp. 340, 342; W. A. Anderson to William Lemke, May 9, 1922; Arthur Le Sueur to J. J. Hastings, March 2, 1922; J. J. Hastings to Dick Brown, May 25, 1922; all Lemke Papers; Gutzon Borglum to William Lemke, April 7, 1922, Borglum Papers.

14. Gutzon Borglum to Senator Joseph S. Freylingson, July 17, 1922, Borglum Papers; Alice J. Johnson, "The Public Career of J. F. T. O'Connor" (unpublished Master's thesis, University of North Dakota), pp. 78–82.

15. Minutes of July 15, 1922, meeting, Lemke Papers.

16. Alice J. Johnson, pp. 91–92; *Lemke v. Farmers Grain Company*, 258 U.S. 50; Blackorby, p. 71; Albert Selke, "A History of the Initiative in North Dakota" (unpublished Master's thesis, University of North Dakota, 1940), p. 41.

17. *Fargo Forum*, October 27, 1922.

18. Warren G. Stone to William Lemke, September 26, 1922, Lemke Papers.

19. *Billings County Pioneer*, November 2, 1922; *Fargo Forum*, September 9, 1922.

20. Minutes of the League convention, Lemke Papers.

21. Interview with A. C. Townley, July 1, 1957.

22. Blackorby, p. 77.

23. William Lemke to Harry A. Weaver, May 29, 1923; to George L. Lewis, May 29, 1923 (quotations); to Benjamin Marsh, October 25, 1923; Covington Hall to William Lemke, October 25, 1923; all Lemke Papers.

24. Calvin Coolidge to E. F. Ladd, November 2, 1923, Lemke Papers.

25. William Lemke to Carl Thompson, November 28, 1923, Lemke Papers.

26. John Pfeiffer to William Lemke, July 2, 1925, Lemke Papers.

27. Attorney General George Shafer to Secretary of State Thomas Hall, February 20, 1924, copy in Lemke Papers; William Lemke to R. C. Bryant, February 22, 1924, Lemke Papers.

28. William Lemke to Covington Hall, May 17, 1924; R. H. Walker to William Lemke, May 20, 1924; William Lemke to John Bloom, July 21, 1924; all Lemke Papers.

29. William Lemke to Thomas Hall, September 29, 1924; to Covington Hall, September 28, 1924; both Lemke Papers.

30. William Lemke to E. F. Ladd, September 28, 1924, Lemke Papers.

31. Ralph Ingerson to William Lemke, January 17, 1925, Lemke Papers.

32. Walter Maddock to William Lemke, January 13, 1925, Lemke Papers.

33. Gerald P. Nye to William Lemke, February 18, 1925, Lemke Papers (quotation); biographical information from interview with Gerald P. Nye, September 2, 1956.

34. Lynn J. Frazier to William Lemke, June 12, 1925, Lemke Papers.

35. William Lemke to Newton Jenkins, July 27, 1925; to Walter Maddock, July 28, 1925; both Lemke Papers.

36. *NonPartisan*, October 28, 1925; *Griggs County Sentinel Courier*, November 12, 1925, p. 2; Gerald P. Nye to R. H. Walker, November 6, 1925.

37. William Lemke to D. H. McArthur, June 28, 1925, Lemke Papers.

38. The facts in this entire account, unless otherwise noted, are from an interview with Gerald P. Nye on September 2, 1956. However, they do not conflict in any way with those given by Sorlie's secretary, Alfred S. Dale, to the author in June, 1938. Dale was present at the hotel meeting; interview with W. O. Skeels, August 30, 1956. Skeels believes the report about the ballots to be correct.

39. Interview with W. O. Skeels, August 30, 1956; Blackorby, p. 89; William Lemke to Newton Jenkins, July 27, 1925, Lemke Papers.

40. William Lemke to Carl E. Lunn, December 1, 1926; to Del Todd, December 29, 1926; to Covington Hall, April 28, 1927; all Lemke Papers.

41. Blackorby, pp. 93–96.

42. *Loc. cit.;* William Lemke to Lynn J. Frazier, November 16, 1927, Lemke Papers.

43. P. L. Aarhus to William Langer, December 15, 1929 (telegram) and December 16, 1930 (telegram); both Lemke Papers; interviews with Ole Gunvaldsen, October 20, 1952; with Herbert Swett, May 23, 1956.

44. William Lemke to Bjorn Johanson, August 11, 1927; to D. H. Hamilton, August 19, 1927; to Lynn J. Frazier, November 16, 1927; Herbert Swett to William Lemke, January 11, 1928; William Lemke to Lynn J. Frazier, April 18, 1928; all Lemke Papers.

45. William Lemke to Bjorn Bjornson, February 5, 1929, Lemke Papers.

46. Theodore Saloutos and John D. Hicks, *Agricultural Discontent in the Middle West, 1900–1939* (Madison: University of Wisconsin, 1951), p. 403. Smith's less than clear and enthusiastic endorsement is mentioned here; C. J. Olson to William Lemke, June 6, 1928. Olson criticized Lemke for his part in the primary election. This is a fair criticism and the analysis of Saloutos and Hicks makes clear that Lemke could be criticized legitimately for his inaccurate representation of Smith's farm policy.

47. Interview with S. A. Olsness, June 7, 1938.

48. William Lemke to Charles Verret, October 5, 1929; to O. S. Gunderson, October 14, 1929; to Lynn J. Frazier, September 28, 1929; to Nelson A. Mason, October 5, 1929; an undated, unaddressed memo; William Lemke to J. H. Greene, November 29, 1929; to Axel Strom, December 6, 1929; P. L. Aarhus to William Langer, December 15, 1929; all Lemke Papers.

49. William Lemke to Herbert Swett, January 29, 1930; to Walter Maddock, January 29, 1930; to L. C. Miller, January 30, 1930; all Lemke Papers.

50. Charles E. Taylor to William Lemke, February 20, 1930, Lemke Papers.

51. William Lemke to E. H. Brant, June 27, 1930; to C. Hall, April 28, 1927, both Lemke Papers; United States Congress, Senate, Committee on Banking and Currency, *Hearings, Senate Bill 1197,* 72nd Cong. 2nd Sess., 1932–33, pp. 11, 41–62; Gilbert C. Fite, "John A. Simpson: The Southwest's Militant Farm Leader" *Mississippi Valley Historical Review,* XXXV (March, 1949), pp. 563–584; interview with E. E. Kennedy, August 31, 1956; John B. Simpson to William Lemke, March 20, 1934, Lemke Papers. This is a letter written to Lemke by one of the Simpson family expressing appreciation to Lemke whom they had asked to talk at Simpson's funeral. One significant comment in the letter was " . . . I can only say that I feel you reflect Dad's ideas more than any other man in the United States."; Arthur A. Schlesinger, Jr., *The Age of Roosevelt: The Crisis of the Old Order* (Boston: Houghton Mifflin, 1957), p. 265. Schlesinger says of Simpson, "Taciturn and unyielding, he had the old Populist hatred for international bankers . . . and a conviction that inflation through the remonetization of silver was the best means of assuring the farmer the cost of production plus a reasonable profit. . . ."; Mrs. John A. Simpson to William Lemke, March 28, 1938, Lemke Papers. " . . . he [Mr. Simpson] loved you, he admired you because you were and are fearless and courageous, dared to stand alone if necessary in fighting for the common people."

52. William Lemke to Covington Hall, July 6, 1929; Covington Hall to William Lemke, August 4, 1929; both Lemke Papers.

53. Herbert Swett to William Lemke, January 5, 1932, Lemke Papers.

54. Blackorby, p. 110; R. R. Smith to William Lemke, March 5, 1932, Lemke Papers.


## VI. A TRUE FRIEND AND A BITTER ENEMY

1. Undated copies of Lemke Addresses, William Lemke Papers, Orin G. Libby Historical Manuscripts Collection, University of North Dakota Library, Grand Forks, North Dakota, hereafter referred to as Lemke Papers.

2. Interview with E. E. Kennedy, August 31, 1956.

3. Much of the information in the preceding paragraphs is taken from Theodore Saloutos and John D. Hicks, *Agricultural Discontent in the Middle West, 1900–1939* (Madison: University of Wisconsin, 1951), pp. 374, 391, 532.

4. Interview with E. E. Kennedy, August 31, 1956.

5. Gilbert C. Fite, *George N. Peek and the Fight for Farm Parity* (Norman: University of Oklahoma, 1954), p. 38; Baldur M. Kristjanson and C. J. Helteness, *Handbook of Facts about North Dakota Agriculture*, Agricultural Experiment Station Bulletin 357 (Fargo: Agricultural College, June, 1949), p. 67; Arthur M. Schlesinger, Jr., *The Age of Roosevelt: The Crisis of the Old Order* (Boston: Houghton Mifflin, 1957), p. 248.

6. Saloutos and Hicks, p. 446; Adam J. Schweitzer, "John Moses and the New Deal in North Dakota" (unpublished Master's thesis, University of North Dakota, 1954), pp. 29–31.

7. William Lemke to Lynn J. Frazier, January 27, 1931, Lemke Papers; see *Farmers Exchange* (New Paris, Indiana), September 9, 1932, for a very complimentary story on Lemke's speech given in that community and for an indication of the wide area in which the Farmers Union used him during this period; for relation between Simpson and Lemke, see footnote 51, Chapter V.

8. United States Congress, Senate, Committee on Banking and Currency, *Hearings, Senate Bill 1197*, 72nd Cong. 2nd Sess., 1932–1933. Mills sent to the committee copies of letters he had written to E. E. Greene on March 8 and 15, 1932; *ibid.*, copies of letters to Senator Charles McNary from Governor of Federal Reserve Board, March 5, 1932, and from Secretary of Agriculture, Arthur Hyde, March 8, 1932; *ibid.*, copy of letter from Senator Peter Norbeck to G. M. Babcock, December 2, 1932.

9. Information in the preceding paragraph taken from copies of Lemke speeches; William Lemke to C. Hall, December 13, 1930; to Burton K. Wheeler, May 14, 1930; Burton K. Wheeler to William Lemke, June 20, 1931 (quotation); Walter Maddock to Franklin D. Roosevelt, October 18, 1932; Herbert Swett to William Lemke, January 5, 1932; all documents and letters in Lemke Papers.

10. H. G. Teigan to William Lemke, April 13, 1931 (quotation); interview with Mrs. William Lemke, June 30, 1957. Mrs. Lemke did not remember the exact date of the visit except that it was in the winter of 1931–32 and before the primary election on March 15, 1932. The entire account of the interview is from Mrs. Lemke's recollection of her husband's conversation about it; the account of how arrangements were made for the Lemke conference with Roosevelt is from the interview with Fred McLean, September 4, 1957.

11. Interview with Herbert Swett, August 13, 1956; Gertrude Almy Schlichter, "Roosevelt and the Farm Program, 1929–1932," *Mississippi Valley Historical Review*, XLIII (September, 1956), p. 241 (quotation); interview with Ole Gunvaldsen, October 20, 1952. Mr. Gunvaldsen stated and later reaffirmed in correspondence that "Lemke was the big wheel in putting the Middle West in Roosevelt's column."

12. Interview with Mrs. William Lemke, June 30, 1956; Frank Freidel, *Franklin D. Roosevelt*, Vol. III: *The Triumph* (Boston: Little, Brown, 1956), p. 285; interviews with Herbert Swett, August 13, 1956 and with Ole Gunvaldsen, October 20, 1952; Gilbert C. Fite, "John A. Simpson: The Southwest's Militant Farm

Leader," *Mississippi Valley Historical Review*, XXXV (March, 1949), pp. 563-584; William Lemke to Franklin Roosevelt, February 27, 1932 (telegram), Lemke Papers.

13. Freidel, pp. 285, 241-242; North Dakota, Secretary of State, *Compilation of State and National Election Returns, 1930-1944;* James M. Burns, *Roosevelt: The Lion and the Fox* (New York: Harcourt Brace, 1956), p. 130; interviews with Ole Gunvaldsen, October 20, 1952; with Fred McLean, September 4, 1957; John Nystul, June, 1951; Herbert Swett, August 13, 1956; E. E. Kennedy, August 31, 1956; Mrs. William Lemke, June 3, 1951.

14. E. C. Blackorby, "Political Factional Strife in North Dakota from 1920 to 1932" (unpublished Master's thesis, University of North Dakota, 1938), p. 111; John M. Holzworth, *The Fighting Governor* (Chicago: The Pointer Press, 1938), pp. 17, 27; copies of Lemke speeches, undated, Lemke Papers.

15. Interview with Earl Duell, May 29, 1954.

16. William Lemke to William Langer, December 31, 1932, Lemke Papers; interview with Herbert Swett, August 8, 1957.

17. William Lemke to Covington Hall, September 13, 1932, Lemke Papers; *Dickinson Press,* October 27, 1932; *Chicago Tribune,* September 19, 1932; North Dakota Secretary of State, *Compilation of State and National Election Returns, 1930-1944.*

18. Freidel, pp. 272-274; A. E. Bonzer to William Lemke, November 28, 1932, Lemke Papers.

19. H. B. French to William Lemke, November 13, 1932, Lemke Papers.

20. Interview with Mr. and Mrs. Herbert Swett, August 8, 1957.

21. William Lemke to Lars Siljan, March 29, 1933, Lemke Papers; interview with Franklin Page, November, 1956. Page served in the North Dakota Legislative Assembly, first in the lower house and later in the Senate where he succeeded Thomas Whelan, through most of this period.

22. Saloutos and Hicks, p. 446.

23. *San Francisco Call Bulletin,* August 9, 1948.

24. Interview with E. E. Kennedy, August 31, 1956.

25. Walter Maddock to Chester Davis, November 24, 1933, Department of Agriculture Papers, National Archives, Washington, D.C., hereafter referred to as Department of Agriculture Papers. Davis was George Peek's first lieutenant in the original Agricultural Adjustment Administration.

26. Chester Davis to Henry A. Wallace, November 29, 1933; Henry A. Wallace to William Lemke, December 4, 1933; both Department of Agriculture Papers.

27. United States, *Congressional Record,* 73rd. Cong. 1st. Sess. (March 9 to April 3, 1933), LXXVII, part 1, p. 203, hereafter referred to as *Congressional Record.*

28. William Lemke to Ben Lemke, March 27, 1933, Lemke Papers.

29. George Webb to Bernard Baruch, April 10, 1933, Lemke Papers (quotation); interview with W. O. Skeels, August 30, 1956.

30. E. E. Kennedy to William Lemke, July 29, 1933. In this letter Kennedy blamed the late July disastrous decline in farm prices to a statement released to the press by the Department of Agriculture which gave surprisingly low estimates of cost of production of farm products, estimates on which support policies would be based. Kennedy, secretary of the National Farmers Union, stated that the

Farmers Union was making a protest to Wallace; William Lemke to Ed Stangler, August 12, 1933. Lemke stated that he was going to Washington to see what could be done about Federal Land Bank policies; Mary Pinche to W. O. Skeels, November 6, 1933, Lemke Papers.

31. William Lemke to John Crawford, May 12, 1933 (quotation); to C. Hall, February 8, 1934 (quotation); both Lemke Papers.

32. Interviews with W. O. Skeels, August 30, 1956; with William Lemke, Jr., August 20, 1956; William Lemke to Lillian Shotten (his sister), April 14, 1934; to Gutzon Borglum, April 7, 1934; both Lemke Papers; *Bismarck Tribune,* June 12, 1934; William Lemke to Seth Richardson, April 30, 1934; to Ben Lemke, May 30, 1934; both Lemke Papers.

33. *Bismarck Tribune,* June 12, 1934; interview with W. O. Skeels, August 30, 1956; Representative Frank Oliver of New York to William Lemke, July 1, 1934, Lemke Papers.

34. Interview with E. E. Kennedy, August 31, 1956; C. C. Daniels to William Lemke, June 19, 1934 (quotation), Lemke Papers.

35. Ray Goldberg, *The Nonpartisan League in North Dakota* (Fargo: Midwest Printing and Lithographing, 1948), pp. 33–34; minutes of the Rumper convention made available to the author and now in his files through the courtesy of John Nystul, chairman of the League Executive Committee from 1932 to 1934; interview with John Nystul, June 4, 1951.

36. William Lemke to Lynn J. Frazier, October 11, 1933, Lemke Papers; interview with Ole Gunvaldsen, October 20, 1952.

37. Interview with Ole Gunvaldsen, October 20, 1952.

38. Schweitzer, p. 38; interview with Ole Gunvaldsen, October 20, 1952; William Lemke to Ben Febe, December 7, 1934, Lemke Papers.

39. Schweitzer, p. 39.

40. Ben Lemke to William Lemke, June 18, 1934, Lemke Papers; interview with Arnold Offerdahl, June 10, 1955. Offerdahl was Lemke's driver for a few days just before the primary.

41. North Dakota Secretary of State, *Compilation of State and National Elections Returns, (1930–1944);* Usher L. Burdick to William Lemke, March 27, 1934, Lemke Papers.

42. Schweitzer, p. 40.

43. Interview with Ole Gunvaldsen, October 20, 1952.

44. C. C. Talbott to William Lemke, December 7, 1934, Lemke Papers.

45. P. O. Sathre to William Lemke, September 4, 1934, Lemke Papers; interview with Jack Riedel, July 17, 1956. Riedel was Lemke's driver through much of the fall campaign; *Congressional Record,* 74th Cong. 2nd. Sess., 1936, LXXX, Part 7, p. 7234; North Dakota Secretary of State, *Compilation of State and National Election Returns 1930–1944.*

46. Interview with E. E. Kennedy, August 31, 1956; *Louisville Joint Stock Land Bank* v. *Radford;* William Lemke to O. S. Gunderson, June 30, 1940; to F. L. Conklin, December 18, 1939; both Lemke Papers; William Lemke, Jr., to author, September 4, 1956.

47. Interviews with E. E. Kennedy, August 31, 1956; W. O. Skeels, August 30, 1956.

48. *Loc. cit.;* Virgil U. Evans to Stephen Early, February 12, 1934; memo

attached to February 12, 1934, letter of Virgil Evans; Henry A. Wallace to Stephen Early, February 21, 1934; all Department of Agriculture Papers.

49. As commonly told at the time (quotation); *Congressional Record,* 74th Cong. 2nd Sess., 1936, LXXX, Part 6, pp. 6922–6933; Part 7, p. 7025 (quotation).

50. *Ibid.,* Part 7, p. 7190.

51. *New York Times,* February 5, 1936 (quotation); May 15, 1936 (quotation).

52. *Congressional Record,* 74th Cong. 2nd Sess., 1936, LXXX, Part 7, pp. 7098, 7167 (quotation).

53. *Ibid.,* p. 7167.

54. *Ibid.,* p. 7163.

55. *Ibid.,* pp. 7097–7140; 7159–7240.

56. *Ibid.,* p. 7230 (quotation); William Lemke to H. A. Bone, May 21, 1936, Lemke Papers.

57. *New York Times,* May 15, 1936.


## VII. IN UNION THERE WAS WEAKNESS

1. See Dixon Wector, *The Age of the Great Depression* (New York: The Macmillan Company, 1948), pp. 206–207 for a description of Smith as a "minor anti-semite and frank admirer of Hitler's Reich."

2. *Loc. cit.*

3. Basil Rauch, *The History of the New Deal, 1933–38* (New York: Creative Age Press, 1944), p. 241.

4. Interview with a person close to Lemke during the campaign of 1936; Nye denied to the author that he had ever been approached as to this candidacy.

5. William Lemke to Covington Hall, July 30, 1935, William Lemke Papers, Orin G. Libby Historical Manuscripts Collection, University of North Dakota Library, Grand Forks, North Dakota, hereafter referred to as Lemke Papers.

6. Grant Heimark to William Lemke, September 25, 1935, Lemke Papers.

7. Interview with Herbert Swett, September 10, 1955; Charles E. Coughlin to William Lemke, June 8, 1936, Lemke Papers; Rauch, p. 243.

8. Interviews with two persons very close to Lemke during the Union party campaign; interview with W. O. Skeels, August 30, 1956. Skeels emphasized how difficult it was for Lemke to finance his campaigns, and that it usually took him nearly a full term to recuperate financially after a campaign.

9. Interview with John Nystul, June 4, 1951. Nystul was national chairman of the Union party and managed Lemke's 1936 campaign. Through his courtesy the author has had the use of a term paper entitled "The Union Party of 1936" written by John Nystul, Jr., when a student at the University of Minnesota. Much of the background and data on the Union party comes from the cooperation of Mr. Nystul and his son; William Lemke to Thomas Charles O'Brien, June 16, 1936, Lemke Papers (quotation); Paul W. Ward, "William Lemke—Crackpot for President," *The Nation,* CXLIII, No. 2 (July 11, 1936).

10. *New York Times,* June 18, 1936; copy of statement in Lemke Papers (quotation).

11. Ellis O. Jones, *Lemke's the Man for President* (Los Angeles: privately printed, 1936), pp. 23–24. These pages contain the Union party platform.

12. Philip La Follette to P. D. Maier, July 6, 1936, Philip La Follette Papers,

Wisconsin State Historical Society, Madison, Wisconsin, hereafter referred to as Philip La Follette Papers; Arthur Naftalin, "A History of the Farmer Labor Party of Minnesota (unpublished Ph.D. dissertation, University of Minnesota, 1948), p. 320. Floyd Olson of Minnesota died in August, 1936, and was replaced by Elmer Benson; Fred A. Shannon, *American Farmers' Movements* (New York: Van Nostrand, 1957), p. 83.

13. *Fargo Forum,* November 18, 1956; Harold L. Ickes, *The Secret Diary of Harold L. Ickes,* Vol. I: *The First Thousand Days 1933–1936* (New York: Simon and Schuster, 1953), p. 645; Howard Carpenter to Charles Dow, July 4, 1936, Philip La Follette Papers; Wallace Stegner, "Pattern for Demagogues," *Pacific Spectator* (Stanford, California), II (Autumn, 1948), p. 407; *New York Times,* October 18, 1936.

14. Interview with W. O. Skeels, August 30, 1956; undated speech delivered when running for President, Lemke Papers (quotation); interview with John Nystul, June 4, 1951; William Lemke to C. Hall, May 2, 1939, Lemke Papers.

15. Poster for a meeting, Lemke Papers; interview with John Nystul, June 4, 1951; E. E. Kennedy to William Lemke, March 15 and April 21, 1937, Lemke Papers.

16. E. M. Sait, *American Parties and Elections* (New York: D. Appleton and Century, 1942), p. 274; *Bismarck Tribune,* October 9, 1936 (quotation).

17. Interview with Herbert Swett, September 10, 1955; *New York Times* October 28, 1936 (quotation).

18. *Minot Daily News,* report of Lemke speech in Minneapolis, October 31, 1936 (quotations).

19. *Minot Daily News,* October 20, 1936; copy of speech made over statewide radio hook-up in North Dakota during campaign of 1936, Lemke Papers (quotation).

20. Samuel Lubell, *The Future of American Politics* (New York: Harper and Brothers, 1951), chapter 7 (quotation), the election totals on states other than North Dakota are as given by Lubell and *Information Please Almanac, 1948* (Garden City: Doubleday and Co., 1947) p. 134, see North Dakota Secretary of State, *Compilation of State and National Election Returns 1930–1944* for county election totals in North Dakota; see Louis H. Bean, *How to Predict Elections* (New York: Knopf, 1948), pp. 96–97 for description of areas where ethnic and religious factors might have been expected to favorably affect Lemke's Union party candidacy in North Dakota; Paul Douglas, "A New Isolationism—Ripple or Tide?" *New York Times Magazine,* August 18, 1957, p. 10.

21. John Nystul to charter members, December 8, 1936; William Lemke to E. B. McCutcheon, July 21, 1938; Mrs. Myrtle Ellsworth to William Lemke, October 22, 1937; to Judson King, February 24, 1940 (quotation); to Kitty Thomas, December 23, 1938 (quotation); to Stephen S. Wise, December 20, 1939; to David Meckler, undated; to Mrs. I. Marklund, May 1, 1939 (quotation); all Lemke Papers.

22. Charles E. Coughlin to William Lemke, March 7, 1941; William Lemke to J. Hefferman, October 4, 1938 (quotation); both Lemke Papers; Lubell, pp. 142–144; John Nystul to William Lemke, November 3, 1938; William Lemke to John Nystul, March 8, 1939; both Lemke Papers.

23. *Fargo Forum,* February 13, 1937.

24. L. B. Hanna to William Lemke, April 6, 1938, Lemke Papers; William Lemke, *You and Your Money* (Philadelphia: Dorrance, 1938); W. H. Harvey, *The Book* (Monte Ne, Arkansas: Mundus, 1930); Charles A. Lindbergh, *Banking, Currency, and the Money Trust* (Washington, D.C.: National Capitol Press, 1913).

25. Speech given January 9, 1936, over a nation-wide radio network, Lemke Papers.

26. United States, *Congressional Record,* 75th Cong. 1st Sess., LXXXI, Part 9 (March 9, 1937), appendix, pp. 483–484 (quotations), hereafter referred to as *Congressional Record.*

27. Robert Page Wright, *v.* Vinton Branch of the Mountain Trust Bank of Roanoke, Va. *et al.,* March 29, 1937; interview by author in August, 1956, name withheld by request.

28. *Congressional Record,* 77th Cong. 1st Sess., LXXXXVII, Part 1, pp. 1108–1121 (February 18, 1941); Part 2, pp. 1363–1370 (February 26, 1941); pp. 1722–1733 (March 4, 1941). These are the long speeches made by Nye in attacks on the Lend-Lease bill; *American Historical Review,* LXII, No. 3 (April, 1957), p. 765. This summarizes the thesis of a paper read by Robert P. Wilkins at the St. Louis meeting of the American Historical Association in December, 1956. The full text is contained in "Middle Western Isolationism: A Re-examination" *North Dakota Quarterly,* Vol. XXV, No. 3 (Summer, 1957), pp. 69–76 (quotation); newspaper release to press by William Lemke, July 26, 1939, Lemke Papers (quotation).

29. William Lemke to C. S. Farnsworth, January 26, 1934 (quotation); newsletter release to press by William Lemke, May 17, 1939 (quotation); both Lemke Papers; Eric Goldman, *Rendezvous with Destiny* (New York: Knopf, 1953), pp. 337–383.

30. Lemke, *You and Your Money,* pp. 8, 22–29, 85–98; phrase used by Roosevelt in his inaugural address (quotation).

31. Interview with W. O. Skeels, August 30, 1956.

32. United States Congress, Senate, Committee on Privileges and Elections, *Report on the Protest by Various Citizens of the State of North Dakota to the Seating of William Langer, as a Senator from the State of North Dakota* (77th Cong. 2nd Sess., 1942), pp. 68–75.

33. William Lemke to Fred Lemke, April 14, 1938; to T. O'Brien, July 2, 1938; to Ole Gunvaldsen, May 31, 1938 (quotation); W. O. Skeels to Gerald P. Nye, June 4, 1938; Gerald P. Nye to William Lemke, June 4, 1938; all Lemke Papers; North Dakota Secretary of State, *Compilation of State and National Election Returns (1930–1944).*

34. Interview with a prominent official of the Democratic party in North Dakota, July, 1938.

35. Adam J. Schweitzer, "John Moses and the New Deal in North Dakota" (unpublished Master's thesis, University of North Dakota, 1954), pp. 82–84; North Dakota Secretary of State, *Compilation of State and National Election Returns (1930–1944).*

36. Henry Lemke to William Lemke, February 9, 1940; William Lemke to Ben Lemke, February 24, 1940; both Lemke Papers.

37. Interview with Charles E. Joyce and with A. C. Townley, both July 1, 1957.

38. William Lemke to Charles E. Joyce, March 13, 1940, copy in possession of Charles E. Joyce, photostatic copy in possession of author.

39. Information in this section is taken from interviews with A. C. Townley and Charles E. Joyce, both July 1, 1957; interview with Herbert Swett, August 13, 1957; and Bismarck Tribune, March 20, 1940.

40. Ole Gunvaldsen to author, April 9, 1957; interviews with Ole Gunvaldsen, October 20, 1952; Franklin Page, February, 1952; A. C. Townley and Charles E. Joyce, July 1, 1957.

41. John Moses to William Lemke, April 22, 1940; William Lemke to I. J. Moe, July 12, 1940 (quotation); both Lemke Papers; William Lemke to C. E. Joyce, April 16, 1940, copy of letter in possession of C. E. Joyce and photostatic copy in possession of author; *The Leader*, April 25, 1940.

42. William Lemke to J. Hoeppel, July 9, 1940, Lemke Papers; North Dakota Secretary of State, *Compilation of State and National Election Returns (1930-1944)*.

43. Interview with Ole Gunvaldsen, October 20, 1952.

44. B. J. Holloway, September 9, 1940; Lloyd Stevens, undated; J. E. Pfeifer, August 12, 1940; Joe LePire, July 12, 1940; all to William Lemke; William Lemke to E. L. Marlow, July 16, 1940 (quotation), Lemke Papers; *Bismarck Tribune*, July 24, 1940; G. A. Haney to William Lemke, July 30, 1940, Lemke Papers.

45. William Lemke to W. H. Edgar, July 16, 1940 (quotation); to Ole Gunvaldsen, July 18, 1940; George A. Dondero to L. P. McAneney, October 29, 1940, all Lemke Papers. The last-mentioned letter is indication that $1000 came to the Lemke campaign from Mr. and Mrs. Thomas Coughlin of Royal Oak, Michigan.

46. William Lemke to O. B. Burtness, November 12, 1940, Lemke Papers.

47. Schweitzer, p. 127; Ole Gunvaldsen to William Lemke, October 7, 1940, Lemke Papers (quotation).

48. O. B. Burtness to William Lemke, September 27, 1940; Al Sundfor to William Lemke, October 5, 1940; both Lemke Papers.

49. William Lemke to Charles E. Coughlin, February 13, 1941, Lemke Papers; interview with W. O. Skeels, August 30, 1956; North Dakota Secretary of State, *Compilation of State and National Election Returns (1930-1944)*.

50. *Labor* (North Dakota Edition), October 29, 1940. This was a special issue of the newspaper published by the railway labor unions.

51. Usher L. Burdick to William Lemke, December 26, 1940; Josephine Efteland to William Lemke, November 8, 1940; copy of speech; William Lemke to J. B. Bridston, October 28, 1940; all Lemke Papers.

52. Schweitzer, p. 127.

## VIII. A PURPOSEFUL LIFE

1. W. F. Seneschal to William Lemke, November 10, 1937, William Lemke Papers, Orin G. Libby Historical Manuscripts Collection, University of North Dakota, hereafter referred to as Lemke Papers; interviews with Herbert Swett, August 13, 1957; Ole Gunvaldsen, October 20, 1952; Theodore Saloutos and John D. Hicks, *Agricultural Discontent in the Middle West, 1900-1939* (Madison: University of Wisconsin, 1951) p. 532.

2. W. H. Smart to William Lemke, January 13, 1941; William Lemke to W. R. Kellogg, March 11, 1941; to Joseph Allegaier, Jr., March 11, 1941; Robert

E. Wood to William Lemke, September 29, 1941 and others; Tom Carroll to William Lemke, October 29, 1941; all Lemke Papers.

3. William Lemke to Robert Wood, January 14, 1942, Lemke Papers.

4. Joe LePire to William Lemke, December 15, 1941; William Lemke to Alfred Fleischner, November 17, 1938; to Joseph Hefferman, September 7, 1939; to A. F. Colwell, September 21, 1939; to Joe LePire, September 21, 1939; to G. E. Hermanstad, March 11, 1941 (quotation); to B. T. Holloway, September 15, 1940 (quotation); to Albert R. Korn, March 26, 1939 (quotation); all Lemke Papers.

5. United States Congress, Senate, Committee on Privileges and Elections, *Report on the Protest by Various Citizens of the State of North Dakota to the Seating of William Langer, as a Senator from the State of North Dakota* (77th Cong. 2nd Sess., 1942), pp. 25–76, hereafter referred to as *Langer Senate Report;* D. D. Riley to William Lemke, January 24, 1941, Lemke Papers.

6. William Lemke to E. H. Burke, April 22, 1941 (quotation); W. O. Skeels to William Lemke, August 15, 1941; both Lemke Papers.

7. *Langer Senate Report,* pp. 63–68; William Lemke to H. C. Lowry, November 1, 1941; to William Langer, December 25, 1922; to Carl A. Hatch, November 30, 1941; S. J. Atkins to William Lemke, January 9, 1950; *Langer* v. *Gray,* 73 ND 437, 15 NW 2nd 732; *Langer* v. *Gray,* 74 ND 709, 24 NW 2nd 399. In these two cases, concerning 1938 income, the taxes were levied by the state tax commissioner and held to be legal and valid; in a third case, *Langer* v. *Gray,* 75 ND 1, 25 NW 89, concerning 1937 income, the taxes levied by the commissioner were held to be non-collectable.

8. *Langer Senate Report,* p. 76; J. B. Bridston to C. R. Verry, December 24, 1941; William Lemke to Robert Dunn, September 3, 1942; both Lemke Papers; *Washington Post,* November 7, 1941; *Time,* April 6, 1942, p. 14.

9. Interviews with Robert Lemke, September 3, 1956; with Gerald P. Nye, September 2, 1956.

10. United States Congress, Senate, Committee on Privileges and Elections, *Hearings, Relative to a Protest to the Seating of William Langer, A Senator from the State of North Dakota* (77th Cong. 1st Sess., November 3 to 18, 1941), *passim;* William Lemke to C. E. Joyce, April 22, 1942, Lemke Papers.

11. *Fargo Forum,* November 8, 1942.

12. William Lemke to Gerald P. Nye, November 9, 1942 (quotation); L. L. Rudrud to William Lemke, November 6, 1942 (quotation); both Lemke Papers; North Dakota Secretary of State, *Compilation of State and National Election Returns 1930–1944.*

13. Roland Young, *Congressional Politics in the Second World War* (New York: Columbia University, 1954), p. 114.

14. Adam J. Schweitzer, "John Moses and the New Deal in North Dakota" unpublished Master's thesis, University of North Dakota, 1954), p. 141; North Dakota Secretary of State, *Compilation of State and National Election Returns 1930–1944.*

15. William Lemke to Ruth Smith, September 22, 1944; to Gerald P. Nye, November 9, 1944; to Bertha Johnson, November 9, 1944 (quotation); all Lemke Papers.

16. Milton R. Young to William Lemke, November 3, 1944, Lemke Papers.

17. Nels Johnson to William Lemke, November 4, 1944, Lemke Papers.

18. Interview with W. B. Allen, February 13, 1957. Fitch was a state legislator from Fargo who strongly disapproved of Lemke.

19. William Lemke to Harry Polk, March 15, 1946 (telegram), Lemke Papers.

20. L. L. Rudrud to William Lemke, August 5, 1946, Lemke Papers.

21. Interview with Russell Reid, September, 1956; William Lemke to John Moses, January 17, 1945, Lemke Papers.

22. Hearings on HR 1441 and HR 4435, held respectively on November 2, 1945, and January 30, 1946; William Lemke to Edward A. Rumely, March 11, 1946; William Lemke to Ann Brown, August 1, 1946; both Lemke Papers; United States, *Congressional Record,* 79th Cong. 2nd Sess., 1946, XCII, Part 8, pp. 10, 791–792.

23. "Truman Signs Bill for Roosevelt Park in N.D. Badlands," *North Dakotan,* May, 1947.

24. Ben Reifel, Superintendent of Fort Berthold Reservation, to William Lemke, June 6, 1949, Lemke Papers.

25. Interview with Mrs. William Lemke, June 3, 1951.

26. Interview with Robert Lemke, September 3, 1956.

27. William Lemke to Hugh Scott, Republican campaign manager, September 17, 1948, Lemke Papers.

28. Milton Rue to Herbert Brownell, November 15, 1948, Lemke Papers.

29. Interview with W. O. Skeels, August 30, 1956.

30. William Lemke to ROC headquarters, May 6, 1948, Lemke Papers.

31. William Lemke to Mrs. Cyrus Clark, December 28, 1949, Lemke Papers; interview with Mrs. William Lemke, June 3, 1951; Theodore Roosevelt McKeldin, "Hats on for General Washington," *American Heritage,* VII, No. 5 (August, 1956), pp. 96–97.

32. Interview with Robert Lemke, September 3, 1956.

33. Interview with Ole Gunvaldsen, former United States Marshal for North Dakota, October 20, 1952. Mr. Gunvaldsen's position with the federal court, his continuing interest in the political life of the state, and his proprietorship interest in the *Normanden,* a newspaper for Americans of Scandinavian origin, have given him an opportunity to know the effect of the farm legislation sponsored by Lemke. The author asked him to state his views regarding this in writing and in a letter of February 9, 1963, he wrote, "Lemke was wholly responsible for the Frazier-Lemke Act. He spent a tremendous amount of time on this and its effect on the economy of the country was very great. When this act became operative it saved thousands of farmers. . . . It made all lending agencies more lenient and made them think twice before foreclosing."

34. From a copy of the resolution adopted by the Tribal Business Council of the Fort Berthold Reservation in possession of the author.

# Bibliography

BIBLIOGRAPHICAL ESSAY

The research for this paper has centered around North Dakota sources and particularly on the voluminous William Lemke papers in the Orin G. Libby Historical Manuscripts Collection at the University of North Dakota Library. The Lemke papers include some 35,000 to 40,000 letters, all of those letters received by Lemke and carbons of those he sent. The volume of this correspondence would seem to indicate that he seldom destroyed a letter and never discarded a file. In addition to his personal correspondence, the papers include the entire files of the Republican national headquarters for the North Dakota campaign of 1916 and most, if not all, of it for the years until 1920. In addition all of the correspondence of the North Dakota Nonpartisan League headquarters during the years Lemke was actively in charge of that organization is included.

A nearly complete collection of court briefs in the cases in which Lemke appeared, copies of his speeches and of his weekly newsletters to constituents, and all of the literature he collected on the topics that constituted his major enthusiasms round out the collection. These include such themes as money, banking, credit, agrarian reform, grain grading, foreign policy, Mexico, and University of North Dakota affairs. It is a rich collection that reaches back to the years in which he was first establishing himself as an attorney. This is by far the most extensive collection in existence on the Nonpartisan League. A number of M.A. theses on North Dakota political history in the same library have been of major assistance, as have the files of pamphlets and campaign literature on North Dakota political campaigns. The papers of A. M. Christianson and A. G. Divet and the microfilms of the John Moses papers, together with the complete newspaper files and the extensive collections of materials on North Dakota political campaigns at the State Historical Library and some material at the State Library Commission and the Secretary of State's office at Bismarck provided a valuable supplement to the materials at the University of North Dakota Library. In one library or another the author has extensively perused five of the daily newspapers printed in North Dakota and some of the weekly newspapers. The *Fargo Forum, Fargo Courier-News, Grand Forks Herald,*

*Bismarck Tribune,* and the *Dickinson Press* together with *The Searchlight, The Cooperators' Herald, The Independent, The North Dakota Leader, The Nonpartisan Leader,* and *The Leader* have all been relied upon extensively. These have been supplemented by many interviews and letters. Some of these have been with or from those who have been prominent in the state political picture and whose names will be familiar to many; others have been with or from persons who, although they never became figures of state-wide renown, nevertheless, have been close to events and have thus been able to illuminate areas that would otherwise be obscure. Often these interviews gave an understanding that could have been gained in no other way. Mrs. William Lemke was of invaluable assistance in explaining and in pointing out sources of information which otherwise would not have been available.

Source materials in other states supplemented to some extent the research done in North Dakota. The theses and dissertations completed at the University of Minnesota bulked the largest among the out-of-state sources, and the author found helpful material in the libraries of both the Minnesota and Wisconsin historical societies. The papers of Henry G. Teigan and those of the National Nonpartisan League in the former institution and those of Philip La Follette in the latter were of assistance. The extensive Gutzon Borglum papers in the Library of Congress and the papers pertaining to Lemke in the Legislative and Department of Agriculture sections of the Archives Building in Washington, D.C., were the most helpful of any of the out-of-state collections. A few references of some assistance were found in the papers of Woodrow Wilson, George Norris, William E. Borah, and Thomas Walsh in the Library of Congress. The interviews in and near Washington, D.C., particularly those with William O. Skeels, Edward E. Kennedy, John M. Baer, Gerald P. Nye, and Robert Lemke, and one with William Lemke, Jr., of Evanston, Illinois, were particularly helpful. The author's indebtedness to the many books on the agrarian movement and contemporary history is indicated by the citations.

There were interviews that the author found it impossible to make, and there are many things he wishes he could have done, but he feels very fortunate in the sources to which he has had access. The accompanying bibliography does not pretend to be exhaustive but refers only to those items or sources cited or those on whom the author depended heavily but did not cite in the text. This is particularly true of government records which were perused. Only those which were actually cited are listed in the bibliography.

## COLLECTIONS OF PAPERS

Lemke, William, Papers, Orin G. Libby Historical Manuscripts Collection, University of North Dakota Library, Grand Forks, North Dakota

Borah, William E., Papers, Manuscripts Division, Library of Congress, Washington, D.C.

Borglum, Gutzon, Papers, Manuscripts Division, Library of Congress, Washington, D.C.

Christianson, A. M., Papers, Library of the State Historical Society of North Dakota, Bismarck, North Dakota

Department of Agriculture Papers, National Archives, Washington, D.C.

Divet, A. G., Papers, Library of the State Historical Society of North Dakota, Bismarck, North Dakota

La Follette, Philip, Papers, Wisconsin State Historical Society, Madison, Wisconsin

Legislative Section, National Archives, Washington, D.C.

Moses, John, Papers (microfilm), Library of the State Historical Society of North Dakota, Bismarck, North Dakota

National Nonpartisan League Papers, Minnesota Historical Society, St. Paul, Minnesota

Norris, George, Papers, Manuscripts Division, Library of Congress, Washington, D.C.

Teigan, Henry G., Papers, Minnesota Historical Society, St. Paul, Minnesota

Walsh, Thomas, Papers, Manuscripts Division, Library of Congress, Washington, D.C.

Wilson, Woodrow, Papers, Manuscripts Division, Library of Congress, Washington, D.C.

## INTERVIEWS AND LETTERS TO AUTHOR

*Interviews with:*
W. B. Allen, February 13, 1957
John M. Baer, August 29, 1956
Einar Berge, numerous
C. E. Blackorby, Hansboro, North Dakota, numerous
Everett H. Brant, February, 1951
Luther A. Bratten, numerous
Chester Brooks, numerous
Usher L. Burdick, October 30, 1954
O. B. Burtness, July, 1937; June, 1938; January 2, 1953
Robert Byrne, July 1, 1954
A. M. Christianson, June, 1938
C. C. Converse, numerous
Peter Crogan, numerous
Alfred S. Dale, June, 1938
W. P. Davies, May and June, 1938
Earl Duell, May 29, 1954

Edward Erickson, numerous
Judge Gudmundur Grimson, numerous
Ole Gunvaldsen, October 20, 1952
John Halcrow, numerous
Thomas Hall, numerous
S. B. Hocking, numerous
Roy P. Johnson, June, 1955
M. Beatrice Johnstone, numerous
Charles E. Joyce, July 1, 1957
E. E. Kennedy, August 31, 1956
Abner Larson, state chairman of the Democratic party, August, 1955
Fred Lemke, Jr., nephew of William Lemke, August 30, 1957
Mrs. Fred Lemke, sister-in-law of William Lemke, August 24 and 30, 1957
Mrs. Henry Lemke, sister-in-law, June 1, 1955
Robert Lemke, son of William Lemke, September 3, 1956
William Lemke, Jr., son of William Lemke, August 20, 1956
Mrs. William Lemke, widow of William Lemke, numerous
Charles Liessmann, numerous
Alex Lind, February 13, 1957
Herbert A. Mackoff, numerous
Vernon McCutchan, May 1, 1957
Fred McLean, chairman of the Democratic State Central Committee for
    many years, September 4, 1957
R. A. Nestos, May, 1938
W. L. Nuessle, February, 1951
Gerald P. Nye, August 28, 1956; September 2, 1956
John Nystul, June 4, 1951
Arnold Offerdahl, June 10, 1955
S. A. Olsness, June 7 and 8, 1938
Ole H. Olson, numerous
Franklin Page, numerous
William W. Phillips, November 5, 1956
Russell Reid, numerous
Jack Riedel, July 17, 1956
Brigadier General Frank Richards, numerous
Margaret Rose, July 1, 1957
George Shafer, June, 1938
Harold Shaft, July, 1938
W. O. Skeels, August 30, 1956
John Steen, June, 1938
J. Lloyd Stone, numerous
Mr. and Mrs. Herbert Swett, numerous
E. J. Taylor, February, 1951
A. C. Townley, January 14, 1951; July 1, 1957
H. L. Walster, June 18, 1957

Walter Welford, numerous
Mr. and Mrs. Harry Wienbergen, numerous

*Letters to Author from:*
John M. Baer, March 5, 1957
C. E. Blackorby, October 4, 1955
Charles A. Brown, Librarian of the *Minneapolis Star and Tribune,* September 15, 1957
Usher L. Burdick, undated (Spring, 1957)
Earl Duell, January 5, 1957; July 6, 1957
Lynn J. Frazier, May 11, 1938
H. E. Gaston, undated
Louis G. Geiger, November 22, 1956
O. S. Gunderson, June 18, 1957
Ole Gunvaldsen, April 9, 1957; February 9, 1963
R. J. Hughes, July 26, 1938
M. Beatrice Johnstone, July 4, 1951
Mrs. William Lemke, numerous
William Lemke, Jr., September 4, 1956; February 28, 1963
W. L. Nuessle, October 26, 1956
George Shafer, August 13, 1938
Kathrine B. Tiffany, July 8, 1957; January 1 and 31, 1957
Cornelius Vanderbilt, Jr., June 25, 1957
H. L. Walster, June 27, 1957
John E. Williams, undated

Letter from E. C. Blackorby to E. M. Sait, June 25, 1938
Letter from William Lemke to Woodrow Wilson, April 22, 1914, in possession of Mrs. William Lemke


PUBLIC DOCUMENTS

*North Dakota*
Secretary of State, *Blue Book,* 1913, 1954
Secretary of State, *Compilation of State and National Election Returns, 1914–1928; 1930–44; 1946; 1948*
*Journal of the House of the Seventh, Fourteenth, Fifteenth, Sixteenth, and Seventeenth Sessions of the Legislative Assembly*
*Journal of the Senate of the Fourteenth, Fifteenth, Sixteenth, and Seventeenth Sessions of the Legislative Assembly*
Secretary of State, *Publicity Pamphlet,* Recall Election, October 28, 1921
Rumper Nonpartisan League Convention, 1934, *Minutes,* John Nystul
*Session Laws,* 1913, 1919

*United States*
*Congressional Record,* Volumes LXXVII, LXXX, LXXXI, LXXXVII, XCII.

Congress, Senate, Committee on Banking and Currency, *Hearings, Senate Bill 1197,* 72nd Cong., 2nd Sess., 1932–1933

Congress, Senate, Committee on Privileges and Elections, *Hearings, Relative to a Protest to the Seating of William Langer, a Senator from the State of North Dakota,* 77th Cong., 1st Sess., November 3 to 18, 1941

Congress, Senate, Committee on Privileges and Elections, *Report on the Protest by Various Citizens of the State of North Dakota to the Seating of William Langer, as a Senator from the State of North Dakota,* 77th Cong. 2nd Sess., 1942

Department of Commerce, *Twelfth Census of the United States, 1900, Population,* Vol. 1, Parts 1, 2

*Unpublished*
Georgetown University, Records, Registrar's Office
University of North Dakota, Records, Registrar's Office
University of North Dakota, Faculty Minutes
Yale University, Records, Registrar's Office


NEWSPAPERS

*Billings County Pioneer*
*Bismarck Tribune*
*Cando Record*
*Cooperators' Herald*
*Chicago Tribune*
*Dickinson Press*
*Fargo Courier-News*
*Fargo Forum*
*Farmers Exchange*
  (New Paris, Indiana)
*Grand Forks Herald*
*The Independent*
*Labor* (North Dakota Edition)

*The Leader*
*Minneapolis Tribune*
*Minot Daily News*
*New York Times*
*NonPartisan*
*Non-Partisan Leader*
*North Dakotan* (Fargo)
*San Francisco Call Bulletin*
*The Searchlight* (Fargo)
*The Student* (Univ. of N.D.)
*Washington Post*
*Williams County Farmers Press*


ARTICLES AND PERIODICALS

*America United,* a reprint of an NBC radio forum, December 14, 1947, Lemke Papers

*American Historical Review,* LXII, No. 3 (April, 1957)

Armstrong, C., "Coughlin and Lemke," *New Republic,* LXXXVIII (September 16, 1936), p. 158

Billington, Ray, "Middle Western Isolationism," *Political Science Quarterly,* Vol. LX (March, 1945)

Bliven, Bruce, "North Dakota—Five Years After," *New Republic*, LXXIV (April 28, 1926)

*The Common Good*

Cooke, Gilbert, "The North Dakota State Mill and Elevator," *Journal of Political Economy*, XLVI (February, 1938)

Coughlin, Charles E., "Third Party," *Vital Speeches*, II (July 1, 1936), pp. 613–616

*Current History*, October, 1936

Davenport, Walter, "Mr. Lemke Stops to Think," *Colliers*, XCVIII (October 17, 1936), pp. 7–8

Douglas, Paul, "A New Isolationism—Ripple or Tide?" *New York Times Magazine*, August 18, 1957

Fite, Gilbert C., "John A. Simpson: The Southwest's Militant Farm Leader," *Mississippi Valley Historical Review*, XXXV (March, 1949)

Glaab, Charles N., "The Revolution of 1906—North Dakota versus McKenzie," *The North Dakota Quarterly*, XXV (Fall, 1956)

*The Goat*, a League publication, May–June, 1920

Hall, Luella J., "History of the Formation of Counties," North Dakota State Historical Society *Collections*, V (1923)

Harris, Herbert, "That Third Party," *Current History*, XLV (October, 1936), pp. 89–92

Huntington, Samuel P., "The Election Tactics of the Non-Partisan League," *Mississippi Valley Historical Review*, XXXVI (March, 1950)

Link, Arthur S., "The Federal Reserve Policy and the Agricultural Depression of 1920–1921," *Agricultural History*, XX (July, 1946)

*Literary Digest*, March 19, 1932

McKeldin, Theodore Roosevelt, "Hats on for General Washington," *American Heritage*, VII, No. 5 (August, 1956)

Mitchell, J., "Liberty Bill Lemke," *New Republic*, LXXXVIII (August 12, 1936), pp. 8–10

Schlichter, Gertrude Almy, "Roosevelt and the Farm Program, 1929–1932," *Mississippi Valley Historical Review*, XLIII (September, 1956)

Stegner, Wallace, "Pattern for Demagogues," *Pacific Spectator* (Stanford, California), II (autumn, 1948)

Sulzberger, C. L., *New York Times Magazine*, October 31, 1956

*Time*, April 6, 1942

Ward, Paul W., "William Lemke—Crackpot for President," *The Nation*, CXLIII, No. 2 (July 11, 1936)

Wilkins, Robert P., "Middle Western Isolationism," *North Dakota Quarterly*, Vol. 25, No. 3 (Summer, 1957)


BOOKS

Bean, Louis H., *How to Predict Elections*. New York: Knopf, 1948

Beard, Charles A. and Mary R., *America in Midpassage*. New York: Macmillan, 1939

Briggs, Harold E., *Frontiers of the Northwest: A History of the Upper Missouri Valley*. New York: D. Appleton Century, 1940

Bruce, Andrew A., *The Non-Partisan League*. New York: Macmillan, 1921

Burdick, Usher L., *History of Farmers Political Action in North Dakota*. Baltimore: Wirth Brothers, 1944

Burns, James M., *Roosevelt: The Lion and the Fox*. New York: Harcourt Brace, 1956

Clark, Dan E., *The West in American History*. New York: Crowell, 1937

Dorfman, Joseph, *Thorstein Veblen and His America*. New York: Viking, 1935

Farley, James A., *Behind the Ballots*. New York: Harcourt Brace, 1938

Fite, Gilbert C., *George N. Peek and the Fight for Farm Parity*. Norman: University of Oklahoma, 1954

Fite, Gilbert C., *Peter Norbeck: Prairie Statesman*. Columbia: University of Missouri, 1948

Fossum, Paul R., *The Agrarian Movement in North Dakota*. Baltimore: Johns Hopkins, 1925

Freidel, Frank, *Franklin D. Roosevelt*, Vol. III: *The Triumph*. Boston: Little, Brown, 1956

Gaston, Herbert E., *The Nonpartisan League*. New York: Harcourt Brace, 1920

Geiger, Louis G., *University of the Northern Plains*. Grand Forks: University of North Dakota, 1958

Goldberg, Ray, *The Nonpartisan League in North Dakota*. Fargo: Midwest Printing and Lithographing Company, 1948.

Goldman, Eric F., *Rendezvous with Destiny*. New York: Knopf, 1953.

Harvey, W. H., *The Book*. Monte Ne, Arkansas: Mundus, 1930

Hofstadter, Richard, *The Age of Reform from Bryan to F. D. R.* New York: Knopf, 1955

Holzworth, John M., *The Fighting Governor*. Chicago: The Pointer Press, 1938

Ickes, Harold L., *The Secret Diary of Harold L. Ickes*, Vol. I: *The First Thousand Days, 1933–1936*. New York: Simon and Schuster, 1953

Jones, Ellis O., *Lemke's the Man for President*. Los Angeles: privately printed, Ellis O. Jones, 1936

Keen, Benjamin, *Readings in Latin American Civilization, 1492 to the Present*. Boston: Houghton Mifflin, 1955

Kramer, Dale, *The Wild Jackasses*. New York: Hastings House, 1956

Kristjanson, Baldur M. and Heltenes, C. J., *Handbook of Facts about North Dakota Agriculture*, Agricultural Experiment Station Bulletin 357. Fargo: Agricultural College, June, 1949

La Follette, Belle C. and Fola, *Robert M. La Follette, June 14, 1855–June 18, 1925.* New York: Macmillan, 1953

Lamar, Howard Roberts, *Dakota Territory, 1861–1889.* New Haven: Yale University, 1956

Langer, William, *The Nonpartisan League: Its Birth, Activities, and Leaders.* Mandan, North Dakota: Morton County Farmers Press, 1920

Lemke, William, *Crimes Against Mexico.* Minneapolis: Great West Printing Company, 1915

Lemke, William, *You and Your Money.* Philadelphia: Dorrance, 1938

Link, Arthur S., *The American Epoch.* New York: Knopf, 1955

Lindbergh, Charles A., *Banking, Currency and the Money Trust.* Washington: National Capitol Press, 1913

Lubell, Samuel, *The Future of American Politics.* New York: Harper and Brothers, 1951

MacDonald, Austin F., *Latin American Politics and Government.* New York: Crowell, 1954

McKean, Dayton D., *Party and Pressure Politics.* Boston: Houghton Mifflin, 1949

Manahan, James M., *Trials of a Lawyer.* Minneapolis: privately printed, 1933

Maxwell, S. R., *The Non-Partisan League from the Inside.* St. Paul: 1918

Mayer, George H., *The Political Career of Floyd B. Olson.* Minneapolis: University of Minnesota, 1951

Morlan, Robert M., *Political Prairie Fire.* Minneapolis: University of Minnesota, 1955

Peterson, Samuel, *Democracy and Government.* New York: Knopf, 1919

Rauch, Basil, *The History of the New Deal, 1933–1938.* New York: Creative Age Press, 1944

Russell, Charles Edward, *The Story of the Nonpartisan League.* New York: Harper and Brothers, 1920

Sait, E. M., *American Parties and Elections.* New York: D. Appleton and Century, 1942

Saloutos, Theodore, and Hicks, John D., *Agricultural Discontent in the Middle West, 1900–1939.* Madison: University of Wisconsin, 1951

Schlesinger, Arthur M., Jr., *The Age of Roosevelt: The Crisis of the Old Order.* Boston: Houghton Mifflin, 1957

Shannon, Fred A., *American Farmers' Movements.* New York: Van Nostrand, 1957

Stedman, Murray S. Jr., and Susan W., *Discontent at the Polls: A study of Farmer and Labor Parties, 1827–1948.* New York: Columbia University Press, 1955

Studenski, Paul and Kroos, Herman E., *Financial History of the United States.* New York: McGraw-Hill, 1952

Taylor, Carl C., *The Farmers Movement, 1620–1920.* New York: American

Book Company, 1953

Thomas, Alfred B., *Latin America: A History*. New York: Macmillan, 1956

Tostlebe, Alvin S., *The Bank of North Dakota: An Experiment in Agrarian Banking*. Columbia University Publications: Studies in History, Economics and Public Law, Vol. CXIV, No. 1. New York: Longmans Green, 1924

Webb, Walter P., *The Great Frontier*. Boston: Houghton Mifflin, 1952

Wector, Dixon, *The Age of the Great Depression*. New York: Macmillan, 1948

Wittke, Carl, *The German Language Press in America*. Lexington: University of Kentucky, 1957

Young, Roland, *Congressional Politics in the Second World War*. New York: Columbia University, 1954


## UNPUBLISHED

Bahmer, Robert H., "The Economic and Political Background of the Non-partisan League" (unpublished Ph.D. dissertation, University of Minnesota, 1941)

Blackorby, E. C., "Political Factional Strife in North Dakota from 1920 to 1932" (unpublished Master's thesis, University of North Dakota, 1938)

Brudvig, Glenn L., "The Farmers Alliance and Populist Movement in North Dakota, 1884–1894" (unpublished Master's thesis, University of North Dakota, 1956)

Glaab, Charles N., "John Burke and the North Dakota Progressive Movement, 1906–1912" (unpublished Master's thesis, University of North Dakota, 1952)

Hagen, E. Bruce, "The North Dakota State Mill and Elevator Association: History, Organization, Administration and Operation" (unpublished Master's thesis, University of North Dakota, 1955)

Johnson, Alice J., "The Public Career of J. F. T. O'Connor" (unpublished Master's thesis, University of North Dakota, 1956)

Johnson, Kenneth C., "The Bank of North Dakota, an Analysis of Its Value" (unpublished Master's thesis, University of North Dakota, 1957)

Koenker, William E., "Banking Trends in North Dakota—1922–1947" (unpublished Ph.D. dissertation, Ohio State University, 1949)

Mader, Joseph M., "The Political Influence of the Non-Partisan League on the Press of North Dakota" (unpublished Master's thesis, University of Minnesota, 1937)

Naftalin, Arthur, "A History of the Farmer Labor Party of Minnesota" (unpublished Ph.D. dissertation, University of Minnesota, 1948)

Norman, Richard M., "The Election of 1912 and the Progressive Party in

North Dakota" (unpublished Master's thesis, University of North Dakota, 1950)

Nystul, John D., "The Union Party of 1936" (unpublished term paper, University of Minnesota, 1949)

Phillips, William W., "The Growth of a Progressive, Asle J. Gronna" (unpublished Master's thesis, University of North Dakota, 1952)

Putnam, Jackson, "The Socialist Party in North Dakota, 1902–1918" (unpublished Master's thesis, University of North Dakota, 1956)

Schweitzer, Adam J., "John Moses and the New Deal in North Dakota" (unpublished Master's thesis, University of North Dakota, 1954)

Selke, Albert, "A History of the Initiative in North Dakota" (unpublished Master's thesis, University of North Dakota, 1940)

Talbot, Ross B., "The Policies of Farm Organizations in North Dakota" (unpublished Ph.D. dissertation, University of Chicago, 1953)

Tweton, D. Jerome, "The Election of 1900 in North Dakota" (unpublished Master's thesis, University of North Dakota, 1957)

Walster, H. L., "History of the North Dakota Agricultural College" (manuscript in preparation at the time of his death)

Wilkins, Robert P., "North Dakota and the European War, 1914–1917: A Study in Public Opinion" (unpublished Ph.D. dissertation, West Virginia University, 1954)

# Index

## DATE DUE

| | | | |
|---|---|---|---|
| | | | |
| | | | |
| | | | |
| | | | |
| | | | |
| | | | |
| | | | |
| | | | |
| | | | |
| | | | |
| | | | |
| | | | |
| | | | |
| | | | |
| | | | |
| | | | |
| | | | |
| | | | |
| GAYLORD | | | PRINTED IN U.S.A. |

FIC
Vincent

Vincent, E. Duke.

The Camelot
conspiracy.

WITHDRAWN

$24.95